THE
Coronado
Expedition

The
Coronado
Expedition

From the Distance of 460 Years

edited by
RICHARD FLINT and
SHIRLEY CUSHING FLINT

University of New Mexico Press
Albuquerque

Library of Congress Cataloging-in-Publication Data

The Coronado expedition : from the distance of 460 years / edited by
Richard Flint and Shirley Cushing Flint.— 1st ed.
   p. cm.
Includes bibliographical references and index.
  ISBN 0-8263-2975-6
1. Coronado, Francisco Vasquez de, 1510–1554—Congresses.
2. Southwest, New—Discovery and exploration—Spanish—Congresses.
3. Explorers—Southwest, New—History—16th century—Congresses.
4. Explorers—Spain—History—16th century—Congresses.
5. Spaniards—Southwest, New—Antiquities—Congresses.
6. Southwest, New—Antiquities—Congresses.
7. Excavations (Archaeology)—Southwest, New—Congresses.
I. Flint, Richard.　II. Flint, Shirley Cushing.
E125.V3C725 2003
979′.01—dc21

       2002151381

Design: Melissa Tandysh

To the memory of Dr. Jack T. Hughes,

whose knowledge of and enthusiasm for Texas Panhandle archeology has

powerfully influenced research about the Coronado expedition

in what might be called the Hughes Province.

Introduction: New Vantages on the Coronado Expedition
by RICHARD FLINT and SHIRLEY CUSHING FLINT   *1*

1. To See Such Marvels with My Own Eyes: Spanish Exploration in the
   Western Borderlands   *11*
   by JOHN L. KESSELL

2. Before the Coronado Expedition: Who Knew What and When Did
   They Know It?   *20*
   by WILLIAM K. HARTMANN and RICHARD FLINT

3. The Financing and Provisioning of the Coronado Expedition   *42*
   by SHIRLEY CUSHING FLINT

4. What's Missing from This Picture? The *Alarde,* or Muster Roll, of the
   Coronado Expedition   *57*
   by RICHARD FLINT

5. Chichilticale: A Survey of Candidate Ruins in Southeastern Arizona   *81*
   by WILLIAM K. HARTMANN and BETTY GRAHAM LEE

6. Spanish Artifacts, a Trail, and a Diary: An Eighteenth-Century Trail
   from Sonora to Zuni, New Mexico   *109*
   by JOHN H. MADSEN

7. Jars Full of Shiny Metal: Analyzing Barrionuevo's Visit to Yuque
   Yunque   *116*
   by ANN F. RAMENOFSKY and C. DAVID VAUGHAN

8. The Mystery of Coronado's Route from the Pecos River to the
   Llano Estacado   *140*
   by HARRY C. MYERS

9. Reconciling the Calendars of the Coronado Expedition: Tiguex to the Second Barranca, April and May 1541   *151*
   by RICHARD FLINT

10. Bison Hunters of the Llano in 1541: A Panel Discussion   *164*
    by DONALD J. BLAKESLEE, DOUGLAS K. BOYD, RICHARD FLINT, JUDITH HABICHT-MAUCHE, NANCY P. HICKERSON, JACK T. HUGHES, and CARROLL L. RILEY

11. The War for the South Plains, 1500–1700   *187*
    by NANCY P. HICKERSON

12. The Jimmy Owens Site: New Perspectives on the Coronado Expedition   *203*
    by DONALD J. BLAKESLEE and JAY C. BLAINE

13. First Arrivals: Coronado, Hank Smith, and the Old Springs of the Llano Estacado   *219*
    by JOHN MILLER MORRIS

14. Spanish Crossbow Boltheads of Sixteenth-Century North America: A Comparative Analysis   *240*
    by FRANK R. GAGNÉ JR.

15. Looking at a Mule Shoe: Sixteenth-Century Spanish Artifacts in Panama   *253*
    by DEE BRECHEISEN

16. Mapping, Measuring, and Naming Cultural Spaces in Castañeda's *Relación de la jornada de Cíbola*   *265*
    by MAUREEN AHERN

17. Two Colonies, Two Conquistadores: Francisco and Juan Vázquez de Coronado   *290*
    by FÉLIX BARBOZA-RETANA

References Cited   *305*

Contributors   *327*

Index   *332*

4.1   A page from the muster roll of the Coronado expedition   *71*

4.2   Transcription of a page from the muster roll of the expedition   *72*

4.3   Conquistador, sixteenth-century Mexico   *75*

4.4   Dress of a rank-and-file European member of the Coronado expedition   *76*

5.1   Rooms excavated by pothunters, Eureka Springs "Crescent Ruin"   *96*

5.2   Wall segment outlining a room, Eagle Pass Site   *101*

6.1   Spanish colonial artifacts: spontoon, spur, stirrup   *112*

6.2   Spanish colonial artifacts: sword, bowl   *112*

12.1   Hearth remnant and associated animal bone, Jimmy Owens Site   *210*

12.2   Sixteenth-century nail in situ, Jimmy Owens Site   *212*

14.1   Diagram of a crossbow bolthead from Hawikuh   *245*

14.2   Scattergram of crossbow bolthead types   *248*

15.1   Mule shoe with nails, Madden Lake, Panama   *258*

15.2   Lead shot from Santiago Pueblo, New Mexico   *261*

15.3   Crossbow boltheads from Santiago Pueblo, New Mexico   *262*

17.1   Juan Vázquez de Coronado y Anaya   *292*

17.2   Genealogy of the Vázquez de Coronado family   *294*

17.3   List of participants in the expedition of Juan Vázquez de Coronado   *296*

ix

1.1   Northwestern Spanish America in the sixteenth century   *7*

5.1   Sulfur Springs Valley, Arizona, showing selected Late Pueblo sites   *86*

6.1   Distribution of Spanish colonial artifacts in southeastern Arizona and southwestern New Mexico   *110*

7.1   Lower Río Chama villages   *123*

7.2   Distribution of Rio Grande glazes and Black-on-white matte-paint ceramics in northern New Mexico   *126*

8.1   Two historic routes of travel from Pecos Pueblo to the Llano Estacado   *142*

10.1   Key sites of the Tierra Blanca and Garza Complexes   *169*

11.1   Culture groups and areas of the South Plains, circa 1500–1700   *191*

12.1   Location and apparent structure of the Jimmy Owens Site   *206*

12.2   The Texas portion of the Coronado route   *214*

15.1   The route of the Camino Real across Panama   *255*

16.1   World map by Pietro Coppo, Venice, 1528   *266*

16.2   Map of "la nueva Tierra de Santa Cruz de la California," 1535   *267*

16.3   Approximate routes of the Coronado expedition, 1540–42   *268*

16.4   "Il Disegno del Discoperto della Nova Franza," 1556   *271*

TABLES

3.1   Balance Sheet for the Coronado Expedition   *46*

5.1   Ceramic Assemblages at Major Sites in the Sulfur Springs Valley, Arizona   *87*

7.1   Possible Sixteenth- and Seventeenth-Century Lower Chama Pueblos   *122*

7.2   Tree-Ring Dates and Luminescence Dates for Lower Chama Pueblos   *124*

9.1   Time Line for the Coronado Expedition, Tiguex to the Second Barranca   *155*

10.1   Key Sites for the Tierra Blanca and Garza Complexes   *170*

14.1   Summary of the Sample of Crossbow Boltheads   *243*

14.2   Metric and Nonmetric Observations for Sample Crossbow Bolthead Specimens   *247*

14.3   Comparison of Crossbow Boltheads from Three Sites   *249*

ACKNOWLEDGMENTS

The conference on which this book is based was made possible through funding from New Mexico Highlands University, the Floyd County (Texas) Historical Museum, the New Mexico Endowment for the Humanities, the First National Bank of Floydada (Texas), the Floyd County (Texas) Chamber of Commerce, and the Texas Council for the Humanities. Without their support, neither conference nor book would have come to life. Special thanks are due to Glen W. Davidson, former provost and vice president for academic affairs at New Mexico Highlands University. His unflagging interest and support were key to the conference's becoming a reality. Many thanks also to Harry Myers, a wizard with Photoshop, and to Jane Kepp for her keen eye and thoughtful copyediting.

New Vantages on the Coronado Expedition

RICHARD FLINT AND SHIRLEY CUSHING FLINT

FOR TWO AND A HALF YEARS, from February 1540 to August 1542, an armed force of perhaps two thousand people, with many thousands of livestock, trekked across the Greater Southwest of North America. They went, at great expense, with the intent of taking political control of sophisticated populations rumored to be living in what the expeditionaries thought of as the periphery of India.

That undertaking has come to be known as the Coronado expedition, after its leader and one of its major underwriters, Francisco Vázquez de Coronado. It was part of a century-long program of reconnaissance and conquest executed mostly at private expense on behalf of the monarchs of Spain. From the date of Columbus's landfall in 1492 until permanent settlement of the distant province of New Mexico in 1598, roughly a hundred major expeditions of conquest (known after 1573 as "pacification") were completed from the Caribbean to California, from South Carolina to Tierra del Fuego.

Beginning less than fifty years after revelation of the Western Hemisphere to Europe, the Coronado expedition marked the first large-scale encounter between natives of what Europeans perceived as the Old World and those of the New in today's Greater Southwest. Although the newcomers expected to find wealthy people of high culture living in the Southwest, reality disappointed them. Nevertheless, they persisted in the search, sending detachments west and north and east, and then farther east, and finally farther east still. All without the hoped-for result: glittering oriental cities.

The Coronado expedition, like most others of the century of conquest, returned to its place of origin empty-handed and in debt. Shortly afterward, other, more solid sources of Spanish colonial prosperity were confirmed and successfully exploited, such as the silver lode at Zacatecas. The places visited by the Coronado expedition—Señora, Cíbola, Tiguex, Cicuique, Quivira—lapsed into distant unhappy memory among veterans of the expedition and their descendants. It was forty years before Europeans again expended the effort to reach the upper Southwest, and almost another two decades after that before they returned to stay.

For the last 160 years, our most important vantage on the actions and attitudes of both the expedition members and their wary and often unwilling "hosts" has been provided by a rich documentary record generated by and resulting from the expedition. In recent years, documentary sources have been increasingly augmented by archeological evidence. For instance, the discovery in the late 1980s of a portion of a campsite of the Coronado expedition near Bernalillo, New Mexico, and the identification during the 1990s of a second campsite in Blanco Canyon, Floyd County, Texas, have significantly increased our knowledge of the expedition. Similarly, the location and analysis of hitherto unstudied documents and the reanalysis of previously known documents continue to modify our understanding of this pivotal event in the history of the Southwest.

The publication in France in 1838 of Henri Ternaux-Compans's French translation *Relation du voyage de Cíbola entrepris en 1540, par Pedro de Castañeda de Nagera* brought a hitherto unknown Spanish colonial Southwestern past to the attention of readers in the burgeoning United States.[1] During the middle third of the nineteenth century, the great era of U.S. national expansion, the heroic tale told by a member of the Coronado expedition, Pedro de Castañeda de Nájera, and published for the first time by Ternaux-Compans struck a chord among proud and recently independent Americans. Already by 1838, British North American colonists and United States expatriates had encroached on the northeastern reaches of Spanish America, seizing the Floridas in 1763, purchasing formerly Spanish Louisiana in 1804, and wresting Texas from the former Spanish colony of Mexico in 1836. Within another decade, the remainder of the old northern Spanish frontier provinces (what now make up New Mexico, Arizona, California, Nevada, Utah, and part of Colorado) would be gobbled up by the United States. This turned Castañeda's exotic history of Renaissance conquest and reconnaissance into part of the story of the United States.

In other ways, too, the timing of Ternaux-Compans's publication of the Castañeda *Relación* was fortuitous. The three decades preceding 1838 had embraced the revolutions of independence from Spain staged and won by creole colonial populations in region after region of the Americas. This, in the wake of the successful rebellion of thirteen British North American colonies, helped fuel a burgeoning New World chauvinism that sought to establish Western Hemisphere counterparts of Old World accomplishments in all fields. Writing of a New World history had begun, a history independent of, or at least equal to, that of the Old World. An American antiquity was being outlined and in some cases fabricated that could rival the wonders of Egypt, Greece, and Rome. Then in 1843 came William H. Prescott's *The Conquest of Mexico,* a long-lived best seller portraying the spectacular civilization of the Mexica that had been destroyed by European conquest some three hundred years before. Painting a marvelous and heroic New World past to rival that of classical antiquity was a political imperative for patriotic writers of the early nineteenth century. Spanish knights extending the frontiers of civilization into the Greater Southwest fit the agenda nicely.

But even in 1838 there were other reasons for writing history than to cement hemispheric identity. It was, after all, a rational age, one committed to impartial, scientific scrutiny and verification. So side by side with New World boosterism came skepticism and a budding awareness that memoirs such as Castañeda's were likely to be incomplete and flavored by the author's social and economic position and the dominant cultural attitudes of the day. One possible antidote to such bias was comparison of "independent" documentary sources dealing with the same events. Furthermore, the opportunity to "ground truth" the documentary sources sometimes presented itself as surveying parties crisscrossed the Southwest following its annexation by the United States. One such reconnaissance was made under James H. Simpson in 1848. Twenty years afterward he published his observations and those of other members of the U.S. Army's Corp of Topographical Engineers as they related to the Coronado expedition, asserting, for instance, "It seems to me that what I have advanced shows most conclusively that Cibola and Zuni are identical localities."[2] Nineteenth-century standards of evidence and proof thus tempered the strong urge to accept without question Castañeda's univocal, linear narrative.

By the end of the nineteenth century it had become clear, as George Parker Winship put it, that "Ternaux had not only rendered the language of the original accounts with great freedom, but that in several cases he had entirely failed to understand what the original writer endeavored to relate."[3] To remedy that situation, Winship published both a transcription of the original Spanish text and an English translation of Castañeda's *Relación,* which he supplemented with translations of eight other documents deriving from the expedition. Relying heavily on the work of the pioneer anthropologists, archeologists, and ethnologists Adolph F. Bandelier, Frederick W. Hodge, J. Walter Fewkes, and Frank Hamilton Cushing, Winship also included a number of annotations in his publication, often in an effort to identify places and place names.

Winship's publication initiated a trend that continues to this day, a trend toward publishing an ever-enlarging corpus of sixteenth-century documents dealing with aspects of the Coronado *entrada*. For example, in 1940 George P. Hammond and Agapito Rey published English translations of twenty-eight such documents, including all those that Winship had previously published.[4] We ourselves, through the Documents of the Coronado Expedition Project at New Mexico Highlands University, are continuing the trend by preparing for publication both Spanish transcriptions and English translations of some thirty-five documents deriving from the expedition.[5] The net effect is a significant enrichment, in both quantity and type of documentary source, of material available for study of the expedition. The corpus of published documents becomes increasingly less dominated by literary narratives and instead is characterized by more mundane sources that shed light on people and aspects of the enterprise previously ignored in favor of strong narrative.

In addition, a number of historians, archeologists, ethnohistorians, geographers, and linguists have brought a wide variety of nondocumentary sources to bear on issues or topics raised by the documents. Perhaps no one has done more to expand the use of such sources than has the ethnohistorian Carroll L. Riley. In a series of publications, Riley has employed documentary, ethnographic, and archeological data to portray the complex constellation of native peoples contacted by the Coronado expedition, as well as the cultural geography of the Greater Southwest in the sixteenth century.[6]

Over the more than 160 years since Ternaux-Compans brought knowledge of the expedition to general attention, the trajectory of awareness of Vázquez de Coronado's venture has been one of increasing complexity. Researchers have spun a web of interconnections between the two-and-a-half-year enterprise itself and people and circumstances seemingly at far remove. Attention has turned, for instance, to the politics of the Spanish royal court, to indigenous warfare on the southern Great Plains, to tales of chivalry, to millenarian Franciscan visions, to extensive native trade and communication networks, and to sixteenth-century narrative styles. It has turned to Panama, Costa Rica, and Peru, to west Africa and China. To the requirements and implications of an imperial administrative system dependent on documentation. To climate and disease. To slavery and servitude. To the trappings and prerogatives of status. To a world of human experience and the environment that sheltered and sustained it.

In the last two decades, we have been pleased to have been involved in the ongoing process of bringing forth a broadening understanding of events that ushered in the modern age in the Greater Southwest. As part of that involvement, we have put together and directed two conferences dealing with the Coronado expedition and its context and consequences. The first was held in August 1992 at New Mexico Highlands University, and the papers resulting from it were published in 1997 by the University Press of Colorado under the title *The Coronado Expedition to Tierra Nueva: The 1544 Route Across the Southwest*. That conference and book stimulated further work on the entrada and contributed, at least in part, to the discovery and identification of a campsite of the expedition in the Texas South Plains.

As the year 2000 approached, the volume of new study of the expedition that had taken place since 1992 warranted another conference, to allow the gathering and dissemination of results and work in progress. In April that year, researchers assembled at two venues for the four-day conference "Contemporary Vantage on the Coronado Expedition through Documents and Artifacts"—one venue again at New Mexico Highlands University, where we are based, and the other in Floyd County, Texas, near the Jimmy Owens Site. Once again, the quality and variety of papers presented was astounding. It is seventeen papers from that 2000 conference that make up this book. They are arranged in accordance with the chronology of the expedition itself, as we outline it next.

The Expedition and Its Ongoing Study

By the late 1530s Nueva España—essentially what was to become the core of modern Mexico—had attracted thousands of men and women from the Iberian Peninsula and elsewhere in Europe. Most were young and had passed their youth in an atmosphere charged by stories of strange peoples who were the custodians of incredible wealth in the Indies. John L. Kessell's "To See Such Marvels with My Own Eyes: Spanish Exploration in the Western Borderlands" (chapter 1) opens the book with the continuing lure of firsthand experience of the fabulous, the grotesque, and the stupendous that drew those thousands to Mexico City and then led them beyond, under the banners of Francisco Vázquez de Coronado, Juan de Oñate, Diego de Vargas, and Juan Bautista de Anza.

With "Before the Coronado Expedition: Who Knew What and When Did They Know It?" (chapter 2), by William K. Hartmann and Richard Flint, we move from general attitudes to specific expectations. A combination of fanciful geography, rumor, firsthand accounts from Tejo, fray Marcos de Niza, and Álvar Núñez Cabeza de Vaca, and a trickle of hard physical evidence led most people of the 1530s to expect the existence of prosperous, sophisticated polities to the north of Nueva España.

These attitudes and expectations came strongly into play when, in the fall of 1539, Viceroy Mendoza announced the raising of an expedition to investigate and subjugate the place fray Marcos said bore the name Cíbola. Hundreds of Europeans answered the call. But more was required than personnel. The mounting of such an enterprise was extremely expensive. Like nearly all Spanish-led expeditions in the New World during the sixteenth century, this one would be privately financed. Shirley Cushing Flint, in "The Financing and Provisioning of the Coronado Expedition" (chapter 3), estimates the cost of the expedition and gives us an idea of who met the heavy expenditures of its outfitting and provisioning.

Once a force had been enlisted and supplies and transportation paid for, in February 1540 at Compostela, the capital of the recently conquered province of Nueva Galicia, the official muster of the expedition took place. In chapter 4, "What's Missing from This Picture? The *Alarde,* or Muster Roll, of the Coronado Expedition," Richard Flint reexamines the surviving documentary record of the muster. A number of significant facts, it turns out, have been overlooked or under-appreciated in the past, including that the bulk of the two thousand or so expedition members were actually Indians from central and western Mexico.

In the last week of February 1540 the whole expedition left Compostela, heading first for the northernmost outpost of Spanish control, San Miguel de Culiacán, in modern Sinaloa (see map, this chapter, and map 16.3). Arriving there at Easter, Vázquez de Coronado, in consultation with his captains and the clergy who accompanied the entrada, decided to proceed to Cíbola with only a part of his force. The remainder was to follow later. Along the trail to Cíbola the expedition was disappointed to find the famous landmark of Chichilticale a mud-walled ruin. In chapter 5, "Chichilticale: A Survey of Candidate Ruins in Southeastern Arizona," William K. Hartmann and Betty Graham Lee present for the first time comprehensive archeological data on a series of late prehistoric town sites in that area. Among them may well be the one known to the Coronado expedition as Chichilticale. In an effort to delineate the route the expedition followed down the San Pedro River valley in southern Arizona to Chichilticale and on to Cíbola, the archeologist John Madsen has been examining artifacts from the region for more than a decade. He reports his findings to date in chapter 6, "Spanish Artifacts, a Trail, and a Diary: An Eighteenth-Century Trail from Sonora to Zuni, New Mexico."

The first serious conflict between the expedition and native people of the Greater Southwest occurred at Cíbola, now identified as one of the ancestral Zuni pueblos in west-central New Mexico. The expedition's *requerimiento,* or formal summons to the indigenous people to submit to Spanish rule, was met with a shower of arrows. In response, the detachment led by Vázquez de Coronado attacked and overran the pueblo. But Cíbola, too, fell short of European expectations, lacking as it did a money economy based on precious metals. In the days

Map I.1. Northwestern Spanish America in the sixteenth century.

following its capture, the expeditionaries and the people of Cíbola reached an accommodation. Soon, natives of other pueblos came to Cíbola to meet and treat with the expedition diplomatically. As a result, the expedition shifted its base in the late fall of 1540 to the Rio Grande of what is now central New Mexico, where dozens of pueblos lined the river. Once again, the wealthy cities the Europeans sought failed to materialize.

In several locations, though, there were hints that sources of precious ores might be nearby. Ann Ramenofsky and David Vaughan, in "Jars Full of Shiny Metal: Analyzing Barrionuevo's Visit to Yuque Yunque" (chapter 7), investigate what the metallic substances seen at the pueblo of Yuque Yunque, associated with modern San Juan Pueblo, New Mexico, might have been and where they might have originated.[7]

Ill-prepared to feed, clothe, and shelter itself, the expedition soon provoked hostility from the Pueblo Indians of the middle Rio Grande Valley with demands for corn, cotton and hide robes, and accommodations. The upshot was the Tiguex war, which raged for several months and left hundreds of natives of the Tiguex area, in the vicinity of modern Albuquerque and Bernalillo, New Mexico, dead, wounded, or homeless. In the spring of 1541, the expedition set off for yet another rumored prosperous polity, the distant land of Quivira.

Stopping briefly at Cicuique—Pecos Pueblo, New Mexico—the entire, huge expeditionary force was led east by natives of the Great Plains. In "The Mystery of Coronado's Route from the Pecos River to the Llano Estacado" (chapter 8), Harry Myers makes a case for reconstruction of the route that the expedition likely followed across east-central New Mexico. Richard Flint deals with the same portion of the expedition's journey, but from a temporal rather than geographical perspective, in chapter 9, "Reconciling the Calendars of the Coronado Expedition: Tiguex to the Second Barranca, April and May 1541." By closely comparing the calendars implied in several sixteenth-century narrative accounts of the expedition, he is able to show their close congruence and the geographical consequences that follow.

Arrived at the eastern margin of the Llano Estacado, the expedition encountered seminomadic people known as Teyas living in one of the great canyons, or barrancas, that characterize the region. Who these people and their immediate neighbors the Querechos were is the subject of the panel discussion recorded in chapter 10, "Bison Hunters of the Llano in 1541." Looking in more detail at the Teyas, Nancy P. Hickerson, in "The War for the South Plains, 1500–1700" (chapter 11), argues that they were identical with the group later called Jumanos, who had close ties with the Tompiros of New Mexico.

The expedition occupied camps in two of the barrancas for a period of several days to two weeks in the early summer of 1541. In 1993 and 1994, the amateur archeologist Jimmy Owens located objects likely to have been associated with the Coronado expedition in Blanco Canyon, Floyd County, Texas. The resulting archeological investigation, directed by Donald J. Blakeslee, has identified Blanco Canyon as one of the barrancas in which the expedition camped. Many of the results and conclusions of that ongoing archeological investigation are detailed in Blakeslee and Jay C. Blaine's "The Jimmy Owens Site: New Perspectives on the Coronado Expedition" (chapter 12). The water sources that made Blanco Canyon attractive as a campsite for both Teyas and the expedition are dealt with by John Miller Morris in "First Arrivals: Coronado, Hank Smith, and the Old Springs of the Llano Estacado" (chapter 13).

Archeological work at the Jimmy Owens Site has revealed several artifact types as characteristic of the Coronado expedition. One of these, copper crossbow boltheads, or dart points, is the subject of chapter 14, "Spanish Crossbow Boltheads of Sixteenth-Century North America: A Comparative Analysis," by Frank R. Gagné Jr. Through detailed morphological analysis, Gagné demonstrates that all known copper crossbow boltheads from North America derive from the same source, the Coronado expedition. Another object found in abundance at the Jimmy Owens Site and occurring at other suspected campsites of the expedition is the caret-head nail. Based on his extensive experience in Panama, Dee Brecheisen, in "Looking at a Mule Shoe: Sixteenth-Century Spanish Artifacts in Panama" (chapter 15), shows that the nail was also plentiful as a horseshoe fastener on the *camino real* that crossed the isthmus during the period of the Coronado expedition.

Convinced that the expedition was being led astray by its Indian guide, at the last barranca Vázquez de Coronado divided his forces. A small contingent went on with the captain general to Quivira while most of the people returned to the Rio Grande. Like the expedition's earlier destinations, Quivira proved disappointing, and the small contingent, too, returned to New Mexico, after executing one of its guides. Another winter passed among the hostile Tiguex people, though apparently without further significant bloodshed. Discouraged by the paltry fruits of its reconnaissance, and with its supply line interrupted by uprisings of native people in Mexico, the expedition abandoned further plans in Tierra Nueva, as the lands in the north were called, and returned south in the spring of 1542, fighting a good part of the way.

One of the legacies of the Coronado expedition was the addition to European geography and sense of the world of some of the peoples and places it had encountered and explored. In chapter 16, "Mapping, Measuring, and Naming Cultural Spaces in Castañeda's *Relación de la jornada de Cíbola*," Maureen Ahern outlines the tentative textual conquest of a vast Southwest by one of the expedition's participant chroniclers.

Historians—perhaps too credulously—have tended to judge the Coronado expedition less harshly than others of the period. Its captain general is most often portrayed as concerned for Indian welfare and mindful of Indian rights. As illusory as that vision may be,[8] the leader's nephew, Juan Vázquez de

Coronado, enjoys a similar reputation regarding his conquest of Costa Rica in the 1560s. That and other parallels between the two conquistador relatives are laid out in the concluding chapter, "Two Colonies, Two Conquistadores: Francisco and Juan Vázquez de Coronado," by Félix Barboza-Retana.

Throughout this book are presented the thought-provoking fruits of the ongoing research of many scholars hard at work disclosing the humanness and modernity of the people who took part in and were affected by the Coronado expedition, the first European incursion into the Greater Southwest. The attitudes, concerns, behaviors, motives, and beliefs of these people have not vanished. The conflicts and accommodations that resulted from the expedition, too, still echo. This volume offers not merely a partial reconstruction of the past but also a signpost to the origins of much of the framework of life in the Southwest today.

Notes

1. Henri Ternaux-Compans, *Voyages, relations et memoires originaux pour servir a l'histoire de la decouverte de l'Amerique,* vol. 9 (Paris: A. Bertrand, 1838). At the time, French, the principal international language, was accessible to many educated people in the young American nation.

2. James H. Simpson, "Coronado's March in Search of the 'Seven Cities of Cibola' and Discussion of their Possible Location," *Annual Report of the Board of Regents of the Smithsonian Institution for 1869* (Washington, D.C.: Smithsonian Institution, 1869), 332.

3. George Parker Winship, ed. and trans., *The Coronado Expedition, 1540–1542,* Fourteenth Annual Report of the United States Bureau of American Ethnology of the Smithsonian Institution, 1892–1893, Part 1, 107 (Washington, D.C.: Smithsonian Institution, 1896; reprint, Chicago: Rio Grande Press, 1964).

4. George P. Hammond and Agapito Rey, eds. and trans., *Narratives of the Coronado Expedition, 1540–1542* (Albuquerque: University of New Mexico Press, 1940).

5. Richard Flint, *Great Cruelties Have Been Reported: The 1544 Investigation of the Coronado Expedition* (Dallas: Southern Methodist University Press, 2002), and Richard Flint and Shirley Cushing Flint, eds. and trans., *"They Were Not Familiar with His Majesty": Documents of the Coronado Expedition, 1540–1542,* in preparation.

6. See, for example, Carroll L. Riley, *The Frontier People: The Greater Southwest in the Protohistoric Period,* rev. and exp. ed. (Albuquerque: University of New Mexico Press, 1987), and Carroll L. Riley, *Rio del Norte: People of the Upper Rio Grande from Earliest Times to the Pueblo Revolt* (Salt Lake City: University of Utah Press, 1995).

7. Such reports from members of the Coronado expedition may well have helped stimulate permanent settlement of New Mexico in 1598 by Juan de Oñate, son of Vázquez de Coronado's lieutenant governor. Indeed, the report that is the subject of chapter 7 may have led Oñate to select Yuque Yunque for the first Spanish settlement in New Mexico, on the basis of a supposition of the presence of nearby silver.

8. See Flint, *Great Cruelties,* for a very different appraisal of the expedition's attitudes and actions toward Native Americans.

ONE

To See Such Marvels with My Own Eyes: Spanish Exploration in the Western Borderlands

JOHN L. KESSELL

TO THE ITALIAN ANTONIO PIGAFETTA, gentleman chronicler of Magellan's fatal voyage, the wonders he first heard about the Ocean Sea were enchanting. "And then and there," he confessed, "I resolved to see such marvels with my own eyes."[1]

Even after a century of revelation, as new-found islands, continents, and oceans crowded the Padrón Real (the official map) at the Casa de Contratación in Sevilla, the climate of wonder persisted. Errant Spaniards had seen countless marvels, invented new ones, and grasped repeatedly for those that receded before them like mirages, all the while seeking to reconcile fable, Christian scripture, and geography.

Father Francisco Escobar, chaplain on Juan de Oñate's trek to the Gulf of California in 1604–5, was no exception. According to contemporaries, he possessed the gift of languages. Just as well, for not far from the Colorado River, an Indian whom Escobar called Otata put him to the test, describing people so strange that the Franciscan was at pains to record them. One tribe had gigantic ears that dragged the ground. Another slept underwater. And a third existed solely on the smell of food, its members born without anuses. Otata must have excelled at pantomime. The men of yet another native nation boasted, in the friar's words, "virile members so long that they wound them four times around the waist, and in the act of copulation the man and woman were far apart."

A circle of Indians nodded assent. Besides, Escobar assured skeptics, there were books that told of equally amazing things. And there was God. "Whosoever reflects on the marvels that God continuously performs in this world will not find it hard to believe that since He is able to create them, He may have done so."[2] In his journal, the Franciscan chose not to speculate that these oddities might have been creatures of Satan, the Dark Side of the Force. Nor did he witness personally to believing them without seeing.

To explorers, seeing such marvels was rarely enough. To experience them personally, to possess them, materially and spiritually, and to enjoy a discoverer's fame—such motives seemed always, in varying proportions, to underlie their travels and inure them to the excruciating hardships they were apt to suffer.

Three great swells of Spanish exploration and discovery rolled north from Mexico across the coasts and high deserts of the western borderlands. The first, set in motion by Columbus, lasted from the medieval (yet visibly Mesoamerican) quest of Francisco Vázquez de Coronado to the failed business ventures of Juan de Oñate and Sebastián Vizcaíno, or from about 1540 to 1610. During the second, in the 1680s and 1690s, questing gave way to imperial defense as Frenchmen challenged Spain's exclusivity west of the Mississippi. By the third, from the 1770s through the 1790s, Spanish explorers who shared the enlightened world of Thomas Jefferson reasserted Spain's quixotic claims, erecting on promontories cairns and crosses before Russians, Englishmen, or Anglo-Americans did.

Not that these three swells rose on a calm sea. Always there was movement; hunters, prospectors, slavers, traders, white Indians—they were always out there even when the authorities, in the interest of consolidation, decreed otherwise. Exploration progressed, sometimes steadily, sometimes fitfully, as Spaniards compiled practical geographical observations, established new bases, and pushed back frontiers and myths.

Too often, perhaps, we have oversimplified explorers' motives, especially those during the first wave. Some of us have embraced or damned Columbus as a brave and practical mariner while, with a postmodern sneer, shunning him in his self-proclaimed role as Christopher, the Christ-bearer, mystical visionary who convinced himself that "he had discovered the 'new heaven and the new earth' prophesied in the Apocalypse."[3]

If only we knew more about the explorers' psyches, we might better understand how and why they saw, or did not see, certain features of the strange new worlds they entered. And we should not forget that most of the exotic scenes they beheld were already peopled by fellow human beings, non-Christian men, women, and children whom the Europeans understood very well, even while arrogantly professing not to. Almost to a man, secular explorers rejected the intimate, all-embracing vision of Álvar Núñez Cabeza de Vaca. Yet more often than not, Europeans, whatever their motives, were led along beaten trails by natives who influenced what they saw.

Contact and Early Initiatives

During the cluster of adventures that clung to Coronado between 1539 and 1542, material and spiritual motives diverged neatly in two men: the youthful leader himself and the obsessed fray Juan de Padilla. Coronado, in keeping with the private enterprise favored by the kings of Spain, had invested heavily of his wife's fortune in the hope of discovering somewhere to the far north of Mexico City peoples and resources richer still than those subdued by Hernán Cortés and his hordes of native allies.

For the cranky Father Padilla, a former soldier, glory lay in revealing and reuniting with Christendom the Seven Cities of Antillia, allegedly founded centuries before on some distant shore by seven bishops fleeing the Muslim invasion of the Iberian Peninsula and since grown fabulously wealthy. Instead, he found death in 1542 at the hands of Plains Indians somewhere in today's Kansas. Coronado, alive but unfulfilled, went home, where his patron, Viceroy Antonio de Mendoza, decreed perpetual silence about the hapless venture.

By their brief passing, however, these steel-age Europeans had broken into the interlocking memory of native peoples from the Colorado River in the west to the plains of central Kansas. Yet nothing the invaders saw, when compared with the Valley of Mexico, was worth the cost of occupation. They imagined no profit in scenic wonders. How, for that matter, could they even relate to someone back in Sevilla the awesome dimensions of the Grand Canyon? The cathedral tower made a poor measuring stick.

Still, this first herculean wave of exploration, which included the contemporaneous failures of Juan Rodríguez Cabrillo up the California coast, Hernando de Soto from Florida to Arkansas, and Ruy López de Villalobos in the Philippines (each fatal to its leader), served to define a reality for the future. From the 1540s onward, Spaniards had a surprisingly accurate idea of the width of North America and the vastness of the Pacific Rim. Colonies would follow for a variety of purposes.

To guard the return route of the silver fleets through the Straits of Florida and expel French Huguenots, Pedro Menéndez de Avilés established a conspicuous Spanish presence at St. Augustine in 1565. That same year, the first galleon from the Philippines caught the Japan Current back across the north Pacific and sailed down the California coast to Acapulco, verifying the theory of an astute Augustinian friar and navigator, the Basque Andrés de Urdaneta. In 1571, Manila took life as a Spanish entrepôt. Thence, for two and a half centuries, on a voyage considered "the longest from land to land on our globe," luxury goods from the Orient flowed to New Spain for transshipment to Europe while Mexican and Peruvian silver ebbed back to transform the economies of the Far East.[4]

The inveterate risk-taker Sebastián Vizcaíno, a merchant and mariner engaged in the Philippine trade whose surname suggests Basque blood, contracted in 1595 to pacify the Californias and develop pearl fisheries, but his beachhead at La Paz quickly foundered. Later, in 1602 and 1603, casting saints' names along the outer coast, he dropped anchor in what he claimed was a superb harbor for the returning China ships. Not for 167 years, however, until Russians and Englishmen threatened on sea and land, did Spain move to occupy Monterey Bay and, soon afterward, San Francisco Bay, which Vizcaíno and the galleons had overshot because of rocky, storm-lashed offshore islands and fog.

Another son of a Basque, the mine owner Juan de Oñate, who disregarded Coronado's fiasco, negotiated a deal the same year as Vizcaíno and founded New Mexico as a corporate venture in 1598. Viceroy Luis de Velasco hoped the dual enterprises would divulge a Strait of Anián. But although Oñate's San Gabriel proved slightly more liveable than La Paz, neither looked out upon a northwest passage between the so-called South and North Seas, the Pacific and Atlantic, respectively.

As New Mexico's poverty sank in and his colonists took flight, proprietor Oñate explored in desperation. His captain Marcos Farfán de los Godos, prospecting in present-day central Arizona, reported veins of rich, multicolored ores "so long and wide that one-half of the people in New Spain could stake out claims in this land." On the Gulf of California, wrote Father Escobar, "according to experienced seamen, we saw the most famous bay or harbor . . . that any of them had ever seen."[5]

Viceroy the Marqués de Montesclaros doubted it. In 1605, the same year Cervantes's *Don Quijote* appeared in Madrid, Montesclaros despaired of the New Mexico project. "I cannot help but inform your majesty," he wrote to Felipe III, "that this conquest is becoming a fairy tale. If those who write the reports imagine that they are believed by those who read them, they are greatly mistaken."[6] Still, disillusion fed illusion, and Frenchmen, a century later, felt the lure westward of bountiful fantasy mines in New Mexico.

Rivals

The middle, transitional wave of exploration broke all along the northern frontier in the 1680s and 1690s amid widespread warfare with native peoples and heightened French activity following the Sieur de LaSalle's descent of the Mississippi in 1682. Once Oñate had withdrawn from New Mexico in 1610, the Spanish crown, at the friars' urging, turned his proprietary colony into a government-subsidized Franciscan ministry to the Pueblo Indians. Abiding for three generations, the

Pueblos in 1680 avenged themselves in fury, not only casting Spaniards out but also shutting down their medieval machine of questing knights, a feudal lord, and the friars' expectant city of God on the Rio Grande.

Between first and second swells, trade kept drawing Spaniards from New Mexico out into the vastness of the Great Plains. The case of the rugged Diego Romero implies at least two generations of far-ranging commerce. Romero, who led a caravan hauling manufactured goods hundreds of miles east from New Mexico in the summer of 1660, had an ulterior motive. He wanted the Plains Apaches to honor him as their head war chief, a title he swore they had once bestowed on his father. At a distant rendezvous that he called the *rancheria* of don Pedro, Apaches feted Romero in an elaborate calumet ceremonial. Afterward, according to eyewitnesses, he entered a new teepee set up for the occasion and had sexual intercourse with an Apache woman. Romero wished, he admitted later, to leave, as his father had, a son among the Apaches. If only he had not stuck the symbolic white feather on his hat, the agent of the Inquisition might never have found out.

Another Spaniard accused and tried by the Holy Office was New Mexico's resourceful, blaspheming governor Diego de Peñalosa. Banished from New Spain in the mid-1660s, don Diego had presented himself at the courts of Charles II in England and Louis XIV in France. As credentials, he carried the falsified diary of a grand exploration he claimed to have made across the plains and a map showing the settlements of New Mexico, one of which he had labeled Santa Fe de Peñalosa. The Spanish swashbuckler's offer to lead an invasion force of pirates and capture for France the mines of northern New Spain, although courteously refused, evidently played into the hands of LaSalle.

As Spanish-French rivalry intensified in the 1680s, so did exploration. Lured eastward by reports of freshwater pearls, bison products, and Indians asking for baptism, civilians and friars from the New Mexico colony in exile around El Paso penetrated central Texas. Farther east, Spaniards mounted coordinated sea and land probes to locate and put to the torch what was left of LaSalle's aborted colony on the Texas coast, a pleasure bestowed in April 1689 on Coahuila's governor Alonso de León and the zealous fray Damián Massanet.

A tireless Jesuit, meanwhile, had begun his notable career as a missionary explorer to the west in Baja California. Although Cortés and Coronado knew it was a peninsula, Father Eusebio Francisco Kino had been taught in Europe that California was an island. His first recorded crossing from the gulf to the Pacific failed to convince him otherwise. Later, however, Kino's methodical explorations of the Gila and lower Colorado River drainages, and his crossing of the Colorado River delta in a big basket to observe the sun rising over the Gulf of California, led him to restore Baja California's peninsularity. Kino's map of 1710, despite the peninsula's swollen girth, is a marvel of accuracy.[7]

Regardless of the almost immediate royal demand that New Mexico's break-away Pueblo Indians be restored to the empire, that feat had awaited Governor Diego de Vargas, the lisping but self-assured Spanish nobleman who took command at El Paso in 1691. Sending the viceroy a sack of salt from salines he discovered east of El Paso, Vargas lamented that the sample was not from the Sierra Azul, an elusive, silver- and mercury-laden range off beyond the Hopi pueblos to the west. Vargas never found it, but that hardly tarnished New Mexico's imaginary luster.

Vargas's grit, meanwhile, combined with Pueblo Indian disunion, resulted in a ceremonial repossession of the Pueblo world in 1692 and, late the following year, a bloody battle for Santa Fe. By the time Vargas died in 1704, the crusading intolerance of the seventeenth-century colony was giving way to a more practical, day-to-day accommodation as Hispanos and Pueblos stood shoulder to shoulder against common nomadic enemies, traded beans and chilies, and became *compadres*.

Vargas and Kino, two European imperialists who rode the turn-of-century swell and died on the northern frontier, both evoked an earlier age. Raised on Spain's past glories and confident of knighthood in the military Order of Santiago, don Diego continued to beseech Our Lady of Remedies while coping with a monarchy in decline. The accomplished Father Kino, mathematician, astronomer, and contemporary of Sir Isaac Newton, saw with medieval eye the comet of 1680 as a dire omen from God.

To Defend Such Vastness

As the third swell of exploration and defensive expansion gained momentum to peak in the 1770s, '80s, and '90s, the imperial map of North America shifted constantly. Earlier, Frenchmen at midcontinent such as Louis Juchereau de Saint Denis had caused Spain mighty discomfort. The concurrent founding in 1718 of French New Orleans and Spanish San Antonio, along with José de Escandón's massive project for Nuevo Santander in the 1740s, was symptomatic. French influence among Plains tribes in the meantime had drawn Pedro de Villasur hundreds of leagues northeast from Santa Fe in 1720 into an early preview of Custer's last stand. Then suddenly, France, biggest loser in the great war for empire, gave over Louisiana and Illinois west of the Mississippi to a revitalized Spain in 1762, while most everything east of the river went to rival England.

Spain, by creating in 1776 almost but not quite a northern viceroyalty (the

General Command of the Provincias Internas) sought to bind from east to west and from west to east frontier colonies founded at different times for different reasons, but always from south to north. On a map, they resembled the extended and widespread fingers (the Californias, Sonora-Arizona, New Mexico, Texas, and Louisiana) of a giant hand with its forearm at Mexico City. To explorers, both military and missionary, fell the task of creating webs of communication between the digits.

No one figured more prominently in this effort than the frontier-born Juan Bautista de Anza. As captain of the presidio of Tubac in southern Arizona, he led exploring, then colonizing, expeditions overland by the Yuma Crossing to Alta California, guided in part by the earthy, unadmiring fray Francisco Garcés. Anza's colonists, ignorant of current events in Philadelphia, founded San Francisco in 1776. Garcés, meantime, traveled solo from Mission San Gabriel eastward across sierras, deserts, and canyons to the Hopi pueblos, where on July 4 the natives dismissed him rudely.

Coastal California's belated occupation, directed by Governor Gaspar de Portolá and fray Junípero Serra in 1769, had been the pet project of José de Gálvez, a brilliant, erratic, high-ranking servant of the enlightened Spanish despot Carlos III. It was Gálvez, as reforming special investigator to New Spain, who expelled the Jesuits from their northwest missionary empire and then experimented, in vain, with converting paternalistic frontier missions into progressive collective farms. He had no quarrel, however, with Franciscans as explorers.

The small party accompanying fray Francisco Atanasio Domínguez and fray Silvestre Vélez de Escalante northwestward from New Mexico in 1776 into the Great Basin learned the hard way that no convenient northern route led from Santa Fe to Monterey. Still, the versatile Bernardo de Miera y Pacheco drew a map of a wild landscape no European had seen before. With a nod to the past, Miera sketched in the upper right-hand corner the pope in triumphal car drawn by the lions of Castile. Here, no colonization followed, and Zion remained open. At the least, the two blue-robed Franciscans had given Utah something to commemorate during the bicentennial of the United States in 1976.

By the last third of the eighteenth century, the rosters of Spanish exploring parties, like those of other European nations, often included surveyors and cartographers, members of the Royal Corps of Engineers, along with scientists bent on collecting, drawing, and classifying the myriad species of nature. Anza, promoted to the governorship of New Mexico, found himself trapping elk live to ship to the royal zoological park in Madrid.

A Spanish naval department at San Blas, meanwhile, resuscitated Pacific coast exploration. While British colonists fought British regulars on the eastern seaboard, venturesome Spaniards like Juan Francisco de la Bodega y Quadra urged their wooden vessels northward against contrary winds and currents as far as the ice floes of Alaska, seeking always that northwest passage. Nootka Sound on Vancouver Island, first visited by Juan Pérez in 1774, saw not only a multinational parade of seaborne scientific expeditions but also Spain's losing, twenty-year bid to maintain exclusive jurisdiction that far north.

From landlocked New Mexico, in contrast, the view appeared to be widening. Governor Anza, in 1786, entered into a far-reaching commercial and military alliance with the Comanches. The aging Domingo Cabello of Texas had also treated with Comanches, which empowered plains trailblazer Pedro Vial to show the way to Santa Fe from San Antonio in 1786–87, from Santa Fe to Natchitoches in Spanish Louisiana and back via San Antonio in 1788–89, and to and from St. Louis in 1792–93. But his timing was off. Instead of ties that bound Spanish colonies, Vial's paths became avenues of Anglo-American penetration. The Louisiana Purchase lay only ten years in the future, and the Adams-Onís Treaty, the Santa Fe Trail, and war with Mexico less than a lifetime.

The day blocky Facundo Melgares rode out of Santa Fe at the head of some six hundred Hispanos and Pueblo Indians in 1806 belatedly to intercept Lewis and Clark, he was not conceding Spanish defeat. Anything but. Spaniards lacked neither will nor experience. What they lacked in the early nineteenth century were manpower and matériel to fight Napoleon at home, fend off European rivals in the Americas, and dissuade their own colonists from opting for independence.

Walter Prescott Webb was right when he observed that the Great Plains offered little that Spaniards wanted but wrong when he implied that the harsh environment and mounted Plains Indians offered obstacles too great.[8] Had Coronado, Oñate, Vargas, or Anza discovered a mountain of silver on the Arkansas, a supply port would have sprung up overnight on the Texas coast, and Tulsa would speak Spanish today. The same can be said of the San Joaquin Valley of California or the Great Basin; Spaniards had explored those expanses but found no compelling reasons to stay.

The North Transfigured

With time, the patterns traced by humans on the landscape were bound to change. When Zebulon Montgomery Pike, under Spanish escort, toured the western borderlands in 1807, by far the largest concentration of Hispanos still lived in New Mexico with the Pueblo Indians. Then Anglos poured into Texas and later into California, followed by Mexican immigrants. Together, they reversed the old reality. The former heartland, New Mexico, turned out to be a void between the great states of Texas and California, which it still is, and, to non–New Mexicans, a fine place to isolate nuclear waste.

One thing has not changed. As long as men and women perceive unexplored realms of the physical and spiritual universe and are drawn to the mysteries that give God and Theoretical Science unknowable faces, they will seek to see such marvels with their own eyes. And for just as long, given the nature of humankind, simply to see will not be enough.

Notes

This chapter is a somewhat reworked version of an article that appeared under the same title in *Montana: The Magazine of Western History* 41, no. 4 (1991): 68–75. I have chosen here for the most part to give references only for direct quotations. For general treatments of Spanish exploration and settlement of New Spain's far northern frontier, see David J. Weber, *The Spanish Frontier in North America* (New Haven: Yale University Press, 1992), and John L. Kessell, *Spain in the Southwest: A Narrative History of Colonial New Mexico, Arizona, Texas, and California* (Norman: University of Oklahoma Press, 2002).

1. Quoted by Irving A. Leonard, *Books of the Brave: Being an Account of Books and of Men in the Spanish Conquest and Settlement of the Sixteenth-Century New World* (New York: Gordian Press, 1964), 12.
2. George P. Hammond and Agapito Rey, eds. and trans., *Don Juan Oñate, Colonizer of New Mexico, 1595–1628* (Albuquerque: University of New Mexico Press, 1953), 2:1024–26.
3. Pauline Moffitt Watts, "Prophecy and Discovery: On the Spiritual Origins of Christopher Columbus's 'Enterprise of the Indies,'" *American Historical Review* 90 (February 1985), 73–102.
4. Quoted by William Lytle Schurz, *The Manila Galleon* (New York: E. P. Dutton, 1959), 238.
5. Hammond and Rey, *Oñate,* 1:413, 2:1023.
6. Hammond and Rey, *Oñate,* 2:1009.
7. See Ernest J. Burrus, *Kino and the Cartography of Northwestern New Spain* (Tucson: Arizona Pioneers' Historical Society, 1965).
8. Walter Prescott Webb, *The Great Plains* (New York: Grosset and Dunlap, 1931), 85–139. Webb simply did not know enough about Spanish activity on the Plains.

TWO

Before the Coronado Expedition: Who Knew What and When Did They Know It?

WILLIAM K. HARTMANN AND RICHARD FLINT

FOR MOST PARTICIPANTS in the Coronado expedition of 1540–42, it was first and foremost a financial enterprise, in which the members and backers invested and from which they expected handsome returns. As Shirley Cushing Flint shows in chapter 3, three major investors, Viceroy Antonio de Mendoza, Francisco Vázquez de Coronado, and Pedro de Alvarado, contributed about 50,000 pesos each—substantial fortunes—to finance the expedition.[1] Most rank-and-file members of the expedition also spent funds to participate, outfitting and supplying themselves, often borrowing money to do so. Total investment in the expedition was at least half a million pesos. The supposition was that investors would see substantial profits in a matter of months, and certainly in no more than two years. On the other hand, if gold or other "hard wealth" could not be appropriated from Cíbola or other nearby communities, then nearly every member of the expedition stood to return south in severely straitened circumstances, as indeed most eventually did.

The huge monetary investment in the expedition testifies to the widespread expectation of extraordinary wealth in Cíbola. On what was this popular presumption based? Modern historical accounts of the Coronado expedition assign to fray Marcos de Niza the role of originator of the belief in Cíbola as a place rich in gold and silver. In this view, fray Marcos's reports, following his six-month trip to the north in 1539, planted visions of a glittering Cíbola in the minds of restless young European adventurers. This explanation greatly oversimplifies the situation in Mexico City, and indeed in Spanish America at large, in the late 1530s.

Our intention in this chapter is to delineate the deep-seated and long-building web of geographical knowledge, belief, and rumor that held fray Marcos and the other European residents of Mexico City even before the friar was appointed to make his famous reconnaissance to the north. What past experience, European folklore, New World stories, official reports, and grapevine facts made up the evolving store of knowledge of Spanish conquest in March 1539 as Marcos and Esteban set off toward the north from Culiacán?

The State of Geographical Knowledge and Surmise in the 1530s

We begin with what members of the expedition itself had to say. Writing in the 1560s, Pedro de Castañeda opened his chronicle of the Coronado expedition by retelling what in his opinion was the earliest account to have been received that specifically told about the seven cities in the north. In his telling, first notice came in 1530 from a native of Oxitipan, whom the Spaniards called Tejo.[2] This Tejo told of having visited seven large towns, so grand that he liked to compare them to Mexico City. In these towns he had purportedly seen streets of silversmiths' shops (*platería*). In Castañeda's version, this news was sufficient to inspire the launching of an expedition of nearly four hundred Spaniards and twenty thousand Indian allies by Nuño Beltrán de Guzmán. Guzmán's expedition—always in pursuit of Tejo's seven cities, according to Castañeda—got only as far as Culiacán, without finding them.[3] It was left to the Coronado expedition ten years later to seek them out.

What Castañeda ignored in his narrative were the many other reports that led European settlers of Nueva España to expect that there were communities far to the north where gold and silver were plentiful. In fact, a crescendo of reports served to prime European residents of Nueva España to hear in messages from fray Marcos in 1539 confirmation of the existence of those seven wealthy cities.

To adequately represent the state of knowledge and belief in 1539 concerning prosperous societies in the interior of the Indies, we must go back much farther than Nuño de Guzmán. To begin with, a robust heritage of thought led Europeans of the sixteenth century to believe that the Indies of Christopher Columbus harbored unimaginable stores of gold and silver and other precious goods. Two powerful notions that were part of the common conception of the world in late medieval and early modern Europe and especially in Spain were, first, a vision of the East as a place of limitless wealth and, second, a tradition of seven Catholic bishops and their congregations who had fled the Muslim invasion of the Iberian Peninsula in the early 700s.

Routine, if perilous, connection between Europe and the Far East had been reestablished by Venetian traders, including Marco Polo, in the thirteenth century. That opening of China, Japan, and the Spice Islands revealed to Europeans cultures and polities much more sophisticated and prosperous than their own, places of unheard of wealth. Marco Polo had written, for instance, about the palace of the Great Khan in Cathay as being carved and gilded throughout and housing his personal treasure of gold, silver, pearls, and other jewels. Nearly two hundred years later, writing to King Alfonso V of Portugal in 1474, Paolo dal Pozzo Toscanelli (who strongly influenced Christopher Columbus's geographical thought) referred to the temples and palaces of Japan as "roofed with massy gold."[4] The lure of such wealth in the East had already motivated more than a century of increasingly intense exploration by Portuguese and Spaniards before the Coronado expedition was conceived. Cíbola, when that name was first heard by Europeans through Marcos de Niza, was for many certainly a place in the Orient. It is worth remembering, in this regard, that more than twenty years after the expedition, Pedro de Castañeda still maintained that the lands north and west of Cíbola and Tiguex were the beginning of greater India.[5]

Coupled in popular European consciousness in the 1530s with belief in an opulent Orient was the lore of seven wealthy cities to the west. The Portuguese refugees in this land called Antillia had supposedly become marvelously wealthy during the succeeding eight hundred years. As Jane Walsh has shown, the belief that seven Christian cities had been established at the time of the Muslim invasion of Iberia in the 700s in a land or island far to the west of Europe was widely held for hundreds of years.[6] An indication that the existence of the seven cities was still part of popular consciousness in Spain in the mid-sixteenth century is fray Bartolomé de las Casas's early 1550s account of several mariners having reportedly reached Antillia in the final decades of the 1400s and having found the soil and sand of the island heavy with gold.[7] These fabulous seven cities were the destination for generations of conquistadores, including those of the Coronado expedition.

The Confirmation and Promise of Precious Metals

By the late 1530s, Europeans had been regularly plying the waters and trekking across the continents of the Americas, heading west to the Orient and expecting in the intervening thousands of leagues to encounter the seven wealthy cities of the Portuguese bishops. Columbus, for instance, took the island of Cuba to be Cipango (Japan), as predicted earlier by Toscanelli.[8]

In addition to this mythic consciousness was another powerful motivator, experience. In the course of nearly six months in the Bahamas and Caribbean islands in the 1490s, Columbus acquired a few items of gold jewelry, and expectations began to build. Already by 1496, placer gold deposits on the island of Hispaniola had yielded a brief bonanza.[9]

Twenty-three years and a succession of short-lived gold strikes later, Indians in what is now Tabasco told Hernán Cortés of the prodigiously wealthy city of Tenochtitlán many miles inland from the Gulf of Mexico coast. When he and his followers arrived in the city known even then as México, they were greeted by its great leader Moctezuma, reportedly riding beneath a canopy with gold and silver embroidery and wearing slippers with soles of gold.[10] The conquistador Bernal Díaz del Castillo's lengthy and spellbound account reads for all the world like Marco Polo's descriptions of Cathay written more than two hundred years earlier.

Cortés soon extorted golden objects from Moctezuma, who in turn levied them from tributary towns, some at great distance. According to Cortés himself, writing to King Carlos in October 1520,

> all of those lords to whom he sent, gave most fully what he had requested of them, both in jewelry and in disks and sheets of gold and silver. [And they gave] feather diadems and [precious] stones and many other valuable things which I apportioned and assigned to your sacred magesty. [All of] which may have amounted to 100,000 ducados in value.[11]

The Spanish conquerors of Tenochtitlán were overawed by the luxury of the city. As Bernal Díaz del Castillo later wrote, "We saw things so astounding that we didn't know what to say to each other or whether what appeared before us was true."[12]

Everywhere was evidence of unheard-of wealth and grandeur; the conquistadores felt they had stumbled into the pages of the fabulous tales of Amadís of Gaul or the *Travels* of Marco Polo. This was the city, it must be remembered, where less than twenty years later the Coronado expedition was planned and organized. More than a quarter of the European men who made up the expedition were under twenty years old in 1540,[13] and they had heard stories and firsthand accounts of the lavish prizes of the Aztec conquest all their lives. Furthermore, in the late 1530s nearly all the European residents of Mexico City (the former Tenochtitlán) had been born since Columbus's great first voyage and had as a tangible background to their lives a mounting flow of rich objects from the Indies, both East and West.

For instance, the dust from the demolition of Tenochtitlán had barely settled when news of other populous and wealthy lands was heard. Learning from native informants of another wealthy and powerful polity, a frequent rival of Tenochtitlán, Spaniards ventured to the west, finding the Tarascan or Purépechan center of Tzintzúntzan, known then as Michoacán. In a *relación* presented to Viceroy Mendoza in 1541, fray Martín de Jesús de la Coruña told of the first entrance of Spaniards to Michoacán in the early 1520s. At that time the Cazonci, or principal leader, placed "wreaths of gold on their heads" and gave each of them "a round, golden shield."[14] Following this first taste of gold at Michoacán, two of Cortés's lieutenants, Cristóbal de Olid and Andrés de Tapia, made separate trips there with armed forces. Each group ferreted out and extorted from the Cazonci hundreds of disks of gold and silver.

Meanwhile, in Mexico City Spaniards were learning about the history of the Mexica (Aztecs) and their neighbors from knowledgeable natives and from pre-conquest painted books. Most active in recording the traditional histories were the Franciscan, Augustinian, and Dominican priests who had arrived in Tenochtitlán–Mexico City as early as 1523. One of the friars most dedicated to interviewing Mexica elders and narrating the contents of their painted records was fray Diego Durán. Born about 1537, he moved with his family to Mexico City as a young child. As he approached adulthood, he became a Dominican friar and took on the task of writing down local native traditions. He eventually wrote three books, one of which, *Historia de las Yndias de Nueva España y yslas de la tierra firme,* is particularly of interest here. In it he wrote:

> The only knowledge I have of the origins of these people, and the Indians know more than they relate, tells of the Seven Caves where their ancestors dwelt for such a long time, and which they abandoned in order to seek this land, some coming first and others later, until those caves were deserted. The caves are in Teocolhuacan, also called Aztlán, which we are told is found toward the north and near the region of La Florida.[15]

To sixteenth-century Spanish ears the story of Aztlán sounded like a version of the Seven Cities of Antillia, where riches abounded. And now the native people themselves appeared to be saying that these places lay toward the north.

Yet other sources pointed some Spanish aspirations northward. In August 1527 a pilot, Luis Cárdenas, wrote to the king about the New World, saying that he had heard rumors of a city called Coluntapan lying more than two hundred leagues north and two hundred leagues west of the area of Pánuco on the Gulf of Mexico coast. Another city was reportedly beyond that, "where they arm themselves with silver and use metal swords."[16]

To add further northward attraction for Spanish conquistadores, in 1508 a new edition of the books of the fictional chivalric adventure hero Amadís of Gaul had been issued with a freshly minted tale, the *Sergas de Esplandián,* about the hero's son. In the course of Esplandián's make-believe battles with the Turks, his enemies were joined by amazon warriors from an island said to be called California, "to the right hand of the Indies."[17] It is perhaps no wonder, then, that less than three years after the fall of the Mexica (Aztec) capital, Tenochtitlán, Cortés was told of a place that sounded very like that wealthy island inhabited only by warlike women. Writing in 1524, he told the king about "an island inhabited totally by women, without a single man. . . . this island is ten days' journey from this province [Ceguatán, Ciguatlán, or Cihuatlán, both in the region of Compostela in what became Nueva Galicia]. . . . They tell me likewise that it is very rich in pearls and gold."[18]

These and similar reports were important motivators for Nuño Beltrán de Guzmán's conquest of Nueva Galicia, which began only six years later. After looting Michoacán yet again, Guzmán sought energetically to find the fabled rich island of women, which he understood was toward the north along the Gulf of California coast. The notion of an island of amazons, coupled with Tejo's story of the seven cities of silversmiths, continually led Guzmán north. Finally, frustrated at not locating the amazons, he turned exclusively to searching for the seven cities. A member of Guzmán's expedition put it this way: "He decided to cross the mountain range to see what there was beyond, since the search he had made for the Amazons had exhausted him. And besides, he wanted to pursue [the search] for the seven cities, of which he had heard at first when he left Mexico City."[19] Guzmán never found them.

Until the 1530s, Spanish activity in the Americas had been for the most part a succession of forays to verify native reports of wealthy population centers located *más allá*, farther on, more toward the interior. More than fifty full-fledged expeditions had been launched to find the fabled riches of the Indies, of which the Americas were then thought to be an extension. We have concentrated here on only a few reports and discoveries of wealthy places toward the west and north of Mexico City. But Spanish America was awash in stories, eyewitness accounts, and native reports of "kingdoms" and "provinces" where gold, silver, pearls, and other gems existed in quantities that had never been heard of or seen before.

While Guzmán chased rumors of the seven cities northward, for instance, news spread like wildfire from the south that the Pizarro brothers and their followers had taken captive the Inca, Atahualpa, in Peru and had briefly spared his life in exchange for the greatest treasure ever, in excess of a million pesos worth of gold and silver. In Peru at the time (the middle 1530s) was a Franciscan friar named Marcos de Niza, who would soon become prominently involved in the search for the seven cities of the north.

Physical Evidence: A Metal Bell from Wealthy Cities in the North

Occasional raids northward along the coast of the Gulf of California in the 1530s turned up pearls and bits of precious metal. Hernán Cortés financed three sea expeditions, the hoped-for destination of which was the amazon island of Califas. He even made a trip to Baja California himself in 1535, in an ill-fated attempt to start a colony. Writing to Cristóbal de Oñate in that year, Cortés told of having found "a great quantity of pearls" on the peninsula.[20] It was not until the next year, though, that seemingly indisputable evidence of the rich northern cities was received.

It came with four survivors of a shipwreck on the Gulf of Mexico coast eight years before. These wanderers, Álvar Núñez Cabeza de Vaca, Alonso del Castillo Maldonado, Andrés Dorantes, and Esteban de Dorantes, had fled westward from native captors toward vaguely known Spanish settlements in Mexico. The tale of their trek became a sensation on both sides of the Atlantic. They told of subsistence as slaves, acceptance as healers, adventures as the first European witnesses of bison. But more especially they told of "towns with many people and very large houses" where the people "wear cotton shirts." These towns, they learned, lay north of where they had journeyed.[21] Furthermore, Cabeza de Vaca and company heard that the people of the north were experienced metalworkers and even saw physical evidence of their handiwork. First, in one town, they were given "some small bags of silver."[22] Then, shortly afterward, according to the so-called Joint Report of the survivors' experiences recorded by Gonzalo Fernández de Oviedo y Valdés, probably in the 1540s, native people "gave the Christians [the Spaniards] a copper hawksbell and some cotton blankets and said [they] came from the north, having crossed the land toward the South Sea [Pacific Ocean–Gulf of California].[23]

Cabeza de Vaca, in his own relación elaborated the story this way:

> From here we began entering the land toward the interior by way of the skirt of the mountain range for more than 50 leagues. At the end of them we found 40 houses. Among the things they gave us Andrés Dorantes had a big, heavy copper bell with a face engraved on it. They showed that they prized it and told that they had obtained it from their neighbors. When asked where they [the neighbors] had gotten it, they told him [Dorantes] that they had brought it from toward the north and that there were many [bells] there, and they were greatly esteemed. We understood that from wherever [the bell] had come, there were foundries and that casting in molds was done.[24]

Later, the Spaniards showed the bell to other Indians who said that "in that place from which [the bell] had come there were many sheets of [metal] buried underground, and that it was a thing that they [the people of that country] prized."[25]

From what the Cabeza de Vaca party heard and saw, its members "inferred that where that [bell] was brought from, even if there is no gold, there is a source [of metal] and they smelt [it].[26]

It is both clear and ironic that the copper bell given to Dorantes played a major role in Spanish deductions about the north. Cabeza de Vaca, with reasonable logic, concluded that metal was being mined and processed at the northern town. The "proof," however, was false. Copper bells were trade items coming from the pueblos north of the castaway's route, but current knowledge indicates that the bells were not Puebloan but originated farther south, in southern Sinaloa, Michoacán, and other parts of western Mexico.[27] The irony was that the bell that helped launch an expedition to the north came originally from lands the Spaniards had already conquered.

The Dorantes bell was, in reality, evidence not of northern metalworking but of vigorous regional trade. It was no doubt assumed by many that Cabeza de Vaca's reports confirmed Tejo's story and supported the supposition that another Mexica- or Inca-scale empire lay beyond the northern frontier. Although nowhere in the Cabeza de Vaca documents are the populous towns of metal-workers in the north called the "seven cities" or "Cíbola," it was widely assumed that the places the "*naufragios*," or shipwreck survivors, had heard of were the same towns told of by Tejo and sought by Guzmán just a few years earlier. And the towns of Tejo were identified with the seven cities of the Portuguese bishops. As Jane Walsh has written, "it seems clear . . . that from the very start, Tejo's account was conflated in Spanish minds with the Seven Cities of Antillia myth."[28] Now, with the coming of Cabeza de Vaca and his companions, there were not just stories but hard physical evidence in the shape of a native-made metal bell.

Seeking Verification of the Northern Cities

Cabeza de Vaca's party reached Mexico City on July 23, 1536, with the bell and their reports. In the fall, Cabeza de Vaca and Dorantes traveled to Veracruz with the intention of leaving for Spain, but their departure was delayed, and Dorantes stayed in Nueva España. It was during these months of late 1536 and early 1537 that Viceroy Mendoza decided an expedition to the north was advisable. Writing to the king on December 10, 1537, he said:

> After [Cabeza de Vaca and Dorantes] had arrived here [Mexico City], they decided to leave for Spain. Understanding that if Your Majesty would be pleased to send some people to that land [to the north] in order to learn for sure what it was, no one would remain [in New Spain]

who could go with them or provide information, I purchased from Dorantes a Black named Esteban for this purpose. Later it happened that the ship in which Dorantes was traveling returned to port. When I learned this, I wrote to him at Veracruz begging him to come here. When he reached this city, I spoke with him, saying that it would be good for [him] to return to this [northern] land with some religious persons and horsemen, which I would provide to him, to reconnoiter and learn for certain what was in it [the northern land].

When he understood my wish and the service I was engaging him in and what he would do through it for God and Your majesty, he replied to me that he was happy to [do] it.[29]

However, as Mendoza later wrote to the king, he spent a considerable sum to outfit Dorantes, but nothing came of it, for reasons that Mendoza said he did not understand.

Instead, the viceroy started over and in mid-1538 arranged an expedition to be led by the well-regarded friar Marcos de Niza, guided by Esteban and accompanied by another friar named Honorato. They were seeking the towns of metalworkers, the streets of silversmiths, the seven cities, the beginnings of Greater India. The notion that this was their destination held true for Esteban, Marcos, and Honorato no less than for Francisco Vázquez de Coronado, the new governor of Nueva Galicia, who accompanied them as far as Culiacán, and for the populace of Mexico City at large. Images of the Indies and the Seven Cities of Antillia naturally flavored the reports of Tejo, Cortés, Guzmán, and Cabeza de Vaca. The reports of the 1530s, in turn, seemed to confirm and expand the older tales. Thus, no manipulation or exaggeration of news from the north was necessary to solidify what was already common knowledge in 1538: seven cities of gold and silver lay far toward the north, and fray Marcos de Niza was headed there.

According to Vázquez de Coronado, fray Marcos and Esteban were being sent to "reconnoiter by land along the coast of this Nueva España, in order to learn the secrets which there are in it, the lands and people who have not been seen [before]."[30] In his written instructions to the priest, Viceroy Mendoza specified that he was to "inquire always for information about the coast" and "take great care to inquire about . . . the minerals and metals which there are in [the northern land]."[31] Furthermore, fray Marcos was always to "try to send information via Indians about how you are proceeding and how you are received and, very especially, what you find."[32] As we will see, this last instruction was to result in unintended confusion in Mexico City about exactly what was discovered in the north, where the discoveries were situated, and by whom they were made.

Information Received and Sent by Marcos de Niza

In the formal report that fray Marcos certified after returning from the north, he wrote that he and Esteban had departed from Culiacán (in modern Nayarít) on March 7, 1539.[33] Only a week to ten days later, natives from islands off the coast told the friar about the existence of pearls in their home territory, though he did not see any himself.[34] He traveled on, passing a valley, or *abra,* where he was told there was gold. Because it would have required a departure from the coast, he decided to leave its exploration for his return trip. About three days farther on he reached an agriculturally productive native settlement known as Vacapa. There he remained perhaps as long as two and a half weeks, enquiring about the surrounding territory and the seacoast. During this hiatus, in order not to waste time in his northward progress, Marcos sent Esteban ahead, giving him instructions to seek information about northern cities and telling him that

> if he received news of a settled and wealthy land (which would be a won-
> derful thing), that he was not to travel farther but instead return in per-
> son or send me Indians with this sign that we agreed on: if the thing
> [found] was moderately important, he was to send me a white cross of
> one palm [in size], if it was of great [importance], he was to send one
> of two palms [in size], and if it were grander and better than New Spain,
> he was to send me a large cross.[35]

Just four days later, probably in very early April, native messengers returned to Vacapa from Esteban bearing "a very large cross the height of a man. They told me on behalf of Esteban that I should, at that [very] moment, set out in pursuit of him, because he had run across people who gave him a report of the grandest thing in the world. He had Indians who had been there. And he sent me one of the Indians who had been in the land."[36]

Two days farther on, Marcos came to a settlement where he learned of seven great cities, and for the first time he learned the name of the place. The people informed him that "from here they traveled in thirty days to the ciudad of Cíbola, which is the first of the seven. Not just one [person] told me about it, but many. And in very great detail they told me [about] the grandness of the houses and their style."[37]

With such astonishing news, it is plausible that Marcos dispatched a messenger to the viceroy at about this time, in conformance with his instructions, so that Mendoza would be apprised of what could be expected ahead, based on eyewitness testimony. Such a message could have reached Mexico City as early as June 1539 and could have told of the friar's friendly reception, reports of pearls on islands off the coast and gold in a valley to the east, his seeing bountiful irrigated valleys, and firsthand accounts of turquoise from the seven multistoried towns known collectively as Cíbola. This interim report would have been free of any of the ominous news that was yet to come.

By early May Marcos reached the last settlement before the long unpopulated region, or *despoblado,* beyond which lay Cíbola. Esteban was still some days ahead of him. Along the way Marcos had received numerous reports of the northern cities from residents of the settlements he passed through. Some had actually lived there; one was a native of Cíbola who had fled from there. And Esteban sent him yet another very large cross. In this final settlement before the great despoblado, Marcos also reported seeing more than two thousand bison hides and even more turquoise than he had seen before, all of which came from Cíbola.

Because fray Marcos had been told that this settlement was four days from the beginning of a fifteen-day trek across an uninhabited land, it is likely that he sent off a final interim message to the viceroy before setting out, now in early May. Because of the important role of Marcos's messages in the unfolding events, we now follow this last possible message in order to demonstrate the latest probable arrival time of a uniformly positive message about the north, referring to pearls, turquoise, and gold.

Marcos indicated that he left this last settlement on May 5 and had traveled no more than thirty-nine days since he left Culiacán, meaning that his hypothetical final interim message could easily have reached Culiacán by mid-June. When the message arrived at Culiacán, it would have found Vázquez de Coronado, then governor of Nueva Galicia, absent. He had gone in search of yet another rumored place rich in gold, known as Topira. Fray Honorato, though, might well have been there, because he had fallen ill shortly after he, Marcos, and Esteban had set out and had been sent back. Honorato himself might have had instructions from Marcos to carry any message about major discoveries back to the viceroy. Either he or another messenger could have traveled the approximately 305 miles from Culiacán to Compostela, capital of Nueva Galicia and Vázquez de Coronado's seat of government, in 13 days at about 23 miles per day. The message would have arrived in Compostela by the end of June. The distance from Compostela to Mexico City, approximately 520 miles, could have been covered in 20 days by horsemen carrying this priority message at a rate of 26 miles per day, putting Marcos's final interim message in the viceroy's hand by late July.

Our estimated 33-day trip is much faster than the 58-day travel time of Cabeza de Vaca's party over the same route, which made the trip in 1536 with an armed escort of 20 horsemen and 500 Indian slaves and was feted along the way.[38] Earlier messages from fray Marcos about the good lands and northern city could have arrived before this. Viceroy Mendoza had instructed him to report in secret, but rumors of these messages clearly leaked out. All this is confirmed by the fact that Cortés wrote to Mendoza on July 26, 1539, about rumors concerning "the news from Marcos" and "the good country" he had found.[39]

Meanwhile, fray Marcos himself had met with a disastrous turn of events, still unknown in Mexico City. Esteban had been killed in Cíbola, and on about May 25 Marcos had approached only close enough to see the city in the distance and confirm its promising multistory appearance before turning and fleeing at top speed back toward Mexico.

On July 8, Francisco de Ulloa sailed from Acapulco under Cortés's orders to explore the north. It is possible that Cortés rushed ahead with this voyage in response to the rumors of Marcos's first messages about a good country to the north, which would have arrived in Nueva España in June.

Events were now unfolding rapidly. Probably around July 13, Vázquez de Coronado returned to Compostela from Topira and apparently was given copies of the various interim messages fray Marcos had sent. On July 15, with good news from Marcos in hand, the governor drafted a letter to the king, telling of "such an excellent land" in the north.[40] That information had to come from a message sent by the friar through couriers, because he himself was still far to the north, traveling south posthaste. It is clear that Marcos was not yet back, because Vázquez de Coronado apparently had no inkling of the death of Esteban, writing instead that the Indians had been treating Marcos and Esteban "very well."

Our insistence on the existence of such interim messages clears up several mysteries that plagued earlier researchers. Carl Sauer, Henry Wagner, and Cleve Hallenbeck, writing separately in the 1930s and 1940s, claimed (strangely) that there were no such messages, and therefore Marcos himself had to have been back in Compostela by July 15 (July 1 by Wagner's reckoning) in order personally to give Vázquez de Coronado the news of the good country.[41] This in turn is the primary rationale for their claim that Marcos did not have time to reach Cíbola, that he stopped short, and that he deliberately lied about seeing Cíbola as part of a conspiracy with Mendoza. The presumed existence of messengers removes most of this rationale.

Probably about a week after the governor dispatched his July 15 letter, Marcos himself reached Compostela, later reporting that he found Vázquez de Coronado there. Now the governor knew of the catastrophe that had befallen Esteban, and he presumably also knew, from interviewing Marcos, that there was as yet no tangible proof of precious metals at Cíbola, although fray Marcos would continue to refer to the *riquezas,* or wealth, there. Fray Marcos and Vázquez de Coronado now rushed to Mexico City to deliver personally to Mendoza what was viewed as very positive news of Cíbola.

By this time, Hernán Cortés in Cuernavaca had already received news of fray Marcos's good discoveries. On July 26 Cortés sent a letter to the viceroy asking for confirmation,[42] which Mendoza supplied by a return letter. On August 6 Cortés wrote back, thanking Mendoza for the good news, "worthy of rendering praise to God." Cortés remarked that he had been very anxious for confirmation "on account of what is being said around here about that country," a phrase which confirms that rumors were already spreading like wildfire.[43] It is interesting that none of these July 15–August 6 letters of Vázquez de Coronado and Cortés refers to gold or jewels, but only to the "good country" or "an excellent land."

By about August 20 fray Marcos and Vázquez de Coronado reached Mexico City, each reporting to his superior-Marcos to the Franciscan provincial Antonio de Ciudad Rodrigo, and Vázquez de Coronado to the viceroy. On August 23, fray Juan de Zumárraga, bishop of Mexico, wrote a letter including a comment that fray Marcos "has discovered a much more wonderful land."[44] In the letter he summarized the friar's discoveries, but with some variance from Marcos's final written report. For example, he said that the people of Cíbola lived in multistory houses of wood. The mistake about wood and the general tone of the letter suggest that the information about the northern land was being remembered from conversation with Marcos rather than paraphrased from a document written by him. This letter reports at some length (correctly) that the people of Cíbola were cultured, had multistory houses, and worshiped the sun and moon, that the men had only one wife, and that Marcos had heard stories of cities grander than Mexico City. Like the other letters, it says nothing about gold or jewels in Cíbola.

Meanwhile, as per instructions, Marcos presumably reported in secret to the viceroy. But regardless of attempts at secrecy, whatever Marcos said or wrote in public and whatever people in Mexico City and elsewhere in Nueva España thought he said created a sensation, adding to the expectations that had antedated his trip.

By August 24, 1539, officials in Mexico City already felt some urgency about an impending exploration to the north. Presumably to stop wildcat planning in response to rumors now heightened by fray Marcos's return, and to block Cortés's plans, Viceroy Mendoza issued a proclamation on that date forbidding anyone to leave the country by sea or land without his permission.[45]

Marcos's Final Report and Its Aftermath

Fray Marcos's formal, written report was dated August 26, 1539, having been certified that day by the Franciscan provincial. Further court certification was made in front of Viceroy Mendoza and other officials on September 2. This relación is thus the official document stating that Marcos saw irrigated, populous, and prosperous towns in the north, was told about the seven cities called Cíbola, saw numerous turquoises and bison hides said to have come from there, and viewed one of those cities from a distance. Although Marcos made no claim that there was gold in Cíbola, he reported that native people to its south considered it a wealthy place where they went to work and trade. The word *oro,* gold, appears just three times in the surviving copies of the report, all three in reference to the abra, or valley, far south of Cíbola. There, Marcos reported (both in his relación and his probable interim messages), Indians had told him of gold in use, but he noted soberly that he had been unable to enter the valley or confirm gold there during a brief foray in that direction as he fled south.

Conflation of this report of gold at the abra with information about the existence of Cíbola surely fueled renewed notions of precious metals at Cíbola. They were only reinforced when the relación noted that hundreds of people from the Sonora area had been willing to accompany Esteban to Cíbola "because they thought [that they would] return rich"[46]—an idea no doubt true in the local people's frame of reference, because they were accustomed to trading there.

The relación's omission of discussion of gold in Cíbola, or even any discussion of attempts to confirm it by showing gold samples to the Indians, seems strange, because gold had been discovered and was already being mined at several locations in Nueva España. One assumes that Marcos must have been grilled on this point by Viceroy Mendoza, and it is possible that any admission in the document that Marcos had been unable to confirm gold in Cíbola, or speculation about such forms of wealth, was deliberately discouraged, in order to allow Mendoza better control over the situation. Marcos's strangely "oblique" report might have been interpreted by general readers (if there were any outside the viceroy's office) as a tacit assumption that Cíbola was rich in gold or other precious metals. Because Marcos described how he carried gold samples and used them to query Indians of other regions on this point, his total silence on any similar efforts to ask about gold in Cíbola is all the more puzzling. In any case, many people, both those who read the report (who must have been few) and those who heard oral versions of what it contained (who were many), came to the conclusion that Marcos had found an empire that was surely full of gold, another Tenochtitlán.

Rumors intensified in Mexico City that the friar had discovered rich and populous lands to the north. About two months later, seven witnesses were interviewed in Havana about what was being said in Mexico regarding Marcos's discoveries. Six out of seven used a phrase similar to "rich and populous land" and did not mention gold. Nonetheless, some individuals who had personal or secondhand contact with Marcos and heard him talk about his trip evidently understood him to say that gold would be found in Cíbola. The father-in-law of Marcos's barber, for instance, testified in Havana in November 1539 that Marcos had told his son-in-law that in Cíbola "the women wore strands of gold and the men golden waistbands."[47] It is difficult to dismiss the barber's story, for in all details other than gold it jibes nearly word for word with Marcos's written report. And even in this, it matches the friar's report except that Marcos wrote "cintas de turquesas" (belts or waistbands made with turquoises, which was almost certainly correct), rather than "cintas de oro."

A month earlier than the Havana testimony, fray Jiménez de San Esteban drafted a letter parts of which he said were based on a conversation with Marcos. In it he described Cíbola much as Marcos had in his written report, with the single addition that he mentioned silk. Still, his overall impression of what the friar told him was of a place that was fabulously wealthy. He was even reluctant to write some of the details, saying, "Of the richness . . . I do not write because it is said to be so great that it does not seem possible."[48] In face-to-face conversations, it seems that Marcos may have been offering speculations that went far beyond his official report.

Jiménez wrote further, "The friar himself told me this, that he saw a temple of their idols, the walls of which, inside and out, were covered with precious stones. I think he said they were emeralds."[49] Because Marcos himself denied entering the city of Cíbola, he clearly would not have described a Cíbolan "temple," and therefore fray Jiménez must have misunderstood this point. We suppose that Marcos was describing smaller shrines he had seen in northern Sonora. Historic and archeological evidence of public architecture and decorated shrines in this area, including comments by Coronado expedition member Pedro de Castañeda, has been summarized by William Doolittle.[50] To Marcos's listeners, all the wonders he described were in the "rich and populous lands" he had discovered in the north, and Jiménez probably associated what he heard with the new empire of Cíbola. Because the letter of fray Jiménez has some of the strongest claims of riches, and because of the accusations that Marcos was trumpeting gold to all who would listen, it is again remarkable that this letter does not mention gold per se in Cíbola.

Even with all the excitement over what Marcos said and implied, the viceroy may have harbored either skepticism at the speculations or anger that Marcos had come so close without proving the presence of gold. While he was investing heavily in mounting a full-fledged expedition to Cíbola to be led by his protégé Francisco Vázquez de Coronado, Mendoza dispatched a second reconnaissance party to Cíbola led by the alcalde of Culiacán, Melchior Díaz, to confirm what Marcos had found. We cannot say for certain whether this reflects uncertainty about Marcos's veracity or accuracy or whether it was simply a prudent follow-up, although the official reason for the Díaz reconnaissance was to locate food supplies in an area where they were said to be scarce.

At any rate, Díaz and a small company were sent off in mid-November 1539. They did not penetrate the final fifteen-day despoblado, being stopped by snow. Mendoza later included a direct quotation of Díaz's report in a letter to the king. Though it contained considerable information about life in Cíbola, it gave little more information than Marcos did on the all-consuming issue of gold. Díaz interviewed many Indians and confirmed Marcos's account of turquoises in Cíbola and the manner of Esteban's death, but he reported tersely, "[The Indians] are unable to give me information about any metal nor do they say that [the people of Cíbola] possess it."[51]

We get a better sense of Díaz's news from eyewitness accounts of the situation. When Díaz's party returned and met the advancing expedition in March 1540 south of Culiacán, its news was apparently considered discouraging. Diego López, one of the Coronado expedition's captains, later recalled that "after the day they met Melchior Díaz, the witness [López] held no hope that they would come across anything [worthwhile] in that land."[52] Similarly, Pedro de Castañeda wrote, "They [the Díaz party] arrived and talked with the general. Despite the privacy in which it was discussed, the bad news was soon rumored."[53] We have the same story from a letter sent by the captain general, Vázquez de Coronado himself, about five months afterward. He wrote to the viceroy saying, "From the people here he [Díaz] learned that nothing would be found farther on except the continuation of the very rough mountains, entirely uninhabited by people."[54]

What those who signed on to the expedition had come to believe, conditioned at least in part by the statements and actions of fray Marcos de Niza, was not confirmed, and it must have been a serious blow to them. In July, when the expedition arrived at Cíbola, it was Marcos who took the blame:

When they [the members of the expedition] saw the first town, which was Cíbola, the curses that some of them hurled at fray Marcos were so strong, that may God not allow him to understand [them]. [rubric] It is a small town crowded together and spilling down a cliff. In Nueva España there are *estancias* which from a distance have a better appearance.[55]

Whether or not Marcos had intentionally misled people about Cíbola, a great many thought he had. As a result, he fled back to Mexico City in fear for his life. At the very least, there is no evidence that he did anything to disabuse anyone of obvious misunderstandings of what he had said and written.

Conclusion

The people of Mexico City in 1539–40 operated-as do all people at all times-within a matrix of tradition, rumor, and direct evidence, some of which eventually proved accurate while other parts did not. The news and copper bell obtained by Cabeza de Vaca's party would have been viewed as viable evidence of northern wealth and metalworking. Marcos de Niza, like most of his contemporaries, probably had an a priori conviction when he began his trip that unimaginable European-style wealth was likely to exist north of Nueva España. During his reconnaissance, he diligently sought information about such a place from knowledgeable native informants. Reading his report now, we can see that he recorded fundamentally accurate information about active and, by native standards, prosperous trading centers. Regardless of what the natives of Sonora *meant* about riches at Cíbola (which is definitely of interest to anthropologists and historians of today), what was *understood* by Europeans back in Mexico City-what the Spanish words conveyed-was that there was European-style wealth there, such as the Spaniards had already found in Tenochtitlán and Peru.

Thus, the words Marcos used in regard to Cíbola, such as *rico* and *riqueza* (perhaps deliberately vague in order to give the viceroy maximum flexibility), naturally led others to believe that silver and gold would be found there in unprecedented quantity, as Marcos himself may also have believed.

By the time of Marcos's return to Mexico City in 1539, the earliest rumors and reports of wealthy lands to the north and the expectations raised by the conquests of Mexico and Peru had been strongly augmented by much more concrete information. We must remember another aspect of the case. As developed in more detail by Michel Nallino and William Hartmann, people in Mexico City in the summer of 1539 witnessed "two waves" of information arriving from the north.[56] The first was the arrival of messengers in June or July with news of newly discovered rich and populous lands. This was no doubt seen as confirmation of everyone's dreams. The second wave was the return of Marcos himself a month or two later with confirmation of the first wave of news but nothing much additional, given that he had not actually entered any of the Seven Cities of Cíbola. It may even have been difficult, by August and September of 1539, to deflate the June–July "discovery" of riches in the north. As Nallino and Hartmann point out, these two waves were transformed by later historians into two different explorations, a 1538 expedition by a captain and two friars who found Cíbola (based on Vázquez de Coronado, Marcos, and Honorato's leaving Mexico City in 1538 and on Honorato's or other messengers' returning in July with news of the basic discoveries) and a 1539 expedition by Marcos to confirm it (based on Marcos's showing up in Mexico after the first news and rumors had circulated).

Marcos's report and public and private statements about Cíbola seemed to further authenticate all preexisting beliefs. A huge expedition like the one subsequently launched, on the scale of a national enterprise with well-known major investors, would never have been mounted without confidence that Cíbola was among the richest places in the Indies.

The Coronado expedition found no wealth, but it did locate people ready for evangelization and good land available for cultivation. Despite that, the participants saw it as a failure and returned home. Souls and soil would have been nice side benefits (at least for the majority, excluding the religious), but clearly the paramount goal of the expedition was to find and acquire European-style wealth.

When Marcos was sent north to determine whether Cabeza de Vaca's reports were true-whether a place already associated with silver and other metals, including gold, really existed-his reply in effect was, "It exists and it must be rich." Although we have no direct evidence that Marcos wrote about or talked about gold in Cíbola, we also have no evidence that he did anything to discourage such conclusions. Publicly, based on the available evidence, he seems to have been much more restrained than is usually described, but the greatest likelihood is that he encouraged high expectations, perhaps offering speculations in private conversations. He was not lying, in that he probably really believed that Cibola was wealthy in a European sense. But to say he was not lying-that is, intentionally telling untruths—does not mean he was producing an accurate and unbiased picture of Cíbola. Images of Tenochtitlán, Peru, China, and the Seven Cities of Antillia naturally flavored the reports of Tejo, Cortés, Guzmán, Cabeza de Vaca, and eventually fray Marcos. Thus, no manipulation or exaggeration of news from the north was necessary to solidify what was already common "knowledge" in 1538 and 1539: seven cities of gold and silver lay far toward the north.

Our reconstruction of the information about Cíbola available to Spaniards in Mexico City in 1539 makes it appear highly unlikely that a conspiracy existed between Marcos de Niza and Viceroy Mendoza to create a flat-out fraud about wealth in the north. The hypothesis of a campaign of lies, such as was popularized sixty years ago by Sauer, Wagner, and Hallenbeck, is simply unnecessary to explain the enthusiasm behind the Coronado expedition. No direct evidence for such a conspiratorial program of disinformation exists; its life owes only to inferences made by its proponents, many of which are no longer deemed to be correct. In particular, it rests on the assumption that fray Marcos did not follow instructions and neglected to send back messengers. Further, it is senseless to suppose that the viceroy would have been a party to such a scheme when he himself stood to lose a fortune if the Coronado expedition failed to find the expected wealth in Cíbola. Neither profit nor prestige would have accrued to Mendoza were he to have mounted a grand expedition to a place he suspected might be devoid of European-style wealth.

Another point of departure between our views and those of earlier authors is our emphasis on Marcos's instructions to explore the coast. Marcos repeatedly spoke of his awareness of these instructions and his attempts to gain information about the coast, whereas Hallenbeck, in particular, claims he ignored them.[57] This is important because Mendoza was in a race with Cortés, who wanted to explore the north by sea, and a key part of Mendoza's expeditionary force of 1540 was the now largely forgotten seaborne arm that took much of the expedition's supplies in an ill-fated plan to rendezvous at the nonexistent "port" of Chichilticale. Marcos's attempts to stay near the coast may even have affected his northward route, which may have lain, in some sections, farther west than the final route of the Coronado expedition.

A more important point of departure between our analysis and earlier work is our reconstruction of events to include interim messages sent by Marcos de Niza to the viceroy or the Franciscan provincial in June and July of 1539. Lansing Bloom was first to suggest that many problems regarding Marcos's trip could be solved by assuming the friar followed the viceroy's instructions and sent back messages as he traveled north.[58] In this we concur. Hallenbeck denied it,[59] and Sauer claimed he could not even understand the suggestion,[60] in spite of Vázquez de Coronado's statement in a now-lost letter, (mis?)dated in March 1539, that he had received a letter from Marcos after the friar left Culiacán, describing what seems to have been the first one or two weeks of his trip. Our view is that a first wave of messages from Marcos, containing optimistic reports of marvelous lands to the north-including mention of gold—not only fits with rumors circulating in Mexico City during July and August 1539 but also is in keeping with Mendoza's instructions. It suggests that pressure for an expedition began to mushroom then, before Marcos's own return to Mexico City. The story of the Coronado expedition is not so much a story of fraud as it is a monumental story of preconceived expectations, all because of what a large number of people thought they knew even before any of them had seen it.

So it was that reports of the wealth of the East and the cities of the seven Portuguese bishops, chivalric tales of amazons, Tejo's story of towns of silversmiths, Mexica traditions of the seven caves of Aztlán, Cabeza de Vaca's secondhand information about towns of metalworkers, and tangible evidence such as a metal bell, turquoise, and bison hides all combined to point north as surely as any mariner's compass.

Notes

1. The list of investors in the expedition continues to grow. Research conducted in Sevilla in 2002 by Shirley Cushing Flint and Richard Flint has revealed two additional significant financial backers, don Luis de Castilla and Luis de León Romano. For details, see chapter 3.

2. Oxitipan has been identified as being in the modern state of San Luis Potosí. Peter Gerhard, *A Guide to the Historical Geography of New Spain,* rev. ed. (Norman: University of Oklahoma Press, 1993), 354.

3. Pedro de Castañeda de Náçera [1563], *Relación de la jornada de Cíbola compuesta por Pedro de Castañeda de Náçera donde se trata de todos aquellos poblados y ritos, y costumbres la qual fue el año de 1540,* Primera Parte, Capítulo 1, fol. 10r–11v. Case 12, Rich Collection 63, Nuevo Mexico, Sevilla, 1596, 157 11, 4° bound, New York Public Library, Rare Books and Manuscripts Division. In Flint and Flint, *"They Were Not Familiar."*

4. Samuel Eliot Morison, *The European Discovery of America: The Southern Voyages, 1492–1616* (New York: Oxford University Press, 1974), 29.

5. Castañeda, *Relación,* Segunda Parte, Capítulo 6, fol. 119v.

6. Jane MacLaren Walsh, "Myth and Imagination in the American Story: The Coronado Expedition, 1540–1542" (Ph.D. diss., Catholic University of America, 1993), 28–34.

7. Bartolomé de las Casas, *Historia de las Indias,* 3 vols., ed. André Saint-Lu (Caracas, Venezuela: Biblioteca Ayacucho, 1986),1:70.

8. Christopher Columbus, *The Diario of Christopher Columbus's First Voyage to America, 1492–1493,* eds. and trans. Oliver Dunn and James E. Kelley Jr. (Norman: University of Oklahoma Press, 1989), 108, 109.

9. Peter Bakewell, *A History of Latin America: Empires and Sequels, 1450–1930* (Oxford: Blackwell Publishers, 1997), 72.

10. Bernal Díaz del Castillo, *Historia verdadera de la conquista de la Nueva España,* ed. Carmelo Sáenz de Santa María (México, D.F.: Alianza Editorial, 1991), 240; Richard Flint translation.

11. Hernán Cortés, *Cartas de Relación* (México, D.F.: Editorial Porrúa, 1993), 61; Richard Flint translation.

12. Díaz del Castillo, *Historia verdadera,* 239; Richard Flint translation.

13. Flint, *Great Cruelties,* 542–45.

14. Eugene R. Craine and Reginald C. Reindorp, eds. and trans., *The Chronicles of Michoacán* (Norman: University of Oklahoma Press, 1970), 68–69.

15. Diego Durán, *The History of the Indies of New Spain,* ed. and trans. Doris Heyden (Norman: University of Oklahoma Press, 1994), 10.

16. Quoted in Carl O. Sauer, "The Discovery of New Mexico Reconsidered," *New Mexico Historical Review* 12 (July 1937): 271–72.

17. Garci Rodríguez de Montalvo, *Las Sergas de Espandián* (Zaragosa: Casa de Simon de Portonariis, 1587; facsimile, Madrid: Ediciones Doce Calles, 1998), 100v; Richard Flint translation.

18. Cortés, *Cartas,* 184; Richard Flint translation.

19. Joaquin García Icazbalceta, ed., "Primera y segunda relaciones anónimas de la jornada que hizo Nuño de Guzmán a la Nueva Galicia" (Mexico, D.F.: Chimalistac, 1952), 15; Richard Flint translation.

20. Hernán Cortés, "Carta de Hernán Cortés a Cristóbal de Oñate," in *Documentos Cortesianos,* ed. José Luis Martínez (México, D.F.: UNAM and Fondo de Cultura Económica, 1992), 4:148.

21. Álvar Núñez Cabeza de Vaca, *Naufragios y comentarios con dos cartas,* 9th ed. (México, D.F.: Espasa–Calpe Mexicana, 1985), 92; Richard Flint translation.

22. Cabeza de Vaca, *Naufragios,* 81; Richard Flint translation.

23. Gonzalo Fernández de Oviedo, *Historia general y natural de las Indias,* ed. Juan Pérez de Tudela Bueso (Madrid: Ediciones Atlas, 1992), 4:307; Richard Flint translation.

24. Cabeza de Vaca, *Naufragios,* 83–84; Richard Flint translation.

25. Cabeza de Vaca, *Naufragios,* 85; Richard Flint translation.

26. Fernández de Oviedo, *Historia general,* 4:307; Richard Flint translation.

27. By means of detailed stylistic comparisons, Victoria Vargas has concluded that all prehistoric and protohistoric copper bells in the Southwest were made in western Mexico and carried north along the very trade route that Marcos de Niza and Vázquez de Coronado were to follow. See Victoria D. Vargas, *Copper Bell Trade Patterns in the Prehistoric U.S. Southwest and Northwest Mexico* (Tucson: Arizona State Museum, University of Arizona, 1995).

28. Walsh, "Myth and Imagination," 54.

29. Antonio de Mendoza, "Letter to the King, Mexico City, December 10, 1537," AGI, Patronato, 184, R. 27, fol. 14v; Richard Flint translation.

30. Francisco Vázquez de Coronado, "Letter to the King, Compostela, July 15, 1539," AGI, Guadalajara, 5, R.1, N.6, fol. 2r, in Flint and Flint, *"They Were Not Familiar."*

31. Fray Marcos de Niza, "Narrative Account by fray Marcos de Niza, Temistitán, August 26, 1539," AGI, Patronato 20, N.5, R.10, fol. 1v, in Flint and Flint, *"They Were Not Familiar."*

32. Marcos de Niza, "Narrative," fol. 1v.

33. Marcos de Niza, "Narrative," fol. 2r.

34. Marcos de Niza, "Narrative," fol. 2v.

35. Marcos de Niza, "Narrative," fol. 3r.

36. Marcos de Niza, "Narrative," fol. 3r.

37. Marcos de Niza, "Narrative," fol. 3v.

38. Rolena Adorno and Patrick Charles Pautz, *Álvar Núñez Cabeza de Vaca: His Account, His Life, and the Expedition of Pánfilo de Narváez* (Lincoln: University of Nebraska Press, 1999), 2:383–85. Regarding this time scale, a simple but important confirming argument can be made that, to our knowledge, has not been advanced before. At the settlement before Cíbola on his northward trek, Marcos was told that it was a nineteen-day journey to Cíbola. He himself traveled to within sight of Cíbola before having to flee rapidly back to the same settlement. Therefore, if he had sent a message to the viceroy from that town before leaving for Cíbola, he would have been traveling the return trail roughly thirty-eight days behind his own message. We know Marcos was probably in Mexico City by August 23. Therefore, it is plausible that the last positive report Marcos sent from his northern journey arrived in Mexico City around mid-July.

39. Hernán Cortés, "Letter from Cortés to Mendoza, Cuernavaca, July 26, 1539," in Henry R. Wagner, "Fray Marcos de Niza," *New Mexico Historical Review* 9 (April 1934): 213.

40. Vázquez de Coronado, "Letter to the King, Compostela," fol. 2v.

41. Sauer, "Discovery of New Mexico"; Wagner, "Marcos de Niza," 214; Cleve Hallenbeck, *The Journey of Fray Marcos de Niza* (Dallas: Southern Methodist University Press, 1987), 63.

42. Cortés, "Letter from Cortés to Mendoza," 213–14.

43. Antonio de Mendoza, "Letter from Mendoza to Cortés, Mexico City, August 3, 1539," in Wagner, "Marcos de Niza," 217.

44. Fray Juan de Zumárraga, "Letter to unknown recipient, Mexico City, August 23, 1539," in Wagner, "Marcos de Niza," 223.

45. A. Grove Day, *Coronado's Quest: The Discovery of the Southwestern States* (Berkeley: University of California Press, 1940), 66.

46. Marcos de Niza, "Narrative," fol. 5v.

47. Hernando Florencio, scribe, "Testimony of witnesses, Havana, November 1539," AGI, Patronato, 21, N.2, R.4, fol. 4r, in Flint and Flint, *"They Were Not Familiar."*

48. Fray Jerónimo Ximénez, "Carta de fray Jerónimo Ximénez de San Esteban a Santo Tomás de Villanueva," in *Cartas de religiosos de Nueva España, 1539–1594,* ed. Joaquín García Icazbalceta (México, D.F.: Editorial Salvador Chávez Hayhoe, 1941), 188; Richard Flint translation.

49. Ximénez, "Carta," 188; Richard Flint translation.

50. William K. Doolittle, *Pre-Hispanic Occupance in the Valley of Sonora, Mexico: Archaeological Confirmation of Early Spanish Reports,* Anthropology Papers 48 (Tucson: University of Arizona, 1988), 3.

51. Antonio de Mendoza, "The Viceroy's Letter to the King, Jacona, April 17, 1540," AGI, Patronato, 184, R.31, fol. 2r, in Flint and Flint, *"They Were Not Familiar."*

52. Fernando Gómez de la Peña, scribe, "Testimony Taken at Culiacán," in "Criminal Process in the Audiencia of Mexico against Nuño de Chaves, Rebel in the Rebellion, Mexico City, 1566," AGI, Patronato, 216, R.2, in Flint, *Great Cruelties,* 396.

53. Castañeda, *Relación,* Primera Parte, Capítulo 7, fol. 27v.

54. Francisco Vázquez de Coronado, "Letter of Coronado to Mendoza, from the city of Granada, province of Cíbola, August 3, 1540," in Hammond and Rey, *Narratives,* 163. See also Giovanni Battista Ramusio, *Terzo volume delle navigationi et viaggi* [1566], fol. 359v, in Flint and Flint, *"They Were Not Familiar."*

55. Castañeda, *Relación,* Primera Parte, Capítulo 9, fol. 34r–34v.

56. Michel Nallino and William K. Hartmann, "A Supposed Franciscan Exploration of Arizona in 1538: The Origins of a Myth," paper presented at the conference "Contemporary Vantage on the Coronado Expedition through Documents and Artifacts" (Las Vegas, New Mexico, 2000).

57. Hallenbeck, *Journey of Fray Marcos,* 84–85.

58. Lansing B. Bloom, "Was Marcos de Niza a Liar?" *New Mexico Historical Review* 16 (April 1941): 244–46.

59. Hallenbeck, *Journey of Fray Marcos,* 84–85.

60. Carl O. Sauer, "The Credibility of the Fray Marcos Account," *New Mexico Historical Review* 16 (April 1941): 233–43.

THREE

The Financing and Provisioning of the Coronado Expedition

SHIRLEY CUSHING FLINT

IT IS IMPORTANT TO EMPHASIZE the overall enterprise of exploration that Spain undertook in the Western Hemisphere in roughly one hundred years. Beginning with Columbus's landfall in 1492 and ending with Juan de Oñate's settlement of northern New Spain in 1598, Spaniards conducted well over one hundred separate major expeditions to explore, conquer, "pacify," and colonize the New World. The vast territory brought under Spanish influence encompassed the Caribbean Islands, what is now the southern United States from Florida to California, Mexico, Central America, and most of the South American continent.

The Coronado expedition of 1540–42 to the frontier of northern New Spain, in what is now referred to as the southwestern United States, was only one of those many explorations. But for those of us living in the Southwest, it was important for having brought to European consciousness a vast territory with the potential for exploitable natural resources, wealth, and expansion. It also exposed the native peoples of the Southwest to Europeans and contributed to the alteration and ultimate enrichment of both cultures.

The Coronado expedition fits into a larger picture of exploration and control of power in New Spain. At the time, several political factions were vying for control of the unexplored territories, and efforts were under way to curb the power of Cortés.[1] Among the important persons in these "grand plans of exploration" were Álvar Núñez Cabeza de Vaca, Hernán Cortés, Pedro de Alvarado, Hernando de Soto, and Antonio de Mendoza. All of these men maneuvered for the right to explore, claim, and exploit territories as yet underexplored to the north, in the hope of personal gain. The Coronado expedition was one facet of Viceroy Antonio Mendoza's plan for getting his share of what might lie in the north and elsewhere, as well as thwarting any attempt by Cortés to expand his political clout and his very large holdings.[2]

In 1540 Francisco Vázquez de Coronado left Nueva Galicia heading the expedition to the fabled Seven Cities of Cíbola, somewhere in the northern frontier of New Spain. After two years he and his party of men, women, servants, slaves, and Indian allies returned empty-handed and discouraged about prospects in the north—prospects for another Mexico City and for Aztec-like wealth. Instead of confirming the stories of Álvar Núñez Cabeza de Vaca and fray Marcos de Niza that fabulous wealth of the type found in Mexico and Peru existed in what was to become the Greater Southwest, he found only hardship and bloodshed. Much has been written and conjectured about his route and abut Indian contact during the expedition, but little about the preparation for such an extensive and expensive undertaking.

In this chapter I explore the methods of conducting and financing Spanish explorations in general and the Coronado expedition in particular. I show who the economic participants were and how much they invested in the expedition, and I document its outfitting. Finally, I discuss what its repercussions were for future Spanish exploration in the New World.

The method used in this chapter is to construct a variation on the modern balance sheet, in which each side is determined independently of the other. First, the monies invested in the expedition—its assets—are determined through documentary evidence and extrapolation from it. The investment is one side of the balance sheet. Second, monies spent on supplies and transportation are derived from documentary evidence, from evidence for other expeditions, and from the prices of items in Mexico City in the late 1530s and early 1540s. The expenditures are the other side of the statement.

The use of a balance sheet helps show whether any particular assumption made of either investment or expenditure is reasonable or improbable. If the estimated investment amount seems probable and yet only half can be shown to have been expended, or if expenditures outstrip known investment, then perhaps there is a flaw in the reconstruction. On the other hand, if each side of the balance sheet nearly approximates the other, then this method of fact-gathering, extrapolation, and comparison is feasible. As it turns out, the balance sheet method does show the validity of the assumptions made.

The Investment

In general, colonial American explorations were made under license of the Spanish Crown but without royal funds. Among the few notable exceptions were the partial royal funding of the Columbus trips, of the Menéndez de Avilés military campaign in South Carolina against the French,[3] and of the Luna expedition to La Florida.[4]

The majority of expedition licensees were required to fund not only their own involvement, which included servants, slaves, and retainers, but also that of other members of the enterprise, both Spaniards and Indian allies, who were unable to supply their own needs, either partially or completely, but who were necessary for its protection. Most grantees of licenses for exploration had full responsibility for the management, provisioning, and success or failure of their expedition. This method of licensure precluded the Crown's funding risky enterprises with attendant possibilities of failure. Yet in the case of a successful endeavor, the Crown would receive its fifth. The Crown risked nothing and gained everything.

Such an ambitious enterprise as the Coronado expedition, with its approximately fifteen hundred to two thousand members and their necessary provisioning, required great expenditure. Current conservative estimates are that it cost in excess of half a million pesos, an enormous quantity. This amount would have been difficult, if not impossible, for one person to possess, as Alonso de Estrada, the royal treasurer, made clear only twenty years before the expedition when he stated that all the goods in New Spain together could be valued at 63,000 pesos[5]—about one-eighth the amount spent on this expedition. Accordingly, investors were a prerequisite.

For such a daring and uncertain enterprise as the Coronado expedition, investors were actually not hard to muster. Because possibilities for partaking of wealth and prestige in Mexico City, Peru, and other parts of Spanish America were dwindling for newcomers and even for those who had gotten in on the first wave of exploitation, it was prudent to seek alternative routes to wealth. The land and Indian wealth and labor had been quickly divided and controlled, leaving few resources for subsequent settlers. There were, however, dreams and rumors of unexplored and untapped resources still to be found in New Spain. By investing in new ventures of exploration, one stood at least a chance of obtaining wealth.

The Coronado expedition had three categories of investors: the Mendoza–Vázquez de Coronado–Alvarado group, the officers, and other members of the expedition.

Mendoza, Vázquez de Coronado, and Alvarado
Viceroy Mendoza created two different partnership arrangements: one with Vázquez de Coronado in nearly equal shares and another with Pedro de Alvarado in a complicated share arrangement. In return, these investors could expect, in the most successful of endeavors, to share in four-fifths of the wealth found in

new regions (one-fifth was automatically the Crown's). If the north yielded any-thing like what had been exploited in Mexico or Peru, these investors could recoup their investment, become extremely rich and powerful, and perhaps be rewarded handsomely by the Crown with titles and privileges.

Under his arrangement with Vázquez de Coronado, Mendoza was the larger funder, contributing over 85,000 silver pesos (table 3.1),[6] or 54 percent of their joint amount.[7] All of his investment came from his own holdings and not from the royal treasury, as was alleged.[8] His monies covered the partial sponsorship of an untold number of other Spanish members, and he contributed to the fund-ing of the Indian component because it was enlisted for the protection of the expedition. In a later investigation of Mendoza's administration, it was stated that he helped various Spaniards and Indians but did not necessarily fund their participation completely.[9] An example is Juan Troyano, his *criado* (retainer), who went as *soldado* (soldier) to Cíbola and who mentioned that he received aid from Mendoza.[10]

The captain general of the expedition, Francisco Vázquez de Coronado, nearly equalled Mendoza's contribution. By Vázquez de Coronado's own account, he invested nearly 71,000 pesos of his own money, or 46 percent of the joint amount.[11] Juan Fernández Verdejo testified that he acted as purchasing agent for Vázquez de Coronado and spent well over 30,000 pesos in gold (approximately 50,000 silver pesos) to provision not only Vázquez de Coronado but also many of the caballeros.[12] The other 21,000 silver pesos of his invest-ment were not specifically accounted for.

After both the land and sea contingents of the Coronado expedition were well under way north, Mendoza contracted a royally sanctioned agreement with Pedro de Alvarado in November 1540 to expand the expedition's scope to include additional coastal exploration.[13] This joint venture also served Mendoza's political schemes. By contracting with Alvarado he essentially neutralized a potential rival in the exploration and conquest of new lands—Alvarado him-self—and also weakened Cortés's efforts in the same endeavors. Alvarado, the governor of Guatemala and Honduras, agreed to supply his nine ships, which were already at anchor in the Port of Santiago de Buena Esperanza in Colima, and three other vessels in Acapulco for the exploration of the western sea and its coastline. He had also equipped three hundred arquebusiers.[14]

No documentary evidence exists at present to confirm the actual peso amount of Alvarado's investment. However, information from the Pedro Menéndez de Avilés expedition of 1565 states that 18,400 silver pesos (13,000 ducats) were spent on three small craft and two ships for that endeavor, along with supplies and munitions at an additional 25,000 pesos (17,681 ducats).[15] If one assumes that the

Table 3.1

Balance Sheet for the Coronado Expedition

	Amount in Silver Pesos
Investments	
Antonio de Mendoza	85,000
Francisco Vázquez de Coronado	71,000
Eleven captains	60,000
Other Spaniards (estimate)	358,000
Total	574,000
Expenses for 2,000 people	
Basic sea ration @ 3.33 pesos/month	159,840
Supplemental food @ 4 pesos/month	192,000
Livestock (estimate)	42,000
Horses (estimate)	40,000
Clothing @ 50 pesos _ 370 Spaniards	17,000
Armaments:	?
100# gunpowder = 3,500 pesos	
Arquebus = 2.5 pesos	
Sword & belt = 2 pesos	
Medicine	?
Trade goods	?
Ships, 3 @ 500 pesos each + supplies	26,000
Total	476,840

43,400 pesos spent to outfit Menéndez's three small craft, two ships, and attendant supplies is comparable to the costs associated with Alvarado's three small
craft, nine ships, and supplies, then it is possible to extrapolate from the known
costs to the unknown. Because Alvarado had more than twice the number of ships,
it would not be unreasonable to double the Menéndez amount for an estimate of
the Alvarado costs, especially considering that prices were higher in New Spain
than in Spain, where Menéndez's expedition was organized. Therefore, in the most
conservative of estimates, the Alvarado-Mendoza arrangement added another
90,000 pesos to the total cost of the enterprise to northern New Spain, which

would enlarge the figure associated with the entire northern expedition to more than 600,000 pesos.

The total amount invested in the Vázquez de Coronado and Alarcón components of the expedition (73 percent of all estimated investments) also includes what other members added from their personal fortunes, borrowed from relatives, or acquired by mortgaging property in order to generate the capital needed to participate. The few individuals known to have funded themselves do not reflect the complete picture of all those who probably did. Most caballeros were expected to pay their own expenses, which would have amounted to about an additional 370 men outfitting themselves, their accompanying women, servants, and enslaved Africans, and their horses and mules. A few of the participants at later times mentioned that they went on the expedition at their own expense and were still paying back the resulting debt. Again, Mendoza and Vázquez de Coronado probably subsidized some of the members of the expedition, but as will be shown, they could not have paid completely for every participant.[16]

Officers

One method of estimating the total investment by the officers is again by means of extrapolation. Juan de Zaldívar, an officer of horsemen, spent 5,000–6,000 (silver) pesos.[17] Because he was a captain, he may have spent this amount of money on himself and his retainers. If it may be assumed that Zaldívar was typical, then the eleven captains together spent on average 5,500 pesos, or a total of 60,000 silver pesos.[18]

Other Members

Among the rank and file, Melchor Pérez, a horseman, claimed to have spent 3,300–5,000 silver pesos.[19] Presumably he funded only a servant or two, and yet he nearly equaled Zaldívar in expenditure. At the other end of the list of known funders, Cristóbal de Quesada spent 1,000 (silver) pesos.[20]

If even the smallest known amount, 1,000 silver pesos, is deemed typical and is multiplied by the 358 remaining participants (not including Vázquez de Coronado and his captains), the additional amount of 358,000 silver pesos is staggering. Again, if we assume a conservative individual expenditure of 1,000 pesos, then the fact that Mendoza funded an unknown number of rank and file members would not significantly alter the total figure for this participant group.

Some evidence to support this scenario can be found in the statements of Cristóbal de Escobar,[21] Rodrigo de Paz Maldonado,[22] and Juan de Paradinas,[23] all of whom said they spent large sums of money for which they never received recompense.

The largest group of investors was the rank and file, at 63 percent of the total amount spent on the Vázquez de Coronado component of the northern explorations—that is, exclusive of the later Alarcón component. Mendoza and Vázquez de Coronado, however, were the largest single investors, accounting for 27 percent of the total.

Sources of Cash

The next obvious question regarding a Mexico deficient in hard currency is, Where did all this cash come from?

Mendoza's yearly salary was 25,000 silver pesos,[24] and Vázquez de Coronado's salary as governor of Nueva Galicia amounted to 3,500 silver pesos. Clearly, their salaries cannot account for the money they expended.

The money needed was not something the main investors had saved. They had to borrow it using property as collateral. Vázquez de Coronado was able to parlay the dowry of his wife, Beatriz, into the necessary investment amount. She had been given one-half of the *encomienda* of Tlapa as dowry by her mother, and her husband used this as collateral to borrow the 71,000 pesos.[25] In New Spain, hard currency was in short supply, and gold currency was strictly forbidden until the establishment of the mint in 1537. Instead, much of the economy ran on promises. In addition to the probable sale of real estate (*huertas* and *suertes de tierra*) in Mexico City and its environs, an *encomendero* would offer as collateral the expected payments of tribute from his encomienda. Even though those amounts were a pittance compared with the amount on loan, the lenders and creditors seemed satisfied that they would receive long-term, yearly income and leverage from all the property they held to secure the loans. Of course great risk was involved that the loans would never be repaid, because of death or bankruptcy. Those who were not encomenderos may have traded their services as retainers, borrowed from relatives, or mortgaged small plots of land.

After the unsuccessful outcome of the Coronado expedition, we find several references to expedition members still repaying their debts long after their return to Mexico. García Rodríguez says in 1578 that he spent much money in gold pesos and was indebted as a result, and that it took him a long time to repay.[26] Melchor Pérez was indebted for more than 500 pesos upon his return.[27]

Vázquez de Coronado himself in 1544 was still in debt for more than 10,000 pesos and was forced to sell real estate and movable goods. Still he was unable to extinguish the debt.[28] It can be safely assumed that there were many others who returned in debt or impoverished and remained so. Thus the creditors, too, suffered economic losses, which would have had repercussions throughout the Mexican economy.

The Expenses

The supplies needed for an enterprise the size of the Coronado expedition would have been enormous. Fifteen hundred to two thousand people would have needed, at a bare minimum, food (including hunting and preparation items), clothing (including sewing implements), shelter, armaments, and horse gear. Such provisioning would have had a tremendous impact on Mexico City's resource base.[29] Shortages, higher prices, and disruptions in local economies could easily have resulted from attempts to supply this expedition. Indeed, concern was voiced and prohibition threatened so that the expedition would not drain the city of *vecinos* (residents with full political rights), to fill its ranks. Vázquez de Coronado made assurances that the men who went on the expedition were not vecinos from Mexico City.[30] Nonetheless, the inevitable disruption and scope of this endeavor may have hampered provisioning and impelled the expedition to plan on acquiring further supplies from native people as they went along. For this reason, the known costs may not accurately reflect the true costs, because more supplies may have been purchased outside of the city itself or commandeered from the natives.

In addition to the necessities of life, we know that among the supplies taken on the expedition were tools and gear, items for blacksmithing, domestic furnishings (including furniture and bedding), games, governmental paraphernalia (including those needed for punishment), jewelry and other forms of adornment, surgical instruments and medicines, musical instruments, navigational devices, items of personal hygiene, scribal items (paper and ink), religious articles, trade and gift items, items for transporting and storing supplies, a few woodworking tools, and hard cash.[31] The six religious members, with their presumed assistants and servants, would certainly have brought paraphernalia for celebrating mass and the necessary wine and bread.

The Mexican Indian component of the expedition would have needed many of the same items and probably were supplementally supplied by the Spaniards. In addition, they probably brought things only they could provide, such as items of adornment, medicine, music, and games.[32] Castañeda says the expedition left with six hundred laden animals.[33]

Hernando de Alarcón was commissioned to resupply the expedition via ship but was unable to rendezvous with Vázquez de Coronado because of a lack of geographical understanding. Alarcón was to set sail twice with supplies of hardware, guns, powder, crossbows, other armaments, wine, oil and *bizcocho* (hardtack).[34] He departed on May 9, 1540, and failed to rendezvous with Vázquez de Coronado. The following year, the Mixtón war interfered with his second attempt. Because Alarcón departed so soon after Vázquez de Coronado, it would seem that the supplies on board were considered a key factor in the success of the expedition. The ground element apparently was counting on the naval element to bring many of the necessary supplies.[35]

The question of the quantity of supplies needed depends also on the length of time the expedition expected to be away. To date we have no documentation regarding a specific time frame. Indeed, Vázquez de Coronado's commission seems to have been open ended. The money spent, however covered expenses for nearly two years, with shortages due to the ships' not meeting the ground expedition and supplying it with items already purchased. In effect, the half million pesos invested in the expedition covered two years' expenses for fifteen hundred to two thousand people and livestock.

Even if it is difficult to determine the quantity of supplies a group of such size would have needed, we have documentation of what was taken and, in some cases, how much those items cost. Price figures exist in the records of the *cabildo* (city council) of Mexico City for some staple items in the late 1530s.[36] A basic sea ration consisted of wine and bizcocho with some supplemental foods such as oil, vinegar, rice, and beans. Other common foodstuffs were meat, cheese, and salt. The basic ration was valued at thirty *maravedis* ($1/272$ of a silver peso) per person per day.[37] It seems that many of the 1540 prices were dependent on supply and demand: chicken and sugar were quite expensive, and meat, inexpensive. The supplemented basic food kit could have averaged seven pesos per person per month.[38] At that basic rate, feeding two thousand people over two years would have cost nearly 352,000 pesos. That is, more than half of the expedition's expenditures went for food alone (table. 3.1).

The expeditionaries took along 5,000 head of livestock,[39] which might have cost 42,000 pesos. The cost of the 1,000 horses, even valued at a low 40 pesos per head,[40] would have totaled 40,000 pesos. This was the value of a horse that had been on the expedition for two years, and it might have been worth more at the time of purchase. Armaments, both Spanish and native, would have accounted for some unknown number of additional pesos. For example, on the Menéndez expedition, 600 arquebuses cost 1,500 pesos.[41] And important items such as medicine and trade goods, although their values are unknown, would have increased the total expenditure as well.

Mendoza supplied more than a thousand horses and mules, a figure that does not include the livestock of the captains and soldiers, and aided three hundred Indian men and their wives with money and provisions. To other Spaniards he gave money, horses, arms, herds of cattle and sheep, and other items. He also provided gifts to be given to Indians whom the expedition might encounter, in order to "buy" corn and other supplies.[42]

Juan de Bermejo, a witness for Vázquez de Coronado, later testified that arms, medicines, foodstuffs, horse tack, livestock, cows, pigs, sheep, trade goods, and clothing were purchased for the expedition.[43] Vázquez de Coronado reportedly took fine horses, pack animals, and arms and provided salaries to many of the participants. In his retinue were servants, pages, and slaves. These expenses amounted to 30,000 *castellanos,* or nearly 50,000 silver pesos, for armaments for himself, for his own horses and mules, and for the horses and other things he gave to his *criados* (retainers) and black slaves.[44] According to his own account, Vázquez de Coronado always paid for items received from Indians: he gave knives, beads, bells, and other things in exchange for what the Indians brought.[45]

It is to be remembered that Pedro de Alvarado would also have provisioned his ships and been responsible for all their associated costs. Because his ships were at anchor in 1540, it is assumed that he spent some considerable amount of money to have them ready—at least 50,000 pesos. His death in the Mixtón war, however, put an end to his participation and further financial investment in the northern expedition.

Others who later testified that they had participated in the expedition also mentioned supplies they had provided. Rodrigo de Paz Maldonado said that he took "many horses and blacks,"[46] and he was seen buying many necessary things for the journey.[47] Melchor Pérez, in a *probanza,* said that he had taken 1,000 hogs and sheep at 8 maravedis (0.03 pesos) per 4 pounds' weight, which would have totaled approximately 1,200 pesos.[48] He also took 7 horses at 40 pesos each (none came back),[49] and he was accompanied by 2 *negros ladinos,* who ran away.[50] Pérez could easily have spent 1,500 pesos supplying himself and his servants. García Rodríguez took horses and two criados on the expedition to Tierra Nueva,[51] and Juan Troyano took horses, slaves, and arms.[52]

During the expedition, some supplies apparently were scarce. Lorenzo Álvarez, a witness in Tiguex, said that some Spaniards were sick there, many horses died, and corn sold for very high prices.[53] The continual lack of corn is mentioned throughout the documents. Clothing and its lack were important factors in the hostilities and hardships of the expedition, whereas hardware and armaments seem to have been in sufficient supply. Among the documents there exist reports that the Spaniards demanded that the Tiguex pueblos supply mantas,[54] that a large number of bison skins were taken from the Teyas,[55] that many members were dressing in skins,[56] and that by 1542 the clothing of expedition member Juan Jiménez was in a poor state.[57] The same Jiménez, however, had plenty of horseshoe nails and farrier's equipment that no one wanted to purchase.[58]

The expedition depended on native people to supply food and clothing when needed,[59] at least partly because of the failure of the naval rendezvous. As matters stood, Spanish ignorance of the natives and their resources seriously hampered the sustaining of the expedition. Yet the Spaniards never expected the natives to resupply them with metal objects, so they made certain to carry enough of those.

The overall result is that the expedition was well provisioned at the beginning, but as time went on and the resupply mission failed, certain supplies became scarce, though others did not. The scant supplies were of the type that the natives were expected to supply and so to the Spaniards were of less critical concern. This expectation was largely unfulfilled and helped precipitate the demise of the expedition.

Conclusion

To put in perspective the funding of the Coronado component of the expedition at a level of 574,000 silver pesos, several comparisons prove useful. In the 1520s, Cortés spent 38,000 pesos in his attack on forces sent by Francisco de Garay and 122,000 pesos in pacification of Indians. These expeditions included large ships, horses, supplies, and several hundred men each.[60] The 1561 Luna y Arellano attempt to settle La Florida totaled 327,000 silver pesos.[61] Menéndez de Áviles (1565–68) defended La Florida against the French at the cost of more than 119,000 pesos.[62] Finally, the largest Spanish expeditionary force, the 1588 Spanish Armada against the English, cost 5.3 million pesos and comprised more than 560 sailing vessels, 30,000 sailors, and 64,000 soldiers for a period of eight months.[63]

In Mexico, Montezuma's "treasure" amounted to 214,500 silver pesos.[64] In 1532 Francisco Pizarro, conqueror of Peru, the wealthiest native region in the New World, received as his share of the booty from the ransom of the Inca, Atahualpa, about 132,000 silver pesos (80,175 pesos in gold), and from Cuzco, another 51,000 pesos.[65] In other words, the financers of the Coronado expedition were willing to spend an incredible sum (nearly as much as others had gained in the most successful conquests and far more than was usually spent in organizing expeditions) for a chance at even greater glory and bigger financial returns than had so far been achieved. None of those hopes was realized, and the sum spent on the expedition was never recovered. Every investor lost his or her money.

The reasons the expedition failed to produce the expected results rest in several places. A major contributing factor was that supplies intended for the expedition never reached it, causing hardship and exacerbating antagonism with the native population. This antagonism also contributed to the leadership's deciding not to remain in the north to await further supplies and forbidding any contingent to remain there. Hostilities with natives both in New Mexico and Sonora were still strong after two years, and any persons left behind to establish a base for resupply would surely have perished once the main body of sufficiently armed men returned to Mexico. Two armed conflicts in Mexico also contributed to the return of the expedition: the Mixtón war and the Sonoran uprising both made resupply from the south very unlikely. The members of the expedition were needed in other, more pressing areas. And finally, the expeditionaries faced the fact that even after penetrating into the middle of the continent, they simply had discovered no wealth of any consequence.

Several subsequent events brought northern exploration to a halt for about twenty years. First, the heavy financial losses incurred by the expedition's investors deterred any immediate return. Second, the fabulous Zacatecas silver strike in 1546 converted gold fever into silver fever, and much of the Spaniards' exploratory energy was channeled into finding more silver in the Zacatecas area—a surer thing than chasing after what might be in the north. It was not until the Ibarra explorations in the 1560s that further northern incursions took place, but the reasons by then were different. Francisco Ibarra was looking for more silver mines, rather than the fabled seven cities of gold. And when Juan de Oñate, a native of Zacatecas, made his colonizing trek north in 1598, he followed, it is interesting to note, in the footsteps of Coronado. He explored essentially the same areas both to the east and the west from his base along the Rio Grande, but he was looking for silver deposits rather than native societies already wealthy in precious metals. In fact, Oñate was following up comments made in the documents of the Coronado expedition regarding "jars full of shiny metal."[66] His hope was to find another Zacatecas, not another Mexico City.

In some ways the Coronado expedition and the money spent on it were not a complete loss to Spain and its colonial goals. They were necessary precursors to the eventual permanent settling of Europeans in northern New Spain. The personal disappointment was that the original investors did not live to see those accomplishments.

Notes

1. Herbert E. Bolton, *Coronado: Knight of Pueblos and Plains* (Albuquerque: University of New Mexico Press, 1949; reprint with foreword by John L. Kessell, Albuquerque: University of New Mexico Press, 1990), 44.

2. Bolton, *Coronado*, 7.

3. Eugene Lyon, *The Enterprise of Florida: Pedro Menéndez de Avilés and the Spanish Conquest of 1565–1568* (Gainesville: University Presses of Florida, 1976), 61.

4. Herbert Ingram Priestley, *The Luna Papers: Documents Relating to the Expedition of don Tristán de Luna y Arellano for the Conquest of La Florida in 1559–1591,* 2 vols. (Freeport, New York: Books for Libraries Press, 1971), 2:143.

5. *Actas de Cabildo de la Ciudad de México,* eds. Ignacio Bejarano and others, 26 vols. (México, D.F.:1889–1904), 1:16.

6. The amounts mentioned in the documents for the various investors are in ducats, but I have converted them into pesos in order to facilitate comparisons. For a helpful discussion of currency, see Thomas C. Barnes, Thomas H. Naylor, and Charles W. Polzer, *Northern New Spain: A Research Guide* (Tucson: University of Arizona Press, 1981), 66–67. The authors suggest an exchange rate of 1 silver ducat to 1.42 silver peso and of 1 silver peso to 272 maravedis.

7. Francisco López de Gómara, *Historia general de las Indias,* 2 parts (Barcelona: Editorial Iberia, c. 1954), 368.

8. [Antonio de Mendoza], "Merits and services of Antonio de Mendoza—(1545)," AGI, Patronato 57, N2, R1.

9. Joaquín García Icazbalceta, ed., "Fragmento de la visita hecha a Don Antonio de Mendoza," in *Coleccion de documentos para la historia de México* (México, D.F.: Antigua Librería, 1866), 2:119.

10. Antonio de Turcios, scribe, "Proof of service of Juan Troyano—(1560)," AGI, Mexico, 206, N.12, fol. 1r, in Flint and Flint, *"They Were Not Familiar."*

11. Francisco A. de Icaza, *Conquistadores y pobladores de Nueva España: Diccionario autobiográfico sacado de los textos originales* (Madrid, 1923), 1:no. 364.

12. Juan de Zaragosa, scribe, "Testimony of Coronado's Purchasing Agent, Juan Fernández Verdejo, Guadalajara, 1553," AGI, Justicia, 336, N.1, fol. 3v, in Flint and Flint, *"They Were Not Familiar."*

13. Under this complicated agreement, Mendoza would receive a fourth interest in all the rights and grants to the land and sea discovered by Hernando de Alarcón in his three ships—the naval aspect of the Coronado expedition—a half interest in what the king had given Alvarado, a third interest in Alvarado's profits from the explorations, and a half interest in Alvarado's ships. Alvarado would receive a half interest in all the rights and grants to the future discoveries, conquests, pacifications, and colonizations made by the Coronado expedition and the Alarcón component, as well as a fifth interest in the profits that might already have accrued to the Vázquez de Coronado and Alarcón expeditions prior to the November date. See [Antonio de Mendoza], "Contract between Antonio de Mendoza and the adelantado Pedro de Alvarado, November 2, 1540," AGI, Patronato, 21, N3, R.2, in Flint and Flint, *"They Were Not Familiar."*

14. Bolton, *Coronado,* 44.

15. Lyon, *Enterprise of Florida,* 227.

16. Evidence has recently come to light that Luis de Castilla and Luis de León Romano paid for *tamemes* (load bearers) on the expedition, and Castilla was scheduled to supply a ship for Alarcón's second voyage. It is probable that others helped finance the expedition without physically participating in it, which would only have increased the investment figure. Antonio de Mendoza, "Probanza made in the name of don Antonio de Mendoza, Zacatula—(1546–47)," AGI, Justicia 263, pieza 1; Antonio de Mendoza, "Viceroy's instructions to Hernando Alarcón, May 31, 1541," Biblioteca del Escorial, códice &-II-7, Docs. 66 and 67, fol. 2v and 3r, in Flint and Flint, *"They Were Not Familiar."*

17. [Juan de Zaldívar], "Proof of service of Juan de Zaldívar, Guadalajara, 1566," AGI, Patronato 60, N5, R4, fol. 25r.

18. The eleven captains were Diego López, Rodrigo Maldonado, Tristan de Luna y Arellano, Rodrigo Diego Guevara, Pablo Melgossa, Juan Zaldívar, Hernando de Alvarado, López de Cárdenas, Francisco de Ovando, Pedro de Tovar, and Diego Gutiérrez de la Caballería.

19. [Melchior Pérez], "Melchior Pérez's Petition for Preferment, 1551," Bancroft Library, University of California, Berkeley, manuscript M-M 1714, fol. 3v, in Flint and Flint, *They Were Not Familiar.*

20. Icaza, *Conquistadores,* 2:no. 1298.

21. [Cristóbal Escobar], "Proof of Service of Cristóbal de Escobar, 1543," AGI, Mexico 204, N14, fol. 1r, in Flint and Flint, *They Were Not Familiar.*

22. [Rodrigo de Paz Maldonado], "Proof of service of Rodrigo de Paz Maldonado, 1571," AGI, Patronato 117, R.5.

23. [Juan Gómez de Paradinas], "Proof of service of Juan Gómez de Paradinas, 1560," AGI, Patronato 63, R.5.

24. John Frederick Schwaller, *Origins of Church Wealth in Mexico: Ecclesiastical Revenues and Church Finances, 1523–1600* (Albuquerque: University of New Mexico Press, 1985), note 12.

25. Zaragosa, "Testimony of Verdejo," AGI, Justicia, 336, N.1, fol. 3r.

26. [García Rodríguez], "Proof of service of García Rodríguez and his grandson, 1617," AGI, Patronato, 87, N.1, R.5, fol. 19v.

27. [Pérez], "Petition for Preferment," fol. 3v.

28. Flint, *Great Cruelties,* 273, 473.

29. See José Ignacio Avellaneda, *The Conquerors of the New Kingdom of Granada* (Albuquerque: University of New Mexico Press, 1995), 29.

30. Juan de León, scribe, "Hearing on Depopulation Charges, Compostela, February 21, 1540," AGI, Patronato, 21, N.2, R.3, 1r, in Flint and Flint, *They Were Not Familiar.*

31. Richard Flint, "The Pattern of Coronado Expedition Material Culture" (M.A. thesis, New Mexico Highlands University, 1992), 78–221.

32. Flint, "Pattern of Coronado Expedition," 78–221.

33. Castañeda, *Relación,* Primera Parte, Capítulo 8, fol. 30v.

34. Díaz del Castillo, *Historia verdadera,* 830.

35. Mendoza, "Viceroy's instructions."

36. According to the *Actas del Cabildo,* vol. 4, bread cost 1 silver real ($^1/_8$ gold peso) per pound (p. 165); oil, 4 pesos per *arroba,* or 25 pounds (p. 187); sugar, 3.5 pesos per pound (p. 135); cheese, $^1/_8$ peso per pound (p. 99); beef, $^1/_{100}$ per 4 pounds (p. 123); and mutton and pork, 0.03 peso per 4 pounds (p. 143).

37. Lyon, *Enterprise of Florida,* 92, 94.

38. Using the Menéndez basic food kit number of 30 maravedis per person per day, or 3.33 pesos per month, and adding in the supplemental foods at 4 pesos per month produces the figure of 7 pesos per person per month.

39. Castañeda, *Relación,* Tercera Parte, Capítulo 8, fol. 152v.

40. Miguel López de Legazpi, scribe, "Disposal of the Juan Jiménez estate, Puebla de Los Angeles, 1550," AGI, Contratación, 5575, N. 24, fol. 64, in Flint and Flint, *They Were Not Familiar.*

41. Lyon, *Enterprise of Florida,* 227.

42. García Icazbalceta, "Antonio de Mendoza," 118–19.
43. Juan de Zaragosa, scribe, "Testimony of Juan Bermejo, Guadalajara, 1553," AGI, Justicia, 336, N.1, fol. 3r, in Flint and Flint, *They Were Not Familiar.*
44. [Francisco Vázquez de Coronado], "Residencia of Francisco Vázquez de Coronado, Guadalajara, 1544–45," AGI, Justicia, 339, N.1, R.1.
45. Pedro de Requena, scribe, "Proceso de Francisco Vázquez, 1544" AGI, Justicia, 267, N.3, in Flint, *Great Cruelties,* 287.
46. [Paz Maldonado, Rodrigo de], "Proof of service of Rodrigo de Paz Maldonado, Quito, 1564," AGI, Patronato, 112, R.2.
47. [Paz Maldonado], "Proof of service, 1571."
48. *Actas de Cabildo,* 4:188.
49. López de Legazpi, "Juan Jiménez," fol. 6r.
50. [Pérez], "Petition for Preferment," fol. 3v.
51. [Rodríguez], "Proof of service," fol. 21r.
52. Turcios, "Juan Troyano," fol. 1v.
53. Gómez de la Peña, "Testimony Taken at Culiacán," 358, 366.
54. Castañeda, *Relación,* Primera Parte, Capítulo 15, fol. 62v.
55. Castañeda, *Relación,* Primera Parte, Capítulo 19, fol. 84v.
56. [Escobar], "Proof of Service," fol. 5v.
57. Richard Flint and Shirley Cushing Flint, "A Death in Tiguex, 1542," *New Mexico Historical Review* 74 (July 1999): 248.
58. Flint and Flint, "Death in Tiguex," 251.
59. Castañeda, *Relación,* Primera Parte, Capítulo 15, fol. 61v.
60. Cortés, *Cartas de relación,* 175–206 passim.
61. Priestley, *Luna Papers,* 2:143, 215.
62. Lyon, *Enterprise of Florida,* 226–27, 89, 43.
63. Garrett Mattingly, *The Armada* (Boston: Houghton Mifflin, 1959), 76.
64. Francisco López de Gómara, *Cortés: The Life of the Conqueror by His Secretary,* trans. and ed. Lesley Byrd Simpson (Berkeley: University of California Press, 1964), 296.
65. James Lockhart, *The Men of Cajamarca: A Social and Biographical Study of the First Conquerors of Peru* (Austin: University of Texas Press, 1972), 79, 104n2.
66. Castañeda, *Relación,* Primera Parte, Capítulo 22, fol. 94v. See also chapter 7.

FOUR

What's Missing from This Picture? The *Alarde,* or Muster Roll, of the Coronado Expedition

RICHARD FLINT

IN THE CENTURY FOLLOWING Columbus's landfall in the Bahamas, more than a hundred major Spanish-led expeditions of conquest and reconnaissance probed the Americas by sea and by land. During the first half of that century of conquest, roughly until the middle 1500s, these undertakings were aimed primarily at locating, establishing authority over, and then milking the wealth of sophisticated and prosperous New World societies. In this regard, most expeditions were only marginally successful at best, obtaining reports merely of phantasms beyond where they had penetrated. In many ways typical of the conquests that preceded the great silver strikes of midcentury was the *entrada* organized by Viceroy Antonio de Mendoza and led by Francisco Vázquez de Coronado from 1539 to 1542, the destination of which was a rumored mineral-rich polity known as Cíbola situated in what is now the American Southwest.

Under the Documents of the Coronado Expedition Project, which we direct at New Mexico Highlands University, Shirley Cushing Flint and I are preparing the first annotated, dual-language edition of thirty-five documents relating to and deriving from the Coronado expedition. Called by the working title *"They Were Not Familiar with His Majesty": Documents of the Coronado Expedition,* the book will include the documents previously published in English only by George Hammond and Agapito Rey in 1940 and the handful of documents George Winship published in both English and Spanish in 1896. It also includes seven documents previously published in Spanish but never before in full in English, and seven others that have never been published in either language.

Some historians, archeologists, and general readers may wonder why the most commonly used sources on the expedition, Hammond and Rey's *Narratives of the Coronado Expedition, 1540–1542* (now out of print) and Winship's *The Coronado Expedition, 1540–1542* (still available in partial reprint as *The Journey of Coronado*) need to be superseded. Part of the answer is that these earlier editions are riddled with errors, misinterpretations, and omissions in English translation. To give an example of the sorts of errors to be found in the earlier editions, I focus here on one relatively brief document that has been available in English translation for more than sixty years. It is the *alarde,* or muster roll, of the expedition, which is preserved as a signed original manuscript document in the Archivo General de Indias (AGI) in Sevilla, Spain, where it is cataloged as AGI, Sección Guadalajara, Legajo 5, Ramo 1, Número 7. Even though it comprises only twenty-four folio sides and is a seemingly straightforward and unambiguous list, the misguidance provided by earlier editions of this short and uncomplicated document has been profound.

On February 22, 1540, at the town of Compostela in the new Spanish province of Nueva Galicia (in what is now the state of Nayarit in Mexico), the scribe Juan de Cuevas prepared a list of 288 men as they passed in review before Viceroy Antonio de Mendoza. Along with each man's name is recorded the number of horses he took with him on the expedition, if any, and a summary of what arms and armor he was equipped with. In Cuevas's own words: "Se hizo El alard*e* de toda la gente q*ue* Va a la tierra nuevame*n*te d*e*scubierta por el padre provy*nci*al frai marcos d*e* nyça" (an inspection was made of all the people who are going to the land newly discovered by the father provincial fray Marcos de Niza).[1]

This was standard procedure at the outset of undertakings of this sort. The alarde was used to verify that the number of persons and amount of equipment promised by the expedition organizers had in fact been raised. Nearly all expeditions of conquest in the sixteenth century were privately organized and financed but were required to obtain license from the king. In order to obtain the license, the aspiring organizers of an entrada had to submit a formal proposal to the king and his advisors, specifying where the expedition was headed, why it should be allowed to go there, how it would be financed, and how many persons would compose it (often including a breakdown of persons with special skills to be recruited, such as arquebusiers, crossbowmen, and artillerymen).[2] Before departure, it was necessary to demonstrate to royal officials that the organizers' promises had been met.

Furthermore, the alarde was used to formally record the organizational structure of the expedition or to facilitate completion of that structure, if it had not already been fully established. The latter was the case with the Coronado expedition; not until sometime after February 22 was the composition of many of the companies set. Even some of the captains had not been appointed by that date. In the instance of the Coronado expedition, there was a further use for the alarde. Accusations had been made that recruitment for the expedition had seriously depleted the citizenry of Mexico City and all Nueva España. To counter those charges, the viceroy arranged to have prominent residents of Mexico City present at the review, in order to certify that very few vecinos would be included in the expedition.[3]

Indios Amigos

The February 22 muster roll has been published three times in the last sixty years, twice in Spanish and once in English. Arthur Aiton, the first researcher to locate the muster roll in the AGI, published a Spanish transcription in the *American Historical Review* in 1939, which he called "a nearly complete and authentic list of those who went on the expedition."[4] A year later, George Hammond and Agapito Rey published an English translation in their important *Narratives of the Coronado Expedition*.[5] In 1992, Carmen de Mora published a new, modernized Spanish transcription in Spain.[6] Shockingly, none of these competent scholars pointed out that the muster is far from complete. It does not begin to list all the people who participated in the massive entrada to Cíbola and beyond. The overwhelming majority of members of the expedition, including the fighting members, is visible in the documentary record only rarely, in one- or two-sentence lightning flashes that momentarily illumine what is otherwise a profound obscurity. Only by seemingly causal inadvertence do they appear at all, slipping in primarily at moments when their presence emphasizes the hardships and assaults endured by the expedition. Thus they serve to enhance the bravery, sacrifice, and perseverance of the men on the muster roll.

Most glaringly absent from the alarde and from scholarly comment on it is mention of the thirteen hundred or more natives of central and western Mexico, the so-called *indios amigos,* who made up the great bulk of the expedition, outnumbering the European members by at least three to one. To demonstrate how easily references to the indios amigos can be missed, consider the viceroy's brief account of the preliminary reconnaissance to the north made by a party headed by Melchor Díaz. Writing to the king in April 1540, Mendoza wrote that Díaz "fuese con algunos de Cavallo" (was to go with some horsemen) to verify fray Marcos's report. It was only later, in explaining why Díaz's party was unable to reach Cíbola, that he mentioned in ten words that it had turned so cold that "*h*elarsele algunos yndios de los q*ue* lleVaban en su conpañia" (some Indians froze [to death], from among those they were taking in their company).[7] The

Indians are never mentioned again. Presumably, if several had not died, they would never have been mentioned at all.

Indios amigos appear equally momentarily in Captain General Vázquez de Coronado's reports. In the lengthy letter he wrote to the viceroy from Cíbola in August 1540, Vázquez de Coronado referred to them fleetingly only five times in seven densely printed folios. Again the allies appear only accidentally, as it were, without a role or even a presence that continues beyond the impositions they make on their European comrades. Certainly, there is not the slightest hint of their numbers or dominating presence. Thus, the captain general reported that he had to send Melchor Díaz out to trade for corn "per darne à gli Indiani amici che conducevamo con noi" (to give to some of the Indian allies whom we brought with us). Shortly afterward some of the indios amigos flash through the captain general's words and disappear again. In recounting the exhaustion of expedition members from carrying heavy loads of supplies, he pointed out that as a result, "partirono alcuni nostri mori, & alcuni Indiani" (some of our Moors and Indians left). The next mention of allies comes when several were poisoned by eating native plants. Vázquez de Coronado wrote that "alcuni Indiani amici & uno Spagnuolo . . . & duoi mori" (some Indian allies, one Spaniard . . . and two Moors) thus perished. Finally, he recounted that several days later, everyone in the expedition was suffering from severe hunger, "massimamente gli Indiani" (especially the Indian [allies]).[8] Keep in mind that up to this point in the chronological sequence of surviving Coronado expedition documents, no outright statement has been made that Indians from Mexico made up a segment of the expedition company. These few mentions of indios amigos could, seemingly, refer to a handful of almost accidental hangers-on.

Of the remaining surviving documents that were written at the time of the expedition, few make any reference to the Indian allies. Yet there are rare passing mentions. The brief anonymous report known as the "Traslado de las nuevas" and another called the "Relación del suceso" repeat the story of the deaths of some indios amigos along the route to Cíbola, again without suggesting either the total number of allies or the number of fatalities. The "Relación del suceso" adds that Indians, apparently meaning Indian allies, were killed at the expedition's base camp at San Gerónimo in Sonora by local natives who rose up against the expedition's severe treatment of them.[9] Another short and fragmentary narrative, possibly written by Hernando de Alvarado, makes no reference whatsoever to the indios amigos.[10] Neither does the "Relación postrera de Cíbola," composed by fray Toribio de Benavente from one or more reports given to him by expedition members, or a letter to the king written by Vázquez de Coronado from Tiguex in modern New Mexico in October 1541.[11]

The expedition's Mexican Indian allies are all but absent from surviving documents written while the expedition was in progress.

When, however, two years after the return of the disappointed expedition to Nueva España, an investigation into its treatment of natives of the Greater Southwest was launched, further information about the Indian allies emerged. During the course of testimony before Lorenzo de Tejada, an *oidor* of the *audiencia*, and before a local magistrate in Nueva Galicia during 1544 and 1545, seven witnesses referred to the presence and roles of the indios amigos. Three witnesses, Lorenzo Álvarez,[12] Juan de Zaldívar, and Vázquez de Coronado,[13] all explicitly placed the Indian allies among the combatants during the Tiguex War in the Rio Grande Valley during the winter of 1540–41. Typical of these witnesses' testimonies is Captain Juan de Zaldívar's statement that at Pueblo de Alameda, "sabe que del dicho Conbate Salieron heridos mas de Se(s)tenta esPañoles amygos" (he knows that more than [seventy] Spaniards [and their] allies came out of the fight wounded).[14]

On March 12, 1545, Captain Diego López testified in Culiacán that in the Tiguex area "hAber muerto Los dichos naturales Un yndio de los Amygos que lleVabamos" (the natives had killed one of the Indian allies "whom we brought along").[15] The same event was referred to with slightly varying details by three other witnesses: García Rodríguez, Gaspar de Saldaña,[16] and Juan de Paradinas.[17] Meanwhile, the captain general justified his sending men to the pueblos of Tiguex to acquire clothing by saying that "çiertos esPañoles soldados e yndios amygos se queXaron A este conFesante que eStaban DeSnudos e morian de Frios" (a number of Spaniards, men-at-arms, and Indian allies complained to the accused that they did not have clothing and were dying of cold).[18] Vázquez de Coronado also told judge Tejada that he had "ynviado A don garcia loPez con yndios de Çibola e amyGos Para Asentarse el Real e (f)hazerSe rrancho donde el dicho Fray juan dezia" (sent don García López and some [Indian] allies, with Indians from Cíbola, to establish the camp and erect shelter where fray Juan suggested).[19] The expedition's former leader also testified that he had sent "dos yndios mexicanos" (two Nahua Indians) to the first pueblo of Cíbola ahead of the advance guard with a cross as a sign of peace. However, "llegado este conFesante A tres leguas de Çibola Adonde (F)hallo los mexicanos que habya enViado e le Dixeron que el Pueblo e ProVincia estaban de guerra e no querian venyr de Paz" (when the accused had gotten three leagues from Cíbola, he found there the Nahuas whom he had sent, and they told him that the pueblo and province were at war and were not willing to come to peace).[20] In these sworn statements, then, the indios amigos appear, however sketchily, as active participants in the expedition, though their numbers remain unknown.

In 1547, the viceroy was the subject of a *visita,* or extraordinary administrative review. The *visitador,* Francisco Tello de Sandoval, lodged forty-four charges against Mendoza as a result of his energetic investigation. In response, the viceroy called hundreds of witnesses to rebut those charges; one of them was Francisco Vázquez de Coronado. Replying to the two-hundredth question of his patron's *interrogatorio,* or questionnaire, the former captain general agreed that thirteen hundred Indian allies had accompanied him on the *jornada* to Cíbola.[21] We see that the Mexican Indians did not make up merely a insignificant fraction of the expedition's membership but instead composed at least three-fourths of it, a bombshell indeed for anyone who has taken literally Arthur Aiton's assertion of the completeness of the muster roll.

Following the written evidence chronologically, not for nearly another twenty years were additional documents prepared that expand our knowledge of the expedition's company of native allies. In the 1560s, two lengthy narrative accounts of the Coronado entrada were written by men who had themselves participated in it, Juan de Jaramillo and Pedro de Castañeda de Nájera. Neither was among the expedition's leadership or apparently figured prominently in the events of the enterprise. Both, however, provided much more detail about the two-year jornada than is available in all the previous surviving documents. In particular, Castañeda's *Relación* fills 316 folio sides and is replete with data to be found nowhere else.

Early on in his report Castañeda wrote about the recruiting of expedition members that took place in Mexico City following the release of fray Marcos de Niza's glowing accounts of his just-completed trek to Cíbola. In Castañeda's words, in a few days "se juntaron mas de tresientos hombres españoles y obra de ochoçientos indios naturales de la nueva españa" (more than three hundred Spaniards were assembled, and about eight hundred Indians native to Nueva España).[22] The figure given here for European (mostly Spanish) members of the expedition seems in approximate agreement with the 360 or so that is our own current count. Perhaps, then, the claim that eight hundred Indian allies were also present is in the right ballpark. But this was not all Castañeda had to say about how many indios amigos took part in the expedition. Much later in his account, in demonstrating the incredible resilience of the grasses of the Great Plains, he wrote that the grass returned immediately to upright even after the passage of "mas de mill y quinientas personas de los amigos y serviçio" (more than fifteen hundred individuals among the allies and servants [of the expedition]).[23] On that basis, Vázquez de Coronado's thirteen hundred indios amigos may not be out of line. And as we will see, the cohort of allies was augmented as the expedition passed through Nueva Galicia, along modern Mexico's west coast, so the assertion that eight hundred natives of Nueva España (modern central Mexico) made the great trek and the later count of thirteen hundred or so total indios amigos may both be accurate. That is made the more probable in that Castañeda wrote once more regarding the size of the indigenous component of the expedition. Having arrived at Culiacán, at the time the northernmost outpost of Spanish occupation in what is now Mexico, the expedition was generously reprovisioned before jumping off into territory beyond Spanish control. As Castañeda told it, "salieron mas de seiçientas bestias cargadas y los amigos y serviçio que fueron mas de mill personas" (more than six hundred loaded pack animals left, as well as the [native] allies and servants, who amounted to more than one thousand persons).[24] No further documentary evidence has come to light regarding the size of the indigenous corp that comprised the bulk of the expedition. Juan de Jaramillo, the second memorialist of the 1560s, for instance, had nothing to say about how many indios amigos were included in the expedition, though he did reveal some important information about them, which is discussed later.

Castañeda, on the other hand, had a considerable amount to say about the part played by the indios amigos in the course of the two years the entrada lasted. He begins by telling us that when Vázquez de Coronado selected "sinquenta de a cavallo y pocos peones" (fifty horsemen and a few footmen) to travel as an advance guard to Cíbola, he also took along "la mayor parte de los amigos" (most of the [native] allies).[25] Thus, when the advance guard arrived at Cíbola (probably Hawikuh, the southwesternmost ancestral Zuni pueblo in west-central New Mexico), it may have numbered one thousand or more, substantially overmatching the number of Pueblo warriors determined to oppose it. Consequently, it hardly seems miraculous that the Spanish-led force quickly overran the pueblo, though the contemporary Spanish accounts convey that sense. Castañeda himself claimed that Cíbola had perhaps as many as "doçientos hombres de guerra" (two hundred fighting men).[26]

After the capture of Cíbola, Captain Melchor Díaz was dispatched in an attempt to locate the marine component of the expedition, which was coasting up the Gulf of California. In another of their fleeting appearances, a party of Indian allies was reported by Castañeda as having accompanied Díaz in what proved to be a long, unsuccessful trek.[27] Castañeda also repeated the information provided by earlier documents that some of the Indian allies served as guards for the expedition's horse herd. After quarters for the winter had been established at Tiguex on the Rio Grande, one or more of the allies were killed in a Pueblo raid on the herd, or *remuda*.[28] In retaliation for this and other gestures of resistance by the Pueblos, one of the Tiguex towns was attacked and sacked, in the course of which, according to Castañeda, "muchos amigos de la nueVa españa" (many allies from Nueva España) lit fires in the ground-floor rooms in an effort to smoke out the defenders.[29] This tactic proved decisive in the assault, and the residents of the pueblo quickly capitulated.

At the end of a winter of nearly continuous fighting between the expedition and the people of Tiguex, the Spanish-led force departed for the east and a reported wealthy settlement called Quivira. Fearing that he was being misled by his Plains Indian guide, Vázquez de Coronado sent out scouting parties. One of these, its return overdue, was located, as Castañeda told it, by some "indios del campo" (Indians from the expedition) who had gone out looking for fruit.[30] Castañeda said little more about activities of the Indian allies, except to mention that late in the expedition, Juan Gallego led a party of reinforcements north from Culiacán that included "amigos" (Indian allies).[31] But he did recount that as the expedition retreated from the Pueblo world in the spring of 1542 on the long march back to Nueva España, "quedaron algunos amigos entre ellos" (some of our [Indian] allies stayed behind among them [the settlements]).[32] Indeed, as Castañeda told it, "en dos o tres jornadas nunca dexaron los naturales de seguir el campo tras la rretaguardia por coger algun fardaje o gente de serviçio" (for two or three days' journey the natives [of Cíbola] never stopped following the expedition, behind the rear guard, in order to pick up a little of the baggage or a few servants), apparently including indios amigos, as will become apparent.[33]

As to exactly where the Indian allies of the Coronado expedition came from, a small amount of documentary evidence exists. As we have already seen, some eight hundred indios amigos were likely natives of Nueva España proper. Castañeda qualified this region of origin by saying that "eran de la nueVa españa y la mayor parte de tierras calientes" (they were from Nueva España and most of them from hot climates), perhaps including today's *tierra caliente,* the coastal plains.[34] Regarding the often repeated claim that Tlaxcaltecas, the earlier allies of Hernán Cortés, were among those who made the trip to Cíbola, there is no documentary evidence whatever, though it would not be unreasonable to suspect that some were present.

With documentary support, though, we can say that at least some natives of the Valley of Mexico served during the entrada. The *Codex Aubin,* a pictorial manuscript glossed in Nahuatl that was completed early in the seventeenth century, records events from the history of Tlatelolco, the companion city to Tenochtitlán in Lake Texcoco at the time of Spanish conquest, which persisted as a barrio of the Spanish Ciudad de México. The entry for the year 1539, the year when members of the Coronado expedition would have departed from the city to rendezvous in Compostela, depicts *tenocha,* or natives of Tenochtitlán, leaving for "yancuic tlalpa*n*" (the lands newly discovered [by fray Marcos de

Niza]).[35] There can be little doubt that these Tenocha represent some of Vázquez de Coronado's indios amigos. From Tlatelolco itself came at least two individuals, a man called Francisco Jiménez[36] and a don Luis de León (a *principal,* or leader, at Santiago de Tlatelolco).[37]

From farther west in Mexico, people of the former Tarascan state are represented in the surviving documentary record by a man "que se dezia Andres" (called Andrés) who stayed in Quivira.[38] Incredibly, forty years after the end of the Coronado expedition, the members of an entrada into New Mexico led by Antonio de Espejo found several indios amigos from the earlier group at Zuni. According to Diego Pérez de Luxán, a member and chronicler of the Espejo entrada, they were "Mexican Indians, and also a number from Guadalajara, some of those that Coronado had brought."[39] The leader of the entrada himself was more specific, providing the names of some of those found at Zuni: Andrés (from Coyoacán), Gaspar (from México), and Antón (from Guadalajara).[40] Joining fray Juan de Padilla in his martyr's mission to Quivira when the Coronado expedition left the Southwest were "dos yndios creo que de çapotlan e de ally" (two Indians who I think were from Zapotlán or thereabouts), one evidently known as Sebastián.[41] Zapotlán was on the fringe of what was at the time the province of Colima.

The sum of the available documentary information tells us that approximately thirteen hundred Indian allies accompanied the Coronado expedition in its journey. Nearly all of them were native to the Nahuatl-, Tarascan-, and Caxcán-speaking regions of central and western Mexico. They made up the overwhelming majority of the expedition as a whole and probably each of its detachments, including that sent on Vázquez de Coronado's final leg of march to Quivira. The indios amigos were, most importantly, part of the fighting force of the expedition; their involvement in combat helps explain the ease with which most of the indigenous communities met were subdued or overawed into pro forma submission. In addition, some of the Indian allies often traveled ahead of even the advance guard, serving as intermediaries and emissaries, as was the case at Cíbola. The indios amigos carried supplies, guarded livestock, and constructed shelter. Their active involvement in the expedition was essential to what success it had. The statement of Pedro de Cieza de León, writing about Spanish expeditions of conquest in Peru in the 1530s, is no less fitting in relation to the Coronado expedition. Writing about the aid of Indians in the Peruvian expeditions, he said that "without abundant service [of Indians] . . . in no way, form, or manner could any expedition have been undertaken."[42]

Joining the expedition primarily as warriors, Mexican Indians made possible the journey of Marcos de Niza and the establishment of a "Spanish" beachhead in the upper Southwest. As in other cases of sixteenth-century Spanish conquest, native groups that had previously submitted to Spanish sovereignty made possible the extension of that control. It is no exaggeration to say that the conquest of the Americas during the sixteenth century was principally the conquest of native groups by other American natives, at least nominally under the direction of Europeans. The Coronado expedition was no different.

Others

Even many Europeans and other Old World natives who went on the expedition to the Tierra Nueva of Cíbola are missing from the muster roll. For instance, as Hammond and Rey mentioned in the brief introduction to their translation of the alarde, none of the six Franciscan friars who accompanied the expedition, nor at least three lay assistants, appears on the muster roll. Nor does a minimum of eighty more men-at-arms who are now known from other documentary sources to have gone on the expedition. Some of these, such as Juan de Zaldívar and Melchor Díaz, were simply not at Compostela at the time. Others, including a contingent from Culiacán, probably did not join the expedition until it moved north of Compostela. The recording scribe Juan de Cuevas himself tells us in the text that concludes the muster roll that some horsemen had "gone ahead with the friars" and some "are awaited from Mexico to join the expedition."[43] Still others may have purposely stayed or been kept away from the review before the viceroy, perhaps to frustrate the simultaneous investigation that was being made into whether a significant number of established vecinos of the settlements of Nueva España was being drawn away by the lure of Cíbola. Yet others do not appear on the muster because they were preoccupied with other preparations or were of a status too humble to warrant counting. In just one example of known expedition members whose names are not listed, a document from the AGI that we recently published for the first time—AGI, Contratación, 5575, N. 24, *bienes de difuntos,* Juan Jiménez, Tenancingo, November 19, 1550—mentions eight men previously unknown to historians: Antón Negrín, Jorge Báez, Diego Gallego, Pedro de Lasojo, Pedro de Huerve (Huelva), Juan Barragán (from Llerena), Juan Pedro, and Pedro, the black *pregonero,* or crier, of the expedition.[44] Even sixty years ago, Hammond and Rey pointed out that some men-at-arms were named in other documents but not listed on the muster roll, and they appended to their transcription of the alarde the names of forty-eight of whom they knew.[45]

Also participating in the expedition but not recorded on the official muster were many slaves and servants. Here, numbers can only be imagined. Surviving *probanzas de méritos y servicios,* or service records, of expedition members report that those men went to great expense to take servants and slaves with them.

Typical was Juan de Zaldívar, whose claim that he had expended thousands of pesos to take with him an unspecified number of "criados y negros" and "servicio" (henchmen, black slaves, and servants) was corroborated by all the witnesses called in 1566 to support his petition for preferment by the king.[46] It would have been unheard of if the hidalgos, or minor nobility, and many individuals of lesser rank on the expedition were not accompanied by servants and slaves. The chronicler Juan de Jaramillo referred in his *Relación* to "un esclavito myo que se dezia *crist*obal" (a young slave of mine called Cristóbal).[47] And he wrote of yet another slave of his who was on the expedition, listing "dos negros Uno myo que se dezia sebastian" (two blacks, one named Sebastián [being] mine).[48] Pedro de Castañeda mentioned "mucha gente de serviçio" (many servants) killed in a disastrous native attack on the expedition's supply base at Suya in modern Sonora.[49] In all likelihood, the number of servants and slaves equaled or exceeded the number of European men-at-arms in the expedition.

Such was clearly the case for other Spanish-led expeditions of the sixteenth century. Even most expeditionaries of relatively low status were attended by servants and slaves. As but two examples, there are Martín López, a little-known, rank-and-file member of the Cortés expedition in the conquest of Tenochtitlán who was accompanied by three personal servants,[50] and Alonso de Contreras, an undistinguished member of Beltrán Nuño de Guzman's 1529 expedition to west Mexico who took with him one servant and two black slaves.[51]

One final group is not only missing from the muster roll but is all but invisible in the documentary record as a whole: women. Only two women who accompanied their husbands on the expedition are known by name: María Maldonado and Francisca de Hozes. Maldonado was particularly well remembered by former expedition members as a nurse in time of sickness.[52] Francisca de Hozes was the first witness called by Lorenzo de Tejada when he investigated the expedition's conduct in 1544.[53] Perhaps not unexpectedly, but with surprising documentation, we meet a third female member of the expedition, an unnamed Pueblo woman who became the wife of expedition member Juan Troyano during the entrada.[54] These three are surely not even the tip of the tip of the iceberg of women who traveled to Cíbola, performing tasks disdained by the conquistadores such as cooking and mending and nursing, not to mention serving as companions and lovers and the makers of field households, and even doing combat service for all we know.

Why Are They Missing?

The documents of the Coronado expedition are far from unique in their scant notice of Native Americans, women, slaves, and servants. Throughout Spain's century of conquest, a privileged male monotone was commonplace in the records of enterprises of subjugation and reconnaissance. As but one of a multitude of possible examples from other expeditions, take Pedro de Cieza de León's lengthy account of the conquest of Peru. After 335 pages of narration without a single whisper concerning women on any of the various Peruvian expeditions of the 1530s, Cieza recorded the story of how a party led by Diego de Alvarado made a brutally cold crossing of the Andes. In the course of his telling, he casually mentioned that because of the severity of the conditions, fifteen Spanish men and six Spanish women died in the snow.[55] But the women expeditionaries vanish and are never mentioned again.

Why the protagonists of nearly all contemporary accounts of Spanish conquest are European men of at least modest rank, even though they were frequently outnumbered by other groups, is clear enough to imagine. Most documents that have been used to study the conquest are what might be called "bragging documents," manuscripts prepared principally to glorify the accomplishments of the conquistadores and portray them in the patterns of the centuries-long *reconquista* of Iberia from the Moors and of the wildly popular romances of chivalry.[56] One of the hallmarks of both the romances and contemporary accounts of the reconquest is stories of a relative handful of Christian knights pitted against and besting vastly more numerous heathen enemies. Consequently, it is not at all remarkable that we find Vázquez de Coronado telling the viceroy in a letter from Cíbola that "noi fossimo pochi" (we were few) and "Indiani . . . erano molti" (the Indians . . . were numerous) during the capture of that pueblo, when in all likelihood his force was at least twice as large as the number of Cíbola's native defenders.[57] Thus, the failure to reveal the presence of a large body of Indian allies, or anyone else, heightened the apparent danger the men of the muster roll faced and increased their worthiness for recognition and reward, the achievement of prestigious positions in the form of titles and authority being one of the principal aims of most conquistadores. Not that premeditated manipulation of the facts was necessary. It went without saying that a man's *criados,* or henchmen, and his household were extensions of himself; their accomplishments were his.

Whereas this might have been widely understood and accepted in Spanish hidalgo society of the sixteenth century, it can easily be missed by modern readers of the documents, because that attitude is out of step with the more egalitarian stance of later times. Unfortunately, this modern blindness has been aggravated by the seemingly innocent and unintentional distortion introduced by the great historian of the Coronado expedition Herbert E. Bolton. It was his intention, he said, to demonstrate that there were Hispanic heroes of the United States to set alongside George Washington and Abraham Lincoln. Francisco Vázquez de Coronado was his chief candidate for that honor. In the contemporary Spanish narratives, Vázquez de Coronado seemed to fit a classic American heroic mold as the leader of a small band facing overwhelming odds. It may have been because the fit seemed so good that Bolton failed to examine the documents with the skepticism typical of historians. He simply accepted the sixteenth-century documents at face value and paraphrased them in his monumental *Coronado: Knight of Pueblos and Plains,* failing to follow the scattered hints of not a small troop of Spaniards pitted against indigenous multitudes but a legion of Spanish-led Mexican Indians accompanying a corps of Europeans with their numerous servants and black slaves, all supported by huge herds of livestock, overmatching native communities generally only a fraction the size.

Organization of the Expedition

As evidence of the size and composition of the expedition, then, the muster roll must be qualified and supplemented. On another matter, though, the original document, AGI, Guadalajara, 5, R.1, N.7, tells us significantly more than its previous American editions do. In fact, by failing to reproduce the format of the manuscript document, those editions have inadvertently but utterly suppressed rare information about the expedition's organization. No one consulting only Aiton's transcription or Hammond and Rey's translation of the muster roll would ever know, for instance, that Rodrigo Maldonado was captain of a company of horsemen that included at least nine men at the time Juan de Cuevas recorded the muster. Those men were Juan de Torquemada, Francisco Gutiérrez, Sancho Rodríguez, Alonso de Medina, Hernando de Barahona, Leonardo Sánchez, one Çepeda, Antón Miguel, Gaspar Guadalupe, and Hernando de Caso Verde. Probably, more men were added to the companies as the expedition traveled north. At least we find that by later in the expedition's course, Juan de Zaldívar's company, for example, comprised seventeen horsemen, including the captain, and Hernando de Alvarado's comprised twenty-one.[58] At the time of the muster itself, however, the great majority of the men listed were not yet assigned to any company. For instance, 127 horsemen were listed in a large group following the six skeleton companies already mentioned.

This information about the composition of companies is available in the document itself but not in the earlier American editions because four folio sides of the manuscript are organized by companies, with each captain's name set against the left margin and the names of the men under his direction indented below his (fig. 4.1). In this manner, six companies of horsemen are delineated.

The six for which organizational information is provided by the manuscript muster roll are the companies led by García López de Cárdenas, Diego Gutiérrez de la Caballería, Diego López, Rodrigo Maldonado, Tristán de Arellano, and Diego de Guevara.

In the previous American editions of the muster roll, on the other hand, the names of all expedition members are aligned with the left margin, thus hiding the delineation of companies (fig. 4.2). This betrays a lack of appreciation of an important historical and cultural difference between lists and censuses of the sixteenth-century Spanish world and those of the modern United States. The overriding organizational paradigm for U.S. rosters is alphabetical ordering by surname, whereas alphabetizing was not practiced for similar sixteenth-century lists. Instead, persons listed next to or near each other on sixteenth-century Spanish lists are likely to have been close associates, but they are shown in hierarchical order if one existed. The first letter of one's surname was completely irrelevant in this schema. What to modern American eyes appears to be a random, hodgepodge list is, in fact, rich in information about the social relations between members of the group being listed.

In the case of the six companies distinguishable on the manuscript muster roll of the Coronado expedition, the men listed below their captains are likely to have been recruited by them and, in many cases, may have been closely associated before the mobilization of the expedition. Often these men remained associated for years afterward, too. In some cases, they may have had business or familial relationships with the captain, even being members of his extended household. The captain may have subsidized the outfitting and upkeep of such persons.

Not only does the format of the muster role provide fascinating information about social relationships among the men listed, but it also reveals, in combination with other documents, otherwise unknown information about how the expedition marched—namely, not generally as a single massive unit but by companies with significant space between them. This was stated explicitly by the expedition member Francisca de Hozes in her 1544 testimony concerning the return of the expedition through Sonora. The scribe recorded what she said this way: "Sabe que mataron los dichos yndios e a otros muchos esPanoles e mataron al dicho don garcia lopez y los que Con el yban sino VolVieran aTras e hobieran soCorro con otro Capitan que çerca venya" (she knows that the Indians killed [Alcaraz] and many other Spaniards and would have killed don García López de Cárdenas and those who went with him, if they had not turned back and gotten ten reinforcements from another captain who was coming close behind).[59] It is also likely that the expedition camped in company enclaves, and so one might

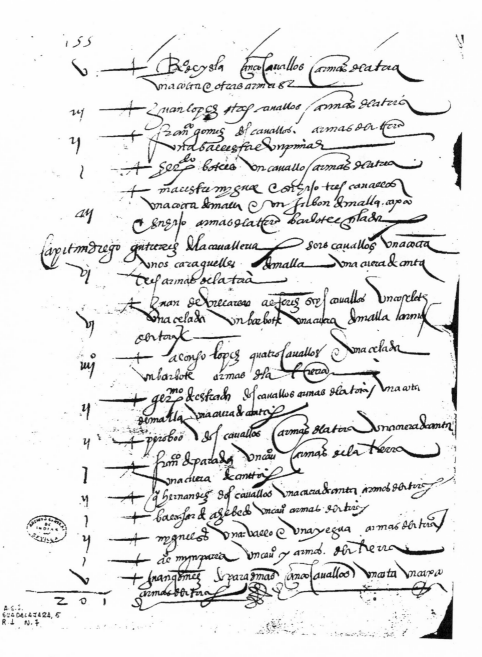

Figure 4.1. A page from the muster roll of the Coronado expedition, February 22, 1540, AGI, Guadalajara, 5, R.1, N.7, fol. 3r. Note the heading at midpage in the name "Capitan Diego Gutierrez de la cavalleria." Reproduced with permission of Spain's Ministerio de Educación, Cultura y Deporte.

Pedro de Ledesma,[20] five horses, one coat of armor, one beaver, one sallet, native arms.

Captain Don García López de Cárdenas,[21] twelve horses, three sets of Castilian weapons, two pairs of cuirasses, one coat of mail.

Juan Navarro,[22] five horses, one coat of mail, native weapons, one sallet with beaver.

Alonso del Moral, ensign of this party, two horses, one beaver, one sallet, native weapons.

Rodrigo de Ysla, five horses, native weapons, one coat of armor, and other arms.

Juan López, three horses, native weapons.

Francisco Gómez,[23] two horses, native weapons, one crossbow, and one dagger.

Hernando Botello,[24] one horse, native arms.

Maestre Miguel and his son, three horses, one coat of mail, one doublet of mail, a helmet, and his son had native weapons, one beaver, and a sallet.

Diego Gutiérrez, captain of the cavalry, six horses, one coat of armor, breeches of mail, one buckskin coat, three native weapons.

Juan de Villareal,[25] ensign, six horses, one corselet, one sallet with beaver, one coat of mail, native weapons.

Alonso López,[26] four horses, one sallet with beaver, native weapons.

20. Ledesma, a native of Zamora, was a witness at the inquiry held by Judge Tejada. He was also a character witness for Coronado at his residencia. In 1552 he testified that he had known Coronado for twenty-four years. He married a daughter of Melchior Pérez, the son of Licentiate Diego de la Torre. See A. G. I., *Justicia*, legajos 336, 339, and 1021, pieza 4; Icaza, *Diccionario*, no. 1166.

21. See the testimony of López de Cárdenas, pp. 337-365.

22. Navarro, from Aragon, came to New Spain with Cortés, serving as a crossbowman. Icaza, *Diccionario*, no. 18.

23. *Cf. Ibid.*, no. 1376.

24. Botello, a native of Alcántara. *Ibid.*, no. 1301.

25. Villareal, a native of Agudo and member of the order of Calatrava, said that the army consumed one thousand pesos worth of cattle which he took along on the expedition. He carried messages from Coronado in Cíbola to the viceroy. Later he was a favorable witness in the residencia of Coronado. Judge Tejada held his residencia as alcalde of Guadalajara on September 7, 1544, and sentenced him to pay a fine of thirty pesos. A. G. I., *Justicia*, legajo 339, pieza 1; Icaza, *Diccionario*, no. 548.

26. López, a native of Córdoba. *Ibid.*, no. 144.

Figure 4.2. A page from the muster roll of the expedition, February 22, 1540, as printed in Hammond and Rey, *Narratives of the Coronado Expedition, 1540–1542*, 91.

hope, at campsites like the Jimmy Owens Site in Texas, to distinguish discrete areas associated with individual units.

Odd Man Out

Leaving aside for a moment group characteristics, let me turn my attention to one of the captains listed on the muster role. The name of the second captain shown on that list, on folio 3r, appears as "Capitan diego gutierrez de la cavalleria" (fig. 4.1). Hammond and Rey, in their 1940 translation, rendered his name as "Diego Gutiérrez, captain of the cavalry" (fig. 4.2).[60] The same man is mentioned in Castañeda's narrative as having become a captain during the initial appointment of the expedition's leadership.[61] During testimony in 1544, on the other hand, the captain general, Francisco Vázquez de Coronado, failed to list Diego Gutiérrez among captains he had appointed. Nor does he appear in narrative accounts of the expedition after the muster at Culiacán in February 1540.

Who was this man, and why does his name appear on the February 1540 muster roll but is absent from subsequent documents? Recent research by Shirley Cushing Flint into the social and financial position of the Estrada family (that is, the family of Vázquez de Coronado's in-laws) in early colonial Mexico City has provided the answer. In about 1537, Francisco Vázquez de Coronado had married Beatriz de Estrada, daughter of Alonso de Estrada, former royal treasurer and briefly governor of Nueva España, and Marina Gutiérrez de la Caballería. Marina, Beatriz's mother and Vázquez de Coronado's mother-in-law, had a brother, Diego Gutiérrez de la Caballería,[62] who in 1537 had become a vecino of Mexico City.[63] Diego Gutiérrez went to Nueva Galicia, apparently with his sister's son-in-law. His participation in the expedition to Tierra Nueva can be seen as part of the Estrada-Gutiérrez-Coronado sponsorship of the venture. Diego Gutiérrez, though, may never have made the long trip to Cíbola. He appears to have died in Jalisco in February 1542, killed by natives, several months before the Coronado expedition as a whole abandoned its mission and returned south.[64] It is possible, therefore, that Diego Gutiérrez de la Caballería never left Compostela or did not go beyond Culiacán, or that he was one of the founders of the expedition's supply and communication base at San Gerónimo de los Corazones in Sonora. In the latter case, he might have been among the Spaniards who fled south from San Gerónimo late in 1541 or early in 1542, when the Ópata of that region rose up in arms and destroyed the base camp. That might even explain his dying not long afterward from wounds inflicted by Indians.

Clearly, many questions remain about Gutiérrez de la Caballería's life and his actual role in the Coronado expedition. A daughter of his, however, married one Alonso Pérez, who also went on the expedition.[65] And a son, also named Diego, went to Costa Rica with Juan Vázquez de Coronado, nephew of Francisco, in the 1560s and was killed there.[66] Nevertheless, it is clear that Diego Gutiérrez de la Caballería, the elder, was at least briefly among the leadership of the Coronado expedition. His name and therefore relationship with the captain general have gone unrecognized because Hammond and Rey misinterpreted "caballería" as referring to the captain's unit, the cavalry, when in actuality it was part of his surname.

Information such as this helps to show that, like most other Spanish expeditions of the period, the Coronado expedition relied significantly for its makeup on people who were related to the organizers, either by birth or place of origin or through habitual social or commercial contacts. It has been commonly assumed that the members of the Coronado expedition were recruited solely by beating the drum on street corners in Mexico City.[67] Though such recruitment surely did take place, the close social connection of expedition members such as Diego Gutiérrez de la Caballería with Vázquez de Coronado (and with Viceroy Mendoza) suggests another, much less random source of membership in the expedition. Thus, Diego Gutiérrez de la Caballería's full and correct name reveals fascinating and important connections between members of the leadership of the expedition that are wholly missing from earlier American editions of the muster roll.

Europeans in American Clothing

What Diego Gutiérrez de la Caballería or any other member of the expedition may have looked like has, in the past, been suggested only in paintings and other artistic representations that have relied on stereotypical and fanciful images. It has not been based on information about specific expedition members or even about the Coronado expedition in particular, and mostly not on the documentary evidence.

Though abundant evidence to the contrary is provided in the manuscript muster roll, the prevailing image of the appearance of the Coronado expedition is that of a troop of ironclad, medieval-looking knights (fig. 4.3). Yet the bulk of the expedition, as we have seen, consisted of Mexican Indians. They certainly did not look like European knights. What about the European members themselves? Of the 288 men whose names were recorded on the muster roll, only 61 declared that they had European-style body armor. In almost every case this amounted only to a coat of chain mail. No more than a handful of men had anything approaching a full suit of armor. Only 45 men possessed European-style helmets; most of them were men who also had body armor. A few other pieces of European armor were carried on the expedition—a stray sleeve of chain mail or a beaver here and there—but the majority of men listed on the muster roll had no European armor at all. By contrast, 90 percent of the men on the muster roll (258 out of 288) declared that they had *armas de la tierra,* or native arms and armor, either solely or supplementing their meager compliment of European armor. This fact is all but invisible in Hammond and Rey's translation of the muster roll, because they almost always translated "armas de la tierra" as "native weapons," rather than including armor in that term.[68] With that evidence obscured, visual images of the Coronado expedition have been at wide variance with its actual appearance.

Even with a fuller rendition of the muster roll, though, what would be a more accurate image has remained in doubt. Recently, independent documentary evidence has come to light that illuminates the subject of armor worn by members of the expedition. While working at the Archivo General de Indias in Sevilla, Spain, in 1997, I happened onto a group of copies of short documents dealing with the disposal of the worldly goods of one Juan Jiménez, a member of the Coronado expedition who died at Tiguex (in the area of modern Bernalillo, New Mexico) in February 1542.[69] At Tiguex an inventory of Jiménez's possessions was made shortly after his death, and soon thereafter they were auctioned off to other expedition members. The whole process was dutifully recorded at the time, as was required by Spanish law. Several years later a copy was made of those documents prepared in Tiguex. It is those copies that are still kept in the AGI.

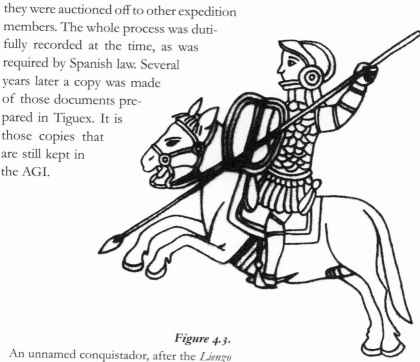

Figure 4.3.
An unnamed conquistador, after the *Lienzo de Tlaxcala,* sixteenth-century Mexico.

From those documents, we learn many things, including that Juan Jiménez possessed no metal armor at the time of his death, but only a native *sayo,* or tunic (presumably of quilted cotton in the pre-Columbian style of central Mexico, a garment known in Nahuatl as an *ichcahuipilli*),[70] a piece of native head armor, or *caperusa de armas de la tierra* (probably the conical headgear typical of Mexica–Aztec warriors, called a *copilli*),[71] and a jerkin with hide sleeves. He had both shoes and sandals and an old hat. In all likelihood his shirt and breeches and whatever else he was wearing when he died were buried with him; at least, they were not inventoried. Jiménez's wardrobe, then, adds support to the suggestion I have made in the past that most of the European members of the expedition looked very different from the romantic vision that has become conventional, a vision of the expedition as a party of ironclad, post-feudal knights.[72] Rather, even the European members of the expedition relied heavily on gear from indigenous central Mexican traditions (fig. 4.4). In this respect, Juan Jiménez was typical.

Implications for Editing the Documents

As a consequence of what I have briefly sketched here about the composition of the Coronado expedition, Shirley Cushing Flint and I, as editors of a new edition of documents of the expedition, would be seriously remiss simply to publish the muster roll without making it clear that it lists only a fraction of the people who made up the entrada. The company itself was much

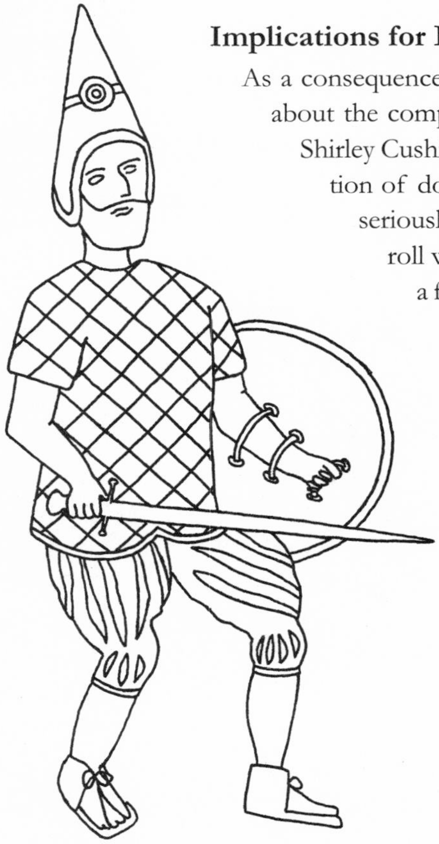

Figure 4.4.
Typical dress of a rank-and-file European member of the Coronado expedition, based on documentary evidence. He wears a central-Mexican-style tunic of quilted cotton and a conical piece of headgear of the type called *copilli* in Nahuatl. Drawing by Richard Flint.

larger and more diverse than the muster roll, standing by itself, would lead one to believe. Without reference to the various components of the expedition missing from the official roster, we would be guilty of perpetuating a partial truth, the myth that a relative handful of European men conquered the native peoples of the Americas. Certainly they were the principal engineers of the conquest, but the undertaking itself was carried out and executed by an array of American, African, and European men and women. Rather than just the 288 European men-at-arms listed on the muster roll, the Coronado expedition probably included between fifteen hundred and two thousand people of various ethnicities and nationalities. Their actions were often amazing, if not quite of mythic proportions, and were the results of a complex matrix of individual motives and cultural values.

Additionally, the muster roll contains valuable information about the composition, organization, and accouterment of the European component of the expedition that has been obscured or ignored in previous editions. Without scrupulous attention to the format of the document, for instance, specific information about the expedition's organization into companies has slipped passed. And with the past absence of thorough contextualization for the muster roll, the presence in the expedition of at least one close relative of Francisco Vázquez de Coronado in a leadership role has been hidden. So, too, has been the pervasive Mexican Indian character and appearance of the expedition, even of the Europeans who participated in it.

These and countless other deficiencies exist in the previous editions of Coronado expedition documents. Unfortunate errors and instances of misinformation, similar to those I have pointed out here but far too numerous to list, are contained in the existing (mostly out-of-print) editions. I do not mean to imply by such examples that George Winship, George Hammond, and Agapito Rey were deficient scholars. In fact, they all produced remarkable works that represented the state of knowledge in their day. However, in the last sixty years (one hundred years in the case of Winship) an extraordinary amount has been learned about the Coronado expedition, the early Spanish colonial period in general, and the protohistoric peoples of the Greater Southwest. Although Winship and Hammond and Rey conveyed satisfactorily the broad outline of events of 1540–42, details in their work are frequently at variance with what we now believe to have been the case, and omissions sometimes seem painfully glaring.

It is to remedy the inadequacy and inaccuracy of documentary editions currently available to general readers and scholars researching the Coronado expedition that we have begun work on a new and expanded dual-language edition. Such an edition is essential if we are to minimize disagreements among scholars that are the products solely of faulty transcription and translation or outdated annotation.

Notes

1. Juan de Cuevas, scribe, "Muster Roll of the Expedition, February 22, 1540," AGI, Guadalajara, 5, R.1, N.7, fol. 1r, in Flint and Flint, *They Were Not Familiar.*

2. The expedition proposal submitted by Viceroy Mendoza to the king, probably no later than 1538, is not known to have survived.

3. For the testimony of the witnesses present during the review, see León, "Hearing on Depopulation Charges." *Vecino* is a complex term that refers to an individual who has full political rights in a town. To be granted vecino status, one ordinarily had to pay a fee and promise to reside in the town for a certain period.

4. Arthur S. Aiton, "Documents: Coronado's Muster Roll," *American Historical Review* 64 (1939): 556–70.

5. Hammond and Rey, *Narratives,* 87–108.

6. Carmen de Mora, ed., *Las siete ciudades de Cíbola: Textos y testimonios sobre la expedición de Vázquez Coronado* (Sevilla: Ediciones Alfar, 1992), 199–211.

7. Mendoza, "Viceroy's Letter to the King," fol. 1r and 1v.

8. Known only from a sixteenth-century Italian translation, see Francisco Vázquez de Coronado, "Letter to the Viceroy, Cíbola, August 3, 1540," in Ramusio, *Navigationi et viaggi,* fol. 360r and 360v, translated into English in Flint and Flint, *They Were Not Familiar.*

9. "Relación del suceso [1540s]," AGI, Patronato, 20, N.5, R.8, fol. 7r, 11v, and 12r, in Flint and Flint, *They Were Not Familiar.*

10. Hernando de Alvarado, "Narrative, 1540," AGI, Patronato, 26, R.23, in Flint and Flint, *They Were Not Familiar.*

11. Fray Toribio de Benavente, "Relación postrera de Cíbola [1540s]," Benson Collection, University of Texas, Austin, JGI 31 XVI C, fol. 123v–124v; and Francisco Vázquez de Coronado, "Letter to the King, Tiguex, October 20, 1541," AGI, Patronato, 184, R.34, in Flint and Flint, *They Were Not Familiar.*

12. "Se mataron algunos naturales . . . ynDios por ser Ellos Reveldes y haber ellos tanbien muerto muchos Españoles E yndios" (some native Indians were put to death [only] because they were rebels and also because they had killed many Spaniards and Indian [allies]). Gómez de la Peña, "Testimony Taken at Culiacán," fol. 15r, 363, 384.

13. "Le hirieron mas de quarenta esPañoles e yndios Amygos" (more than forty Spaniards and Indian allies were wounded). Requena, "Proceso de Francisco Vázquez," fol. 114v, 290, 308.

14. Requena, "Proceso de Francisco Vázquez," fol. 96v, 258, 266–67. Both scribal and editorial deletions are preserved in the transcripts but are identified as deletions by being enclosed between standard parentheses. All emendations, additions, and expansions are rendered in italics.

15. Gómez de la Peña, "Testimony Taken at Culiacán," fol. 21v, 393, 400.

16. To question seven of the *interrogatorio* of Vázquez de Coronado's agent Francisco Pilo, García Rodríguez and Gaspar de Saldaña both assented, and Saldaña gave a detailed reply. The question asked whether they knew that the people of the Tiguex Province "aporrearon e hirieron alg*un*os (h)inDios Amigos De los q*ue* guardaban las d*ic*has bestias e murieron algunos de (h)ellos" (clubbed and wounded some of the Indian allies who were guarding the animals and killed some of them). [García Ramírez de Cárdenas], "Report extracted from the affidavit prepared for don García Ramírez de Cárdenas," AGI, Justicia, 1021, N.2, Pieza 2, fol. 2r, in Flint, *Great Cruelties,* 439, 449.

17. Paradinas stated that the Tiguex had killed "A çiertos yndios Amigos que las fueron a buscar" (some Indian allies who had gone to find the stock). Requena, "Proceso de Francisco Vázquez," fol. 16v, 80, 85.

18. Requena, "Proceso de Francisco Vázquez," fol. 110v, 287, 304.

19. Requena, "Proceso de Francisco Vázquez," fol. 110r, 286, 304.

20. Requena, "Proceso de Francisco Vázquez," fol. 102v, 280, 297.

21. Arthur S. Aiton and Agapito Rey, "Coronado's Testimony in the Viceroy Mendoza *Residencia*," *New Mexico Historical Review* 12 (July 1937): 314.

22. Castañeda, *Relación*, Primera Parte, Capítulo 4, fol. 19r, 19v.

23. Castañeda, *Relación*, Tercera Parte, Capítulo 8, fol. 152v.

24. Castañeda, *Relación*, Primera Parte, Capítulo 8, fol. 30v.

25. Castañeda, *Relación*, Primera Parte, Capítulo 8, fol. 30v.

26. Castañeda, *Relación*, Primera Parte, Capítulo 9, fol. 34v. Cristóbal de Escobar, testifying in 1544, on the other hand, estimated there had been three hundred to four hundred warriors at Cíbola, still probably less than half as many as the advance guard. See Requena, "Proceso de Francisco Vázquez," fol. 44v, 146, 154.

27. Castañeda, *Relación*, Primera Parte, Capítulo 10, fol. 42r.

28. Castañeda, *Relación*, Primera Parte, Capítulo 15, fol. 63v, 64r.

29. Castañeda, *Relación*, Primera Parte, Capítulo 15, fol. 65r.

30. Castañeda, *Relación*, Primera Parte, Capítulo 19, fol. 83v.

31. Castañeda, *Relación*, Tercera Parte, Capítulo 7, fol. 150r.

32. Castañeda, *Relación*, Tercera Parte, Capítulo 4, fol. 141r.

33. Castañeda, *Relación*, Tercera Parte, Capítulo 5, fol. 141v.

34. Castañeda, *Relación*, Primera Parte, Capítulo 10, fol. 44r.

35. *Códice Aubin,* "Record of Mexican Indians Participating in the Expedition," in Códice Aubin, British Museum, Add MSS 31219, fol. 45v, in Flint and Flint, *"They Were Not Familiar."*

36. Fray Pedro Oroz, *The Oroz Codex,* ed. and trans. Angélico Chávez (Washington, D.C.: Academy of American Franciscan History, 1972), 314.

37. Lewis Hanke, *Los virreyes españoles en América durante el gobierno de la casa de Austria, México* (Madrid: Ediciones Atlas, 1976), 1:70.

38. Juan Jaramillo, "Narrative [1560s]," AGI, Patronato, 20, N.5, R.8, fol. 5v, in Flint and Flint, *"They Were Not Familiar."*

39. Diego Pérez de Luxán, "Diego Pérez de Luxán's Account of the Antonio de Espejo Expedition into New Mexico, 1582," in *The Rediscovery of New Mexico, 1580–1594: The Explorations of Chamuscado, Espejo, Castaño de Sosa, Morlete, and Leyva de Bonilla and Humaña,* eds. and trans. George P. Hammond and Agapito Rey (Albuquerque: University of New Mexico Press, 1966), 184.

40. Antonio de Espejo, "Report of Antonio de Espejo," in Hammond and Rey, *Rediscovery of New Mexico,* 225.

41. Jaramillo, "Narrative," fol. 5v.

42. Pedro de Cieza de León, *The Discovery and Conquest of Peru,* eds. and trans. Alexandra Parma Cook and Noble David Cook (Durham, North Carolina: Duke University Press, 1998), 384.

43. Cuevas, "Muster Roll," fol. 9v.

44. Flint and Flint, "Death in Tiguex," 247–70.

45. Hammond and Rey, *Narratives,* 104–8.

46. [Zaldívar], "Proof of service."

47. Jaramillo, "Narrative," fol. 5r.

48. Jaramillo, "Narrative," fol. 5v.

49. Castañeda, *Relación,* Tercera Parte, Capítulo 3, fol. 137v.

50. C. Harvey Gardiner, *Martín López: Conquistador Citizen of Mexico* (Lexington: University of Kentucky Press, 1958), 20.

51. Gardiner, *Martín López,* 103–4.

52. [Gómez de Paradinas], "Proof of service."

53. Requena, "Proceso de Francisco Vázquez," fol. 6v–10v, 58–62, 66–70.

54. Juan Troyano, "Letter by Juan Troyano, Dec. 20, 1568," AGI, Mexico, 168.

55. Cieza de León, *Discovery and Conquest,* 336.

56. See Leonard, *Books of the Brave.*

57. Vázquez de Coronado, "Letter to the Viceroy, fol. 360v, 361r.

58. Requena, "Proceso de Francisco Vázquez," fol. 91r, 106r, 253, 262, 282, 300.

59. Requena, "Proceso de Francisco Vázquez," fol. 10v, 61, 70.

60. Hammond and Rey, *Narratives,* 91.

61. Castañeda, *Relación,* Primera Parte, Capítulo 5, fol. 21r.

62. Francisco Fernández del Castillo, "Alonso de Estrada: Su familia," *Memorias de la Academia Mexicana de la Historia* 1, no. 4 (1942): 400.

63. *Actas de Cabildo,* 3:188.

64. Juan Sánchez Bermejo, "Encomienda grant to Juan Sanchez Bermejo, (1542)" AGN, Mercedes, vol. 1.

65. Icaza, *Conquistadores,* 1:no. 133–34.

66. Ricardo Fernández Guardia, *Cartas de Juan Vázquez de Coronado, Conquistador de Costa Rica* (Barcelona: la viuda de Luis Tusso, 1908), 55, 61.

67. Bolton, *Coronado,* 51.

68. Shirley Cushing Flint's and my study of hundreds of sixteenth-century documents leaves no doubt that the term referred to both weapons and armor. As Spain's first important lexicographer put it: "arma puede ser ofensiva, como la espada, la lanza, etc. . . . y defensiva, como la cota, el casco, la rodela, el coselete, etc." Sebastián de Covarrubias Orozco, *Tesoro de la lengua castellana o española* (Madrid: Editorial Castalia, 1995 [1611]), 118.

69. López de Legazpi, "Disposal of Juan Jiménez estate."

70. Patricia Rieff Anawalt, *Indian Clothing before Cortés: Mesoamerican Costumes from the Codices* (Norman: University of Oklahoma Press, 1981), 46.

71. Frances Berdan and Patricia Rieff Anawalt, *The Essential Codex Mendoza* (Berkeley: University of California Press, 1997), 184.

72. Richard Flint, "Armas de la Tierra: The Mexican Indian Component of Coronado Expedition Material Culture," in *The Coronado Expedition to Tierra Nueva: The 1540–1542 Route Across the Southwest,* eds. Richard Flint and Shirley Cushing Flint (Niwot: University Press of Colorado, 1997), 57–70.

FIVE

Chichilticale: A Survey of Candidate Ruins in Southeastern Arizona

WILLIAM K. HARTMANN AND BETTY GRAHAM LEE

THE LATE PUEBLO PERIOD in southeastern Arizona, especially south of the Gila River, is the intriguing time from about 1275 to 1400 when above-ground, pueblo-style complexes, often with kivas, began to appear along with distinctive pottery, walled compounds, and other traits.[1] At some sites these traits represent direct incursions of ancestral Pueblo (Anasazi)–related people,[2] whereas at others the traits mixed with or partially replaced older, local traditions involving pithouse villages, as at University Ruin in the Tucson Basin and Tres Alamos on the San Pedro River.[3] Many sites of this period are part of the "Salado phenomenon" and have been called Salado pueblos, although this term has different interpretations among investigators.

The Coronado expedition passed through this general region and reported stopping at a large, fortresslike ruin named Chichilticale and crossing a nearby pass and mountain range of the same name. The expedition's chroniclers regarded the Chichilticale region as a major point on the trail to Cíbola. We believe the Chichilticale ruin was one of the Late Pueblo structures in the northern Sulfur Springs Valley and adjacent Aravaipa headwaters (map 5.1).

That region was thickly settled during the Late Pueblo period and has one of the largest concentrations of still visible pueblo-style ruins in Arizona. The valley connects to the northeast through Eagle Pass to the Thatcher-Safford-Solomonville area of the Gila Valley, which in the 1800s was known as Pueblo Viejo because of its even higher concentration of large ruins, still visible at the time. The Pueblo Viejo ruins were virtually destroyed by nineteenth- and twentieth-century farmers, and neither the Pueblo Viejo sites nor the ruins of the Sulfur Springs Valley have received much professional study. In this chapter we concentrate on still visible ruins (principally foundations), mostly of Salado pueblos, in the Sulfur Springs Valley, Aravaipa headwaters, and Eagle Pass areas. Although nearly all the sites included here lie on private ranch land, pothunters unrelated to the owners have made clandestine forays into the area, especially in the 1980s and 1990s. They have dug into many rooms and removed much material, and the sites are deteriorating. Starting in 1969, when the sites were more nearly pristine, Betty Graham Lee (BGL) made many visits to them, recording field notes and interviews. And we both visited the sites in the 1990s. In the hope of preserving a database about their early condition and stimulating further interest in the area, we report survey results from thirty years of field investigations at many of these sites and compare them with sites in nearby areas.

Because of its many springs and streams and its pleasant setting, the northern Sulfur Springs Valley was relatively more important and more traveled in historic times than it is today, when it has been bypassed by an interstate highway and railway. In the mid- and later 1800s it lay on a significant route from New Mexico Territory to military camps on the San Pedro River, such as Camp Grant, because it avoided the lower, hotter, dryer land and sulfurous springs of southern Sulfur Springs Valley and the area of the Willcox Playa. By means of a wagon road through Eagle Pass (probably superimposed on a prehistoric route), it also offered a route from Tucson, Camp Grant, and later Fort Grant to settlements on the Gila River in the Safford area. Many ranches were established in the area in the 1870s to supply Fort Grant and travelers with provisions.

The most recent published overview of major pueblo sites in the valley was that of Carl Sauer and Donald Brand, who called this area "a neglected corner" of Arizona, which it still is. In 1930 Sauer and Brand surveyed the area and made many prescient observations about it. For example, they noted that "archaeology is of common interest: cattleman and peon know the places and the outlines of the ancient sites, and the ranch house may harbor an important collection." They also wrote that "the finest sites and largest settlements south of the Gila were met with [in the Aravaipa Valley]. Apparently they have never been reported on, and have been viewed only by local amateurs."[4]

These statements are surprisingly true seventy years later, in spite of abundant publications on the archeology of Hohokam sites in neighboring valleys to the west. The concentration of ruins in the Aravaipa headwaters and northern Sulfur Springs Valley is surprisingly little known to professional archeologists, and some ruins reported here still have no site cards in the Arizona State Museum.

The contemporary degradation of sites in the Sulfur Springs and Aravaipa drainages is a modern repeat of the destruction of many other extraordinary

Late Pueblo ruins by settlers at the end of the 1800s. Many travelers in the 1800s commented on mounds, pottery, standing walls, and irrigation canals visible then in southeast Arizona. James Ohio Pattie, who traveled down the Gila in 1824–25, remarked on the "great quantities of broken pottery . . . scattered over the ground, and . . . distinct traces of ditches and stone walls, some of them as high as a man's breast."[5] This particular site seems to have been along the San Pedro River, but it gives an impression of the ruins that were still prominent roughly 420 years after their abandonment and 284 years after the Coronado expedition.

Lack of attention to all these ruins has biased scholars' understanding of Arizona prehistory in general and the Coronado expedition in particular.

Location of the Chichilticale Province

Where was Chichilticale? Where was the Coronado expedition's route? The two questions are linked. As reviewed by William K. Hartmann,[6] William A. Duffen and Hartmann,[7] and others, the Coronado expedition probably traveled about four days downstream on the San Pedro River and then turned east for a few days, possibly traveling up the Sulfur Springs Valley and over Eagle Pass. This fits reports by expedition members Juan Jaramillo and Pedro de Castañeda that they traveled north up the "Senora" Valley past a town called Ispa or Arispa (modern Arispe?), then four days across an uninhabited region, then two days downstream on the "Nexpa" (San Pedro?) before turning "right to the foot of the mountain range in two days' travel, where we were told it [the mountain range] was called Chichiltiecally."[8] Jaramillo says they had heard of this famous mountain range three hundred leagues to the south, and it contained a pass that they also called Chichilticale. Beyond this lay the fifteen-day despoblado, or unpopulated region, leading to Cíbola.

The San Pedro fits the "Nexpa," and the two days farther downstream on it would have taken the expedition some 48–64 kilometers to a region between present-day Sierra Vista and Benson, Arizona, where there are many village sites, such as the late prehistoric site at Tres Alamos. A turn of two days to the right (east) would have taken them into the Sulfur Springs Valley, somewhere between the western Chiricahua Mountains and the Aravaipa headwaters.

As for the Chichilticale ruin, Castañeda says it was "reduced to a ruined roofless house" that appeared once to have been a "strongly fortified dwelling." He says it was "clearly perceived to have been built by civilized and warlike foreigners [who] had come from far away," and it was "made of bright red earth." Later in the same narrative, he writes that it had been "inhabited by people who split off from Cíbola" and had been "abandoned because of the [local] Indians of that land [who were] uncivilized."[9]

Marcos de Niza described a similar route in the previous year. He did not mention the place names Nexpa or Chichilticale, or the ruin, but Castañeda says Marcos's party discovered it and that Indians from that area had traveled to Cíbola with Marcos's companion, Esteban.[10] Because Marcos and the expedition traveled the same route, the Chichilticale location can be better understood by correlating their reports.

Marcos's commentary about the last populated valley before the despoblado (i.e., the Nexpa–San Pedro) is confused but suggests that he traveled at least three days along it. This could have put him near modern Benson. He waited three days at a large, prosperous village because the natives wanted to prepare to go with him to Cíbola. There, he learned that it took four days to go from this village to the beginning of the great fifteen-day despoblado to Cíbola. Noting from the Coronado narratives that the final fifteen-day despoblado started around Chichilticale Pass or the Gila, where the thorny vegetation ended, we can identify Marcos's additional four days from the final populated valley (Nexpa–San Pedro) to the Gila as corresponding to Jaramillo's turn to the right for two days to the Chichilticale Mountains, plus another day or two across the pass to a deep river (the Gila?). Thus, it is in the general area two to four days east of the San Pedro that Chichilticale Pass and the Chichilticale ruin are to be found, near the Sulfur Springs Valley.[11]

A similar route was known in the twentieth century as the "Hopi trail" to the Hopi-Zuni country (map 5.1). Sauer and Brand, Herbert Bolton, and interviews between BGL and Safford-area ranchers indicate that the Hopi trail ran from the San Pedro Valley through the Galiuro Mountains via Hooker Hot Springs, then via Post Office Canyon and Rattlesnake Creek into the Aravaipa headwaters, across Eagle Pass to the Gila, north through one of the low gaps in the Gila Mountains, such as Gila Gap, and on to the Hopi pueblo country.[12]

A better understanding of the Late Pueblo ruins in southeast Arizona and their relation to the Coronado *entrada* records will perhaps offer a chance to pin down the expedition's route in southeastern Arizona and allow identification of the specific Chichilticale ruin. It may also let us understand more clearly the Spaniards' Chichilticale province and their conception of it and clarify our understanding of late prehistory by tying the eyewitness accounts deriving from the expedition to more precise locales.

Environment and General Description

The northern Sulfur Springs Valley and Aravaipa headwaters offer a great variety of ecological zones and resources, which apparently supported a sizable population in the 1300s. Sauer and Brand estimate that "the several villages on the Aravaipa, of which [the Haby Site] is the chief, may possibly have accommodated a couple of thousand people."[13] A curiosity of the valley is that although it appears as a single valley between two mountain ranges, it does not have a major central stream like the San Pedro Valley. Instead, it has a high point in the middle, west of Bonita. Thus, the Sulfur Springs Valley and streams near Fort Grant drain south into the Willcox Playa, and Aravaipa Creek drains north and feeds through the narrow, rugged, Aravaipa Canyon west into the San Pedro River.

The ruins along the valley tend to lie in the foothills on either side and among the Aravaipa headwaters at the northwest end. These areas have abundant springs, small creeks, and opportunities for both agriculture and hunting-gathering. Vegetation is sparse on the terraces and lower mesas around many of the sites and includes catclaw, cholla, and a few junipers. The lower valley has mesquite and cottonwood, sycamore, and walnut. Nearby foothills have oak, rabbit, deer, javelina, turkey, and bear. The Coronado expedition chroniclers recorded that they encountered many mountain sheep and mountain goats in this general area, and modern local ranchers confirm seeing them in the neighboring hills. The Pinaleños Mountains, on the northeast side of the valley, include Arizona's second highest peak, and runoff from them feeds many streams entering the valley, including Grant Creek. Similar runoff and springs feed Aravaipa Creek from the Galiuro Mountains on the southwest.

Brief Site Descriptions

The order of the sites in the descriptions that follow is somewhat arbitrary, but our intent is to start with the largest or more important sites in the northern Sulfur Springs Valley and Aravaipa headwaters area, in terms of prehistoric population and population density.

Map 5.1 shows the general locations of the sites discussed and a few earlier sites. Among the potsherd samples mentioned here, sherds we observed in situ were left on site, and additional samples were observed in the collections of the Arizona State Museum. Table 5.1 summarizes the percentages of the most widely found types within the total datable sample from each site.

1. The Haby Ranch Site (Arizona BB:3:16; Sauer and Brand site 31).
This site, also known as the Garden Springs Site, consists of a multiroom pueblo atop a gravelly ridge approximately 65 meters high, immediately above Haby Spring and the Haby Ranch house. Rooms are also terraced down the southeast

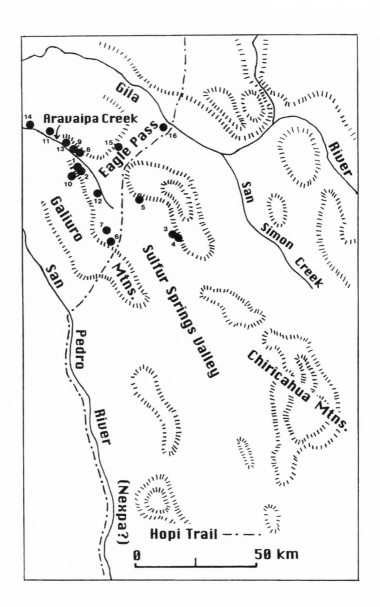

Map 5.1. Chichilticale Province: the Sulfur Springs Valley, Arizona, showing selected Late Pueblo sites. 1, Haby Ranch Site; 2, Haby Ranch Site, older eastern outlier; 3, Fort Grant Ruins; 4, Fort Grant Eastern Ruins; 5, 76 Ranch Ruins; 6, Eureka Springs Ranch House Site; 7, Eureka Springs Ranch, "Crescent Ruin"; 8, "Pentagon" Ruin Site; 9, Wooten-Claridge Terrace Site; 10, Rattlesnake Mesa Ruin; 11, Citadel Ruin; 12, Eastern Arizona College Field School Site; 13, Klondyke Cemetery Site; 14, Pottery Hill Site; 15, Eagle Pass Ruin; 16, Skinner Site.

Table 5.1

Ceramic Assemblages at Selected Major Sites in the Sulfur Springs Valley, Southeastern Arizona

Type	Assigned Duration	1 Haby	3 & 4 Fort Grant	5 76 Ranch	7 Eureka Crescent	10 Rattlesnake Mesa	11 Citadel	16 Skinner Site	Goat Hill	Curtis Salado Bldg	Kuykendall	University Ruin Salado Mound (Tucson)
Total no. sherds		97	92	32	1,041	43	42	108	1,730	976	6,052	1,719
Source (see key)		LHA	A	LHA	L	L	L	LHA	WA	Mills	Mills	Hayden
Tucson Polychrome	1300–1400	—	4%	—	—	2%	—	5%	—	1%	—	3%
Gila Polychrome	1275–1400	88%	53%	78%	92%	60%	74%	45%	1%	82%	52%	15%
Tonto Polychrome	1260–1400	4%	—	9%	1%	—	2%	4%	—	15%	34%	—
San Carlos R/Br	1275–1385	4%	1%	—	2%	—	—	11%	—	2%	—	<1%
Gila Bl/R	1250–1350	—	23%	3%	—	—	—	11%	—	2%	—	2%
Maverick Mt. Poly.	1265–1290	—	—	—	4%	5%	10%	1%	92%	<1%	—	—
Ramos Polychrome	1250–1400	—	—	—	—	—	—	1%	—	—	<1%	—
Pinto Polychrome	1200–1300	—	—	—	—	—	—	1%	—	—	—	—
St. Johns Bl/R	1175–1300	—	3%	3%	—	—	—	—	—	—	—	—
St. Johns Polychrome	1175–1350	—	4%	—	—	—	—	2%	—	<1%	—	—
El Paso Polychrome	1100–1350	—	—	—	—	—	—	—	—	<1%	12%	—
Tularosa Fillet-rim	1100–1300	—	1%	—	—	—	—	2%	<1%	—	—	—
Wingate Bl/R	1050–1400	7%	—	—	—	—	10%	6%	—	—	—	—
Mimbres Bl/W	1050–1300	—	1%	—	—	9%	2%	—	—	<1%	—	—
Encinas R/Br	900–1100	—	2%	—	—	21%	—	—	—	—	—	—
Total		99%	92%[a]	93%[a]	99%	97%	90%[a]	89%[a]	93%[a]	101%	100%	20%[a]

Note: Sherd types are listed as percentages of total datable sample, favoring sites with large samples.
Key to sources of samples on which observations are based:
L   Betty Graham Lee field observations
H   W. K. Hartmann and Gayle Harrison Hartmann field observations
A   Arizona State Museum collections
W   Woodson 1999:Table 2
Mills   Jack and Vera Mills
Hayden   Julian Hayden
[a] Additional unlisted sherds include:
Fort Grant: Reserve Bl/W 3%, Pinedale Plychrome 1%, Cedar Creek Polychrome 1%
76 Ranch: Santa Cruz R/Buff 3%, Casas Grandes 3%
Citadel Ruin: Tularosa Bl/W 2%
Skinner Ruin: Tanque Verde R/Br 6%, White Mt. Polychrome 3%, White Mt. Redware 2%,
        Four Mile Polychrome 1%, Tularosa Bl/W 1%
Goat Hill: Tucson Bl/R 6%
University Ruin Salado Mound: Pantano R/Br 63%, Tanque Verde R/Br 18%, both local Tucson area wares

WILLIAM K. HARTMANN AND BETTY GRAHAM LEE   87

side of the ridge. Additional room outlines are seen on a flat terrace on the east base of the ridge, and another block of rooms lies due east a few hundred meters farther across a shallow, flat valley at the base of another pediment.

Cold-water springs exist at the north base of the hill, draining into Aravaipa Creek. In historic times, the spring attracted homesteading by Colonel John Bridwell, associated with Camp Grant, and construction of the adjacent ranch house, occupied from about 1870 to 1900. According to local informants, including former owner Margaret Haby in 1986, the spring at Haby Ranch used to provide much more water and originally bubbled out a four-inch-wide stream of water, but it went dry during the period of the 1920s to 1940s after the sinking of 25- to 35-meter wells nearby. This spring was an attractive site for early travelers. Rattlesnake Creek drains northward into the Aravaipa just south and east of the ranch house and ruin.

Sauer and Brand recorded this site in the following terms:

> The defensive position of the major [hilltop] settlement is superior to any site visited. . . .
>
> [It] seems to have been completely surrounded by a heavy wall. The heaviest walls, however, belong to the inner structure. Six and even nine rows of large cobbles mark the thickness of an inside structure. Traces of a commodious central citadel are to be seen. Cedar posts protrude from the ground. The lower village seems to have been without defenses and was also composed of houses placed in less orderly fashion.
>
> The Haby citadel yielded a virtually pure Middle Gila polychrome assemblage, lacking even the common, fine (Little Colorado) [*sic*] ware that seems to have been freely traded in elsewhere. The absence of this ware may indicate the cessation of such trade and a late decadent period for the origin of the town.[14]

Sauer and Brand also stated that this "fortress site is so situated as to defend one of the principal routes of prehistoric communication—the so-called Hopi trail."[15]

BGL visited and took notes on the site in the early 1970s, when the original room outlines were still visible atop the ridge.[16] She estimated fifty to sixty room units on the ridge summit, with thirty to forty at the north end, ten in the middle, and two major mounds at the south end with numbers of rooms. Rooms were large, paced off as 4 to 5 meters square. She could not recognize any "heavy wall" at that time. Rex Gerald, from the University of Arizona, reportedly excavated two rooms about that time as part of his research for a Ph.D. dissertation.

This ruin had been well protected until late 1975, when some excavation was conducted by the owners at that time. BGL noted abundant Gila Polychrome but no Mimbres Black-on-white Black-on-white, Encinas Red-on-brown Red-on-brown, or Sacaton Red-on-buff on the ridge top, although these were frequent at other, smaller sites within about 500–800 meters distance.[17] Among other materials removed by the owners, BGL noted fifteen to twenty slab metates, a few trough metates, a tripod metate, many 25-centimeter-long manos with groves along the sides, many three-quarter-grooved axes, mescal knives, a *Glycymeris* shell bracelet fragment, and many other lithic materials, all said to be from the roomblocks at the north end of the ridge. The tripod metate may indicate importation from northern Mexico. BGL later verified from Laura Haby Botts that her mother had also collected a tripod metate of volcanic rock nearby along the creek.

At the time of our 1995 visit, after construction of the new Hughes house, the top of the hill was dominated by a large bulldozed hole with two large mounds of debris, one on either side, and a road up the south side disturbing some of the site. Crude stone alignments along the perimeter of the hilltop probably mark the site of the wall reported by Sauer and Brand. BGL in 1995 regarded the hilltop as radically altered from its former appearance, concluding that the great ruin as reported by Sauer and Brand no longer existed, although the site was clearly a major Salado-era habitation.

Our sherd sampling indicates a high percentage of Gila Polychrome (88 percent of 97 sherds in the sample) and a plausible date in the late A.D. 1200s to 1400. Sauer and Brand interpreted the site as one of the latest in the valley; they hypothesized that earlier sites were in open areas and that during a later period of unrest, communities grouped in walled, hilltop, defensive positions. More recent work supports this idea.[18]

East and south of the Haby Site, about 600 meters across the shallow Rattlesnake Creek drainage, is another ridge. At the foot of it, in a position similar to the lower terraces of the main Haby ruin, lies another concentration of material noted by BGL as either a trash mound or possibly a roomblock. Much charcoal, sooty material, and burned bone were noted. The small sample of sherds recorded in this material matches that from the main Haby Site in being primarily Gila Polychrome. Near this latter site, uphill to the south, informants of BGL's made photographs of rock alignments and room outlines. Their sketch map suggests more than a dozen rooms. The photos also show five Gila Polychrome sherds, one probable San Carlos Red-on-brown, and one probable Tonto Polychrome, plus several additional plain ware sherds and one corrugated piece. We infer that these sites mark an occupation area contemporaneous with the main Haby Site.

2. Haby Ranch Site, Older Eastern Outlier

Below the last area, from the ridge northeast to the creek, BGL noted additional sherds. These apparently lack the Gila Polychrome material and average earlier in time. In our sample of seven sherds, we found 29 percent (± 20 percent) each of Casa Grande Red-on-buff, Maverick Mountain Polychrome, and Pinto Polychrome. We suspect this site may mark a separate occupation nearer to the stream.

3. Fort Grant Ruins (Arizona CC:5:5, CC:5:16, and CC:5:1; Sauer and Brand site 28)

This site is one of the major habitation areas of the northern Sulfur Springs Valley and yet is one of the least documented. The area of the site is somewhat ill defined and has an interesting history. Note that Arizona CC:5:16 and CC:5:5 are one or two site diameters apart on the east bank of Grant Creek, south of the current Fort Grant Prison installation. CC:5:1 is several site diameters east of the other two. Referring to the whole terrace from Fort Grant to the 76 Ranch area, Sauer and Brand wrote that the "vicinity of Fort Grant abounds in remains, scattered over [an] area about 16 kilometers long (northwest to southeast) and perhaps 3 miles [5 kilometers] broad."[19] CC:5:5 and CC:5:1 have similar sherd mixes (respectively, 58 ± 15 percent and 50 ± 10 percent of Gila Polychrome among datable painted sherds, for example), whereas CC:5:16 has no Gila Polychrome and an earlier mix.

Sauer and Brand's brief account was based in part on an earlier description by E. J. Hands, a "pioneer settler and amateur archaeologist [and] a shrewd observer of Indian antiquities." They said,

> No defensive character. Mounds of varying size and height are scattered all over the mesquite-grown pediment slopes. . . .[E. J.] Hands considers the main village to have been on Stockton Pass road about a mile and a half from Fort Grant. Important mounds are southeast of the Shirley ranch house [located near Bonita]. A good deal of random pot-hunting has been done, but no excavation of systematic character. An immense amount of broken pottery has been thrown up, as well as great numbers of manos, metates, broken hoes, and axes.
>
> Mr. Hands reports . . .: "Several slab lines showed rooms nearly square, between 10 and 12 feet [3 n>4 meters]. . . . work done by Shirley [a local rancher] followed an adobe wall down for five feet [1.5 meters] to a floor and uncovered part of three sides of a room, 11½ by 12 feet [4 meters square]. Walls had been well plastered. The room was in the

middle of a ridge that I felt sure was made by the falling walls. I think, on excavational trial, that this and other ridges will be found to represent rooms of two stories. There are reports of old ditches."

The site is predominately Middle Gila polychrome as to pottery and apparently as to architecture. Indistinct indications of an older culture are also represented by a few sherds.[20]

On the basis of our own observations among the nearby 76 Ranch Ruins, we infer that the mounds are mostly remains of pueblo roomblock structures, possibly more than one story in height. The description of the room excavation exactly matches excavations by William Duffen at the 76 Ranch Site in the mid-1930s, including adobe walls extending about 1.5 meters down to floors of rooms of typical dimension about 4 meters by 5 meters with a kiva about 5 meters by 8 meters.[21]

With good water because of the stream, this area was chosen in 1872 as the location of Fort Grant, when old Camp Grant was moved from the San Pedro River. It served as a cavalry post until 1905. It was all but deserted from 1905 to 1912. From 1912 to 1973 it was a four-thousand-acre state industrial school (a boy's and girl's correctional facility), and in 1973 it became part of the state prison system. On a prehistoric mound west of Grant Creek was the old Luna Hotel, said to be the site of an 1877 arrest of Billy the Kid for his first murder, which occurred at nearby Bonita.[22] BGL noted that the remains of this hotel were still visible in the 1960s, but she found neither the hotel foundations nor the prehistoric rooms to be easily visible in 1990, although a few sherds were scattered nearby.

During both the fort and prison periods, extensive, random, and undocumented excavation was conducted throughout the area.[23] In addition, informants indicate that families who visited the prisoners typically held picnics on the grounds and pothunted among the ruins, and that this practice resulted in removal of so much material that such picnics were eventually prohibited. It is said that large amounts of artifactual material ended up among families of inmates over the decades. In addition, there are reports of extensive private collections made by workmen laying pipe, grading roads, building tanks, and digging silos for the facility. Informants have mentioned materials including copper bells, many three-quarter-grooved axes, clay and stone figurines, turquoise beads, and shell pendants.

In 1982, William G. White, who worked at the facility, contacted BGL to report continuing destruction of the archeological site. Because the facility paid inmates in a work-study program, he suggested that inmates might be given classes in archeology and be trained and paid to conduct digs. BGL proposed that Eastern Arizona

College conduct such classes, but faculty was unavailable for classes at Fort Grant and the idea was abandoned. About the same time, Keith Kintigh from the University of Arizona phoned BGL to report that he had contacted Governor Bruce Babbitt's office, which (through a chain of calls) approached the staff at the Fort Grant facility about the continuing destruction of archeological resources. Fort Grant staff reported an internal investigation of this charge and concluded that the reports were mostly rumor and that no new building construction was resulting in the bulldozing of sites. There was further discussion of organizing joint crews of volunteers from Safford and the University of Arizona to pursue excavations, but these ideas, too, were abandoned.

BGL searched for what Sauer and Brand called the "main village" site and was unable to locate it. The area appears generally disturbed today, although some mounds probably contain undisturbed rooms.

4. Fort Grant Eastern Ruins (Arizona CC:5:1)
This site may be distinct from the other Fort Grant Ruins, but is discussed under item 3.

5. 76 Ranch Ruins (Arizona BB:8:1)
This is the site mentioned by Emil Haury as his favorite candidate for Chichilticale.[24] Our work on this site is described by Duffen and Hartmann.[25] A sample of thirty-two painted sherds gave 78 percent Gila Polychrome and 9 percent Tonto Polychrome.

6. Eureka Springs Ranch House Site
The Eureka Springs lie at the eastern base of the Black Hills, which are eastern foothills of the Galiuro Mountains. This was an area of marshy springs, "a group of springs that formed an oasis,"[26] near where Black Canyon from the west and President Canyon from the east drain into Aravaipa Creek. Together, these sources help form the headwaters of Aravaipa Creek.

This group of springs, marking the beginning of the Aravaipa drainage, has long attracted travelers, but the historic record is somewhat complicated because, several springs originally lay within perhaps 2 kilometers or less of the present Eureka Springs Ranch house, and place names may have shifted in the 1800s. Some records indicate that the present Eureka Springs complex was originally called Bear Springs,[27] and the name Eureka Springs may have been applied to other, nearby springs. Also, reports indicate that the modern configuration of the springs on the Eureka Springs Ranch and environs has changed somewhat because of the dropping water table.

Members of Lieutenant John G. Parke's railroad survey parties in 1854 and 1856 recorded stopping at the springs, then known as Bear Springs. William Bell described a trip across Arizona in 1867, during which he and his party entered the Sulfur Springs–Aravaipa Valley from the east and kept close to the Galiuro foothills, "because most of the springs lay on that side." Riding overnight during a period of some hours, they stopped at springs they called Bear Springs, Kenedy's Spring, Eureka Springs (described as "warm and sulphurous"), and, 16 kilometers beyond it, a lush camp and spring adjacent to a hill "covered with the stone foundations of many buildings" and pottery (possibly the Haby spring and ruin).[28]

Within a few years, a traveler's station was operated at the site, by then known as Eureka Springs. According to the *Arizona Citizen*, "Mr. George H. Stevens . . . bought the Eureka Springs Station" and constructed the first Eureka ranch house, surrounded by a six-foot adobe wall, near the springs and on a ridge about 100 meters southeast of the present ranch house.[29] Current evidence indicates that the original ranch house was constructed atop a large prehistoric occupation site. The present ranch house was built in 1880.

Sauer and Brand apparently did not see the major sites of the Eureka Springs Ranch; they stated that "[E. J.] Hands reported his inability to find ruins at Eureka Springs."[30] The Arizona State Museum apparently did not have a site card designation for the Eureka Springs Ranch House Site prior to our study. Records as early as 1976 indicate that no vestige of the first ranch house was visible at that time. Ridgway refers to "fragments of pottery and an assortment of artifacts" being prominent around "this delightful watering spot."[31]

The 1880 house, occupied by the ranch managers, and several nearby outbuildings now occupy an area several hundred meters on a side, facing Aravaipa Creek. Water from the springs flowed into a pond near the current house, but this pond has dried up since the 1980s, according to the present manager. Also, according to this source, the owner in 1939, a Mr. Jesscott, built two houses atop the ridge where the original house stood. This ridge still yields many artifacts, but the present managers have no records of materials found at that time.

About 1997, a backhoe dug 1.5 to 3 meters into the ridge in the process of installing an electric line, yielding large quantities of metates, manos, sherds, and various lithics. Also found at that time was what was described as a 10- to 15-centimeter white spear point without notches. Sherds and other artifacts continue to be picked up over the whole area of several hundred meters around the existing buildings. Nonetheless, known collections from this area are not extensive. Those we know of are dominated by Gila Polychrome. In a sample of fifteen painted sherds, we found 93 percent Gila Polychrome and 7 percent San

Carlos Red-on-brown. Additional corrugated, plain-ware sherds, a *Conus* shell "tinkler," and other materials were found. Around three dozen metates are displayed at the ranch house, including basin and slab types.

Unfortunately, it remains unclear whether there is a major pueblo site at Eureka Springs or merely accumulated campsite materials.

7. Eureka Springs Ranch, "Crescent Ruin"

This is a well-defined site atop an isolated ridge about 5.8 kilometers north-northwest of the Eureka Springs Ranch house, on the southwest bank of Aravaipa Creek. A large, multiroom pueblo complex follows about 250 meters along the crescent shape of the ridge top, with the open side of the crescent facing the creek. The ridge lies some 200–300 meters southwest of the creek. Sauer and Brand did not report this site.

The room and wall units appear mostly contiguous, especially in large groupings atop the north and south ends of the ridge. Rooms in the middle part of the ridge lie at a slightly lower elevation and at the base of the ridge, and a road cuts through this area. It is unclear whether there was one continuous pueblo or several roomblocks on the ridge. Some rooms formed terraces on the upper slopes of the ridge. There also appeared to be some separate rooms in the flats, especially at the north base of the ridge. The number of rooms is uncertain, but from the general dimensions of the ruin and the spacing of rooms, we estimate that the total complex may involve 70–150 rooms.

Local ranchers say that the ridge-top site was virtually covered for years with flat, irregularly shaped "flagstones," and that ranchers throughout the valley had removed these from the site over the years and used them to construct walks and patios (for example, the front walk of the Eureka Springs Ranch house and a patio at the Deer Creek Ranch). A number of these are still visible at the site. They are typically roughhewn slabs, 30–50 centimeters in length and a few centimeters thick. Their geologic source and purpose is unknown. They may have been material from collapsed walls of a multistory structure.

A flat, football field–sized space lies between the ridge and the creek. The creek side of this field is lined (parallel to the stream) by a straight wall, 101.7 meters long, of deeply embedded, contiguous, low posts, which historic ranchers say have "always been there." In the 1980s, the posts were easily visible, extending above the surface as much as a foot. They may be juniper. By very shallow excavation, BGL found that the above-ground posts are the survivors of an unbroken wall formed by contiguous posts below the surface, which gives the appearance of having been watertight. The purpose of this unusual wall, whether water control, livestock control, or something else, is uncertain. Samples were supplied to the University of Arizona's Laboratory of Tree-Ring Research, but a definitive report has not been issued.

About 1980, Kim Lackner, the wife of the range manager, Don Lackner, reported that large pits were being dug at night by pothunters and that many sherds and other artifacts were being excavated and left scattered on the surface. What material was actually removed is unknown. Mrs. Lackner requested a visit from BGL and advice on the nature of the site and what could be done. The Lackners and BGL then mapped the site and removed many boxes of sherds and other exposed surface materials and stored them at the ranch in the hope of making the site appear less rich. This had no effect; illegal pothunting continued.

A visit by William K. Hartmann (WKH) and Gayle Harrison Hartmann in 1995 revealed a badly damaged site. Pothunters had excavated more than a dozen large pits, so closely spaced that only narrow walkways were available between them (fig. 5.1). One room with intact walls was carefully exposed, but other pits were amorphous in shape. Kneeling boards and a broken shovel were abandoned on the site, and many heaps of up to two dozen sherds each were left on the rims of the holes.

After a 1997 arrest of pothunters, artifacts recovered were reportedly turned over to a Graham County deputy sheriff, but they were reportedly not returned to the ranch, and their disposition is unknown.

With the owners' permission, BGL, Don and Kim Lackner, and various family members assisted in excavations in 1987 that expanded two pothunter pits into two different, slightly trapezoidal rooms, about 3.4 by 3.9 meters and 2.6 by 3.8 meters, respectively. The walls of these rooms were constructed of boulders covered with heavy, hard plaster. The plaster was reddish brown on the upper wall and gray on the lower wall. Fallen adobe wall material was very hard, even concretelike, and difficult to excavate. The first room included a 43-centimeter-deep post hole, an unplastered firepit containing ash, and walls 30 to 40 centimeters thick. A test pit in the south-southeast corner indicated that the wall extended at least 50 centimeters below the floor surface, raising the question of whether the structure was two-storied. This question was unresolved.

The second room, 2.6 by 3.8 meters, contained an inverted San Carlos Red-on-brown bowl covering the skull of an infant burial on the floor in the northeast corner. The body was flexed, lying east-west with the head at the west. The age was estimated to be two to three years; the maxilla contained nine teeth, with one missing tooth, and the intact mandible contained ten teeth. A polished redware bowl and two large, thin manos were recovered from the well-preserved floor of the same room.

In 1996, BGL went through the complete collection of material that had

Figure 5.1.
Pits mark the remains
of rooms excavated
by pothunters at
Eureka Springs
"Crescent Ruin",
examined by Gayle
Harrison Hartmann,
March 1995. Photo by
William K. Hartmann.

been recovered from the site (primarily from the northeast end of the crescent) and found mostly sherds left from the pothunters' excavations. This yielded an inventory of 2,933 sherds, including 1,032 painted sherds and other material such as copper bells. In a sample of 1,041 painted sherds, we found 92 percent Gila Polychrome, 4 percent Maverick Mountain Polychrome, and 2 percent San Carlos Red-on-brown. Intrusives included Mimbres Black-on-white (three sherds), Pinto Polychrome, Encinas Red-on-brown, Tucson Polychrome, Reserve Black-on-white, and Tularosa Fillet (one each). In addition, there remained an even larger collection of 205 pounds of uncounted sherds. Like the tabulated material, it appeared to be dominated by plain ware, Gila Polychrome, and corrugated ware. The data suggest a late prehistoric, possibly multistoried, stone-walled pueblo structure.

In approximately January 2000, the ranch was purchased by new owners. The Lockners were asked to move out on short notice. The entire collection of artifacts had been removed from its locked storage area, and its whereabouts are unknown.

One kilometer north of the Crescent Ruin is the beginning of the very old wagon road that starts up the mouth of Lindsay Canyon and leads across Eagle Pass. This road was used in the 1800s to carry military supplies between Fort Grant and Fort Thomas. Wagons left Fort Grant, stopped at Eureka Springs (the Ranch House Site) for water, and continued over the pass. The modern dirt road over the pass lies several kilometers farther north. We believe it likely that this old wagon road marks a prehistoric route. The Crescent Ruin might well have been perceived in 1540 as a single, decaying defensive structure on this trail and thus makes a not implausible candidate for the Chichilticale ruin.

8. "Pentagon" Ruin Site (BB:3:18, Sauer and Brand site 31 or 32)

This is a site across the Aravaipa Creek and the Klondyke road about 0.75 kilometer northwest of the Haby Site. It lies on the east side of Buford Canyon behind the old Wooten-Claridge Ranch house, atop a small flat knoll or terrace behind the house. The knoll is partly covered by mesquite and other brush. In the flat area, alignments of football-sized boulders, usually one to two boulders wide, outline a more or less pentagonal, asymmetric enclosure 18 to 32 meters on a side. The longest axis through the pentagon is nearly true north and extends 41 meters. The shortest side is a line of single rocks. The walls or foundations defining the pentagon are not on the rim of the knoll summit but more in the middle of the flat area.

This area includes many room outlines and features defined by rock alignments, and a few additional room outlines are found outside the pentagon, out to a distance of about 50 meters. No obvious contiguous pueblo roomblock is visible, but the area has been heavily trampled by cattle and is brushy, so such features are difficult to make out. We believe that the features inside the pentagon are smaller, separate room features. We estimate that there may be one to three dozen rooms in and around the pentagon. A sample of eighty-four painted sherds gave 39 percent Encinas Red-on-brown and 37 percent Gila Polychrome as the main types, suggesting an extended period of occupation.

9. Wooten-Claridge Terrace Site (BB:3:19, Sauer and Brand site 31 or 32)

This is a ruin on a low gravel ridge behind and slightly west of the old Wooten-Claridge Ranch house. It is just below and about 100–200 meters west of the Pentagon Site. In 1977, Roy Claridge put a road from the ranch house area into

Buford Canyon, which crossed the site. Within a few weeks, BGL observed the site and artifacts taken from it. The site included foundations of perhaps ten rooms. A sample of fourteen painted sherds was dominated by 39 percent Encinas Red-on-brown, 18 percent Mimbres Black-on-white, and only 14 percent Gila Polychrome. The site appears to have a long time span of occupation.

10. Rattlesnake Mesa Ruin

This site came to BGL's attention in 1985 when Eleanor Claridge reported it and took BGL for a visit. Another visit was made in 1990. It is located on Rattlesnake Mesa, an elevated, tilt-topped terrace descending 2 to 3 kilometers north-northeast from the mountains. It lies southwest of, and overlooks, the Haby Ranch Site and the Pentagon Site, as well as the Aravaipa Valley. The summit area includes juniper, mesquite, sotol, piñon, and catclaw.

At least three separate house clusters were noted east of the poor jeep road across the mesa, and a possible ditch along the west edge of the pediment. The northernmost of the observed room clusters forms a rectangle around an open plaza. Pothunting had destroyed some rooms and alignments. About 20 meters south of this was another row of rooms, and south of that was still another row of rooms that may have shared a communal courtyard with it. The site is estimated to include three dozen rooms or more. The sample of forty-two painted sherds gave 60 percent Gila Polychrome and 21 percent Encinas Red-on-brown.

11. Citadel Ruin (Cobre Ranch or Proctor Site)

This site, on a rounded knoll about 65 meters above the junction of Stowe Gulch and Aravaipa Creek, was known in the area as the Citadel. In 1975, when this was still the Proctor Ranch, BGL was taken to the site. Room outlines could be seen over several acres, with some erosion and abundant pottery visible on the surface. The ranch is locally considered to be in an especially favored site in terms of water and environment.

Later, probably in the early 1990s, a buyer prevailed on a new ranch owner to sell about ten acres of land containing the site, under the pretense of wanting to build a house. The buyer made a small down payment, pothunted the site with a bulldozer and backhoes, and then pulled out. The site was essentially destroyed during this episode. Douglas A. Johnson reports a similar vandalization of Fourmile Ruin.[32]

The total extent of the original ruin is uncertain, but it was locally considered to have been a major site. BGL's inventory of forty-two painted sherds noted during the 1975 visit gave 74 percent Gila Polychrome and 10 percent Maverick Mountain Polychrome.

12. Eastern Arizona College Field School Site

This multiroom pueblo site lies about 2 kilometers southeast of the junction of the Eagle Pass road and the Klondyke-Bonita road, on a small hill in the valley floor between the latter road and Aravaipa Creek. It was first reported to BGL in 1976 by a Thatcher family that was excavating artifacts there, including some pots they collected for sale, along with bone awls and other materials. The excavations produced Gila Polychrome and Tonto Polychrome as well as plain-ware bowls and/or jars.

The hilltop is roughly 40–50 meters on a side, and the top is marked by mounds up to 1.5 meters high and rock alignments defining roomblocks. A 1976 sketch map shows roomblocks 34 meters or more in length surrounding a courtyard on at least three sides. The dimensions of three rooms visible on the surface were 4 by 6 meters, 4 by 6 meters, and 4.5 by 5.5 meters. The hilltop pueblo structure is judged likely to have contained fifteen to twenty rooms, assuming a one-story structure. The 1.5-meter mound may indicate two-story construction.

Classes at Eastern Arizona College used the site for field-school work in the late 1970s, under Tom Scott, head of the Social Science Department, but this work was never published. WKH and Gayle Harrison Hartmann visited the site in 1995, after the Eastern Arizona College excavations had ended, and noted numbers of roughly square rooms marked out by alignments of football-sized rocks. Some rooms were contiguous and others appeared to be detached.

No sherd count statistics are available. A qualitative preponderance of Gila Polychrome and the roomblock designs suggest that this is a typical Salado pueblo site like the nearby Haby Site. A bird pendant of Hohokam style, found below the site, suggests possible trade with Hohokam people to the west.

13. Klondyke Cemetery Site (Arizona BB:3:20)

This site, on the north side of Aravaipa Creek about 2 kilometers southeast of Klondyke, is contiguous with the historic cemetery dating from the early twentieth century or before. The site lies on a low mesa with a good view of the valley. Many stone alignments define rooms, and some of the stones piled on the modern graves appear to have come from the ruins. The digging of many of these graves has unearthed pottery fragments.

In 1985 BGL noted the following sherd types without tabulating numbers: Encinas Red-on-brown (67 percent of nine sherds), Mimbres Black-on-white, corrugated (mostly large and crude), some obliterated corrugated, polished red ware (polished inside and out), and smudged plain ware (some with tan or pinkish paste, possibly Hohokam, and others with brown paste). No Gila Polychrome was seen during the 1985 visit. The Arizona State Museum has a tiny sherd collection from the Klondyke Cemetery Site, dominated by Encinas Red-on-brown. The Encinas Red-on-brown and Mimbres Black-on-white recorded probably predate A.D. 1150, although these types may show up later as trade ware.[33] These data suggest that this site is somewhat earlier than many of the other pueblo sites in the valley.

14. Pottery Hill Site

The designation "Pottery Hill" is a local name for a ridge just west of Morago Canyon, northeast of Aravaipa Canyon. BGL's informant in 1998 remarked that pottery had been dug on this hill by children "for a hundred years, mostly by children living in the area." Our records include only two sherds, both Gila Polychrome.

The site appeared to BGL to be possibly terraced on the steep east slope, which faces onto a field that is now a grassy pasture. The hill has tall grass and thorny brush, which hampered the survey. Her observations indicated that the site contained a pueblo of about twenty rooms, or possibly more if the terracing down the east side included rooms.

15. Eagle Pass Ruin (BB:4:1)

This is a multiroom, masonry-walled pueblo with a central courtyard, described in more detail by BGL, who excavated two rooms.[34] Her maps indicate about twenty-five to thirty rooms, including a long roomblock running roughly east-west with five to ten rooms and an attached courtyard, and another roomblock of four to six contiguous rooms. Also present were circular, probably older detached rooms or pithouses. A thin scatter of surface sherds was seen but not counted during the study. The two rooms together yielded a number of whole vessels, including five Gila Polychrome, one San Carlos Red-on-brown, four corrugated jars, and eleven plain-ware vessels. During our brief visit on March 12, 1995, the only painted sherds observed were three Gila Polychrome.

The Eagle Pass Site is notable for having well-laid rock masonry walls with a red clay mortar, perhaps the best rock masonry construction of any of the sites we have described (fig. 5.2). By reconstructing fallen wall materials, BGL estimated that the rock walls once reached nearly 2 meters in height from the floor level.

These data appear sufficient to establish the Eagle Pass Ruin as a typical Gila Polychrome–dominated site. BGL has suggested that the Eagle Pass Ruin was a candidate for the Chichilticale ruin of the Coronado records, based on site location, red clay, and its position on a well-traveled prehistoric trail across Eagle Pass from the Aravaipa–Sulfur Springs Valley to the Gila. By way of illustration, she points to a finely made, 7-centimeter-long crucifix found in 1915 at nearby Indian Springs, a camp spot on the trail about 3 kilometers from the Eagle Pass Ruin.[35] The age is not known, but an early Spanish origin has not been excluded.

Figure 5.2. Wall segment outlining a room in the Eagle Pass Site, examined by Betty Graham Lee, March 1995. Photo by William K. Hartmann.

16. Skinner Site (CC:1:7)

This is a multiroom pueblo site at the northern foot of the current Eagle Pass road, nearly on a line between Eagle Pass and Pima Gap, a historic route into the White Mountain country. It could be the first Gila River pueblo encountered by a traveler going north through Eagle Pass on the late prehistoric route referred to by Sauer and Brand as "the so-called Hopi trail," a possible Coronado expedition route through the area.

The site has long been known locally as a source of prehistoric pots, axes, and other artifacts. To our knowledge, no site description has been published, although Sauer and Brand's sites 19 and 20 are mapped as nearby. The railroad track across the area disturbed the site, and several modern houses and outbuildings have also. During our 1999 visit, BGL remarked on the much greater number of pothunting excavations than she had seen earlier. A mound 1 to 2 meters high in a corridor between the modern houses and the railroad track marks one of the pueblo roomblock structures, in which room outlines were once easily visible. In 1999, the room outlines could scarcely be seen.

The site does not have as high a percentage of Gila Polychrome (45 ± 6 percent) as most Sulfur Springs Valley sites, but rather contains a substantial percentage of White Mountain wares (for example, Wingate Black-on-red, St. Johns Polychrome, totaling around 18 percent). As distinct from Salado sites farther east in the Safford Valley, this site lacks substantial Casas Grandes and other Chihuahuan intrusives. These data suggest that the Skinner Site was not heavily involved in trade with Casas Grandes but instead may have been a stop on a north-south trade route coming up through western Mexico. Routes from Chihuahua, New Mexico, and the Casas Grandes area may, however, have entered the Safford Valley from the east, in view of the fact that sites tabulated by Sauer and Brand east of Safford and also east of the Chiricahua Mountains tend to have higher fractions of Mimbres and Casa Grandes ceramics.

The Late Pueblo Ruins of Chichilticale Province and the North-South Trade Route

We have shown that the broad "Chichilticale province" east of the San Pedro River, and in particular the Sulfur Springs Valley, contain many multiroom Late Pueblo ruins. Most of these sites are strongly dominated by Gila Polychrome (ca. 1275–1400). Some of these ruins may have been on or near sites occupied earlier, based on a moderate percentage of Encinas Red-on-brown (ca. 900–1100) and smaller amounts of the other early wares. However, most of the ruins we discuss are chiefly Salado, dominated by late wares.

The Late Pueblo sites of this region fit a hypothetical model derived from work of M. Kyle Woodson, William Hartmann and Richard Flint, Julian Hayden, Carr Tuthill, and others, in which ancestral Pueblo–related immigrants from the north established pueblo communities in the Chichilticale area in the late 1200s.[36] The earliest of these communities brought in northern ware, such as the unusual 92 ± 2 percent incidence of Maverick Mountain Polychrome among painted sherds at Goat Hill (CC:1:28), a site near Safford, Arizona (table 5.1). But in the 1300s they evolved toward production of "standard" Salado wares, dominated by Gila Polychrome. Indeed, among these "pure" Puebloan sites, the painted wares are dominated almost entirely by four types: Gila Polychrome, Tonto Polychrome, Gila Black-on-red, and Maverick Mountain Polychrome, all dating from the period between about 1250 and 1400. The proportions vary from site to site, but the total remains remarkably constant at 81 percent to 100 percent.

Intrusives show that these pueblos maintained widespread trade. We suspect that whereas some of the more eastern and southern sites show evidence of trade from the east or from Casa Grandes, the Sulfur Springs Valley sites show a stronger preponderance of trade to the north. To assess this, let us consider Maverick Mountain Polychrome the "original" northern type as brought in at Goat Hill and then define "other northern trade types" somewhat arbitrarily as indicated by the sum of Fourmile, Cedar Creek, Pinedale, St. Johns, and other White Mountain Red Wares plus St. Johns Black-on-red, Wingate Black-on-red, Pueblo Black-on-red, and Reserve Black-on-red.

Having made this definition, we note that a sample of 6,052 sherds tabulated by Jack and Vera Mills at the Kuykendall Ruin (south of Willcox near the Chiricahua foothills) contains zero Maverick Mountain and four "other northern" sherds for a total of only 0.07 percent, but 728, or 12 percent, El Paso Polychrome and 104, or 1.7 percent, Ramos-Carretas Polychrome.[37] These data suggest that Kuykendall lies off the main north-south trade route—that is, too far to the southeast. Similarly, of 972 sherds tabulated by Mills and Mills at the Curtis Site Salado building, east of Safford, none is Maverick Mountain or "other northern," but eight, or 0.8 percent, are El Paso Polychrome, Ramos Polychrome, and Mimbres Black-on-white.[38] Again, we conclude that this site lies off the main north-south trade route (too far east).

Similarly, University Ruin in Tucson, classified as a Late Pueblo Salado ruin, in a sample of 1,719 datable sherds from the "Salado mound," gave no Maverick Mountain Polychrome and less than 1 percent northern sherds and may thus lie west of the main Cíbola trade route. It also had only 15 percent Gila Polychrome; it was dominated by 63 percent Pantano Red-on-brown and 18 percent Tanque Verde Red-on-brown, both local Tucson Basin wares, a reflection of the site's location at the western edge of the distribution of Salado sites.[39]

In contrast, among the 1,361 sherds we have tabulated at the "pure" late Salado sites in Sulfur Springs Valley (dominated by 1,041 sherds from Eureka Crescent Ruin, plus other sherds from Haby, Fort Grant, 76 Ranch, Eureka Ranch House, Citadel, Klondyke Road BB:3:17, and Pottery Hill), we have 49 Maverick Mountain, or 3.6 percent, and 25 "other northern," or 1.8 percent, but only 6, or 0.4 percent, El Paso Polychrome, Ramos Polychrome, Tularosa Black-on-white, Mimbres Black-on-white, or Casas Grandes ware. The ratio of northern to "southeastern" intrusives is thus reversed, and we infer that the northern Sulfur Springs Valley is on the northern trade route. This agrees with the Coronado entrada evidence that the route lay two to four days east or northeast of a point on the San Pedro River around Benson.

In this context, a site mentioned briefly by Sauer and Brand is of special interest. They state that Pinery Canyon, a site in a valley on the west side of the Chiricahua Mountains, east of the Kuykendall Site, had a very large number of sherds, "unusually mixed" in type. "Mimbres is prominent enough to suggest an occupation from that culture center. Most striking, however, are the shards of northern associations, black on red and bright orange in both fine and crude application, and other shards suggesting Hawikuh ware." This finding is somewhat at odds with our finding that the Kuykendall Site is east of the main north-south trade route, but it is consistent with our suggestion that the route includes part of the Sulfur Springs Valley. Sauer and Brand noted room outlines and various walls and floors but stated that all evidence of walls at the main site were destroyed when an orchard was planted on the site. We do not know the current condition of this site. The Pinery Canyon Site, with its Cíbola-area sherds, lies at the foot of the mountains where the ranges begin to turn west, and a day's journey south of the well-used Apache pass. It therefore fits several criteria for Chilchilticale and remains a candidate for Coronado's lost ruin.

In context of the Cíbola route, the Skinner Site, at the north mouth of Eagle Pass, on the south terrace of the Gila River west of Safford, is also of interest. Among 108 counted sherds, it contained fourteen, or 13.0 percent, "other northern," as well as one, or 1 percent, Maverick Mountain, but only one, or 1 percent, "southeastern" intrusives (Ramos Polychrome in this case). This is consistent with our hypothesis that in the 1300s (and probably as late as the 1500s), a major northern trade route exited in the Sulfur Springs Valley through Eagle Pass, which is thus a prime candidate for Chichilticale Pass.

In the late 1800s, as scholarly exploration began in the Southwest, physical evidence that could have been tied to the Coronado expedition, such as the Chichilticale ruin or artifacts associated with campsites, would have been easier to find than it is today. But the records of the expedition were not well understood at the time, and no concerted searches for Chichilticale were made. Today, the route and artifacts of the expedition are better understood, but scholars may miss ties between the Coronado entrada record and the archeological evidence because so much of the latter has been destroyed since the 1890s. The identification of a campsite of the expedition in Blanco Canyon, Texas, gives us a better idea of the artifactual material that might help identify the Chichilticale ruin.[40]

We believe that an internally consistent picture of the Southwest at the time of the Coronado expedition can be obtained by tying together the early Spanish documents and travelers' documents of the 1500s to early 1900s with the archeological record.

For example, the report of Álvar Núñez Cabeza de Vaca supports the existence of widespread indigenous trade networks in the 1500s, including the "maize route" through Sonora.[41] When Marcos de Niza traveled north through Sonora in 1539, he confirmed Cabeza de Vaca's implication of a trade route to a northern trade center, which Marcos learned was called Cíbola. As far south as central Sonora (a few days north of Corazones), he talked with many people who had traveled to Cíbola to trade, and even with a resident of Cíbola who had moved south to escape a conflict. There he also obtained detailed reports from Sonoran natives of multistory, stone-walled architecture in Cíbola, the practice of putting turquoises in doorways,[42] the Cíbola clothing style, and the way local Sonoran people traveled north to trade and work in Cíbola, acquiring what he called "cow hides" (bison hides), which he saw in abundance in Sonoran villages. Marcos described the "road" to Cíbola and campsites that had been used by previous travelers.

In view of Marcos's direct testimony in 1539 about a well-established prehistoric trade route from central Sonora to Zuni, and of Castañeda's report that Chichilticale had been built by people from the north, the somewhat tortured arguments among archeologists about the existence and extent of such trade and migration are surprising.

Although Coronado expedition chroniclers speak only of the single ruin along their route, Chichilticale, they may have been aware of the large number of ruins in the Chichilticale region. As evidence, Hartmann and Flint point to a little-known document found by Richard and Shirley Cushing Flint during their work in the Archivo General de Indias in Sevilla. It describes the return of Melchior Díaz from the Chichilticale region after his reconnaissance in 1539–40 and the disappointment of the Coronado expedition over Díaz's having found only "ruins" (plural) in that area.[43]

A "Neglected Corner": The Salado Problem and the Coronado Eyewitness-Era Records

An instructive exercise is to go back to the literature of the first archeological observers who saw Arizona ruins prior to their destruction by modern farming and pothunting and to compare the questions they asked with the progress that has been made since.

Sauer and Brand, in an introductory section headed "A Neglected Corner," remarked that "the neglect of this extreme corner of Arizona is partly to be explained by the fact that the peripheries of the Pueblo country have been regarded in general [as] of little significance . . . though what is periphery and what is [center] may not be certain yet."[44] Partly because University of Arizona archeologists focused on Salt-Gila-Hohokam sites and avoided the southern Arizona summer heat by establishing summer field schools in the White Mountains, the multiroom pueblos of southeastern Arizona never attained a significant place in the public imagination or in the archeological literature.

Furthermore, the identification of these pueblos with the Salado phenomenon has also been treated to some extent as a semantic problem deriving from "words we have used in the past."[45] Stephen Lekson, at the Second Salado Conference, concluded a review by asking, "Is Salado really a problem? Or is Salado just a phase we all go through?"[46] Had Arizona history evolved on a slightly different course, however, and had the great pueblo ruins of the Safford Valley been excavated, they might have been considered a grand climax of southern Arizona archeology, and the Hohokam might have been considered only poorer and earlier cousins of the western valleys. The region of the Sulphur Springs Valley to the Chiricahua Mountains on the east and the Gila River near Safford and Duncan on the north was known as Chichilticale, and the ruin known by that name, where Esteban Dorantes, Marcos de Niza, Melchior Díaz, and Francisco Vázquez de Coronado all probably camped, is one of the Salado ruins in that region.

Notes

1. Many sites we include here are classic "Salado" pueblo sites with Gila Polychrome ceramics. We have given some preference to the more general term "Late Pueblo sites," referring to imposing, above-ground buildings built in southeastern Arizona. We intend not to be drawn into larger, long-standing arguments about the origins, definitions, and history of the broader Salado culture. For such discussion see, for example, Richard C. Lange and Stephen Germick, eds., *Proceedings of the Second Salado Conference, Globe, Arizona* (Phoenix: Arizona Archaeological Society, 1992).

2. M. Kyle Woodson, "Migrations in Late Anasazi Prehistory: The Evidence from the Goat Hill Site," *Kiva* 65 (1999): 63–84. See also William K. Hartmann and Richard Flint, "Migrations in Late Anasazi Prehistory: 'Eyewitness' Testimony," *Kiva* 66, no. 3 (2001): 375–85.

3. Julian Hayden, *Excavations, 1940, at University Indian Ruin,* Southwestern Monuments Association Technical Services 5 (Globe, Arizona: Gila Pueblo, 1957); Carr Tuthill, *The Tres Alamos Site on the San Pedro River, Southeastern Arizona,* Amerind Foundation Paper no. 4 (Dragoon, Arizona: Amerind Foundation, 1947).

4. Carl Sauer and Donald Brand, "Pueblo Sites in Southeastern Arizona," *University of California Publications in Geography* 3, no. 7 (Berkeley: University of California Press, 1930): 424.

5. James O. Pattie, *The Personal Narrative of James O. Pattie* [1831] (reprint, Lincoln: University of Nebraska Press, 1984), 62.

6. William K. Hartmann, "Pathfinder for Coronado: Reevaluating the Mysterious Journey of Marcos de Niza," in Flint and Flint, *Coronado Expedition to Tierra Nueva,* 73–101.

7. William A. Duffen and William K. Hartmann, "The 76 Ranch Ruin and the Location of Chichilticale," in Flint and Flint, *Coronado Expedition to Tierra Nueva,* 190–211.

8. Jaramillo, "Narrative."

9. Hartmann and Flint, "Migrations in Late Anasazi Prehistory," 380.

10. Hammond and Rey, *Narratives,* 251.

11. Sauer accepted a very similar reconstruction. Carl O. Sauer, *The Road to Cíbola* (Berkeley: University of California Press, 1932), 36–37.

12. Bolton, *Coronado,* 32, 105–6; Sauer and Brand, "Pueblo Sites," 424–25. BGL interviewed rancher Ted Lee (see Eagle Pass Site), who recalled driving cattle with his father along this route in the early twentieth century.

13. Sauer and Brand, "Pueblo Sites," 424.

14. Sauer and Brand, "Pueblo Sites," 424.

15. Sauer and Brand, "Pueblo Sites," 424.

16. She filed an Arizona State Museum site card in 1976.

17. This agrees with the comment by Sauer and Brand, "Pueblo Sites," 424.

18. Jefferson Reid and Stephanie Whittlesey, *The Archaeology of Ancient Arizona* (Tucson: University of Arizona Press, 1997).

19. Sauer and Brand, "Pueblo Sites," 436.

20. Sauer and Brand, "Pueblo Sites," 436–37.

21. Duffen and Hartmann, "76 Ranch Ruin," 197–200.

22. William Ryder Ridgway, "Billy the Kid Killed First at Bonita," *Journal of Graham County History* 5, no. 1 (1969): not paginated.

23. Informants have indicated to BGL that inmates were used to excavate sites throughout the valley, as far away as the Haby Ranch, and we infer that some excavation by prisoners may have occurred in the Fort Grant area itself.

24. Emil W. Haury, "The Search for Chichilticale," *Arizona Highways* 60, no. 4 (1984): 14–19.

25. Duffen and Hartmann, "76 Ranch Ruin," 197–200.

26. William Ryder Ridgway, "Eureka Springs Ranch," *Eastern Arizona Courier,* March 24, 1976; reprint in *Mt. Graham Profiles,* vol. 2, ed. Glenn Burgess (Safford, Arizona: Graham County Historical Society, 1976), 82–83.

27. Ridgway, "Eureka Springs Ranch," 82–83.

28. William A. Bell, *New Tracks in North America* (London: Chapman and Hall, 1870; reprint, Albuquerque: Horn and Wallace, 1965), 296–97.

29. *Arizona Citizen,* November 15, 1873, cited in Ridgway, "Eureka Springs Ranch," 82–83.

30. Sauer and Brand, "Pueblo Sites," 437.

31. Ridgway, "Eureka Springs Ranch," 82–83.

32. Douglas A. Johnson, "Adobe Brick Architecture and Salado Ceramics at Fourmile Ruin," in Lange and Germick, *Proceedings of the Second Salado Conference,* 131.

33. David A. Breternitz, *An Appraisal of Tree-Ring Dated Pottery in the Southwest* (Tucson: University of Arizona Press, 1966); Steven LeBlanc, "The Mimbres Culture," in *Mimbres Pottery,* eds. J. J. Brody, Catherine J. Scott, and Steven LeBlanc (New York: Hudson Hills Press, 1983), 23–37; and Michelle Hegmon, Margaret C. Nelson, and Susan M. Ruth, "Abandonment and Reorganization in the Mimbres Region of the American Southwest," *American Anthropologist* 100, no. 1 (1998): 148–62.

34. Betty Graham Lee, *The Eagle Pass Site: An Integral Part of the Province of Chichilticale,* Museum of Anthropology Publication no. 5 (Thatcher: Eastern Arizona College, 1996).

35. Lee, *Eagle Pass Site.*

36. Woodson, "Migrations"; Hartmann and Flint, "Migrations in Late Anasazi Prehistory"; Tuthill, *Tres Alamos Site.*

37. Jack P. Mills and Vera M. Mills, *The Kuykendall Site: A Prehistoric Salado Village in Southeastern Arizona,* Special Report for 1967, no. 6 (El Paso, Texas: El Paso Archeological Society, 1969).

38. Jack P. Mills and Vera M. Mills, *The Curtis Site: A Pre-Historic Village in the Safford Valley* (self-published, 1978).

39. Hayden, "University Indian Ruin," plate 22 (sherd distribution), 234.

40. Donald J. Blakeslee, Richard Flint, and Jack T. Hughes, "*Una Barranca Grande:* Recent Archeological Evidence and a Discussion of Its Place in the Coronado Route," in Flint and Flint, *Coronado Expedition to Tierra Nueva,* 370–83.

41. Álvar Núñez Cabeza de Vaca, *Castaways: The Narrative of Álvar Núñez Cabeza de Vaca* [1555], ed. Enrique Pupo-Walker (reprint, Berkeley: University of California Press, 1993).

42. This practice was confirmed at Zuni in the 1880s by Frank Hamilton Cushing, as was reported by Bandelier in 1886. Adolph F. Bandelier, *The Discovery of New Mexico by the Franciscan Monk Friar Marcos de Niza in 1539,* trans. Madeleine Turrell Rodack (Tucson: University of Arizona Press, 1981), 99.

43. Gómez de la Peña, "Testimony Taken at Culiacán," fol. 24r–24v. See discussion in Hartmann and Flint, "Migrations in Late Anasazi Prehistory."

44. Sauer and Brand, "Pueblo Sites," 416.

45. J. Scott Wood, "Toward a New Definition of Salado: Comments and Discussion on the Second Salado Conference," in Lange and Germick, *Proceedings of the Second Salado Conference,* 344.

46. Stephen H. Lekson, "Para-Salado, Perro Salado, or Salado Peril?" in Lange and Germick, *Proceedings of the Second Salado Conference,* 336.

SIX

Spanish Artifacts, a Trail, and a Diary:
An Eighteenth-Century Trail
from Sonora to Zuni, New Mexico

JOHN H. MADSEN

SINCE ABOUT 1990, I have been collecting information on the distribution of Spanish colonial artifacts found throughout southeastern Arizona and southwestern New Mexico (map 6.1). These objects, dating from the sixteenth, seventeenth, eighteenth, and early nineteenth centuries, were lost or discarded on overland journeys and sometimes cached away in remote places only to be forgotten. They have survived the years because they are made of iron, lead, copper, or, occasionally, silver or gold. They have been collected from the landscape by ranchers, farmers, hunters, and hikers who recognized them as curiosities. Today they are mounted on stable walls, displayed proudly in fanciful glass boxes on dining room tables, or packed away in cardboard boxes in forgotten places. Some of these important artifacts have made their way to museums.

Lying on the ground, in the middle of nowhere, these metal artifacts may seem completely out of context to important events in Spanish or Mexican history. In some instances, I believe these artifacts represent the lost or discarded property of Spanish traders and explorers who passed through the wilderness of the northern frontier between Nuevo México and Sonora. They may also mark the locations of long-past journeys, either by Apaches or their allies returning from successful borderland raids in Sonora or Chihuahua or by their pursuers, the presidio troops, who seldom were successful in retrieving the loot.

My recording of Spanish colonial artifacts found in southeastern Arizona and southwestern New Mexico was sparked by an interest in early Spanish exploration. In 1991, the year before the five-hundredth anniversary of Columbus's landfall in the Americas, the Arizona State Museum attempted to

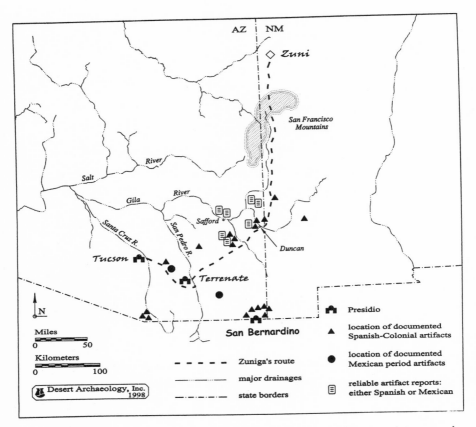

AZ | NM

◇ *Zuni*

San Francisco
Mountains

River

Salt

Gila   *River*

Safford

Santa Cruz R.

San Pedro R.

Tucson

Terrenate

Duncan

↑
N

Miles
0   50

Kilometers
0   100

🦎 Desert Archaeology, Inc.
                    1998

San Bernardino

🏰 Presidio

▲ location of documented
    Spanish-Colonial artifacts

● location of documented
    Mexican period artifacts

🗒 reliable artifact reports:
    either Spanish or Mexican

– – – – Zuniga's route

———— major drainages

–··–··– state borders

Map 6.1.   Distribution of Spanish colonial artifacts in southeastern Arizona and southwestern New Mexico. Copyright Desert Archaeology, Inc., 1998.

gain funding for archeological research designed to identify Coronado's route from Sonora to Zuni. One aspect of the project was to search city, county, and state museums and private collections for sixteenth-century artifacts. I had hoped that artifacts from the expedition were lying unrecognized in museums and that they might have provenances traceable to the trail followed by Coronado himself from Sonora to Cíbola (Zuni) or perhaps even to his own campfires along the trail.

The examination of museum collections for sixteenth-century Spanish artifacts quickly proved fruitless, but unexpectedly, metal artifacts from the eighteenth and early nineteenth centuries, although not abundant, turned out to be common. Most had been acquired through donations from people who had found them lying on the ground in some remote location.

It was now time to examine private collections. I had a hunch that the best source of information would be the ranching communities along the borderlands of Arizona and New Mexico. These people knew the land, and generations of family members had covered most of the ground on horseback. Finding Spanish artifacts with useful provenance information continued to be the goal.

I was fortunate to find a collaborator in this endeavor, Thomas Dees. Tom is a Coronado researcher in his own right and had in his possession Spanish colonial artifacts found by his father in 1928. Having family ties to Duncan, Arizona, Tom knows how and where to seek out private collections. In addition, I made a flyer showing a Spanish colonial horseshoe, and with the help of Tom and other friends, this poster was distributed in a triangle between Tucson, Arizona, and Lordsburg, New Mexico, and as far north as Reserve, New Mexico. The results were rewarding.

Almost immediately I received an invitation from a ranching family to look at their collection of Spanish artifacts, which included spurs, horseshoes, and coins. The flyer also sparked interest in many other people who wanted to share their discoveries of odd metal objects in the desert. Since 1992, fifty-three artifacts have been inventoried, and of these, about twenty-five are Spanish colonial objects. None of the artifacts appears to be from the Coronado expedition. Artifacts can be assigned to one of three categories: horsemen's hardware, including spurs, stirrups, bits and accessories, and horse and mule shoes; armament, including spontoons, swords, and knives; and miscellaneous objects, including coins dating from 1775 to 1821, a copper bowl, and buttons from a horse bit (figs. 6.1, 6.2).

In addition to the survey of artifacts, I am also collecting local legends and lore, reading history magazines and archeological manuscripts, and checking flea markets and antique stores.

There are a surprising number of unwritten accounts about recovered Spanish armor. These stories include a report by members of a U.S. Forest Service crew that they saw a full set of Spanish armor lying in a cave as they flew in a helicopter over the Galiuro Mountains of Arizona. They had been hurrying to put out a fire and could not retrace their flight path.

A land surveyor claims to have found a full set of Spanish armor in a cave in the Blue Ridge country on the Arizona–New Mexico state line. A hunter in the same region claims to have found two small bronze canons. He returned to the area with equipment to retrieve the guns, but the Blue River had flooded and the site could not be relocated.

A brochure for a land sale near Dragoon, Arizona, includes a picture of a conquistador's helmet and claims that two of Coronado's men were found buried nearby.

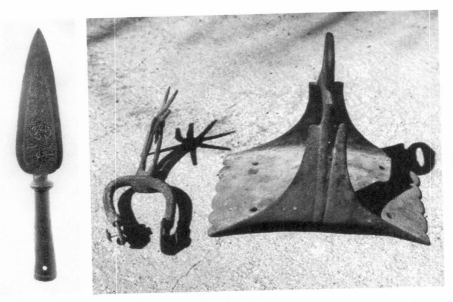

Figure 6.1. Spanish colonial artifacts. From left: spontoon, spur, stirrup.
Courtesy of Thomas Dees. Photos by John Madsen.

Figure 6.2. Spanish colonial artifacts. The "Joe Place" sword (left) and "Coronado's
cereal bowl," found near Duncan, Arizona, in 1914 and 1928, respectively. Courtesy
of the Arizona State Museum, University of Arizona. Photos by Ken Matesich.

Other reports include that of a conquistador's breastplate lodged in the bark of an old cottonwood tree near Bisbee, Arizona. Another Spanish breastplate was supposedly found on Ash Peak near Duncan, Arizona. The artifact was stored in the basement of a house in Duncan that was devastated by the Gila River floods of 1983. Anyone willing to excavate the river sediments from the entire basement is welcome to photograph the armor.

Collecting this type of material regardless of origin or factuality is important, because not recording it could easily lead to a missed opportunity.

Magazines that cater to stories of the West, particularly those published before 1950, provide endless accounts of recovered Spanish artifacts. Some articles that pertain to the region under study are worthy of further investigation. Other magazines cater to the sale and auction of Spanish colonial artifacts, but it is difficult to trace the origins of the materials. A review of archeological manuscripts from the region has provided information on a bronze medallion bearing the picture of Pope Paul V, who was pope from 1605 to 1621, a copper spoon, and a Spanish mule shoe recovered from a cave.

Current Trail Study

What does one do with this type of information in light of the conclusion that none of the artifacts dates to the period of the first Spanish *entrada?* When plotted on a map (map 6.1), some of the artifacts cluster around eighteenth-century presidios. For instance, numerous items have been found in Arizona just opposite San Bernardino in Sonora.

The Spanish artifacts lost, discarded, or cached far from presidios are of particular interest to my trail study. Some of these artifacts were found in a corridor described in eighteenth-century letters as a potential road for commerce between Santa Fe and Sonora. The trail led from Zuni southward to the Gila River by way of the San Francisco River. Could this be the wilderness route followed by Coronado?

As early as 1747 there were reports of a pass through the San Francisco Mountains linking the Gila River region with the eastern margins of the Colorado Plateau. In 1788 a detachment from the Sonoran presidio of Santa Cruz entered the wilderness from the south and confirmed the existence of the pass. However, exhaustion overtook the party, and they were unable to reach Zuni. They returned to Sonora after making a map of the region between the Gila River and the San Francisco Mountains.

In 1795 an expedition under the command of Captain don José de Zúñiga made a successful trip from Sonora to Zuni. The expedition began in Tucson on

April 9, reached Zuni on May 1, and was back in Tucson on May 29. Zúñiga's force included 8 Apache scouts, 151 horsemen, and a "main body" of unknown size. The Zúñiga expedition is an obscure event in Arizona and New Mexico history, but it was of major importance to merchants in New Mexico and Sonora and to religious leaders who were eager for a short route to the Pueblo region and to Santa Fe. Zúñiga's journal is the basis of my current and future research.[1]

Zúñiga's journal contains a description of the "beaten path" he followed and names of landmarks he passed along the way. Many of the landmarks in the desert region were known to Zúñiga because they were identified on a variety of regional maps of the time. But as Zúñiga crossed the Gila River and entered the watershed of the San Francisco River, he carried the only known map of the region, a map made during the 1788 reconnaissance previously mentioned and now lost. Except for the San Francisco River, San Francisco Mountains, and the Mogollon Mountains, no other landmarks in this drainage mentioned in his journal have recognizable names today. It is not until he reaches the place he calls the "Beautiful Salinas," the modern Zuni Salt Lake, that we can trace his route with confidence to the mission at Zuni.

I am compelled to squeeze the rivers and landmarks along a portion of Zúñiga's eighteenth-century trail into the sixteenth-century setting described in the chronicles of the Coronado expedition. But for now, the dust of the Zúñiga expedition is still settling on this trail. I believe I have an opportunity for tangible results by pursuing an archeological study of the trail used by Captain Zúñiga.

Portions of the trail are clearly visible between Zuni Salt Lake and Zuni Pueblo, because the expedition followed the salt trail. Conducting an archeological survey to locate the trail south of the Salt Lake will present many challenges, because the character of the country changes dramatically. The open mesa, scrub, and grasslands of the Zuni region give way to dense pine forest in the San Francisco Mountains. As one descends into the valley of the San Francisco River, the terrain alternates between gorges and narrow, cultivated valleys until it meets the rolling country of the Gila River.

In the near future I plan to look for trail segments in the vicinity of Spanish artifacts found near the Gila River at Duncan.[2] Following this survey I will turn my attention to finding the pass through the San Francisco Mountains and several of the springs mentioned by Zúñiga.

Notes

1. George P. Hammond, "The Zúñiga Journal, Tucson to Santa Fe: The Opening of a Spanish Trade Route, 1788–1795," *New Mexico Historical Review* 4 (January 1931): 40–65.

2. A spontoon blade found in Carlisle Canyon, Grant County, New Mexico, has been dated to the last quarter of the eighteenth century by Sidney B. Brinckerhoff and Pierce A. Chamberlain, *Spanish Military Weapons in Colonial America, 1700–1821* (Harrisburg, Pennsylvania: Stackpole, 1972), 106–7, plate 207. See also Marc Simmons and Frank Turley, *Southwest Colonial Ironworks: The Spanish Blacksmithing Tradition from Texas to California* (Santa Fe: Museum of New Mexico Press, 1980), plate 6. Carlisle Canyon is in proximity to, if not directly on, the route followed by Zúñiga. The "Joe Place Sword" was found nearby, on the Gila River between Duncan and Sheldon. In addition to these artifacts, a copper bowl was found in a rock crevice with twenty-four buttons and a rotting velvet bolero with silver braids. In an adjacent rock shelter is a charcoal drawing of a person perched on a horse and sitting on what appears to be a high-back saddle. This set of finds overlooks a pass that links San Simon Creek to the Gila River at Duncan, along the route most likely taken by Zúñiga in 1795.

SEVEN

Jars Full of Shiny Metal:
Analyzing Barrionuevo's Visit to Yuque Yunque

ANN F. RAMENOFSKY AND C. DAVID VAUGHAN

THE YEAR 1998 MARKED the four-hundredth anniversary of Spanish settlement in New Mexico. Newspaper articles, the publication of the don Juan de Oñate stamp, and the construction of the Oñate statue at the newly established Oñate center north of San Juan Pueblo suggested that 1998 would be marked by joyous celebration. Instead, the Cuarto Centenario triggered tricultural conflict and demonstrated that New Mexicans were deeply divided over this anniversary. They questioned whether the year was a time for celebration or mourning. The Oñate statue, symbol of Spanish settlement, stood at the center of the conflict. It took two years of emotional and acrid debate to resolve the controversy and to determine where to display the sculpture. The front-page article of the *Albuquerque Tribune* for March 8, 2000, encapsulated the nature of the resolution: "Oñate gets his day; City Council approves statue of controversial conquistador but moves it to the Albuquerque Museum after an ugly, emotional meeting."

Although a single event, the controversy over don Juan de Oñate as a historical symbol epitomizes both the rewards and difficulties of historical and archeological research into the early period of Spanish colonization in New Mexico. On the positive side, New Mexicans care deeply about their history, even though they are alternately proud of and troubled by it. Because of this inherent interest, historians and archeologists could make genuine and substantial contributions to unraveling the myths of history and perhaps healing old wounds. On the other hand, the Oñate controversy underscores the quagmire into which the historical researcher can fall. This quagmire is a product of several factors: historical and archeological tradition and the nature of historical and archeological records that attend the period of initial colonization.

Spanish borderlands history begins with the vision of Herbert Bolton.[1] In focusing on the borderlands, Bolton made Spaniards into mythical figures and downgraded native populations and interactions between Spaniards and indigenous peoples. Conquistadores became knights, and Franciscan missionaries were "explorers and diplomatic agents" who made the frontier safe for colonists.[2] As suggested by the writings of more recent borderlands historians,[3] this perspective is giving way to a more even treatment of the different cultures of contact. In addition, relative to the eastern Spanish borderlands, New Mexico is poor in documentary descriptions, especially for the sixteenth and seventeenth centuries. There are few types of documents, and those that do exist are not rich in detail. The relative scarcity of written material makes it difficult to cross-check and analyze observations. Although both ecclesiastical and civil documents from this period survive,[4] what we do not have is as significant as what we do have. There are no mission birth and death records, no wills, no land grant documents, and only a few mining claims. Piecing together even the simplest description, such as the number of encomenderos,[5] is challenging.

Although historical archeology could, at least, fill some of the gaps resulting from an impoverished historical record, archeological contributions to historical understanding have been limited in scope. There are several reasons for this situation.

First, prehistory has always been the major research focus in Southwestern archeology, having been the subject of sustained investigations for more than one hundred years.[6] Historical archeological investigations, by contrast, have been more sporadic, with only two periods of rather intense research. The earlier effort occurred during the initial decades of the twentieth century.[7] With the exception of Frederick Hodge's work at Hawikuh,[8] these field projects focused on mission complexes at a time when archeologists were building prehistoric chronologies.[9] For this reason, the historic period assemblages were either cursorily analyzed or were simply footnotes to the prehistory. The more recent period of historical archeology began in the 1980s and is fueled by new and fundamentally different questions.[10]

The second reason for limited contributions by historical archeologists is an accident of history. In the eastern Spanish borderlands, there are extensive archival descriptions but limited cultural survival. In the southwestern borderlands, the archival record is far less extensive, but cultural survival has been significant. In other words, what is missing from documents can be investigated in living traditions. For instance, both twenty-first-century and sixteenth-century pueblos have or had village-level political structures. Moreover, there appears to have been continuity in the geographic locations of linguistic groups in New Mexico. Given these links between past and present, it is easy to assume stasis throughout the historic period. Yet continuity in village location, linguistics, and politics does not mean that organization is static. The success of the Pueblo Revolt demonstrates unquestionably that at least one period of multivillage polity formation existed. To force the Spaniards out of the colony required coordinated and sustained effort.[11]

The sporadic archeological examination of the historical archeological record, coupled with the scanty archival record, has resulted in a particular approach to historical archeology. Rather than independently mining and evaluating the historical archeological record, archeology has been fitted between the lines of history and ethnography. The end result is that archeology and history tell the same story. As revealed by the Oñate controversy, that story may be far from accurate.

In this chapter on the shiny metal at Yuque Yunque we make an effort to depart from the traditional practice that makes historical archeology the stepchild of history and prehistoric archeology. The problem that informs this investigation of the Coronado entrada is a geographic and geological one that follows from the expedition's exploration of the northern Rio Grande. Over the years, numerous questions have been raised regarding the Coronado route.[12] The focus of this chapter is a short description of one part of the journey in northern New Mexico. In it we investigate questions regarding the route of travel and the accuracy of Spanish observations regarding shiny metal. Did members of the Coronado party visit Yuque Yunque, located in San Juan Pueblo at the confluence of the Rio Chama and the Rio Grande? If the party was not at Yuque Yunque, then where were they? Although we do not completely resolve the question, history, archeology, geology, and geography are brought to bear on it. Each source of information is evaluated and weighed against other information so that in the end, our understanding is, at the least, enriched. This enrichment may, in the final analysis, shed light on the complexities of the first sustained encounters between Spaniards and Pueblo peoples.

Textual Description

The description of the shiny metal, written by Pedro de Castañeda, appears in Book 1, chapter 22, of his *Relación*. The visit to Yuque Yunque occurred in 1541 after the expedition had just returned to Tiguex from its trip out to the Great Plains.

According to Castañeda, as soon as don Tristán de Arellano arrived in Tiguex in the middle of July 1542 (actually 1541), he asked that provisions for the approaching winter be gathered. He dispatched Captain Francisco Barrionuevo with some people upstream along the river toward the north. On it he found two provinces, one of seven pueblos called Jemes and the other called Yuque Yunque.

> The [people of the] towns of Jemes came out in peace and provided food supplies. While the [Spanish] camp was being set up, those of Yuque Yunque abandoned the two very beautiful towns, between which was the river, and went to the mountain chain where they had four very strong towns in rugged land. It was not possible to go to them on horseback.
>
> In these two towns there were many provisions and very beautiful pottery, glazed, intricately worked, and in many shapes. Also, many jars were found full of choice shiny metal, with which [the Indians] glaze their pottery. This was an indication that in that land there were sources of silver, if they had been looked for.[13]

There are both strengths and weaknesses to this passage. On the one hand, Castañeda states the direction of travel and names the provinces visited. These details lend a degree of authenticity to the account. On the other hand, the description is vague, imprecise, and superficial. These shortcomings, in addition to the geographical contradictions, raise questions about the route the party traveled and whether it actually visited Yuque Yunque.

The Castañeda account was not written at the time of the expedition. Although Castañeda clearly kept notes during the journey, he wrote the description at least twenty years after the return to Mexico City. Unfortunately, the 1560 manuscript was lost, but a copy was made in the 1590s. The copy has survived. Additional evidence suggests that the copy differs in some details from the 1560 manuscript. Whether or not these differences include the description of Yuque Yunque is unknown.[14]

If Castañeda remembered the provincial names correctly, then the three locations are three nodes of a geographical triangle. There is substantial historical agreement that Tiguex was in the vicinity of the confluence of the Jemez River and the Rio Grande, somewhere near Santiago Pueblo (LA 326) and the recently excavated Coronado campsite.[15] The Jemez province lies northwest of Tiguex in the valleys and mesas of the Jemez Plateau. Yuque Yunque, the third node of the triangle, was located in the lower Río Chama valley at the confluence of the Río Chama and the Rio Grande (map 7.1).

Given these locations, it would have been possible, as stated in the document, to travel north from Tiguex and reach the pueblo of Yuque Yunque. If the description of the direction of travel is correct, then Barrionuevo's party did not visit Jemez. Instead, it may have stopped by the Keres province, situated directly north of Tiguex. Like the Jemez province, the Keres province was composed of seven pueblos.[16] If the stop between Tiguex and Yuque Yunque was in one or more of the Keres pueblos, then Castañeda switched the names of the provinces.[17]

On the other hand, if the Barrionuevo party visited the Jemez province, then it traveled northwest, not north. To travel from Jemez to Yuque Yunque on the lower Río Chama would have necessitated traversing northeast through the Jemez Mountains, perhaps even through the Valle Grande, and emerging at the southern or southeastern edge of the lower Río Chama.

The analysis of the direction of travel relative to pueblo or provincial locations points to contradictions in the documents. Although it is possible that Barrionuevo visited all three provinces, the route was not directly north. Moreover, the travel from Jemez to Yuque Yunque would have included some of the most spectacular scenery in northern New Mexico. To have excluded a description of this area would have been peculiar. A few more geographic or environmental details, or a lengthier discussion of the time involved in the travel, would have been a great benefit to later scholars. Unfortunately, the nature of this part of the documentary description does not permit resolution of places visited or direction of travel.

Evidence Supporting the Identification of Yuque Yunque

Substantial scholarly agreement exists that the Barrionuevo party visited Yuque Yunque.[18] This agreement is due to the relative concordance between certain parts of Castañeda's description and the geology of the lower Río Chama, the geography of Yuque Yunque, and the location of other lower Río Chama pueblos. In what follows, we consider each of the traditional sources of supporting evidence and add the new information of archeological dating and glaze-paint ceramics that support the identification of Yuque Yunque.

Geography and Geology: Yuque Yunque and the Lower Chama Pueblos

Yuque Yunque was an important place in the early Spanish colonial history of New Mexico. Not only was it likely visited by the Barrionuevo party in 1541, but it was also the location of the first permanent Spanish settlement. In 1598, don Juan de Oñate established the earliest recorded Spanish colony there, which survived until 1604.

The lower Chama region is a roughly triangular area within the Española Basin, one of the many fault troughs along the Rio Grande.[19] The faulting created a series of uplifts including the Sangre de Cristo Mountains. Tectonic action was followed by extensive infilling throughout much of the Pleistocene. Incising by streams has further modified the landscape, creating a series of relatively narrow floodplains and high terraces adjacent to modern streams. The Chama River is the major drainage, joining the Rio Grande at San Juan Pueblo at the western margin of the valley. Small tributaries including the Rio del Oso, Ojo Caliente, and El Rito feed into the Chama. Base elevation in the region ranges between 1,525 and 1,830 meters. Pueblos are located primarily on the dissected terraces overlooking drainages.

In the Coronado chronicles, Castañeda described Yuque Yunque in two ways: both as the capital of a province consisting of six pueblos and in terms of its physical location and composition. He reported that it straddled a river and was composed of two villages. Again, this physical description of Yuque Yunque corresponds to what we know about the region and the pueblo.

Florence Hawley Ellis excavated at Yuque Yunque in the late 1950s and early 1960s.[20] She stated that it was part of San Juan Pueblo. Essentially, San Juan and Yuque Yunque were two parts of the same native settlement. San Juan Pueblo lay on the east side of the Rio Grande, and Yuque Yunque, on the west.

While excavating at Yuque Yunque, Ellis collected considerable Spanish colonial material. Although the bulk of it derived from the Oñate colony, Ellis described one Spanish helmet that dated morphologically to the late fifteenth or early sixteenth century. The helmet could have been from the Barrionuevo exploration, but Ellis believed it was an heirloom piece of the military dress that belonged to one of the Oñate colonists.[21]

Further support for the visit to Yuque Yunque is provided by Castañeda's mention of four Tewa pueblos in the hills beyond Yuque Yunque. Although Castañeda named none of these pueblos, Albert Schroeder suggested several possibilities—Psere, Te'ewi, Ku, and Tsama—based on descriptions from the Castaño de Sosa journal of 1591 and Schroeder's extensive archeological and geographical knowledge of the region (table 7.1).[22] Although on first glance the extrapolation from 1591 to 1541 seems logical, the identification of villages is less secure than one would like. No Tewa village names appear in the Castaño de Sosa journal. Schroeder inferred Castaño's route of travel from geography and from the descriptions of particular villages. The 1591 village identifications were then retrofitted back to 1541. This retrofitting not only collapses time but raises questions about the accuracy of the identifications.

By considering the geographic locations and available archeologically determined dates of lower Chama pueblos, however, we can begin to suggest which pueblos were possible retreats for the fleeing Yuque Yunque people. In late prehistory, or Fred Wendorf's Classic period,[23] seventeen pueblos were aggregated in the lower Chama, Ojo Caliente, and Rio del Oso drainages (map 7.1).[24]

Table 7.1
Possible Sixteenth- and Seventeenth-Century Lower Chama Pueblos

Source	Number of Villages	Pueblos with Tree-Ring Dates	Pueblos with Luminescence Dates
Castañeda 1541	Yunque + 4 unnamed 　pueblos in hills		
Schroeder and 　Matson 1965	Yunque Psere Te'ewi Ku Tsama		
Schroeder 1979	Sepawé		
Wendorf 1953		Te'ewi	
Robinson and 　Warren 1971		Hupobi	
Ramenofsky 2000			Tsama Nuté Ponsipa-Akeri

Ground room estimates for each of these pueblos are upwards of one thousand. Currently, Nuté is the only ruined pueblo surviving on the floodplain; all others are located on dissected terraces overlooking streams. Some of the sites, such as Ku, Te'ewi, Hupobi, Tsama, and Tsiping, are extremely difficult to reach. The relative inaccessibility of these villages indirectly supports Castañeda's mention of four of the province's pueblos in the mountains.

We can limit the number of potential retreats by adding calendrical dates to the list of pueblos. Doing so shrinks the number of possible pueblo retreats from sixteen (that is, excluding Nuté) to five (table 7.1). The sizes of the lower Chama pueblos make it difficult to construct accurate histories of occupation without extensive excavation, and none of the lower Chama pueblos has been subjected to this kind of work. Nonetheless, three tree-ring dates from two pueblos suggest occupation in the sixteenth century. At Te'ewi, Wendorf collected a datable noncutting tree-ring sample from each of two rooms.[25] Both dates are minimal dates that fall in the second decade of the sixteenth century (table 7.2). From Hupobi in the Ojo Caliente drainage comes a single, unprovenienced, near-cutting date of 1502.[26]

More recently, one of us (Ramenofsky) has undertaken topographic mapping, systematic surface collecting of flaked stone and ceramics, analysis of ceramics, and luminescence dating of some surface ceramics at four lower Chama pueblos. Some of the luminescence dates are relevant to this discussion.

Luminescence dates are direct dates of ceramics that tell us when a vessel was last heated to 450° C.[27] This temperature typically corresponds to the time when the vessel was manufactured. So far, there are four reliable luminescence dates from the sixteenth and seventeenth centuries—two dates from Biscuit B sherds and two from Sankawi Black-on-cream sherds (table 7.2). The error terms of the two Biscuit B dates and one of the Sankawi dates overlap with each other and with a possible 1541 visit to Yuque Yunque. The second luminescence date from a Sankawi Black-on-cream sherd suggests that some ancestral Tewas were still living at Tsama at the time of the Pueblo Revolt. Corroboration of post-1540 native use of Tsama is suggested by Ellis's limited excavation of the pueblo. From one kiva, metal and a sheep horn core were recovered.[28]

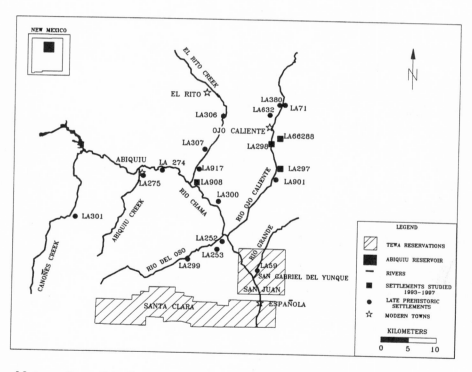

Map 7.1. Lower Río Chama villages. LA 59, Yuque Yunque; LA 71, Howire; LA 252, Ku; LA 253, Te'ewi; LA 274, Poshu; LA 297, Ponsipa-Alkeri; LA 275, Abiquiu; LA 298, Nuté; LA 299, Psere; LA 300, Leaf Water; LA 301, Tsiping; La 306, Sepawé; LA 307, Cerro Colorado: LA 380, Hupobi; LA 632, Posi; LA 908, Tsama; LA 66288, Hilltop.

Table 7.2

Tree-Ring and Luminescence Dates for Lower Chama Pueblos
Occupied in the Sixteenth and Seventeenth Centuries

Pueblo	Tree-Ring Dates		Luminescence Dates		
	Location	Date	Location	Ceramic Type	Date
Te'ewi	Room 14	1412p–1529+vv			
	Room 21	1421np–1529 +vv			
Hupobi	No provenience	1445p–1502v			
Ponsipa-Akeri			Surface transect	Biscuit B	I531 ± 39
Tsama			Surface transect	Biscuit B	578 ± 51
			Surface transect	Sankawi Black-on-cream	552 ± 35
Nuté			Surface transect	Sankawi Black-on-cream	680 ± 27

Note: *vv* refers to a noncutting date, unknown number of missing rings; *v* refers to a near cutting date, within two or three years of cutting date.

Suffice it to say that current archeological knowledge of lower Chama villages indicates that any of five pueblos might have served as refuges for people fleeing Yuque Yunque upon the arrival of Barrionuevo's party: Te'ewi, Tsama, Hupobi, Nuté, and Ponsipa. Four of those pueblos are on dissected terraces and would have required some effort to reach.

Glaze-Paint Ceramics

The last piece of historical and archeological evidence suggesting a visit to Yuque Yunque by members of the Coronado *entrada* is the reference to glaze-paint ceramics. In his *Relación,* Castañeda provides two similar descriptions of these ceramics: one from the visit to Yuque Yunque, quoted earlier, and one from the Tiguex province.[29] The glaze-paint ceramics seen in the Tiguex province had elaborate designs and came in a variety of shapes. At Yuque Yunque, too, the beautifully glaze-painted ceramics occurred in many shapes. Castañeda's references to the shape and beauty of these ceramics suggest that he was impressed by their quality.

What does archeological knowledge of glaze-paint ceramics suggest about the pueblo visited by Barrionuevo? Do glaze-paint ceramics occur at Yuque Yunque? If so, then are they of the same age—the mid-sixteenth century—as the Coronado expedition?

Archeological interest and knowledge of glaze-paint ceramics in the Rio Grande began with Alfred Kidder's chronological work at Pecos and continued with Harry Mera's surface collections in the Rio Grande area.[30] The beauty, diversity, and abundance of the glaze-paint ceramics have made them index fossils for establishing chronological divisions of the late prehistoric and historic periods in the Rio Grande region. Although numerous schemes and numerous problems are involved in clearly associating the sequence with calendrical dates,[31] archeologists generally agree that glaze-paint manufacture in the region began in the early fourteenth century and continued, with considerable modification, through the seventeenth century. Simply, glaze-paint ceramics came into use before Spanish contact and continued to be manufactured by Pueblo people through the time of the Pueblo Revolt.

Glaze-paint vessels occur throughout the region. In central and northern New Mexico, they appear as far east as Pecos and as far west as the Jemez Mountains. On the Pajarito Plateau, the ceramics co-occur with matte-paint, black-on-white wares.[32] The only region where glaze-paint wares are rare to non-existent is the lower Chama, which includes Yuque Yunque (map 7.2). In the lower Chama, matte-painted wares dominate the decorated assemblages. In his surface ceramic assemblages from the lower Chama, Mera only rarely noted glaze-painted sherds.[33] Wendorf's small excavation at Te'ewi produced similar results. Among the decorated ceramics, Wendorf found only 72 glaze sherds, or 2 percent of the total. Our systematic surface collections in the lower Chama villages are similar. Of the 8,500 potsherds Ramenofsky collected from the surfaces of lower Chama pueblos, only 29 were glaze-painted (less than 1 percent). The rarity of glaze-paint wares and the abundance of matte-painted wares in the lower Chama warrants closer investigation.

The proportions of glaze-paint wares just described are stunningly different from those of two other ceramic collections from the lower Río Chama. Mera made a surface collection at San Juan Pueblo in the 1930s,[34] and Ellis's excavation at Yuque Yunque produced the second sample of glazes.

Mera's summary of the Yuque Yunque decorated ceramics shows them to have been dominated by matte-painted black-on-white wares, but he collected sixteenth- and seventeenth-century glaze-paint types as well.[35] Ellis's excavated ceramics from Yuque Yunque form a far more extensive collection than Mera's. It includes 1,350 glaze-paint sherds, and all temporal types of the glaze-paint sequence are present. In addition, glaze-paint decoration occurs on non-native vessels known as colonowares: low-fired, hand-built native ceramics constructed in European styles.[36] These forms include soup plates, straight-sided bowls, cups, and even candlestick holders.

The abundance of glazes in Ellis's collection from Yuque Yunque differs from their proportions in both Mera's collection from the same pueblo and collections made at other pueblos in the lower Chama. The differences may be a function of where each archeologist worked. On the other hand, they may hold

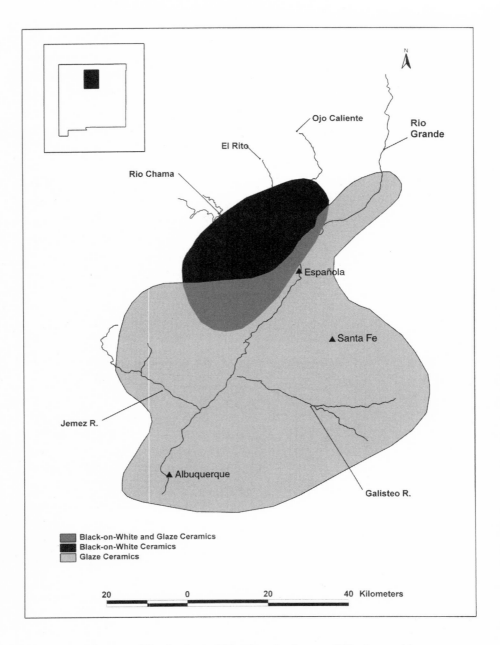

Map 7.2 Distribution of Rio Grande glazes and Black-on-white matte-paint ceramics in northern New Mexico.

significance for two parts of the Castañeda identification. The relative abundance of glaze-painted ceramics at Yuque Yunque suggests that Spaniards could have seen "shiny metal" there—that is, the ore for the glaze paints, as we discuss shortly—indirectly supporting Castañeda's identification. Second, the patterned difference between the frequency of glaze-painting at Yuque Yunque and at other lower Chama pueblos could reflect the status of Yuque Yunque as the provincial "capital." If this is the case, then the origin of that status predates the presence of any Spaniard by at least two hundred years.

In summary, sleuthing into the physiography, geography, and some of the archeology of Yuque Yunque and the lower Chama region offers independent and indirect support for a Coronado-period visit to the area. The geographic location of Yuque Yunque, the minimal description of the surrounding region, and the presence of glaze-paint ceramics tend to confirm its identification. Were all such historiographic research so straightforward, the field would offer little challenge. In the case of Yuque Yunque, however, the positive identifications are balanced by ambiguous references in the descriptions. We consider these next.

Ambiguous Evidence Regarding the Identification of Yuque Yunque

The references to mineralogy, including the jars full of shiny metal and the silver deposits in the region, are the parts of Castañeda's Yuque Yunque description that are the least clear and, therefore, the least reliable. The descriptions are vague, and the association of shiny metal with nearby silver ores suggests that the Barrionuevo visit was to a pueblo or pueblos other than Yuque Yunque.

The references to shiny metal and sources of silver in the region are logically and empirically connected. As documented by archeologists and geologists, the source of the metallic sheen on Rio Grande glaze-paint ceramics is a lead flux that is added to an alumina-silicate base.[37] The most easily smelted form of lead is galena, which is a lead sulfide (PbS). Geological deposits that contain lead also frequently contain silver.[38] Galena, then, is the most obvious interpretation of the "shiny metal" used in manufacturing glaze paints at Yuque Yunque. Schroeder's interpretation of Castañeda's description is just this: the jars full of shiny metal were filled with galena.[39] If we assume that the Spaniards traveling with Coronado understood mineral associations, then the presence of galena could have signaled to them the presence of the more precious metal silver, thus explaining the reference to silver ores in the region.

Before making this inference, however, we must break the descriptions down. Are there other references to glaze painting in the Castañeda manuscript? Are the references consistent? Did the Spaniards with the Coronado expedition have mineralogical knowledge? In other words, can we trust their references to metallic minerals? Finally, does the geology of the lower Chama support the reference to silver deposits in the region? If so, where are these deposits? If there are none, then where are the closest mineral deposits that could have been exploited for glaze paints and silver metal?

Glaze-Paint Metal References

There are three references to glazing material in Castañeda's descriptions. Although none of them specifically mentions lead, one of the references is to a mineral that is geologically associated with lead.

The reference to metal at Yuque Yunque is the least specific. All we know is that the party saw something they perceived as shiny metal. It could have been galena, but many other sulfide minerals fit this description, including sphalerite, pyrite, pyrrhotite, and chalcopyrite. Moreover, the possibility that they saw non-metallic minerals is even greater. Micaceous minerals including chlorite, lepidolite, muscovite, and biotite are shiny, glassy, or pearly and are abundant in the lower Chama region. Adolph Bandelier believed that the shiny metal from Yuque Yunque was mica.[40] These minerals were used to make clay slips that coated many of the ceramics in the region.

When describing the Rio Grande pueblos generally, Castañeda mentioned the presence of "silver ores" that native artisans employed in making glazes. This reference is nearly as vague as that for Yuque Yunque. Although the silvery color could implicate lead (and silver by association), the vagueness also suggests many other metallic minerals.

The most specific reference to glazing material appears in Castañeda's description of the Tiguex province. In it, he mentions the use of antimony to glaze ceramics and as an ingredient in face paint.[41] Antimony (Sb) is a tin-white, metallic semimetal that naturally co-occurs with lead and silver. Because of its natural associations, it is possible that some antimony could be present in a lead ore. Like lead and silver, antimony is relatively soft and could be ground into a powder and used in face painting. Ruth Bunzel, for instance, mentions that the Zunis were using a quartz sphalerite and galena powder to paint their faces before wearing masks.[42]

Of the three references, only that from Tiguex is sufficiently detailed to suggest that Spaniards actually saw a mineral that was related to the metallic mineral employed to make the glaze paints. The other two descriptions might implicate lead, but they could also implicate many other shiny metallic or non-metallic minerals.

Spanish Knowledge of Minerals and Mining

From the beginning to the end of the sixteenth century, the Spanish quest for mineral wealth changed from looting to mining and the practice of metallurgy. This development is important for a preliminary understanding of the Spanish search for mineral wealth in sixteenth-century New Mexico.

Historians generally seem to agree that early Spanish explorers and colonizers were unsophisticated about metals. In the first half of the sixteenth century, the mining experts were Mexican Indians, perhaps Tarascans. They were the ones who identified mines and smelted ores for the Spaniards. By the 1530s, letters were being conveyed to the Crown requesting that mining and metallurgical experts be sent to New Spain.[43] This startling lack of broad mineralogical knowledge is made real in a passage by Cieza de León, who interviewed participants in the Pizarro conquest of Peru:

> [The Spaniards] took . . . many fine emeralds, which at that time were worth a great treasure any place, but because those who were there had seen few, they were unfamiliar with them. Most of [the emeralds] were lost because of a remark by a friar there named Fray Reginaldo, who said that the emerald was harder than steel and could not be broken; thus believing that they were striking glass, they shattered with hammers most of the stones that they took."[44]

This situation had changed by the mid-sixteenth century. In 1556, Agricola (Georg Bauer) published the first modern mining text, and it quickly became the standard mining reference in Europe.[45] The volume includes descriptions of mining methods, fire assaying and smelting, cupellation, smelting facilities, and ore recognition. Spanish miners and entrepreneurs capitalized on this knowledge. Spain was one of a few expanding European powers in the sixteenth century to thoroughly and exhaustively organize mining activities in a colonized territory. Mexico and South America had rich deposits of gold and silver, and even the most powerful native populations posed no long-term threat to the invaders.[46] The renowned patio process, for instance, extracted low-grade silver by using mercury as the reagent to create a silver-lead amalgam. Although Bartolomé de Medina, a Spanish immigrant to New Spain, is often credited with the invention of the specific process used there,[47] the development of the patio process probably had its roots in Birringucci's *Pirotechnia,* published in the 1540s. Moreover, by the mid-sixteenth century, central European miners had arrived in New Spain.[48] By 1550, then, metallurgical expertise in New Spain was more sophisticated and extensive than it had been even a decade earlier.

What we are suggesting is that during the first half of the sixteenth century, Spaniards were largely looting and melting down Indian gold and silver objects. This pattern began to change in the 1540s as the silver lodes in central Mexico were discovered and worked.[49] The active exploration and extraction of metal continued and increased in the second half of the sixteenth century with the mining and smelting of the rich silver ores of Potosí and the implementation of the patio process.[50]

This larger metallurgical trend in sixteenth-century New Spain is reflected by the contrast between the metallurgical knowledge of members of the Coronado expedition and that of members of the later Oñate expedition. In the Coronado expedition documents, there are few references to either gold or silver. Although it is clear that one of the goals of the expedition was the discovery of silver and gold, the party was not prepared to find or exploit ore bodies. Unlike all later expeditions into New Mexico, no Spaniard listed on the Coronado muster roll appears to have been knowledgeable about ores or smelting. Perhaps the Mexican Indian allies fulfilled this role. Additionally, there is no evidence that the expedition carried any mining or assaying equipment. Instead, pieces of gold and silver constituted Coronado's metallurgical "equipment." Our impression is that the search for minerals or finished products was a kind of show and tell. The conquistador held up the pieces of metal and asked Pueblo people whether they had anything similar.

The Oñate colony of 1598, on the other hand, was entirely different. Juan de Oñate himself was a mining engineer. In 1625 he organized the publication of the mining laws of Spain. After leaving New Mexico, he returned to Spain and, in 1624, became the chief inspector of Spanish mines.[51] In the New Mexico venture, he carried equipment for blacksmithing, mining, and smelting. Jars of mercury were included with the smelting equipment.[52] In addition, at both Yuque Yunque and San Marcos pueblos, the Spaniards fire-smelted and/or tested ore bodies.[53] Oñate intended to find, mine, and extract silver.

Although the members of the Coronado expedition hoped to find gold and silver, we suggest that they lacked the knowledge and equipment to make this goal a reality. Sixty years later, when Oñate established his short-lived colony at Yuque Yunque, this was not the case. If we are correct in this assessment, then the general lack of written documentation regarding Spanish metallurgical knowledge in 1540 has implications for Castañeda's reference to shiny metal and ore deposits at Yuque Yunque. There is reason to question what the Spaniards saw, whether they knew what they saw, and whether they were sufficiently informed to connect the possible identification of lead with silver ore deposits.

Geography of Mineral Deposits

The last aspect of this analysis considers whether or not silver-lead ores exist in the lower Chama region. Is the region rich in these minerals? If not, where are the closest such deposits, and what are the implications of these locations for the references to shiny metal and silver deposits at Yuque Yunque?

Although lead, silver, and gold deposits are known from regions to the north and south, the lower Chama area is poor in these minerals. Historically, there is only one known reference to a metallic ore in the area. In the 1910 USGS survey of New Mexico, Waldemar Lingren described a series of mine shafts near Abiquiu that, according to earlier reports, contained copper sulfide, iron, and malachite.[54] These mines supposedly had been worked by Spaniards, but Lingren did not revisit the area and could not assess this reference.

Although the lower Chama apparently lacks silver ore deposits, other mining districts in northern and central New Mexico contain lead, silver, or both in the form of lead-silver ores. In Taos County, Lingren recorded nine mines west of the Rio Grande trench that contained copper, silver, and gold.[55] The most southerly mine was at Copper Mountain in the vicinity of Picurís. The others extended north and east of Taos up through the Red River.

Another series of mining districts lies to the south of the lower Chama region, in Santa Fe and Sandoval Counties. Ore deposits containing lead, copper, zinc, silver, and gold run south from the Cerrillos Hills through the Ortiz Mountains and the San Pedro Mountains. Although the Cerrillos Hills are the only source of lead listed by Lingren, lead also occurs in the San Pedros. The identification of workable lead sources in the Cerrillos area has been independently confirmed by several studies. At the turn of the last century, lead was being commercially smelted in the Cerrillos Hills.[56] In a lead isotope analysis of native glaze-paint pottery, Judith Habicht-Mauche and colleagues were able to associate the lead flux from native ceramics with lead deposits in the Cerrillos district.[57]

Given this baseline geologic knowledge, several interpretations of the reference concerning Yuque Yunque are possible. As discussed earlier, it is possible that the Spaniards did not know what they were seeing. When they recognized something shiny that could have been used in glazing, they simply assumed that the presence of metallic-looking minerals meant there were silver deposits in the vicinity. Alternatively, the error could be Castañeda's. Twenty years passed between the expedition and the writing of his chronicle, and in that time Castañeda could have forgotten or confused some of the details. In other words, Castañeda may be responsible for making the link between the existence of shiny, metallic material and the presence of silver ores.

Still another possibility is that Castañeda's memory lapse relates to the place rather than what was seen. In this case, the Spaniards were correct in identifying the presence of surrounding silver ore deposits, but Castañeda misidentified where they were. In other words, the Spaniards might actually have visited a pueblo that was located near a silver deposit, but that pueblo was not Yuque Yunque.

So Where Were They?

The Galisteo Basin, located approximately fifty miles east-northeast of Tiguex, contains several possible candidates for this potentially misidentified pueblo. These include Pueblo Blanco, Pueblo Colorado, Galisteo Pueblo, She Pueblo, San Cristóbal Pueblo, San Lázaro Pueblo, and, most importantly, Pueblo San Marcos.

The Cerrillos Hills are located within sight of Pueblo San Marcos, and the six features that make up this prominent group of hills are known to contain moderately rich lead-silver ore deposits, notably silver-bearing galena.[58] The Cerrillos Hills also contain evidence of old Indian workings for turquoise and of Spanish silver mining, including the famous Mina del Tiro shaft mine.[59] Modern lead isotope analyses of glaze wares from San Marcos have also identified the Cerrillos Hills as the source of the lead used in making native glaze paints.[60] Most recently, we have recovered strong evidence that metallurgy was in use at San Marcos in the sixteenth and seventeenth centuries. Our surface collections recovered pieces of metallurgical slag, and our magnetometry survey identified signatures suggestive of buried smelters.[61]

The Ortiz Mountains, lying only about a mile south of San Marcos and San Lázaro Pueblos, are known for their gold placers rather than for silver or lead deposits. The Ortiz Mountains adjoin the San Pedro Mountains to the south. Argentiferous galena is present there as replacement deposits in limestone.[62] Finally, South Mountain, where silver is present as lead-silver ores in limestone deposits, is less than fifteen miles south of the San Pedros.[63] Any of these sources would have been easily accessible to Indian potters living in the pueblos of the Galisteo Basin.

Although any one of the Galisteo Basin pueblos is situated closer to metallic mineral deposits than Yuque Yunque, it does not follow that the Barrionuevo party actually visited any of the Galisteo Basin towns. The location of these pueblos relative to Tiguex does not accord well with Castañeda's description. Entering the basin from Tiguex would have required the Barrionuevo party to cross the Rio Grande rather than parallel it. No mention is made of such a crossing to reach the place where shiny metal was observed. Rather, Yuque Yunque is described as straddling the Rio Grande.

In summary, Castañeda's description does not match the geological distribution of metallic minerals. This lack of agreement creates further ambiguities in the description. There are no lead or lead-silver deposits close to Yuque Yunque. If the shiny material described by Castañeda was lead, then it could have been obtained through exchange or by direct procurement. The Cerrillos Hills are the closest source of lead. An alternative interpretation is that the Barrionuevo party was not at Yuque Yunque when the shiny metal was seen. Perhaps Castañeda integrated two places into one description. At Yuque Yunque, for example, the party observed mica, and on a separate visit to a Galisteo Basin pueblo, the group observed lead. Unfortunately, we have no evidence to suggest that this blending of events actually happened. Finally, given the suggested mineralogical naiveté of the Coronado expedition members, it is possible that Castañeda simply misidentified a micaceous mineral as galena. In this case, the Barrionuevo group was at Yuque Yunque and observed something shiny, but the sheen was actually one or another form of mica, not galena.

Conclusion

We have shown that Castañeda's apparently straightforward historical description of the Coronado expedition's exploration of the northern Rio Grande region is fraught with indefiniteness and ambiguity. Did the Barrionuevo party visit Jemez? Or was the provincial name switched by accident? Did the party travel through the Jemez Mountains to reach Yuque Yunque? What shiny material did they actually observe? Is it possible that during this exploration or at some other time they also visited a pueblo in the Galisteo Basin where lead or lead-silver was observed? Of all the possibilities, the simplest interpretation is that Barrionuevo traveled north from Tiguex to Yuque Yunque. On that journey the party explored one or more of the Keres pueblos that Castañeda misidentified as the Jemez province. At Yuque Yunque, the Spaniards saw mica, but Castañeda mistakenly identified the material as metal.

It will require substantially more research to resolve this passage in Castañeda's account. Our approach, which utilizes history, archeology, geology, and geography, is both necessary and important to create a more accurate rendering of historical events. The Coronado expedition documents, like most of the surviving sixteenth- and seventeenth-century descriptions of New Mexico, are too thin in details to enable us to reach definitive conclusions. Precisely because the documentary descriptions are so sketchy, fleshing out the historical events requires an interdisciplinary approach. The integration of all available sources of information not only illuminates the initial encounters between Spaniards and Pueblo people but also suggests still further avenues of investigation.

Notes

We thank Richard and Shirley Flint for their helpful and insightful suggestions during the researching and writing of this chapter. Jennifer Boyd and Julia Angel helped in separating and identifying glaze-paint sherds in the excavated collection of Florence Hawley Ellis. Shawn Penman helped in drafting several of the maps. Although errors in the interpretation of shiny metal from Yuque Yunque are ours alone, we hope that our analysis clarifies rather than obscures the historical text.

1. John Francis Bannon, ed., *Bolton and the Spanish Borderlands* (Norman: University of Oklahoma Press, 1964); David J. Weber, "Reflections on Coronado and the Myth of Quivira" and "Turner, the Boltonians, and the Spanish Borderlands," both in *Myth and the History of the Hispanic Southwest* (Albuquerque: University of New Mexico Press, 1988), 1–17, 33–54.

2. Herbert E. Bolton, "The Mission as a Frontier Institution in the Spanish American Culture," in Bannon, *Bolton and the Spanish Borderlands,* 197.

3. See Flint and Flint, *Coronado Expedition to Tierra Nueva;* Elizabeth A. H. John, *Storms Brewed in Other Men's Worlds: The Confrontation of Indians, Spanish, and French in the Southwest, 1540–1795* (College Station: Texas A&M University Press, 1975); John L. Kessell, *Kiva, Cross, and Crown: The Pecos Indians and New Mexico, 1540–1840,* 2d ed. (Albuquerque: University of New Mexico Press, 1987); Andrew L. Knaut, *The Pueblo Revolt of 1680: Conquest and Resistance in Seventeenth-Century New Mexico* (Norman: University of Oklahoma Press, 1995); Weber, *Spanish Frontier.*

4. See France V. Scholes, *Church and State in New Mexico,* Publications in History 7 (Albuquerque: Historical Society of New Mexico, 1937); France V. Scholes, *Troublous Times in New Mexico 1659–1670,* Publications in History 11 (Albuquerque: Historical Society of New Mexico, 1942).

5. See David H. Snow, "A Note on Encomienda Economics in Seventeenth-Century New Mexico," in *Hispanic Arts and Ethnohistory in the Southwest,* ed. Marta Weigle (Santa Fe: Ancient City Press, 1983), 347–58.

6. See Adolph F. Bandelier, *Final Report of Investigations among the Indians of the Southwestern United States, Carried on Mainly in the Years from 1880 to 1885,* Parts 1 and 2, Papers of the Archaeological Institute of America, American Series, 3 and 4 (Cambridge, Massachusetts, 1890–92; reprint, New York: AMS Press and Kraus Reprint Company, 1976).

7. See James E. Ivey, *In the Midst of a Loneliness: The Architectural History of the Salinas Missions,* Southwest Cultural Resources Center Professional Papers 15 (Washington, D.C.: National Park Service, 1988); Joseph H. Toulouse Jr., *The Mission of San Gregorio de Abo: A Report on the Excavation and Repair of a Seventeenth-Century New Mexico Mission,* School of American Research Monograph 13 (Albuquerque: University of New Mexico Press, 1949); Alfred V. Kidder, "The Glaze Paint, Culinary, and Other Wares," in *The Pottery of Pecos,* vol. 2, eds. Alfred V. Kidder and Anna O. Shepard (New Haven: Yale University Press, 1936), 1–388; Alfred V. Kidder and Charles Avery Amsden, *The Pottery of Pecos,* vol. 1, *The Dull Paint Wares* (New Haven: Yale University Press, 1931).

8. Frederick W. Hodge, *The History of Hawikuh: One of the So-called Cities of Cibola* (Los Angeles: Southwest Museum, 1937).

9. See Kidder, "Glaze Paint"; Kidder, *Pecos New Mexico: Archaeological Notes,* Robert S. Peabody Foundation Archaeological Papers 5 (Andover, Massachusetts: Phillips Academy, 1958); Kidder and Amsden, *Pottery of Pecos.*

10. See Flint and Flint, *Coronado Expedition to Tierra Nueva;* Jonathan Haas and Winifred Creamer, "Demography of the Protohistoric Pueblos of the Northern Rio Grande, A.D. 1450–1680," in *Current Research on the Late Prehistory and Early History of New Mexico,* ed. Bradley J. Vierra (Albuquerque: New Mexico Archaeological Council, 1992), 21–27; Frances Levine and Kurt Anschuetz, "Adjusting Our Scale of Analysis: Observations of Protohistoric Change in Pueblo Land Use," paper presented at the annual meeting of the Society for American Archaeology, Seattle, 1998; Mark T. Lycett, "Archaeological Implications of European Contact: Demography, Settlement, and Land Use in the Middle Rio Grande Valley, New Mexico," Ph.D. diss., University of New Mexico, 1995; Michael P. Marshall, "El Camino Real de Tierra Adentro: An Archaeological Investigation" (Santa Fe: New Mexico Historic Preservation Division, 1990); Michael P. Marshall and Henry J. Walt, "Rio Abajo: Prehistory and History of a Rio Grande Province" (Santa Fe: New Mexico Historic Preservation Office, 1984); Ann F. Ramenofsky, "Decoupling Archaeology and History: Northern New Mexico," in *The Entangled Past: Integrating History and Archaeology. Proceedings of the Thirtieth Chacmool Archaeological Conference,* eds. Matthew Boyd, J. C. Erwin, and M. Hendrickson (Calgary: University of Calgary, 2000), 5–64; Ann F. Ramenofsky and James K. Feathers, "Documents, Ceramics, Tree-Rings, and Luminescence: Estimating Final Native Abandonment of the Lower Chama Region," *Journal of Anthropological Research* 58, no. 1 (2002): 121–59; Diane Lee Rhodes, "Coronado Fought Here: Crossbow Boltheads as Possible Indicators of the 1540–1542 Expedition," in Flint and Flint, *Coronado Expedition to Tierra Nueva,* 44–56; David Snow, "'Por alli no ay losa ni se hace': Gilded Men and Glazed Pottery on the Southern Plains," in Flint and Flint, *Coronado Expedition to Tierra Nueva,* 344–64; Katherine A. Spielmann, "Colonists, Hunters, and Farmers: Plains-Pueblo Interaction in the Seventeenth Century," in *Columbian Consequences,* vol. 1, ed. David H. Thomas (Washington, D.C.: Smithsonian Institution Press, 1989), 101–14; Katherine A. Spielmann, "Coercion or Cooperation? Plains-Pueblo Interaction during the Protohistoric Period," in *Farmers, Hunters, and Colonists: Interaction between the Southwest and the Southern Plains,* ed. Katherine A. Spielmann (Tucson: University of Arizona Press, 1991), 36–50; Steadman Upham, "Population and Spanish Contact in the Southwest," in *Disease and Demography in the Americas,* eds. John W. Verano and Douglas H. Ubelaker (Washington, D.C.: Smithsonian Institution Press, 1992), 223–36; David Vaughan and Ann F. Ramenofsky, "Mining Slag for Knowledge," poster presented at "Founders, Smiths and Platers: An International Conference on Metal Forming and Finishing from the Earliest Times," sponsored by the Materials Science–Based Archaeology Group, Department of Materials, St. Catherine's College, University of Oxford, Oxford, U.K., 1999; Bradley J. Vierra, ed., *Current Research on the Late Prehistory and Early History of New Mexico* (Albuquerque: New Mexico Archaeological Council, 1992); Bradley J. Vierra and Stanley M. Hordes, "Let the Dust Settle: A Review of the Coronado Campsite in the Tiguex Province," in Flint and Flint, *Coronado Expedition to Tierra Nueva,* 249–61.

11. Christopher Pierce, "Toward Explaining Complex Patterns of Cooperation and Conflict during the Protohistoric Period in the American Southwest," paper presented at the Summer Workshop on Modeling Complexity in Social Systems at the Colorado Center for Chaos and Complexity (Boulder: University of Colorado, 1998); Christopher Pierce and Ann F. Ramenofsky, "Investigating Patterns of Cooperation and Conflict during the Contact Period in New Mexico," paper presented at the Sixth Biennial Southwest Symposium, Hermosillo, Mexico, 1998.

12. See Flint and Flint, *Coronado Expedition to Tierra Nueva,* for a review.

13. Castañeda, *Relación,* Primera Parte, Capítulo 22, fol. 94r–94v.

14. Richard Flint to Ann Ramenofsky, personal communication, 2000.

15. Bradley J. Vierra, "A Sixteeth-Century Spanish Campsite in the Tigues Province: An Archaeologist's Perspective," in Vierra, *Current Research,* 165–74; Vierra and Hordes, "Let the Dust Settle," 249–61.

16. George P. Hammond, *Coronado's Seven Cities* (Albuquerque: United States Coronado Exposition Commission, 1940), 258.

17. Other examples of name switching occur in the Oñate journals. See Hammond and Rey, *Oñate* 1:320, 337, 346, 416; and for a summary see Albert H. Schroeder, "Pueblos Abandoned in Historic Times," in *Handbook of North American Indians,* vol. 9, *Southwest,* ed. Alfonso Ortiz (Washington, D.C.: Smithsonian Institution Press, 1979), 250.

18. Elinore M. Barrett, *Conquest and Catastrophe: Changing Rio Grande Settlement Patterns in the Sixteenth and Seventeenth Centuries* (Albuquerque: University of New Mexico Press, 2001); Elinore M. Barrett, *The Geography of Rio Grande Pueblos as Revealed by Spanish Explorers, 1540–1598,* Research Paper Series 30 (Albuquerque: Latin American Institute, 1997); Adolph F. Bandelier, "Documentary History of the Rio Grande Pueblos, Part 1, 1536–1542 (Concluded)," *New Mexico Historical Review* 2 (April 1930): 154–85; Bolton, *Coronado;* Hammond and Rey, *Narratives;* Schroeder, "Pueblos Abandoned."

19. Vincent C. Kelley, *Geology and Mineral Resources of the Española Basin, New Mexico* (Socorro: New Mexico Bureau of Mines and Mineral Resources, 1977), map 48.

20. Florence Hawley Ellis, *San Gabriel del Yunque as Seen by an Archaeologist* (Santa Fe: Sunstone Press, 1989); Florence Hawley Ellis, "The Long Lost 'City' of San Gabriel del Yungue, Second Oldest European Settlement in the United States," in *When Cultures Meet,* papers from the October 20, 1984, conference held at San Juan Pueblo, New Mexico (Santa Fe: Sunstone Press,1987), 10–38; Florence Hawley Ellis and Andrea Ellis Dodge, "A Window on San Gabriel del Yunque," in Vierra, *Current Research,* 175–84.

21. Ellis, "Long Lost 'City.'"

22. Albert H. Schroeder and Dan S. Matson, *A Colony on the Move: Gaspar Castaño de Sosa's Journal, 1590–1591* (Santa Fe: School of American Research, 1965).

23. Fred Wendorf, "A Reconstruction of Northern Rio Grande Prehistory," *American Anthropologist* 56, no. 2 (1954): 200–27; Fred Wendorf and Eric Reed, "An Alternative Reconstruction of Northern Rio Grande Prehistory," *El Palacio* 62, nos. 5–6 (1955): 37–52.

24. For review see John D. Beal, "Foundations of the Rio Grande Classic: The Lower Chama River, A.D. 1300–1500," manuscript on file, New Mexico Office of Cultural Affairs, Historic Preservation Division, Santa Fe (Santa Fe: Southwest Archaeological Consultants, Inc., 1987); Patricia L. Crown, Janet D. Orcutt, and Timothy A. Kohler, "Pueblo Cultures in Transition: The Northern Rio Grande," in *The Prehistoric Pueblo world, A.D. 1150–1350,* ed. Michael A. Adler (Tucson: University of Arizona Press, 1996), 188–204; John A. Jeançon, *Excavations in the Chama Valley, New Mexico,* Bureau of American Ethnology Bulletin 81 (Washington, D.C.: U.S. Government Printing Office, 1923); John A. Jeançon, "Ruins at Peseduinque," *Records of the Past* 11 (1912): 28–37; Ralph A. Leubben, "The Leaf Water Site," in *Salvage Archaeology in the Chama Valley, New Mexico,* ed. Fred Wendorf, School of American Research Monograph 17 (Santa Fe: School of American Research, 1953), 1–33.; Harry P.

Mera, *A Survey of the Biscuit Ware Area in Northern New Mexico,* Laboratory of Anthropology Technical Series Bulletin 6 (Santa Fe: Museum of New Mexico, 1934); Ramenofsky, "Decoupling"; Ramenofsky and Feathers, "Documents, Ceramics"; Fred Wendorf, "Excavations at Te'ewi," in *Salvage Archaeology in the Chama Valley, New Mexico,* ed. Fred Wendorf, School of American Research Monograph 17 (Santa Fe: School of American Research, 1953), 34–124.

25. Wendorf, "Excavations at Te'ewi."

26. William J. Robinson and Richard L Warren, *Tree-Ring Dates from New Mexico C–D: Northern Rio Grande Area,* (Tucson: University of Arizona, Laboratory of Tree-Ring Research, 1971); Ramenofsky and Feathers, "Documents, Ceramics."

27. James K. Feathers, "The Application of Luminescence Dating in American Archaeology," *Journal of Archaeological Method and Theory* 4 (1997): 1–66; Ramenofsky and Feathers, "Documents, Ceramics."

28. Florence Hawley Ellis, "Hiways to the Past," *New Mexico Magazine* 53 (1975): 18–40; Thomas Windes, "Report on Excavations at Tsama, LA 908, near Abiquiu, New Mexico: West Mound, West Rooms, and West Mound Kiva." Manuscript, 1970.

29. Hammond, *Coronado's Seven Cities,* 256.

30. Kidder, "Glaze Paint"; Harry P. Mera, *A Proposed Revision of the Rio Grande Glaze Paint Sequence,* Laboratory of Anthropology Technical Series Bulletin 5 (Santa Fe: Museum of New Mexico, 1933); Harry P. Mera, *Population Changes in the Rio Grande Glaze Paint Area,* Laboratory of Anthropology Technical Series 8 (Santa Fe: Museum of New Mexico, 1940).

31. Mera, *Proposed Revision* and *Population Changes;* Peter J. McKenna and James A. Miles, "Bandelier Archaeological Survey Ceramic Manual," manuscript on file at the Branch of Cultural Research, Southwest Regional Office (Santa Fe: National Park Service, 1991); Janet D. Orcutt, "Chronology," in *The Bandelier Archaeological Survey,* vol. 1, eds. Robert P. Powers and Janet D. Orcutt (Washington, D.C.: National Park Service, 1999), 85–116; Ramenofsky and Feathers, "Documents, Ceramics"; Snow, "Por alli."

32. Mera, *Biscuit ware* and *Population changes;* Orcutt, "Chronology"; James M. Vint, "Ceramic Artifacts," in *The Bandelier Archaeological Survey,* vol. 2, eds. Robert P. Powers and Janet D. Orcutt (Washington, D.C.: National Park Service, 2000), 389–467.

33. Mera, *Biscuit Ware;* Ramenofsky and Feathers, "Documents, Ceramics."

34. Mera, *Biscuit Ware.*

35. Mera, *Biscuit Ware.*

36. Kathleen Deagan, "Accommodation and Resistance: The Process and Impact of Spanish Colonization in the Southeast," in *Columbian Consequences,* vol. 2, ed. David H. Thomas (Washington, D.C.: Smithsonian Institution Press, 1990), 297–314; Leland Ferguson, *Uncommon Ground* (Washington, D.C.: Smithsonian Institution Press, 1992); Shawn L. Penman, "Colonowares at Pecos: A Study in Acculturation" (Ph.D. diss., University of New Mexico, 2002); Vicki L. Rolland and Keith H. Ashley, "Beneath the Bell: A Study of Mission Period Colonowares from Three Spanish Missions in Northeastern Florida," *Florida Anthropologist* 53, no. 1 (2000): 36–61; Richard H. Vernon and Ann S. Cordell, "A Distribution and Technological Study of Apalachee Colono-Ware from San Luis de Talimali," in *The Spanish Missions of La Florida,* ed. Bonnie McEwan (Gainesville: University Presses of Florida, 1993), 418–43.

37. Judith A. Habicht-Mauche, Stephen T. Glenn, Homer Milford, and A. Russell Flegal, "Isotopic Tracing of Prehistoric Glaze-Paint Produce and Trade," *Journal of Archaeological Science* 27 (2000): 708–13; Anna O. Shepard, *Rio Grande Glaze Paint Ware,* Publication no. 528 (Washington, D.C.: Carnegie Institution of Washington, 1942), 221–25, 255–56.

38. R. F. Tylecote, *The Prehistory of Metallurgy in the British Isles* (London: Institute of Metals, 1986).

39. Schroeder, "Pueblos Abandoned," 250.

40. Bandelier, "Documentary History," 164.

41. Richard Flint to Ann Ramenofsky, personal communication, 2000.

42. Ruth H. Bunzel, *Zuni Katchinas,* Annual Report of the Bureau of American Ethnology 47 (Washington, D.C.: Government Printing Office, 1932), 861.

43. Robert C. West, "Early Silver Mining in New Spain, 1531–1555," in *An Expanding World: The European Impact on World History 1450–1800,* vol. 19, *Mines of Silver and Gold in the Americas,* ed. Peter Bakewell (Aldershot, U.K.: Variorum, 1997), 41–56.

44. Cieza de León, *Discovery and Conquest,* 149.

45. Agricola [Georg Bauer], *De Re Metallica,* Translated from the First Latin Edition (1556) with Bibliographic Introduction, Annotations and Appendices upon the Development of Mining Methods, Metallurgical Processes, Geology, Mineralogy and Mining Law from the Earliest times to the Late Sixteenth Century by Herbert C. Hoover and Lou H. Hoover (London: *Mining Magazine* [1912]).

46. Peter Bakewell, "Introduction," in Bakewell, *Mines of Silver and Gold,* xxi–xxii.

47. Alan Probert, "Bartolomé de Medina: The Patio Process and the Sixteenth-Century Silver Crisis," in Bakewell, *Mines of Silver and Gold,* 96–130.

48. Bakewell, "Introduction."

49. West, *Early Silver Mining.*

50. Peter Bakewell, *Silver and Entrepreneurship in Seventeenth-Century Potosí* (Albuquerque: University of New Mexico Press, 1988).

51. Homer E. Milford, Richard Flint, Shirley Cushing Flint, and Geraldine Vigil, *Nuevas leyes de las minas de España de Juan de Oñate,* Congreso Internacional de Historia de la Minería, Facultad de Minas (Guanajuato, Mexico: Universidad de Guanajuato, 1998).

52. Flint, "Pattern of Coronado Expedition," 145.

53. Hammond and Rey, *Oñate.*

54. Waldemar Lingren, Louis C. Graton, and Charles H. Gordon, *The Ore Deposits of New Mexico,* USGS Professional Paper 68 (Washington, D.C.: U.S. Government Printing Office, 1910), 149.

55. Lingren, Graton, and Gordon, *Ore Deposits,* 82–91.

56. Alan E. Disbrow and Walter C. Stoll, *Geology of the Cerrillos Hills Area, Santa Fe County, New Mexico,* Bureau of Mines and Mineral Resources Bulletin 48 (Socorro: New Mexico Institute of Mining and Technology, 1957); Lingren, Graton, and Gordon, *Ore Deposits;* Homer E. Milford, *Cultural Resource Survey for the Real de los Cerrillos Abandoned Mine Lands Project, Santa Fe County, New Mexico,* New Mexico Abandoned Mine Land Bureau Report 1996-1 (Santa Fe: Mining and Minerals Division; Energy, Minerals, and Natural Resources Department, 1996).

57. Habicht-Mauche et al., "Isotopic Tracing."

58. Disbrow and Stoll, *Cerrillos Hills;* Lingren, Graton, and Gordon, *Ore Deposits,* 163.

59. Milford, *Cultural Resource Survey.*

60. Habicht-Mauche et al., "Isotopic Tracing."

61. C. David Vaughan, "Investigation of Spanish Colonial Mining and Metallurgy," in *Summary Report of the 2000 Season of Archaeological Research at San Marcos Pueblo (LA98) by the University of New Mexico,* ed. Ann Ramenofsky (Santa Fe: New Mexico Historic Preservation Division), 66–80.

62. Lingren, Graton, and Gordon, *Ore Deposits,* 172.

63. F. A. Jones, *Mines and Minerals of New Mexico, with Some Reference to the Geological Associations in the Various Camps of the Territory* (Santa Fe: New Mexico Bureau of Immigration, 1901), 60.

EIGHT

The Mystery of Coronado's Route from the Pecos River to the Llano Estacado

HARRY C. MYERS

IN THE SPRING OF 1541, Francisco Vázquez de Coronado and his expedition of close to 2,000 people and animals (approximately 300 Spaniards, 1,500 Indians, 1,000 horses, 500 cows, and 5,000 rams) made the journey from the valley of the Rio Grande near present-day Bernalillo, New Mexico, to Pecos Pueblo and from there to the Llano Estacado in the Panhandle of Texas.[1] The expeditionaries crossed the Llano in a southeasterly direction, through herds of bison, until they made at least one camp on the eastern edge of the Llano Estacado in Blanco Canyon, Texas. Much speculation surrounds the route they took from Pecos Pueblo to the Llano. The only places in which archeological indicators of the route have been found are Pecos Pueblo, New Mexico, and Blanco Canyon, near Floydada, Texas. And although the river that the party bridged is now generally accepted as having been the Pecos, researchers have also speculated that it was the Canadian River that posed an obstacle to the expedition. Additionally, a captured Plains Indian called "the Turk," who had been living at Pecos, was supposed to have been Coronado's guide to the plains and the riches that Coronado believed were there.

It has been thought that for much of Coronado's journey, the party followed existing Indian trails, and this makes good sense. In a land where water could not be taken for granted, the trails and roads of the Indian people followed springs, creeks, and rivers where water flowed clear and cool. Indeed, the latter-day Santa Fe Trail and all other routes of travel did the same, until modern-day auto travel. Route segments without water were described as such—the *jornado del muerto,* or dead man's journey, on the Camino Real in southern New Mexico is a prime example. That appellation both warned that water was unavailable and advertised what would happen if you did not carry your own water.

Another consideration of traveling was the terrain and the mode of travel being used. A person afoot can go places that a dog travois cannot. A person on horseback can go places that a wagon or cart cannot. And even people walking will avoid gullies and canyons and sharp slopes if they can go around these obstacles and still reach their destination without too great a detour, and if they can find fresh water along the route.

Long before Coronado or any other European set foot on the continent, trade was taking place between the people who lived on the Llano Estacado in the general vicinity of Amarillo, Texas, and the Pueblo people of the Rio Grande Valley, with the pueblo of Pecos serving as a way station and trade broker. It was probably no coincidence that Pecos sat out on the edge of the Pueblo world and was both a broker in trade and the strongest Pueblo, with the ability to defend itself against the people of the plains.

The Plains people brought products of the bison (meat, hides, sinew, etc.) to trade for the agricultural products that the Pueblo people grew with irrigation along the Rio Grande. The route between the plains and the pueblos had to provide regular water, a reasonable topography for the dog travois, and a fairly direct route into the interior of the Pueblo world.[2]

And indeed, two very old and historic routes to the Llano Estacado have recently been delineated. They were used long after the Coronado expedition passed through, and probably long before. One route ran from Pecos Pueblo via Bernal, the other from Galisteo, New Mexico, via Cañon Blanco (not the same place as Blanco Canyon, Texas). They joined at Chupains (Chupaines, Chupinas) Spring, east of Anton Chico, and tracked together east about ten miles to Gallinas Spring (Park Spring) on the Gallinas River (see map 8.1). There, what could be called the "upper" route headed a little bit north of east via Conchas Spring and the Angosturas (the Narrows), to the plains. Meanwhile, what could be called the "lower" route headed southeast past Cuervo Hill and Tucumcari Mountain to the plains. Both are old, and both were heavily used over the years.

The Upper Route

In July 1598, don Juan de Oñate brought permanent European settlement to New Mexico. Having to finance this project himself and not finding immediate riches, he, like Vázquez de Coronado, planned a journey to the Great Plains and Quivira in search of wealth. On June 23, 1601, Oñate led his expedition south out of San Gabriel (San Juan Pueblo) and headed for Galisteo. There he stopped for several days while the participants gathered and prepared for their journey. Once set, they headed east along Cañon Blanco and within five days reached the Pecos River in

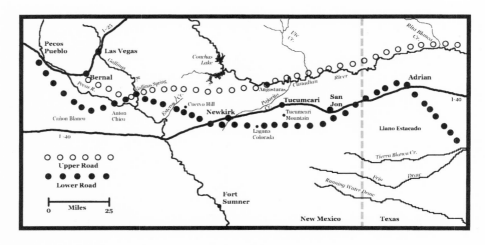

Map 8.1. Two historic routes of travel from Pecos Pueblo to the Llano Estacado. Map by Harry Myers.

the vicinity of Anton Chico. They crossed it without comment and the next day continued over some "wide Plains" and reached another river they named the "Bagres" (Catfish), which has been identified as the Gallinas River.

It is fairly certain that they were at Gallinas Spring and the crossing of the Gallinas. In three days of marching Oñate reached a third river, which he called the Magdalena (Madalena) because he reached it on her feast day. Oñate's comment on the part of the river his party reached is instructive about its identity: "At first we did not think much of it, because we struck it at a place where it was hemmed in by rocks, making its banks unattractive."[3] A nineteenth-century description of the area said that Mesa Rica extended for several miles along the right bank, and on the left bank a series of lower, broken mesas pressed in on the river, causing it to flow, narrower and swifter, between high banks and cliffs for about six miles through the "Angostura."[4]

That description of the Canadian River in 1860 is strikingly similar to Oñate's of 1601 and leaves little doubt that Oñate was at the Angosturas east of Conchas Dam and on the upper road. This road struck the Canadian River in the vicinity of the Angosturas. Elsewhere the Canadian River is a wide, easy-flowing river that is unconstricted once it passes out of the eight-hundred-foot-deep Canadian Canyon.

The Martínez map of 1602 details Oñate's route.[5] It is a fascinating and accurate map. Although it was not drawn to an exact scale, many features can be made out on it, such as Ute and Rita Blanca Creeks flowing into the Canadian (Río de la Madalena), and the river's various meanders and fords. This map confirms that the Oñate expedition struck the Canadian River at the Narrows.

One hundred and thirty-nine years later, another published account described a journey to the Great Plains along this route. In 1739, Paul and Pierre Mallet traveled to Santa Fe from the Illinois country.[6] They are credited with being the first Frenchmen to enter Santa Fe. Although they lost all their trade goods, they spent nearly a year in New Mexico before they were allowed to return home.

On the first of May 1740, the Mallet group left Santa Fe, reaching Pecos Pueblo on the second. They stayed there two days, then headed east, camped on the Pecos River on May 4 and 5, and left it on the sixth. On May 7 they reached another river that flowed in the same direction as the Pecos. This river was the Gallinas, which they then left on the eighth. On the tenth they reached another river, which they thought flowed into the Red or Arkansas River. This was the Canadian, and they followed it to the Mississippi. They, too, like Oñate, took three days to cover the distance between the Gallinas and the Canadian.

In 1792 Pedro Vial led an expedition to St. Louis from Santa Fe. On May 21, his group headed for Pecos and the Pecos River and on the twenty-sixth reached the "Gallinas River," as Vial called it. This party, too, took three days to reach the Canadian, leaving the Gallinas on the twenty-seventh and arriving on the Canadian on the twenty-ninth.[7]

In a period of about two hundred years, then, at least three groups headed east and took the same time, three days, to pass from one river to another. It is no coincidence, because they were traveling on the same road and stopping at the same springs, waterholes, and campgrounds.

In the ensuing years, other expeditions would be documented as coming into New Mexico the same way: Francisco Amangual in 1808, coming from San Antonio, Texas; the Meredith Miles Marmaduke Santa Fe Trail caravan of 1824, coming from Missouri via Cold Spring, Oklahoma; and the Josiah Gregg caravan of 1839, coming from Fort Smith, Arkansas. In 1841, one part of the Texan–Santa Fe Expedition came into New Mexico to the Angosturas and ended up arrested and detained at San Miguel del Vado on the Pecos River.[8] This upper road is well documented over a long period of time.

The Lower Route

Other expeditions that came out of New Mexico, however, followed the same road to Gallinas Spring but then diverged to head southeast from the Gallinas River crossing and to follow the lower (Gallinas–Cuervo Hill–Tucumcari Mountain) road.

On September 15, 1598, a scant two months after Juan de Oñate arrived in New Mexico and settled at San Gabriel (San Juan Pueblo), he sent his nephew, Vicente de Zaldívar Mendoza, with about sixty men eastward from Pecos, headed for the plains. Four days later the party reached the Gallinas (Bagres) River, where they caught five hundred catfish that day and even more the next. Also the next day they were greeted by four Vaquero Indians. Zaldívar gave them presents and asked for "a guide to the cattle [bison] and they furnished one very willingly."[9]

After staying near the Indians for a day, Zaldívar and his men traveled ten leagues, or twenty-six miles, in three days, which places them on Pajarito Creek south of Newkirk, New Mexico. There they saw their first bison, an old bull who was slow of pace.[10] They soon saw more than three hundred at some small lakes as they marched on another seven leagues in three days,[11] which places them close to Barranca Creek just a little southeast of Tucumcari. Zaldívar went to the Canadian River, about six leagues away, and ran into another group of Vaquero Indians who were returning from trading with the Pueblo people of Taos and Picurís.

Zaldívar's encounter there is good confirmation of his location. The eight-hundred-foot Canadian escarpment north of Tucumcari turns and runs north-south from the river to south of present-day Clayton, New Mexico. The Vaqueros would either have met and traded with the Taos and Picurís people at Cejita de los Comancheros (in northeastern Harding County) or followed the route from Cejita into Taos and Picurís Pueblos themselves.[12]

On his return, Zaldívar came upon a ranchería of fifty teepees. Determined to capture some bison, on October 5 the group moved east to a point about five miles inside the present Texas state line and set up a corral, which failed dismally to capture any animals. Zaldívar made a foray of about eighty miles onto the Llano Estacado before he returned to San Gabriel with cured bison meat for the winter.

Nearly two hundred years later, in July 1787, José Mares led an expedition from Santa Fe to San Antonio de Béxar (San Antonio, Texas). Mares's group left the Pecos River on August 1, 1787, and camped at Bernal for the night. The next day they traveled southeast and camped at the Gallinas River. Traveling seven leagues farther, they reached an arroyo that Mares called Nombre de Dios, which places them on or near Esteros Creek. They next set out east and camped on an arroyo close to a mesa and a mountain, having traveled thirteen leagues. This would place them south of present-day Montoya, close to Laguna Colorada (Laguna Colorado) on the Guadalupe–Quay County line.

They next marched east along Charco Creek to Tucumcari Mountain and Plaza Larga Creek and arrived in the Canadian River valley proper. They had run into Comanche people, for Mares noted that he inquired of them about the permanency of a creek. Two more days' march brought them east of the modern-day Texas–New Mexico state line, where they surmounted the Llano and reached the head of Tierra Blanca Creek.[13]

The next year, Santiago Fernández and Francisco Fragoso wrote journals of their expedition to Natchitoches with Pedro Vial. Even though they traveled together, their diaries of daily travel and their place names are different. A comparison of their diaries, however, shows they were following the same route.[14]

They left Santa Fe on June 24, 1788, with seven others (three of them cavalrymen) and arrived at Bernal on the twenty-fifth. The next day they reached the Gallinas River and camped for the night. A march of eight leagues brought them to Pajarito Creek on the twenty-seventh, and they remained there on the twenty-eighth. They traveled east on the twenty-ninth and camped at a mesa they called San Pedro. Their mileage would place them close to Laguna Colorada.

They next traveled along Charco Creek in a valley they called Santana (St. Ana), which was bounded on the north by "two small hills of red slabs and a small mesa,"[15] arriving south of Tucumcari Mountain. A short march on July 1 placed them in a Comanche village—this was a location where few travelers along the route failed to find a village of Indian people. They traveled on and camped overnight at a place they called Santa Rosa, which places their camp southeast of San Jon and not in the present-day location of Santa Rosa, New Mexico.

Another day of marching brought them ten leagues past some white mesas noted by both Captain Marcy and Lieutenant Simpson in 1849,[16] to the spring called in Fragoso's diary "El Puerto" and, on the Vial map, "Ojo de Agua." This places the group at Rocky Dell on Agua de Piedras Creek, a little north of Adrian, Texas. There they arrived without comment atop the Llano at the headwaters of Tierra Blanca Creek. Before reaching Natchitoches they followed the Tierra Blanca, which becomes the Red River, to the Jumanos villages near Wichita Falls, Texas.[17]

Josiah Gregg, the famous chronicler of the Santa Fe Trail, also traveled this lower route in 1840. He left Santa Fe on February 25 with twenty-eight wagons, roughly three hundred sheep and goats, and nearly two hundred mules and arrived at San Miguel del Vado on March 1. His stated course from San Miguel was to Bernal (called San Miguel Spring by the traders) and then via the Gallinas River (near Gallinas Spring), Esteros Creek, Cuervito Creek, Pajarito Creek, and Laguna Colorada to Arroyo de Monte Revuelto (east of Tucumcari), where he arrived on March 9. There his party found three bison bulls and killed two for meat.

At the next campsite east of Trujillo Creek the party was attacked by Pawnees, but none of Gregg's men was killed. On the eleventh they reached Agua de Piedras, or Rocky Dell Creek (near Adrian, Texas), and on the twelfth they "rose upon the

Table land," the Llano Estacado. They then followed the Canadian River valley back to Fort Smith, from where Gregg had set out a year earlier.[18]

In 1841 the second group of the Texan–Santa Fe expedition came into New Mexico this way and, while camped at Laguna Colorada, were captured by Mexican troops. Perhaps the most famous travelers on this lower route were Captain Randolph B. Marcy and Lieutenant James H. Simpson in 1849. Both their expedition and the Amiel W. Whipple survey of 1853 came along the Canadian River from the east, followed the valley of Plaza Larga past Tucumcari Mountain, and continued up Charco Creek past Laguna Colorada to the crossing of Pajarito Creek. They then journeyed past Cuervito Peak to Esteros Creek, which they called Hurrah Creek, and on to the Gallinas River crossing. They continued to Chupains Spring, where the road that both Marcy and Whipple took headed on to cross the Pecos River, enter the town of Anton Chico, and run through Cañon Blanco to Galisteo and Albuquerque. The other road headed northwest to Bernal, San Miguel, Pecos, and finally Santa Fe. It was Marcy who called it the Fort Smith road, and though it already had been in use for several hundred years, the name stuck.[19]

Testimony taken in the dispute over what would become known as the Preston Beck land grant would confirm that this was an old road. Santiago Gonzalez, from Anton Chico, said that the road running along Pajarito (Cuervo) Mesa was called the "Cibuleros (Cibolero) road." Lorenzo Labadie, a long-time Indian agent and scout in the area, testified that it was the "Road of the Cibuleros and Comancheros."[20]

Coronado's Route to the Llano

None of the eighteenth- and nineteenth-century diaries of travel that is specific enough to enable a determination of location delineates a route other than these two—the upper route to Gallinas Spring and then to the Angosturas and along the Canadian River, and the lower route from Gallinas Spring to Pajarito Creek and Tucumcari and then the Llano Estacado. A reconstruction of Coronado's route through this area, from Pecos Pueblo to the east, ought to focus on these two routes, in the absence of evidence that the expedition went a drastically different way.

We know that other routes to the plains below the Canadian escarpment were in use throughout prehistoric and historic times. One road came from Taos over the Sangre de Cristo mountains and split near Rayado, one branch going directly east onto the plains and into the northern Panhandle of Texas and the other heading northeast into southeastern Colorado and eastern Kansas. Just south of this Taos Trail ran another trail that came down through the Mora Valley to present-day Fort Union National Monument and then out to the plains.

Yet another road via Cañon Blanco reached Anton Chico and then forked. One fork went down the west side of the Pecos River, perhaps crossing the Pecos in the vicinity of Puerto de Luna. It then followed the east side of the river to Bosque Redondo at Fort Sumner. The other fork headed east from Anton Chico to Gallinas Spring and Esteros Creek and then headed south on the east side of the Pecos to Bosque Redondo.[21] It is evident from the narratives, however, that the Coronado expedition did not travel to the Llano Estacado via the Taos Trail, nor did it travel closely along a river for any distance on the outbound leg of the trip. Thus, we can eliminate the likelihood that it used the various Bosque Redondo trails.

Looking at the most recent scholarship on the journey, we find that Herbert Bolton, Waldo Wedel, and Richard and Shirley Flint route the expedition in the general vicinity of the two corridors I have called the upper and lower routes east from Pecos Pueblo. Because the Coronado narratives do not mention a river the magnitude of the Canadian soon after the bridging of the Pecos, the expedition's route must have been the lower one, the route passing through Gallinas Spring, Esteros Creek, Pajarito Creek, Laguna Colorada, and Tucumcari Mountain and on to the Llano Estacado.

On April 23, 1541, the Coronado expedition left Tiguex and proceeded four days to Pecos Pueblo. After the party left Pecos, the narratives say that it took three or four days to reach what has been generally accepted as the Pecos River. Had the expedition gone via San Miguel del Vado to Bernal to Gallinas Spring, it would have easily reached the Pecos within a day and a half. Perhaps because it was a wet year the expedition ascended Rowe Mesa and went south to Cañon Blanco.[22] Coronado reached the Pecos River at Anton Chico, and there the expedition would have built its bridge.

Although Richard and Shirley Flint have suggested the bridge's location to have been about ten miles downstream from there, no other recorded expedition heading for or returning from the Great Plains went that way. All recorded travel from the east, whether following the upper route or the lower one, came to Gallinas and Chupains Spring and then either went up Cañon Blanco to Galisteo or turned northwest for Bernal and San Miguel del Vado.[23]

After halting four days to build the bridge and cross the Pecos, the expedition continued east, reaching the "plains" in another day (or just after crossing the Pecos), according to the narratives. Indeed, the character of the land east of the river valley becomes plains almost immediately. Once past the end of Chupains Mesa, the country becomes increasingly open and flat. The expedition next reached Gallinas Spring at the Gallinas River, where it would have camped. It then crossed without comment the Gallinas, which does not run as high or as long from spring runoff as does the Pecos, and took a southeastern bearing. In succeeding days it would have camped at or passed Esteros Creek north of Santa Rosa, Cuervo Creek, and Cuervo Hill, from where it would have crossed to the south of future Interstate 40 and headed more easterly to Pajarito Creek.

According to Waldo Wedel's timetable,[24] along with Castañeda's statement of daily travel of between six and seven leagues a day, it was in this vicinity that the party encountered its first bison. This was the same place in which Vicente de Zaldívar Mendoza ran into his first bison, too. With the scarp of the Llano Estacado now on their right, they reached Laguna Colorada, passed Captivas Peak and Whipple's Pyramid, and would have camped on or near Plaza Larga south of Tucumcari Mountain. In later years virtually every traveler on this route would encounter an Indian village east of Tucumcari. Again, statements from the Coronado narratives and Wedel's timetable place the first Querecho village nearby. From there the expedition went on to encounter a second Querecho village and reach the Llano Estacado possibly at Puerto del Arroyo or at Agua del Piedra (north of Adrian), where there are easy approaches up to the Llano. Then the expedition headed southeast, perhaps to Blanco Canyon in Texas or another point on the eastern escarpment of the Llano.

Although there are possible variations of this route, it is certainly compelling that all published journals telling of going to the plains or returning from them describe travel via Gallinas Spring. Coronado's expedition would have needed all those essentials of the trail that later people needed, and Coronado, with his accompanying fifteen hundred men and women, two thousand sheep, and other animals, needed them in good supply. Abundant water, travel free of canyons, and lack of blocking ridges or escarpments is what Francisco Vázquez de Coronado found on this route from Pecos Pueblo to the plains.

Notes

1. Pedro de Castañeda, "Translation of the Narrative of Castañeda," in *The Journey of Coronado, 1540–1542* [1896], ed. and trans. George Parker Winship (New York: Dover, 1990), 75.

2. Trade between the Rio Grande pueblos and the Plains people is documented in Spielmann, *Farmers, Hunters, and Colonists*. A wonderful and comprehensive history of Pecos Pueblo is Kessell's *Kiva, Cross, and Crown*.

3. Hammond and Rey, *Oñate*, 2:747.

4. Lt. Col. Benjamin S. Roberts, "Report from Hatch's Ranch, New Mexico, December 8, 1860, to Captain Dabney H. Maury, Asst. Adjutant General, Department of New Mexico, Santa Fé," *Letters Received by the Department of New Mexico* (Washington, D.C.: National Archives and Record Service), microfilm 1120, roll 12, frames 414–19. See also Robert Frazer, "Fort Butler," *New Mexico Historical Review* 43 (October 1968): 262–63, for Frazer's

description, which also closely matches Oñate's and led me to realize that both were talking about the same place.

5. See "Martínez Map," in George P. Hammond and Agapito Rey, eds. and trans., *The Rediscovery of New Mexico, 1580–1594: The Explorations of Chamuscado, Espejo, Castaño de Sosa, Morlete, and Leyva de Bonilla and Humaña* (Albuquerque: University of New Mexico Press, 1966), endpapers; and in Carl I. Wheat, *Mapping the Trans-Mississippi West, 1540–1861,* vol. 1, *The Spanish Entrada to the Louisiana Purchase, 1540–1804* (San Francisco: Institute of Historic Cartography, 1957), map 34. Wheat calls the map a "precious memento" and says that another century would pass before another map of actual experience in the region would be produced. Carl I. Wheat, *Mapping the American West, 1540–1857* (Worcester, Massachusetts: American Antiquarian Society, 1954), 33. On the map one can easily make out the Pecos River (Rio Salado), the Canadian River (Rio de la Madalena), and two unnamed streams that run into the Canadian. They are, from west to east, Ute Creek and Rita Blanca Creek.

6. The return journal of the expedition is reprinted in Donald Blakeslee, *Along Ancient Trails: The Mallet Expedition of 1739* (Niwot, Colorado: University Press of Colorado, 1995), 50–51. Blakeslee (165) says that the Mallet's River of the Mare is the Gallinas and that the party was following a trail well documented in later years.

7. Noel M. Loomis and Abraham P. Nasatir, *Pedro Vial and the Roads to Santa Fe* (Norman: University of Oklahoma Press, 1967), 372–75.

8. For Amangual's diary, see Loomis and Nasatir, *Pedro Vial,* 500–509. See also Harry C. Myers, "Meredith Miles Marmaduke's Journal of a Tour to New Mexico, 1824–1825," *Wagon Tracks* 12 (November 1997): 8–16; Josiah Gregg, *Commerce of the Prairies* (Reprint, Norman: University of Oklahoma Press, 1954), 259–60; George W. Kendall, *Across the Great Southwestern Prairies,* vol. 1 (London: David Bogue, Fleet Street, 1845), 277–78; Thomas Falconer, *Letters and Notes on the Texan Santa Fe Expedition 1841–1842* (Chicago: Rio Grande Press, 1963), which contains many references to the Angosturas; and H. Bailey Carroll, "The Texan Santa Fe Trail," *Panhandle-Plains Historical Review* (1951): 141–42.

9. Hammond and Rey, *Oñate,* 1:398.

10. Hammond and Rey, *Oñate,* 1:398–404; Vicente de Zaldívar Mendoza, *Zaldívar and the Cattle of Cíbola: Vicente de Zaldívar's Report of His Expedition to the Buffalo Plains in 1598,* ed. Jerry R. Craddock, trans. John R. Polt (Dallas: William P. Clements Center for Southwest Studies, Southern Methodist University, 1999), 32–36.

11. Captain Randolph B. Marcy, at this point along the trail in 1849, noted, "June 21. After marching seven miles this morning through a grove of cedars, we crossed an arroyo with many large pools of water, about 400 yards to the right of the road, where there is good camping ground, with timber and grass." Randolph B. Marcy, "Route from Fort Smith to Santa Fe: Report Prepared by Captain Randolph B. Marcy, February 21, 1850," Secretary of War, 31st Cong., 1st sess., Executive Document no. 45, Serial 577, 46.

12. Harry Myers and Mike Olsen, "'We Found the Rocks Very Troblesom': The Taos Trail in New Mexico," in *The Prairie Scout,* vol. 6 (Abilene: Kansas Corral of the Westerners, 1996), 80–97. Glenn R. Scott, comp., "Sectional Map of Colfax and Mora Counties, New Mexico, Compiled from the Original Plats in the Surveyor General's Office at Santa Fe, New Mexico, and from Private Surveys by the Maxwell Land Grant Company, 1889," in *Historic Trail Maps of the Raton and Springer 30' by 60' Quadrangles, New Mexico and Colorado,* sheet 2 of 2, Miscellaneous Investigations Series, Map I-1641 (U.S. Geological Survey, 1986), shows trails from Taos headed "to Fort Bascom" near Zaldívar's location.

13. Loomis and Nasatir, *Pedro Vial,* 289–91. A comparison of the leagues Mares traveled with descriptions in the journals of Santiago Fernández and Francisco Fragoso in 1788 and Josiah Gregg in 1839 places Mares along this route.

14. A wonderful map of the journey exists, titled *Mapa del territorio comprendido entre la provincia de Nuevo Mexico y el fuerte de Natchitoches y Texas,* the original of which is in the Archivo General de Indias in Sevilla, Spain. The map is based on Francisco Fragoso's journal and, although mainly a straight line, is accurate in terms of landmarks and distance traveled according to the scale.

15. Loomis and Nasatir, *Pedro Vial,* 319.

16. See Marcy, "Route from Fort Smith to Santa Fe," 43, and Lieutenant James H. Simpson, "Route from Fort Smith to Santa Fe," in Marcy, "Route from Fort Smith," 17.

17. Loomis and Nasatir, *Pedro Vial,* 318–22, 328–31.

18. Josiah Gregg, *Diary and Letters of Josiah Gregg: Southwestern Enterprises, 1840–1847,* vol. 1, ed. Maurice Garland Fulton (Norman: University of Oklahoma Press, 1941), 43–46.

19. Falconer, *Letters and Notes,* 90–92; Carroll, *Texan Santa Fe Trail,* 164–65, 177–79. The two most accessible accounts of the Marcy and Whipple expeditions are both by Grant Foreman: *Marcy and the Gold Seekers* (Norman: University of Oklahoma Press, 1939) and *A Pathfinder in the Southwest* (Norman: University of Oklahoma Press, 1968). The map accompanying Marcy's account was prepared by James H. Simpson and came in four sections. The last section (map 4), showing the Gallinas and Pecos Rivers, does show a road crossing just below the junction of the two rivers, in addition to one crossing at what would be the Gallinas crossing. The road crossing below the junction has the legend, "This road said to be shorter, but not practicable for wagons." Lieutenant James H. Simpson, *Maps of the Route from Fort Smith to Santa Fe, Made by Lieut. James H. Simpson of the Corps of Topographical Engineers, January 14, 1850,* Secretary of War, 31st Cong., 1st sess., Senate Executive Document no. 12, Serial 554.

20. [Juan Estevan Pino], Merced del Sitio del Ojito del Rio de las Gallinas dada a favor de Don Juan Esteban Pino con el tiendo de Hacienda de San Juan Bautista del ojito del rio de las Gallinas. Año de 1823, Preston Beck (Juan Estevan Pino) Grant. Spanish Archives of New Mexico 1, Land Records of New Mexico, 1824 (Santa Fe), SG 1, Roll 12.

21. Myers and Olsen, *Prairie Scout;* James H. Gunnerson, "Documentary Clues and Northeastern New Mexico Archaeology," *New Mexico Archaeological Council Proceedings* 6, no. 1 (1984): 45–76; Blakeslee, *Ancient Trails,* 150–51; José Antonio Cháves and Captain Juan José Arrocha, *1829 Diaries of José Antonio Cháves and Captain Juan José Arrocha,* Mexican Archives of New Mexico, roll 9, frames 870–78; Henry Judd, "Report of a Scout along the Rio Pecos by Captain Henry Judd, March 30, 1850," Arrott's Fort Union Collection, Donnelly Library, New Mexico Highlands University, Las Vegas, New Mexico, 47:153–58.

22. Two possible gentle access routes that have been suggested are directly at Rowe (see Richard Flint and Shirley Cushing Flint, "The Coronado Expedition: Cicuye to the Rio de Cicuye Bridge," *New Mexico Historical Review* 67 [April 1992]: 130) and at Glorieta.

23. Pedro de Castañeda, "Castañeda's History of the Expedition," in Hammond and Rey, *Narratives,* 234–38; Francisco Vázquez de Coronado, "Letter of Coronado to the King from the Province of Tiguex, October 20, 1541," in Hammond and Rey, *Narratives,* 186–87; Flint and Flint, "Cicuye to the Rio de Cicuye Bridge," 123–38.

24. Waldo R. Wedel, "Coronado's Route to Quivira 1541," *Plains Anthropologist* 15 (August 1970): 161–68.

NINE

Reconciling the Calendars of the Coronado Expedition: Tiguex to the Second Barranca, April and May 1541

RICHARD FLINT

THE QUESTIONS "WHEN?" AND "WHERE?" are basic to most historical and archeological research. Without answers to those questions, however tentative, events and even larger patterns of behavior are adrift in a jumbled past that permits little understanding. For both disciplines, context is indispensable to the process of comprehension, and time and place are the two essential anchors of their contextual placement. For the pivotal events of the Coronado expedition of 1540–42, it is surprising how imprecise is the information about places and times that has been teased out of the documents by historians and sifted out of the ground by archeologists. Beyond bracketing time by years and seasons and place by geographical regions, researchers have rarely been able to pin down the location of the expedition, the native peoples it encountered, the specific terrain it passed through, or the interactions among these three elements, either in time or in space. That is not for lack of trying—witness several chapters in this volume alone that detail painstaking efforts to more precisely delimit the places and peoples witnessed and affected by the expedition (see chapters 5, 6, 8, and 10).

Very slowly over the past century and a half, historians, archeologists, ethnohistorians, and geographers have been able to locate with some certainty a few spots in the Greater Southwest—principally indigenous communities—where American natives and Europeans, as represented by the Coronado expedition, first came together: Culiacán, Petatlán, the Zuni pueblos, Acoma Pueblo, the southern Tiwa pueblos, Zia Pueblo, San Juan Pueblo, Taos Pueblo, Pecos Pueblo, Blanco Canyon (Texas), and Rice County (Kansas). And it has become increasingly likely that the expedition passed through or spent time in a number of other places over its four-thousand-mile course: the Sonora River valley, the San Pedro River valley, the Sulfur Springs Valley, Santiago Pueblo, Cañon Blanco (New Mexico), and the Canadian River valley. All in all, though, we can place the expedition with assurance at only a relatively few, widely separated points.

As scant as our specific geographical knowledge is with regard to the Coronado expedition, researchers have devoted significantly less attention to its precise placement in time. There are some notable exceptions, including chapter 2 of this volume and William Hartmann's earlier work on the reconnaissance of fray Marcos de Niza.[1] Nevertheless, many stretches of time during the course of the expedition have not been carefully studied. One in particular is the time between late April and late May 1541, during which the expedition traveled from its base in the Rio Grande Valley of New Mexico to an area known to at least some natives as Cona, on the eastern fringe of the Llano Estacado. The documentary basis for study of this interval seems confused and often contradictory. A more precise definition of the chronology of events during this month, however, would significantly affect efforts to define the expedition's geographical position over a great expanse of territory. It would also help in locating and therefore identifying the seminomadic peoples the expedition encountered on the Great Plains.

Documentary Sources, April and May 1541

Crucial information used for more than a hundred years in attempts to determine the route of the Coronado expedition from its base in Tiguex to Cona and then on to Quivira has been the dates assigned to expeditionary events in three contemporary documents: AGI, Patronato, 184, R.34, Vázquez de Coronado's letter to the king, Tiguex, October 20, 1541; New York Public Library, Rich Collection, no. 63, Pedro de Castañeda's *Relación* (Culiacán) (1560s), copy made in Sevilla, October 26, 1596; and AGI, Patronato, 20, N.5, R.8, Juan de Jaramillo's narrative (New Spain) (1560s). Though all were written by members of the expedition, the dates provided in the three documents appear at first to be at wide variance and, if used singly and uncritically, seem consistent with divergent possible itineraries. I suggest instead that if several plausible, indeed likely, assumptions are made, then most of the apparent discrepancies vanish, and the documents are in substantial congruence and therefore point to a much narrower range of route possibilities.

All documentary sources agree that between the spring and fall of 1541 the Coronado expedition, comprising perhaps as many as two thousand persons and several thousand head of livestock, traveled from the Tiguex area near modern

Bernalillo, New Mexico, to a series of large barrancas, or canyons, in or adjacent to the area called Cona, probably in the Texas Panhandle or South Plains. There, most of the company was ordered back to Tiguex while the captain general and a small group proceeded on to Quivira, quite likely in the area of present-day Lyons, Kansas.

The Calendar Change, Julian to Gregorian

Despite broad documentary agreement, researchers trying to trace the daily progress of the expedition meet difficulty from the beginning. The captain general, writing to the king shortly after his return to Tiguex in the fall of 1541, said that he had left from Tiguex "a Veynte y tres del mes de abryll" (on April 23).[2] Juan de Jaramillo did not report the date of departure, whereas Pedro de Castañeda's *Relación* reported unequivocally that "salio el campo de tiguex a çinco de mayo" (the expedition left Tiguex on the fifth of May).[3] This presents a discrepancy of twelve days between the dates provided by Vázquez de Coronado's letter and Castañeda's *Relación*.

The difference can be partially reconciled by taking into account when the documents were written. With regard to Vázquez de Coronado's letter, what has been preserved in the Archivo General de Indias in Sevilla, Spain, is the signed original, dated at Tiguex "xx de octubre de 1UDxli años" (October 20, 1541) in the Julian calendar,[4] which was then the calendar of the Roman Catholic world. From internal evidence, it is clear that Pedro de Castañeda wrote his undated *Relación* during the 1560s, still under the Julian calendar. The original document, however, is not known to exist. Instead, what survives is a copy made in Sevilla "a veinte y seis de octubre de mill y quinientos y noventa y seis anos" (October 26, 1596).[5] What happened between the 1560s and 1596 is that Pope Gregory XIII promulgated a new calendar, dropping ten days from the year 1582. By papal decree, October 4, 1582, was followed immediately by October 15. Spain adopted the new calendar immediately. Thus, the scribe who prepared the 1596 copy of Castañeda's *Relación* lived and worked under the Gregorian calendar. That becomes relevant to reconciling the Vázquez de Coronado letter with Castañeda's *Relación* because scribes of sixteenth-century Spain almost never, except for very short documents, made exact or verbatim copies when they "duplicated" documents. They regularly altered texts in making copies, when they suspected errors or when their own usages differed from those of the original scribe. I suggest that in this case the 1596 scribe, *licenciado* Bartolomé Niño Velásquez, modernized the dates given in the original, converting them to New Style, or Gregorian, dates.

Travel of the Expedition in Spatially Separate Units

By itself, this assumption would account for ten of the twelve days that separate the statements in Vázquez de Coronado's letter and the copy of Castañeda's *Relación*. The remaining two-day difference might have come about in one of a couple of ways. One possibility is again scribal. If the scribe in the 1560s had used arabic numerals to designate April 23, the 1596 scribe might have read the *3* as a *5*, a not uncommon mistake among both sixteenth-century scribes and modern paleographers. Thus, he might have thought he was modernizing April 25 in the Julian calendar, which would yield May 5 in the Gregorian.

Another possibility, and the one I accept, is that the unit of the expedition that included Castañeda actually left Tiguex on the second day after the captain general. It is clear that the expedition did not generally travel as a monolithic mass, but rather as companies with an interval of space and time between each succeeding unit.[6] So it is conceivable, though hardly proven, that both documents are accurate—that the captain general departed from Tiguex on April 23 (Julian), as he wrote, and the group including Castañeda got under way on April 25 (Julian), or May 5 (Gregorian) (table 9.1). At any rate, I assume that the two documents record the same event of departure and are in essential agreement about when that event occurred. In my reconstruction, the entire expedition was, in any case, back together again at the crossing of the Río de Cicuique, as will be seen shortly.[7]

Total Elapsed Time and Two Major Stages

Before going on to individual segments of travel as the expedition progressed away from Tiguex and toward Cona and Quivira (see map 8.1), let me deal with the time taken by the expedition to complete the next two large stages of its march. That is, how long did it take to reach the second barranca or canyon on the edge of the Llano Estacado, and when did the party reached the Río de San Pedro y San Pablo on the march to Quivira? According to Castañeda's *Relación,* the expedition "hicieronse hasta aqui treinta y siete jornadas de camino de a seis y de a siete leguas" (had made thirty-seven days of travel of from six to seven leagues each up to this point [the second barranca]).[8] Thus, I would expect the date of arrival at the second barranca to have been about May 31 (Julian), or June 10 (Gregorian).

From the second barranca the captain general ordered the bulk of the expedition to return to Tiguex while he and a small, select unit continued toward Quivira. The select unit proceeded probably in a generally northerly direction, reaching a large river on the "dia de san pedro y san pablo" ([feast] day of Saints Peter and Paul).[9] As it is today, that feast was celebrated in 1541 on June 29 (Julian). Jaramillo reported that it took the select unit "mas de treynta dias U casi

Table 9.1

Time Line for the Coronado Expedition, Tiguex to the Second Barranca

Date (Julian)	Day	Date (Gregorian)	Days Elapsed		Event
			Coronado	Castañeda	
4/23	Sat	5/3	1	—	Departure from Tiguex (Cor)
4/24	Sun	5/4	2	—	
4/25	Mon	5/5	3	1	Departure from Tiguex (Cas)
4/26	Tues	5/6	4	2	Reached Cicuique (Cor)
4/27	Wed	5/7	5	3	
4/28	Thur	5/8	6	4	
4/29	Fri	5/9	7	5	Reached Río de Cicuique (Cor)
4/30	Sat	5/10	8	6	Reached Cicuique (Cas)
5/1	Sun	5/11	9	7	
5/2	Mon	5/12	10	8	
5/3	Tues	5/13	11	9	Bridge finished (Cor)
5/4	Wed	5/14	12	10	Reached Río de Cicuique (Cas)
5/5	Thur	5/15	13	11	River crossed (all)
5/6	Fri	5/16	14	12	
5/7	Sat	5/17	15	13	
5/8	Sun	5/18	16	14	Saw first bison (Jar)
5/9	Mon	5/19	17	15	
5/10	Tues	5/20	18	16	
5/11	Wed	5/21	19	17	
5/12	Thur	5/22	20	18	Saw first bison (Cas)
5/13	Fri	5/23	21	19	Encountered Querechos (Cor) (Probably also Jar)
5/14	Sat	5/24	22	20	Encountered Querechos (Cas)
5/15	Sun	5/25	23	21	
5/16	Mon	5/26	24	22	Second Querechos (Cas)
5/17	Tues	5/27	25	23	
5/18	Wed	5/28	26	24	Reached Llano (Cor)
5/19	Thur	5/29	27	25	López dispatched (Cas)
5/20	Fri	5/30	28	26	
5/21	Sat	5/31	29	27	
5/22	Sun	6/1	30	28	Maldonado dispatched (Cas)
5/23	Mon	6/2	31	29	
5/24	Tues	6/3	32	30	
5/25	Wed	6/4	33	31	
5/26	Thur	6/5	34	32	Reached first barranca (Cas)
5/27	Fri	6/6	35	33	Exploring parties dispatched (Cas)
5/28	Sun	6/7	36	34	
5/29	Mon	6/8	37	35	
5/30	Tues	6/9	38	36	
5/31	Wed	6/10	39	37	Reached second barranca (Cas) Left second barranca (Jar)
...	...	...			
6/29	Wed	7/9	68		Reached Río de San Pedro y San Pablo (Jar)

Key: "Cor" denotes Coronado's account, "Cas," Castañeda's, and "Jar," Jaramillo's.

treynta dias de camino" (more than thirty days or nearly thirty days of travel) to get from the second barranca to the Río de San Pedro y San Pablo.[10] This would put departure from the second barranca on about May 30 or 31 (Julian), which jibes well with arrival at the second barranca on May 31 (Julian), as already determined independently.[11]

Thus, it seems clear that in looking at the expedition's travel between Tiguex and the second barranca, the individual segments in aggregate cannot extend beyond May 31 (Julian). With that knowledge, let me now turn to individual travel segments.

Tiguex to the Querecho Rancherías, April 23–May 18

The available documentary testimony about the first segment of travel from Tiguex comes from Juan de Jaramillo, who wrote, like Castañeda, in the 1560s: "Vamos por otros dos pueblos que no se como se llaman En quatro hornadas a çicuyque" (we went by way of two other pueblos, the names of which I do not know, in four days' journey to Cicuique).[12] That puts at least the foremost unit of the expedition at Cicuique, or Pecos Pueblo, on April 26 (Julian).

For the next segment of travel, from Cicuique to the Río de Cicuique, we have two slightly divergent documentary statements regarding time of travel. Jaramillo reported "tres Hornadas" (three days' journey),[13] whereas the Castañeda *Relación* had "quatro dias andados de camino" (four days traveling on the road).[14] Again, this discrepancy may actually reflect the spread of units along the route of travel, so that the unit which included Jaramillo arrived at the river some hours or even days ahead of Castañeda's unit. Some credence is lent to this possibility by noting that Jaramillo on a number of occasions traveled with the advance guard, whereas Castañeda customarily traveled with the main body of the expedition. The advance guard evidently left Cicuique the day after it arrived, or April 27 (Julian), and arrived at the Río de Cicuique on April 29 (Julian).

At this point, the Castañeda narrative states, it was necessary to build a bridge to cross the river, which was flowing very deep and fast. That project, again according to the Castañeda *Relación,* "acabose en quatro dias" (was finished in four days).[15] That time would have allowed all of the trailing units of the expedition to catch up with the vanguard, so that as the Castañeda narrative says, "hecha paso todo el campo y ganados por ella" (when [the bridge] was finished, the whole expedition and all the livestock crossed by means of it).[16] This places the entire expedition on the east side of the Río de Cicuique (Pecos River) on May 4 (Julian), or May 14 (Gregorian). Twenty-seven days remained, therefore, before it was to arrive at the second barranca.

As Jaramillo wrote, at this point "començamos A Entrar por los llanos donde hay las Vacas" (we began to enter upon the plains where there are bison).[17] And indeed, the character of the land east of the Pecos becomes immediately more level. As the expedition headed east through the broad drainage of the Canadian River, the men saw wide corridors of gently undulating terrain. However, writes

Jaramillo, "no las hallamos a mas de a quatro U çinco hornadas" (we did not find them [the bison] for more than four or five days' travel),[18] that is, not until May 7 or 8 (Julian) or perhaps somewhat later.

By contrast, the Castañeda narrative relates that in "otras diez jornadas" (another ten days' travel) after crossing the bridge, the expedition encountered rancherías of nomadic Querechos.[19] The report goes on to say that "havia dos dias que se havian visto vacas" (it had been two days since [bison] had [first] been seen).[20] That would have been May 12 (Julian) or May 22 (Gregorian), allowing one day for the river crossing itself. It is quite possible that the coming of the advance guard forced the first group of bison eastward, effectively clearing the route of bison for some distance, so that the following units (including the one Castañeda was in) did not see their first bison until considerably farther to the east than did the vanguard. This would explain the difference of four days between the Jaramillo and Castañeda documents in regard to the first sighting of bison.

According to the Castañeda narrative, then, the expedition first met Querechos in their camps on May 14 (Julian), or May 24 (Gregorian). It is possible to check that date with information contained in Vázquez de Coronado's October 1541 letter to the king and with Jaramillo's narrative. The periods of travel referred to at this point in all three documents are remarkably congruent. In the captain general's letter, he wrote that "a los diez y siete dias de camino tope Una rrancheria de yndios . . . querechos" (after seventeen days of travel [from Tiguex] I encountered an encampment of Indians . . . [called] Querechos).[21] On the face of it, that would put the first meeting with Querechos on May 10 (Julian). I suggest, though, that Vázquez de Coronado, quite naturally, was not counting the four days spent building the bridge as days of travel. If that is the case, then seventeen travel days would correspond to a total elapsed time of twenty-one days, putting the encounter with the nomad Querechos on May 13 (Julian), in close agreement with the Castañeda document, restored to Julian time. Under this assumption, the expedition was still spread out, with the unit including Castañeda a day behind the one in which Jaramillo and the captain general traveled. Though less clear cut, the Jaramillo narrative points to a natural period in the expedition's march at this same time. He writes, "AnduVimos como hasta ocho U diez dias" (we traveled eight or ten days).[22] The three documents seem to echo a single milestone in the expedition's course, a point worthy of remark: the first encounter with bison-hunting Indians on May 13 or 14 (Julian), with seventeen to eighteen days remaining until arrival at the second barranca.

From this first Querecho camp onward, the expedition's chief guide, a Plains native whom the Spaniards called El Turco, led the whole party "a mas que al este" (farther to the east).[23] Seeing this, a second guide, known as Isopete, dramatically insisted, according to Jaramillo's account, that "no havia de yr por ally ny Era Aquel nuestro Camyno" ([he] must not go that way nor was that our route).[24]

"Desde a dos dias que todavia caminaba el campo a el rrumbo" (after two days during which the expedition was still traveling on the [same] course),[25] says Castañeda, more encamped Querechos were seen, which takes us to May 16 (Julian). At this point, again according to Castañeda, Garcia López de Cárdenas, the *maestre de campo,* broke his arm, and a man became lost "por ser la tierra muy llana" (because the land is very flat).[26] The comment about flat land probably signals the arrival of the expedition on the Llano Estacado, although the apparent conjunction of arrival at the Llano and the presence of the second Querecho village is probably misleading. In the first place, Vázquez de Coronado, in his October letter, wrote that "camine otros çinco dias hasta llegar a Unos llanos Tan sin seña como si estoVieramos engolfados en la mar" (I traveled another five days until I arrived at some plains so without landmarks that it was as if we were in the middle of the sea).[27] This indicates that the expedition saw Querechos only *before* reaching the Llano, which did not occur until three days' travel beyond the second Querecho encampment, or May 18 (Julian) for the vanguard.

The captain general's timing of arrival at the Llano seems more credible than that recorded in the Castañeda narrative because of evidence from another document, the "Relación del suceso." Its anonymous author wrote—probably shortly after the expedition's return to Mexico City in 1542—that the maestre de campo injured his arm only "Dos dias Antes" (two days before) the decision was made at the second barranca to send most of the expedition back to Tiguex.[28] In other words, the injury befell López de Cárdenas not on May 16 (Julian), as is implied in the Castañeda document, but nearly two weeks later, about May 29 (Julian). If this conclusion is correct, then Castañeda's accounts about López de Cárdenas's broken arm and the man straying away from the expedition are misplaced. Their seeming coincidence with arrival at the Llano is the product of composition of the narrative and not reflective of a linear progression of time.[29]

The Llano Estacado, May 18–31

From the vanguard's arrival at the Llano Estacado on May 18 (Julian), then, only thirteen days remained before the expedition reached the second barranca. The Castañeda narrative informs us that the following events must be fit into those thirteen days:

1. Diego López was dispatched to travel east for two days and then rejoin the

body of the expedition, which apparently kept traveling. In all likelihood this consumed at least three days total.

2. Rodrigo Maldonado was also sent ahead of the expedition. After four days of travel he and his company reached the first barranca, in which there was a large settlement of people called Teyas.

3. From the first barranca the captain general sent out exploring parties. They located other Teya settlements spread over an expanse equivalent to four days' travel, a territory known collectively as Cona. A minimum of one day and a maximum of four days may have been consumed by this scouting operation.

4. The expedition "rested" for at least one day in the first barranca.

5. The body of the expedition moved from the first barranca to the last of the Teya settlements and then proceeded to the second, or "last," barranca, which was evidently unoccupied by any native people, that summer at least. The Jaramillo narrative indicates that at least part of this movement occupied one day: "fuimos Una hornada Adelante todos" (all of us went onward for one day's travel).[30]

Assuming these were discrete, consecutive events, they total ten to thirteen days. The lower figure is three days less than the amount of time available, according to the calendars implicit in the Jaramillo and Castañeda documents. It is evident that the events must, in fact, have succeeded each other in quick succession, with the López reconnaissance starting almost as soon as the Llano was reached and followed immediately by that of Maldonado. I suggest, further, that the explorations sent out from the first barranca did not occupy four days, as has often been assumed. Instead, the figure of four days' travel really seems to apply to the geographical space inhabited by the Teyas, the extent of Cona. Thus, in my reconstruction, the expedition reached the second barranca on May 31 (Julian), the thirty-seventh elapsed day since the unit including Castañeda departed from Tiguex, just as he reported. Possibly that same day, Vázquez de Coronado and his thirty select companions left the expedition behind and headed toward Quivira, arriving twenty-nine days (nearly thirty days, as Jaramillo wrote) later, on June 29 (Julian), "el día de San Pedro y San Pablo," at the river they named in honor of the two saints.[31]

It is apparent from this reconciliation of documentary calendrical evidence that the expedition was almost constantly on the move from April 23 until May 29 (Julian), with the possible exception of days spent in the Canadian River valley. In addition, it encountered bands of Querechos only north or northwest of the Llano Estacado and Teyas only on the eastern margin of the Llano, suggesting that the immense herds of bison on the Llano itself made it too risky a place to establish camps. It would have been subject to stampedes, for example, and was characterized by fetid and fouled water. Although my reconstructed calendar does not lead inexorably to conclusions about precisely where these various native groups were located in the late spring of 1541 (but see chapter 10), it does delineate the parameters of expeditionary travel that any hypothesis about their location would have to meet. It also demonstrates that the documentary data, though superficially divergent, can be seen as in essential agreement, at least as to travel time.[32]

What Follows from the Calendar Reconciliation

The implications of this calendar for reconstruction of the expedition's route are several. First, as I mentioned earlier, it appears that Querechos were met only before the expedition reached the Llano Estacado and that the Llano itself may have been all but devoid of human occupants. Second, the expedition, once on the Llano, had to move steadily and directly to the first barranca. There simply is no surplus time that could be attributed to wandering. The expedition may have been "lost" in the sense that it was not going in the direction it wanted to go, but it was not moving either slowly or randomly. Third, the expedition was almost certainly traveling in discrete units at some distance from each other.

Perhaps the oddest thing about the calendar is the amount of time the expedition evidently took to travel from the Río de Cicuique (Pecos River) to the Llano Estacado, two full weeks. The most plausible suggestions about where the Llano was ascended put that spot along or just east of the Texas–New Mexico state line, east of Tucumcari, New Mexico (see chapter 8). If that was indeed the case, then in those two weeks of travel the expedition made only 120–130 miles, an astonishingly slow pace. One would expect the expedition to have covered that distance in eight to ten days, rather than fourteen (using the rate of six to seven leagues per day reported by Castañeda). And indeed, just previously, the expedition had covered almost exactly the same distance (around 128 miles) from Tiguex to the Río de Cicuique in eight days of travel.

If we take Castañeda at his word, then the expedition traveled thirty-seven days from Tiguex to the second barranca at a rate of at least 6 leagues a day, for a total of at least 222 leagues, more than one and a half times the probable straight-line distance. However, the aggregate documentary evidence indicates that both from Tiguex to the Río de Cicuique and from the ascent of the Llano to the second barranca, travel must have been very direct and almost exactly at the six to seven league rate. Therefore, all of the excess travel, if there actually was such, had to have occurred between the Río de Cicuique and the Llano, something not specifically pointed out in the documents.

As a first approach toward accounting for the lengthy travel time between the Río de Cicuique and the Llano, Harry Myers (chapter 8) points out the likelihood that crossing the river by bridge occupied more than a single day, given the large size of the human company and the livestock herd. Further, he reminds us that virtually all historic parties, when encountering bison for the first time, were distracted by chasing and hunting the beasts, making it not unlikely that the Coronado expedition behaved similarly, perhaps delaying for a day or two. To such factors that would have tended to slow travel can be added the time-consuming task of herding thousands of livestock around or through extensive bison herds. At first this probably proved to be a slow, almost impossible, process. Furthermore, like most long-distance travelers, the Coronado expedition could be expected to have taken rest days, although none is specifically mentioned in the contemporary documents. Although these factors are plausible ingredients in the expedition's apparently slow travel after reaching the Río de Cicuique, convincingly accounting for as many as six "extra" days of travel remains a problem facing anyone who attempts to reconstruct the expedition's route in this section.

The reconciliation of the expedition's calendar put forward here also shows that the expedition spent no more than four days in the first barranca, where it was hit by a tremendous hail and wind storm, and perhaps only one or two days. In addition, it seems clear that during the whole period of about five weeks occupied in travel from Tiguex to Cona, major decisions affecting the expedition (to send out exploring parties and in what directions, to send most of the expedition back to Tiguex, and to go in search of Quivira toward the north) were reached quickly and without hesitation and were put into effect with equal speed. There seems to have been little disagreement, if any, among the leadership of the expedition until Vázquez de Coronado, certainly following customary consultation with captains and other important persons, decided to split the expedition at the second barranca. Even in that situation, the captain general executed his decision swiftly, perhaps departing for Quivira that same day.

All in all, on the subject of time, the sixteenth-century documents mesh remarkably well, especially given their apparent conflict at first glance. The calendar that fits the documents and is outlined here raises new questions regarding rates of travel over different portions of the route, but it also severely restricts the possible locations of places such as where the expedition ascended the Llano (almost certainly at least as far east as the area of modern Adrian, Texas) and where the first barranca was (probably no farther south than Yellow House Canyon and no farther north than Quitaque Canyon in the Texas South Plains, no more than a total of about 180 miles from the Adrian area, including marches in at least two directions as so eloquently sketched by John Morris in his *El Llano Estacado,* chapter 4).[33] With the discovery nearly ten years ago of a campsite of the expedition in Blanco Canyon in Floyd County, Texas (see chapter 12), certainly Blanco must be considered the prime candidate for that first barranca. What at first seemed a tangle of inconsistencies has, in the end, allowed much more precise location of the Coronado expedition in both space and time.

Notes

This chapter had its impetus and origin in an afternoon spent with Jack Hughes in 1996, during which we made a good start on the calendar presented here. Jack continued to provide insightful comments and suggestions in the intervening years, without which the rat's nest of documentary dates would have remained just that, a rat's nest. His death in May 2001 knocked the wind out of many whom he taught and collaborated with, including myself. This chapter is especially dedicated to Jack's memory.

1. Hartmann, "Pathfinder," 73–101.
2. Vázquez de Coronado, "Letter to the King, Tiguex, 1541," fol. 1r.
3. Castañeda, *Relación,* Primera Parte, Capítulo 18, fol. 79v–80r.
4. Vázquez de Coronado, "Letter to the King, Tiguex, 1541," fol. 2v.
5. Castañeda, *Relación,* Tercera Parte, Capítulo 9, fol. 160r.
6. For instance, it is clear from Castañeda's *Relación* that while the expedition was crossing the Texas Panhandle in 1541, the rear guard was far enough behind the main body of the expedition to be out of sight. Castañeda, *Relación,* Primera Parte, Capítulo 19, fol. 84r.
7. What the customary distance was between companies on the march is not known. Bernardo de Vargas Machuca, writing in 1599, suggested that units did not get out of earshot of each other. Bernardo de Vargas Machuca, *Milicia y descripción de las Indias* (Madrid: Librería de Victoriano Suárez, 1892), 1:180–81. Nevertheless, it is clear that on several occasions during the Coronado expedition a vanguard preceded the main body by intervals of days and even weeks.
8. Castañeda, *Relación,* Primera Parte, Capítulo 20, fol. 87v.
9. Jaramillo, "Narrative," fol. 3v.
10. Jaramillo, "Narrative," fol. 3v.
11. It should be noted that additional evidence that the date of the expedition's arrival at the second barranca was May 31 or thereabouts is contained in Baltasar de Obregón's 1584 *Historia de los descubrimientos antiguos y modernos de la Nueva España* (México, D.F.: Editorial Porrúa, 1988), 23: "Desde estos llanos fué marchando el campo hasta en fin de Mayo" (the expedition was marching [through] these plains until the end of May).
12. Jaramillo, "Narrative," fol. 2v.
13. Jaramillo, "Narrative," fol. 2v.
14. Castañeda, *Relación,* Primera Parte, Capítulo 19, fol. 80v.
15. Castañeda, *Relación,* Primera Parte, Capítulo 19, fol. 81r.
16. Castañeda, *Relación,* Primera Parte, Capítulo 20, fol. 81r.
17. Jaramillo, "Narrative," fol. 2v.
18. Jaramillo, "Narrative," fol. 2v.

19. Castañeda, *Relación,* Primera Parte, Capítulo 19, fol. 81r.

20. Castañeda, *Relación,* Primera Parte, Capítulo 19, fol. 81r.

21. Vázquez de Coronado, "Letter to the King, Tiguex, 1541," fol. 1r.

22. Jaramillo, "Narrative," fol. 3r.

23. Jaramillo, "Narrative," fol. 3r.

24. Jaramillo, "Narrative," fol. 3r.

25. Castañeda, *Relación,* Primera Parte, Capítulo 19, fol. 82r.

26. Castañeda, *Relación,* Primera Parte, Capítulo 19, fol. 82r–82v.

27. Vázquez de Coronado, "Letter to the King, Tiguex, 1541," fol. 1r.

28. "Relación de suceso," AGI, Patronato, 20, N.5, R.8, fol. 4v.

29. The work of Shirley Cushing Flint and myself in completely retranscribing and retranslating the Castañeda *Relación,* in the course of the Documents of the Coronado Expedition Project, has made it clear that the manuscript is a quite sophisticated literary creation, organized at least partly for dramatic effect rather than always in strict conformance with chronology. See Flint and Flint, *"They Were Not Familiar."*

30. Jaramillo, "Narrative," fol. 3v.

31. Vázquez de Coronado could have left the second barranca a day or two later and still have spent nearly thirty days on the way to the river. How much travel (time and distance) was involved in getting from the first barranca to the second is still highly debatable. Much of the problem revolves around the highly ambiguous particle "a" in the phrase "desde alli emVio el general a descubrir y dieron en otras rrancherias a quatro jornadas." Does this mean that the exploring parties encountered other rancherías of Teyas *within the space of* four days' travel or *after* four days' travel? Both are possible translations of the Spanish. I incline toward the first possibility, "within the space of," partly because the statement would then seem virtually to repeat the information that comes just a few lines later: "duraban estos pueblos de rrancherias tres jornadas." In this case, clearly, a spatial distance and not a travel time is meant. This way, the necessity of having the main body of the expedition sit in the first barranca awaiting the discovery of other rancherías after four days can be dispensed with. This would allow the expedition instead to keep moving right behind the scouts (as apparently it often did), traveling through Cona for perhaps three or even four days. Then it would have traveled one day farther with Teya guides to the "last" barranca, making a total travel time between the first and second barrancas of as much as five days and a distance of as much as perhaps seventy-five miles. Castañeda, *Relación,* Primera Parte, Capítulo 19, fol. 86r.

32. A subject about which the Coronado expedition documents are silent is whether and how often the expedition stopped along its march in order to rest and recover. It seems hardly credible that marching would have continued every day without break. Instead, in all probability some of the days listed on the calendar were spent in camp, recuperating and repairing for continuation of the march, although there is no documentary mention of days of rest. A similar lack exists for other contemporary expeditions, such as that led by Hernando de Soto. Although there were occasional stops at native settlements during the Soto expedition's march, what the hidalgo de Elvas wrote remains true—that " most of the time they were on the march." Lawrence A. Clayton, Vernon James Knight Jr., and Edward C. Moore, eds., *The De Soto Chronicles: the Expedition of Hernando de Soto to North America in 1539–1543* (Tuscaloosa: University of Alabama Press, 1993), 1:77.

33. John Miller Morris, *El Llano Estacado: Exploration and Imagination on the High Plains of Texas and New Mexico, 1536–1860* (Austin: Texas State Historical Association, 1997), 45–57.

TEN

Bison Hunters of the Llano in 1541: A Panel Discussion

DONALD J. BLAKESLEE, DOUGLAS K. BOYD,
RICHARD FLINT, JUDITH HABICHT-MAUCHE,
NANCY P. HICKERSON, JACK T. HUGHES,
AND CARROLL L. RILEY

EARLY IN THE SUMMER OF 1541 the Coronado expedition met several encampments of bison-hunting nomadic or seminomadic people as the expedition moved generally eastward from Cicuique–Cicuye–Pecos Pueblo in New Mexico. After some thirteen or fourteen days of travel from Pecos, the expedition came upon a tent settlement of people they understood were called Querechos by the Pueblos. According to what Vázquez de Coronado and Pedro de Castañeda, one of the members of the expedition, wrote, the Querechos subsisted almost entirely by hunting bison. After perhaps only twelve hours the Querechos broke camp and parted company with the expedition, using large numbers of dogs to transport their belongings.

Two days later the expedition saw other Querechos, who reported large native settlements farther to the east. This took place on very level land on which the expedition traveled for some eight more days until it found a settlement of other tent-dwelling Indians in a barranca, or canyon. Reconnaissance parties sent out from there ran across other settlements of people known at Teyas. The territory where their camps were was known as Cona and could be traversed in three days. Again according to Castañeda, with corroboration by Juan de Jaramillo, another expedition member, the Teyas lived off the bison and were all but indistinguishable from the Querechos, with whom, the captain general wrote, they were enemies.

During a panel session held as part of the conference in 2000 from which this book arose, moderator Richard Flint submitted a series of questions to each of six distinguished panel members. The questions dealt with the distinction between the archeological Garza and Tierra Blanca complexes, whether that distinction has cultural significance, and whether it is appropriate to equate the distinction with that between the Querechos and Teyas of the Coronado documents. The panel included Donald J. Blakeslee, Douglas K. Boyd, Judith Habicht-Mauche, Nancy P. Hickerson, Jack T. Hughes, and Carroll L. Riley.

The main issues were, Who were the Querechos and Teyas, and what evidence can archeology and ethnohistory bring to bear on the question? Specifically, correspondence between the distinctions Garza–Tierra Blanca and Teya-Querecho (or lack of such correspondence) is extremely important for investigating and understanding the Jimmy Owens Site in Blanco Canyon, Floyd County, Texas, and the route of the Coronado expedition in Texas more generally.

The Discussion

The discussion opened with a couple of questions of a theoretical nature, regarding the legitimacy of linking archeological "complexes" with cultural groups.

Q: What are the difficulties involved in equating any archeological complex with specific groups such as tribes, biological populations, ethnic groups, or speech communities?

Blakeslee: The Coronado documents give us essentially three names. Two names are applied apparently by a Puebloan or Quiviran guide to local groups of people, Querechos and Teyas. The third name is different; Cona is evidently a name the Teyas said applied to a geographical entity within which they lived,. So we have here names of two ethnic groups and a name of a territory. Speaking just in terms of the cultural present of ethnography, one can't jump from a name applied by outsiders to the assumption that it refers to a single biological population (within which people find their marriage partners and not outside it). You can't leap to the conclusion that those people all spoke the same language. And you can't leap to the conclusion that they had a political system that defined them. And you can't assume that they had a single political organization, either.

We in the modern world live in societies that tend to create correlations between political units, biological populations, and language communities. The societies that Coronado encountered on the Plains were not organized in that fashion. Many Plains Indians lived in multilingual societies. The Kiowa tribe included Apache speakers, the Cheyenne tribe included Siouan speakers, and the northern Shoshone included Paiute speakers. These groups did not have strong, centralized political authorities that might have enforced some sort of uniformity; in fact, it is a misnomer to speak of an Apache tribe as opposed to many completely independent Apache bands.

Habicht-Mauche: Since ethnogenesis is primarily a discursive process, this process is not obviously or necessarily manifested materially, either in the archeological record or in modern material culture. However, that is not to say that it is never reflected in the material record. In fact, under certain circumstances identity and cultural differences are displayed and marked with material culture. This is especially true in situations where there is intense and socially ambiguous interaction between peoples—where there is potential for conflict or competition, or where identity or social boundaries may be ambiguous or under negotiation.

That being said, when I look at the archeological complexes that have been identified in the southern Plains for the sixteenth century, I do not see any evidence, in the materials that have come down to us, for conscious social or ethnic marking. Of course, this material is only a very small fraction of material culture that was extant in the sixteenth century. References in the ethnohistoric record to tattooing and body painting by some southern Plains groups and not others may be indicative of such a material process for marking ethnic differences. But in the stone and bone tool collections and in the ceramic materials, I do not see a strong example of people consciously marking social identity through differences in material style.

There is another way that archeologists think about and define the notion of style, however. Style can also be imbedded in broad technological traditions that are learned in social contexts, passed down from one generation to another. In this sense, style represents a particular way of doing something and does not necessarily reflect a conscious attempt at communication or symboling. Such technological traditions tend to be associated with basic lifeways and the tools that people use in pursuing these lifeways. Such technological traditions are not necessarily so reflective of specific group identities. Certainly groups that speak different languages and who would self-identify, or that others would identify, as belonging to different ethnic groups can and do share many technological traditions.

During the period we are concerned with here, the sixteenth century, we see much technological convergence among groups on the southern Plains, so that peoples from very different historical, ethnic, and linguistic origins came to share very similar technological styles and traditions. For example, everybody used small triangular projectile points with either no notches or two or three. So the distribution of Garza points is not likely by itself to distinguish different ethnic groups.

All the southern Plains peoples were hunting bison; they all used teepees and followed dog nomadism. I would argue, however, that the folks we see on the Llano in the sixteenth century were not generic hunters and gatherers; they were not generalized foragers; they were specialized bison hide producers. They were commodity producers, not self-sufficient hunters and gatherers. In the period from about 1400 to 1450, this highly specialized, highly mobile bison-hunting mode of life spread to the southern Plains. This commodity producing mode displaces an earlier farming mode for people here. Resident Plains Village folk, such as the Antelope Creek people, are being displaced as Athapaskan groups move in, bringing this highly mobile lifestyle with them. Other resident Plains Village groups that had been in the area for a long time or who were moving in from the east also adopted this very mobile and specialized lifestyle. I think the archeology of the Llano Estacado really shows this demographic and economic transition as it played out in the fifteenth and sixteenth centuries. As a result, the technological traditions of these different groups, both immigrant Athapaskans and resident Plains Villagers, were converging at this time, making it very hard, but not impossible, to sort them out in the archeological and material record.

Boyd: Linking protohistoric archeological remains with specific groups of people (ethnic, biological, or linguistic) is especially tricky even under the best circumstances. The best case scenario for ethnographic evidence is when there are numerous contemporary observations of Native American groups within a region and the observations are full of pertinent details about the distinguishing characteristics of each group. The best case scenario for archeological evidence is when a complex or phase is well defined based on extensive excavation data, including discrete components from a variety of sites that may be reasonably linked together as representing a single culture in time and space. Unfortunately, understanding the Native American cultural groups in the Texas Panhandle–Great Plains during the centuries of European contact is particularly challenging because of limitations on both these fronts.

The problem is further compounded by the fact that Native American groups during the centuries of European contact were changing rapidly. Decimated by diseases and displaced by population pressures and intersocietal warfare, native peoples' lifestyles changed dramatically during this time, and material culture reflects some of these transformations. In the archeological record, for example, we see the importance of certain stone tool technologies and of distinctive implements such as arrow points diminish throughout the protohistoric period. Archeologically, it is difficult enough to recognize a specific group of people and interpret what their lifestyle was like even during long periods of cultural stability. It is much more difficult for the protohistoric period, a relatively short time span characterized by radical cultural changes.

Q: What kinds of evidence were used to define the Tierra Blanca and Garza complexes? What is the likelihood that these kinds of evidence (lithic sources, point styles) correlate with ethnographic entities such as tribes, bands, languages, etc.?

Habicht-Mauche: Actually, Jack Hughes defined these two complexes and saw them as distinct. Tierra Blanca sites are concentrated in the Red River drainage, extending as far east as Palo Duro Canyon [see map 10.1, table 10.1]. The complex consists of two site types: temporary camp sites and base camp sites. Temporary camp sites are very ephemeral on the landscape, being exposed by small blowouts on the northern Llano. Entire surface collections from two or three of these sites can fit into a single small box. They usually consist of a small lithic scatter, a pot drop, and or the remains of a teepee ring. In contrast, base camps are located on the first terrace of the river in more protected areas, below the rims of canyons. The major difference between the two kinds of Tierra Blanca sites is in the amount and diversity of material, which is probably related to both the size and duration of occupation at each. Trade items such as obsidian, turquoise, and Southwestern pottery are recovered from the base camp sites more often than from temporary camp sites.

Hughes: After much experience trying to connect archeological complexes with historic tribes, I'm very reluctant to have any fixed opinions whatsoever. I am acutely aware of the pitfalls and problems and I would like to emphasize that to have any luck at all, we need to come at it from as many directions as possible.

The difference between the two types of Tierra Blanca sites is function. There are the wintering-over or base camp sites, and then the little hunting sites are bison processing sites. Tierra Blanca base camp sites are littered with imported trade ware, Rio Grande polychrome from Galisteo or some other pueblo. Also bean pot utility ware was being exported from the pueblos. A site at Quitaque, for example, is littered with this same ware: a dark, thin, spittoon shape used for bean pots. It is the most common ware in our part of the world for the last several centuries. The big sites have glaze polychrome storage vessels and some of the bean pot ware. The tiny bison processing sites have bison bone, hide scrapers, Harahey knives, and, if you're lucky, a broken pot, usually one of these bean pots. These bean pots are what Kidder called Pecos plain striated. I think what we find here should properly be called Pecos plain striated. Kidder did not limit it to Pecos; it was a utility ware for much of the eastern pueblos.

The arrow points from the bison processing sites are triangular; they are not like the ones from Antelope Creek, or Panhandle Aspect, or Can-Ark or any Canadian breaks people who had side-notched points. Washitas and Harrell

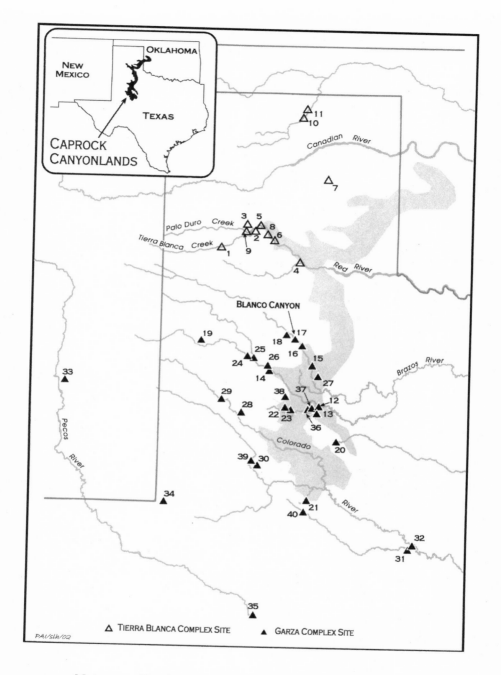

Map 10.1. Key sites of the Tierra Blanca and Garza Complexes, as defined by Douglas K. Boyd in *Caprock Canyonlands Archaeology*, figs. 98 and 99, tables 85 and 89. Map by Sandy Hannum.

DONALD J. BLAKESLEE, DOUGLAS K. BOYD, RICHARD FLINT, ET. AL. 169

Table 10.1
Key Sites of the Tierra Blanca and Garza Complexes

Map Key	Site Name (Number)	Site Type	Source
Tierra Blanca Complex Sites			
1	Tierra Blanca (41DF3)	Residential base or base camp	Holden 1931; Spielmann 1982, 1983
2	Blackburn (41RD20)	Residential base or base camp	Spielmann 1982, 1983
3	Fifth Green (PPHM-A1363)	Bison kill or hunting camp	Kalokowski 1986
4	Tule Mouth sites (41B73, 81, and 83)	Bison kill or hunting camp	Katz and Katz 1976
5	Palisades (PPHM-A530)	Bison kill or hunting camp	See Boyd 1997
6	Cita Mouth (PPHM-A288)	Bison kill or hunting camp	See Boyd 1997
7	Fatheree (41GY32)	Bison kill or hunting camp	Hughes et al. 1978
8	Water Crossing no. 2 (PPHM-A148)	Bison kill or hunting camp	See Boyd 1997
9	Canyon City Club Cave (PPHM-A251)	Rockshelter (with burial)	Hughes 1969
10	Broken Jaw (41HF8)*	Residential base or base camp	Quigg et al. 1993
11	Unnamed Shelter (41HF86)*	Rockshelter	Quigg et al. 1993
Garza Complex Sites			
12	Longhorn (41KT53)	Residential base or base camp	Boyd et al. 1993; Boyd 1997
13	Headstream (41KT51)	Residential base or base camp	Boyd et al. 1993; Boyd 1997
14	Slaton Dump (41LU6)	Residential base or base camp	Riggs 1968; Brown 1972; Booker and Campbell 1978
15	Pete Creek (SMU-X41CB1)	Residential base or base camp	Parsons 1967
16	Bridwell (41CB27)	Residential base or base camp	Parker 1982, 1990
17	Montgomery (41FL17)	Residential base or base camp	Word 1965; Northern 1979
18	Floydada Country Club (41FL1)	Residential base or base camp	Skinner 1975; Word 1963, 1991
19	Yellow Houses Ruins	Residential base or base camp	See Boyd 1997
20	Greene Springs	Residential base or base camp	Portis et al. 1968
21	Davis Hackberry Spring (41ST87)	Residential base or base camp	Riemenschneider 1996
22	Garza (SPAS-41GA40)	Bison kill or hunting camp	Runkles 1964
23	Lott (41GR56)	Bison kill or hunting camp	Runkles and Dorchester 1987
24	Lubbock Lake (41LU1)	Bison kill or hunting camp	Green 1962; Johnson et al. 1977; Johnson 1987
25	Canyon Lakes sites (41LU26/35)	Bison kill or hunting camp	Bandy et al. 1980
26	Johnson Creek (TTC 17-6)	Bison kill or hunting camp	Wheat 1955
27	Red Mud Creek (SMU-X41DK2)	Bison kill or hunting camp	Parsons 1967
28	Unnamed (41LY42)	Bison kill or hunting camp	Hart 1976
29	Hogue (41TY2)	Bison kill or hunting camp	Pope 1991
30	Mitchell Lake (41MT41)	Bison kill or hunting camp	Alvey 1978
31	Elm Creek (41CN95)	Bison kill or hunting camp	Treece et al. 1993
32	Unnamed (41CN78)	Bison kill or hunting camp	
33	Garnsey Spring sites (LA-18399/18400)	Bison kill or hunting camp	Speth and Parry 1978, 1980; Speth 1983; Parry and Speth 1984
34	Blue Mountain Rockshelter	Rockshelter	Holden 1938
35	Red Bluff Shelter (SMU-X41CX8)	Rockshelter	Lorrain 1968
36	Boren Shelters no. 1 and 2 (41GR546/559)	Rockshelter	Boyd et al. 1994; Boyd 1997
37	Reed Shelter (41GR54)	Rockshelter	Riggs 1966
38	Garza County Cave (SPAS-GR269)	Rockshelter	Harper and Shedd 1969
39	Garza Burial (SPAS-41MT40)	Burial	Gates and Hart 1977
40	Garza-U-Ranch Burial	Burial	See Boyd 1997

* Site is classified as "Tierra Blanca–like."

triple-notched are rather different looking from the ones we see with the Tierra Blanca complex. Those points are narrow based with a sinuous head, a little constriction above the base. They are more like the eastern Texas points, Talco points. Some are tiny, some short, but they all have the narrow base. They are exceptionally well made. These Tierra Blanca people made incredibly fine points from Alibates chert. One thing these Tierra Blanca sites do not have is Garza points. It is almost as if it were a different world, in terms of points. These Tierra Blanca bison hunters were not going to go out and kill a bunch of buffalo and process them, too. The women did that dirty work, skinning, butchering, and cooking; thus, the broken bean pots. That is why you find the butchering tool kit: Harahey knife, hide scraper, end scraper, tiny arrow points, and bean pots.

Boyd: Based on my archeological research in the Texas Panhandle–Plains, it is clear that there are many large gaps in our understanding of the Tierra Blanca and Garza complexes, especially regarding the diagnostic material remains that characterize them and their overall cultural similarities and differences. Of the two complexes, Tierra Blanca is the least well defined. Only at nine sites—two base camps, six bison kills–hunting camps, and one rockshelter—have investigations yielded substantive data that contributes to our understanding of this cultural group. The Garza complex is better defined, with ten residential-base camps, twelve bison kills–hunting camps, and five rockshelters attributed to the culture.

Not all of these investigations have yielded the same quality of data. I consider this to be a very small and, in some ways, inadequate archeological sample for defining these cultures. I also consider the potential links between the ethnographically recognized Querechos-Teyas and the archeologically recognized Tierra Blanca–Garza complexes as tenuous for a variety of reasons. The ethnographic evidence consists of only a handful of Spanish observations, both primary and secondary, that are spread thin through time and across space. The accounts provide tantalizing clues but precious few details that help distinguish one group from another. Ethnographic accounts are open to various interpretations because it is often unclear what the observers saw or meant when they wrote down their thoughts. Similarly, the current archeological evidence has many problems that limit how far we can (or should) go with our interpretations.

In a nutshell, much of our lack of understanding of the Tierra Blanca and Garza complexes boils down to sampling problems and inadequate data sets. Too few sites have been excavated, and for many of those where substantive work has been done, the evidence has not been adequately analyzed or reported. Here are two examples. First, out of the thirty-six sites mentioned before, sediment flotation and recovery and analysis of charred macrobotanical remains has been done and reported for only four sites (two Tierra Blanca and two Garza). Thus, the limited information on plant use by these peoples is obviously due to poor sampling. Second, at many of the main residential or base camp sites commonly attributed to the Garza complex (for example, Bridwell, Floydada Country Club, Montgomery, Longhorn), researchers have lumped all of the cultural materials together and treated them as single-component assemblages (that is, materials left by a single group at one time period). It has often been difficult, if not impossible, to separate these materials into different occupation episodes, yet it is clear that some of these sites contain materials deposited for over several hundred years and by multiple cultural groups. Given the nature and limitations of the current archeological database, I think that much more archeological work is needed before we can link the Tierra Blanca and Garza complexes to ethnic groups with any degree of certainty. However, I do feel that we should be exploring these ideas when examining existing archeological data and as new archeological information comes to light.

Habicht-Mauche: With the Garza complex we are talking about very similar tool kits: triangular points, more traditional Harrell and Washita points, and you do get some Garza points. But there are not so many Garza points up in the Blanco Canyon area. It is unfortunate that the Garza complex is named after the Garza point, because that point type is not necessarily a distinctive or unique feature of the complex. In addition to triangular points, you get the steep-edged, snub-nosed scrapers, the four-edged Harahey knives. In the Blanco Canyon area you see richer and more diversified assemblages than in either the Tierra Blanca complex sites or in Garza sites further south, but that is probably because the Blanco Canyon sites were larger and occupied for a longer period of time.

What is most distinctive about the Garza assemblages in the Blanco Canyon area is the presence of plant processing tools, such as grinding stones, as well as reports of possible agricultural tools. Reports of a large, circular stockade at the Bridwell site also suggest a more substantial occupation in this area, and one that has close ties to contemporaneous Plains Village groups in Oklahoma, where similar structures have been found.

The ceramics from Garza sites, especially those in the Blanco Canyon area, also seem to tie this complex to Plains Village groups to the east. Garza sites are characterized by a Plains-style utility ware that has strong technological and stylistic connections to sites in southwestern Oklahoma, where similar pottery has been referred to as Edwards Plain. These pots are made by the paddle-and-anvil method typical of Plains Village ceramics. They generally have either sand or crushed rock temper. Often they are decorated with finger indenting around or near the rim. The majority of the ceramics from Garza sites are of this Plains Village style. Also present as trade wares is a significant amount of Southwestern ceramics, including Rio Grande Glaze Ware. There is also Jornada Brown Ware, Chupadero Black-on-white, and some eastern Caddo-style ceramics coming in as trade wares mixing with the indigenous Plains Village ceramic types.

Thus, I believe that there are ways in which we can distinguish broad differences between the Tierra Blanca and Garza complexes and that these differences represent long-standing adaptational and occupational histories among populations that were resident in the Llano Estacado in the sixteenth century. The most important distinction is between immigrant bison-hunting groups (Tierra Blanca–Athapaskans) who were moving into the area and who were not part of the older, local Plains Village tradition and those populations who were connected to the agricultural and semiagricultural Plains Village traditions to the east (Garza-Caddoans).

We can recognize the Garza complex as descendants of earlier Plains Village groups by the vestigial remnants of their former agricultural lifestyle, including plant processing and agricultural tools and an eastern-style, Plains Village ceramic tradition. In contrast, locally produced ceramics on Tierra Blanca sites reflect a Southwestern rather than a Plains-style technological origin. These different ceramic traditions are not things one can learn by superficial copying. They are distinctions that one learns through habitual practice and through apprenticeship with skilled craftswomen. The Southwestern and Plains-style potting traditions involve very different cognitive and motor skills. They reflect very different ways of conceiving the construction of the pots and the manipulation of clay. Once you learn to make a pot a certain way, you tend to make pots that way the rest of your life. Ethnographic studies have shown that potters do not easily or readily change their primary forming methods. Thus, these distinctions in technological style point strongly to different cultural and historical origins for the Tierra Blanca and Garza populations.

Q: For many years historians, archeologists, and ethnohistorians have disagreed about who these native groups called Querechos and Teyas were and even where the Coronado expedition was when it met them. Since 1993, though, with identification of the Jimmy Owens Site as a likely campsite of the expedition, there can be little doubt that the Teyas must have lived, at least during summer months, in the canyons along the eastern margin of the Llano Estacado and that the Querechos lived somewhere between there and Pecos Pueblo, but closer to the Teyas than to Pecos.

We can confidently say that the expedition ascended the Llano somewhere in its northwest quadrant, say, between Rocky Dell near Adrian, Texas, and the Portales Valley near Taiban, New Mexico. In late May 1541, within ten days' travel (approximately 152 miles) west or northwest of the Llano's eastern escarpment, a Querecho band was camped. More Querechos were in camp about thirty miles closer to the escarpment. This would seem to place the Querechos west of and in the vicinity of the modern Texas–New Mexico state line, in the western portion of the Llano or in the Canadian or Pecos River valleys along the Llano's northern and western edges.

Given what is now known about the protohistoric cultures of the Llano, is there more than one candidate for who the Querechos were?

Boyd: Yes. While I like the ideas that Querecho equals Tierra Blanca and Teya equals Garza for their inherent simplicity and neatness, it would be foolish to think that we know all the answers. We should not rule out the possibility that both Tierra Blanca and Garza represent different groups of Apachean peoples and that we have not yet recognized the remains of the Teyas. We also should keep open minds and not rule out the possibility that Tierra Blanca does not represent the Querechos.

With that cautionary note said, I think there are some strong lines of circumstantial evidence that suggest these possible connections have considerable merit. There admittedly are serious gaps in our archeological knowledge of the Texas Panhandle–Plains region, but Tierra Blanca and Garza are the only archeological complexes currently recognized as representing protohistoric peoples. Geographically they are in the right place and the right time to be the prime candidates for Querechos and Teyas. Perhaps the best evidence is the clear ethnographic observations that the Querechos and Teyas were enemies, coupled with what seem to be well-defined and mutually exclusive territories of the Tierra Blanca and Garza complexes.

Q: Are the protohistoric Querechos specifically distinguishable in the archeological record? More precisely, does what has been called the Tierra Blanca complex represent a distinct cultural group, and if so, does it correspond to the Querechos? Or on the other hand, is the artifact assemblage that defines the Tierra Blanca complex not exclusive to a particular cultural group or not able to be associated with the Querechos?

Boyd: I think there is some reality to the Tierra Blanca complex representing a distinct group of people, and the most likely candidate is the Querechos or Apaches. As I said earlier, however, we should be cautious before jumping to conclusions, and we really need to get more reliable archeological data from more sites and conduct more intensive comparative studies of existing data. The danger is that researchers will begin to indiscriminately interpret archeological remains using this model rather than testing the model using archeological data. Here is one clear example of how ethnographic evidence has been misused in the past. For many years there has been widespread and careless use in the archeological literature of the term "Apache pottery" to denote any micaceous ware found out on the southern Plains. By inference, then, a site yielding micaceous pottery becomes an "Apache" site, a designation that has been used many times. The simple fact is that this is extremely misleading at best and probably dead wrong in many cases. There is still a lively debate as to which Apache groups made pottery, how much they made, and where they were when they made it.

What is certain is that large amounts of micaceous pottery were made in the northern Rio Grande pueblos and that these wares were traded to many different Plains groups, not just Apaches. Coupled with this problem is the simple semantic issue that has yet to be defined: How much mica does it take to be micaceous?

Habicht-Mauche: Yes, I think there is a correlation between Tierra Blanca and Querecho and between Garza and Teya.

Riley: Assuming that Tierra Blanca and Garza are separate traditions, with the dating we have, I think that Tierra Blanca equates with Querecho and Garza equates with Teya.

Hickerson: I don't really have the expertise to posit archeological connections, but based on the geographical distribution, I agree with Cal Riley that there is a relationship.

Blakeslee: What we have is two names for ethnic groups in the documentary record and two archeological complexes. While working on the Jimmy Owens Site, I have pondered the possible relationships many times, and a simple one-to-one correlation between the two names in the documents and the two archeological complexes fits the record. The Jimmy Owens Site is either the camp in the first barranca or the camp in the last and largest barranca seen by the Spaniards. If the Garza complex represents the Teyas, the Jimmy Owens Site is at the northern end of Cona, as the Garza complex is mostly south of Blanco Canyon. This would imply that the first camp is in a smaller canyon south of Blanco by more than one day of travel, as the documents say clearly that the Spaniards traveled through the Teya country from the first camp and then one more day of travel to the second. In their explorations of Cona, the Spaniards would have had to have missed Yellow House Canyon, which is far larger than Blanco.

If the Jimmy Owens Site is the location of the first meeting with the Teyas, then the Spaniards would have had to explore south from there, as the Garza country is to the south. Yellow House Canyon would be a good candidate for the last and larger barranca, but this makes the expedition's route back to New Mexico something of a mystery. The best route across the Llano Estacado from Yellow House Canyon is straight up Yellow House Draw, but the documents make it very clear that part of the route back lay up on the trackless plains. If, for whatever reason, the expedition backtracked to a Teya village in Blanco Canyon and then went across the plains, two problems arise. The first is that no one has found any early Spanish trade goods in any of the Garza sites in the canyon. The second is that the route back would have been nearly as long as the route eastward, and the documents make very clear that the homeward leg of the journey was much shorter than the outward portion.

Hence, I conclude that the archeological division between Tierra Blanca and Garza probably has nothing at all to do with the differences between the Querechos and the Teyas.

Q: For how long after the 1540s are the Querechos identifiable in the historic and archeological record?

Riley: The Querechos were never lost. They are transparently early Apachean groups who probably reached the region of the Canadian (and upper Red River?) drainage sometime in the thirteenth century, perhaps toward the end of that century. At some point, perhaps in the mid-1500s, certain of these groups spread westward, where they were contacted by Espejo's party near Acoma in 1583. A slightly earlier Spanish party had run across the Querechos in 1581, calling them Vaqueros. The term "Apache" may have been first used by Jusepe, a servant with the outlaw Humaña-Leyva party in the mid-1590s.

In the seventeenth century, or perhaps as early as the latter part of the sixteenth century, the Apaches began a spread southward and westward, gradually swamping the Teyas and a number of other groups, some of whom became gradually "Athapaskanized," taking on the language and other cultural attributes of the dominant group. This situation led certain anthropologists—for example, Jack D. Forbes—to consider a whole variety of groups along the southern frontiers of the present-day United States to be Apachean. Forbes believed that the Janos, Jocomes, Mansos, and Sumas, as well as the Jumanos, were Apachean from the beginning. More recent work has shown this to be untrue—for example, Naylor demonstrated that as late as the 1680s the Suma in the Casas Grandes area spoke a non-Apachean language.

J. Charles Kelley in the mid-1940s also considered, as one possibility among others, that the Jumano in the sixteenth century were Apache speaking, but by the time of his Juan Sabeata article was reluctant to make a linguistic designation. He did suggest the Jumano be identified with the archeological Toyah Focus and the spread of Perdiz points. I also suggested in a book written a number of years ago that the Jumano might have been Apachean speaking, but I have long since discarded this idea. It seems to me now totally unlikely that any of these various southern New Mexico, Texas, and Arizona groups and ones in nearby northern Mexico were Athapaskan speaking in the sixteenth century. Indeed, the process of Athapaskanization was only beginning in the seventeenth century, though actual Apache groups had infiltrated the mountainous country of southern New Mexico and Arizona by the end of that century. By the eighteenth century, however, the various groups such as Jumano, Jano, Jocome, Suma, and Manso had largely disappeared, at least in part absorbed into the Apache.

Boyd: Most ethnohistorians are confident of the link between the people the Spanish called Querechos (and later Vaqueros, Faraones, and various band names) and the modern Athapaskan-speaking peoples called Apaches. It appears that Apache peoples are traceable through time in the ethnographic record, and the story that emerges is one of Plains buffalo hunters who became increasingly involved in annual migrations to various eastern frontier pueblos. For almost two centuries at Pecos Pueblo, for example, the Spanish observed the annual arrival of various Plains traders. While ethnographic accounts show that there were other Plains groups who also traded at Pecos and other pueblos, the Apaches are mentioned more consistently and for a longer period of time than any other group. While I do think that the Querechos were Apache peoples and that they may be traced in the historical record from early contact to modern times, each historic observation must be studied carefully to see what it can or cannot contribute to our understanding of these people.

Tracing the Querechos in the archeological record is problematic. The ethnographic evidence suggests that the Apaches and other Plains groups were very similar in terms of their lifestyle and material culture. Perhaps their most distinguishing cultural characteristics, such as tattoos and dress, do not survive in the archeological record. Consequently, I believe it will be much more difficult to trace such groups archeologically.

Q: Can anything be said with confidence about the extent and limits of their territory? Did that territory fluctuate or shift over time?

Habicht-Mauche: Tierra Blanca sites are concentrated in the Red River Valley and numerous sites in Palo Duro Canyon. The Garza boundary is somewhere between Tierra Blanca Creek and the headwaters of the Brazos. It starts there and extends somewhere south.

Hughes: Most of the Querecho–Tierra Blanca–early Apache sites are on the Tierra Blanca and range as far north as Oklahoma; how far south I don't know. By the time you are here at Blanco Canyon, you are in the Garza complex. Somewhere between here and there the Tierra Blanca complex ends.

Boyd: Using Pecos as the example, ethnographic and archeological evidence suggests that the Querechos (Apaches) commonly came to Pecos to trade in the fall and early winter, during harvest time. They probably returned to spend the coldest part of the winter in the deep creek valleys (that is, Palo Duro and Tierra Blanca) at the headwaters of the Red River. In the spring and summer they would range over the Llano, the Canadian and Red River valleys, and the rolling plains hunting buffalo and exploiting the diverse plant resources. After having built up a stockpile of buffalo trade goods (principally hides), they would return to the pueblos in the fall to start the cycle all over again. This is an overly simplistic model, but it seems to fit the majority of evidence and is probably applicable in a general sense for the Teya peoples as well.

I suspect that the geographic range of the Tierra Blanca complex is underestimated due to inadequate sampling. There are probably many more sites in northeastern New Mexico and the Texas Panhandle that represent these people. Because so little archeological work is being done in these areas, the site database grows very slowly. It is likely that the territory inhabited by Tierra Blanca peoples fluctuated through time. This is especially true given the ethnographic evidence suggesting that the Querechos and Teyas were enemies. If they were, it may be surmised that the boundary between them, located somewhere between the headwaters of the Brazos and Red Rivers, was constantly in a state of flux.

Riley: There was a Pueblo occupation which pushed way out beyond the Pecos River in the eleventh century. There was a whole series of sites on the Gallinas and Tecolote and they pulled back between 1250 and 1300. Why?

Hughes: I really think that the Tierra Blanca complex began in the 1300s and had quite an effect. A lot more trade goods up in the Canadian breaks, in the big Caddoan-speaking villages. Those people got along very well, with the Apaches being the trade mediators between Pueblos and Antelope Creek people for a long time. I'm an adherent of the raid-and-trade theory about Pueblo and Apache interactions. When times were good, both parties liked to trade, but when times were bad, heaven help both the Pueblo and Plains villages who didn't have surplus corn. The Apaches were forced to take it, kill people, burn villages. There is plenty of archeological evidence of this.

Another important point that supports this idea of southward movement of Apaches in the 1300s is the sequence of abandonment dates from southern Colorado to the Guadalupe Mountains in West Texas. During that same time all those eastern pueblos vanish; the Apaches (Querechos) move back west. Look at the sites, the sequences, reports, the distributions; even look at the avocational reports, they give you the picture. It sure looks like the Athapaskans were moving down the Canadian and Pecos Rivers and displacing the eastern frontier Pueblos. And it is hard to imagine another reason for the disappearance of western Plains Caddoans from Nebraska on south to the Oklahoma Panhandle except the in-migration of the Apaches. The disappearance of those complexes, Upper Republican, Apishapa, Optima, all take place in successive chronological order beginning about A.D. 1100 in the north and moving on down to the Texas Panhandle.

I have a strong feeling that the Canadian breaks that are full of slab-house villages, huge village sites (little settlements earlier), were for a while a refugium for Caddoan-speaking, western Plains Villagers from western Nebraska and Kansas moving southward away from these Apaches and congregating in greater numbers southward in the Texas Panhandle. I suspect this is not a novel theory. There has been a theory of a coalescence in the upper Missouri region of village peoples to the east, a withdrawal from Montana and Wyoming. I suspect a similar coalescence of Caddoan village people in the Texas Panhandle, particularly beginning in about A.D. 1300. You get an enormous diversity of village traits from that time on in the Texas Panhandle. Then all of a sudden by A.D. 1450, nothing; the village stuff is gone. Here and there the village house sites are found with skeletons spread across the floor; they were never properly buried. At Buried City the complex there disappears about A.D. 1450; nearly every house has a pile of rocks at the corner with a flexed skeleton or two hastily buried under that pile of rocks, as if the refugees came back just to do some kind of burial. We just don't have enough information.

Q: People called Teyas were first encountered by the Coronado expedition in a barranca, or canyon, on the Llano's eastern edge. That first encampment evidently represented one edge of a Teya cultural territory called Cona, which, according to Pedro de Castañeda, extended for three or more days of travel. The Teyas' way of life was very similar to that of the Querechos; in fact, the Spaniards distinguished the two groups mainly on the basis of the Teyas' use of body painting or tattooing.

Does it appear from historical and archeological evidence that in the middle sixteenth century the Caprock canyons were occupied or utilized exclusively by a single cultural group, or was that territory "shared" by different cultural groups? Can that group or one of those groups be confidently identified with the Teyas?

Riley: Even though Coronado does not specifically locate his Teya in any given canyon, it boggles the mind that they were not in one or the other. Theories as to a Canadian River location or one to the south of the Llano Estacado have been pretty much discounted. The real question is "Which canyon(s)?"

Boyd: I think the historical and archeological evidence points to occupation or use of the Caprock Canyonlands by several different groups during the protohistoric period. Ethnographic evidence clearly indicates that the Teyas were living there, but it does not rule out the probability that other peoples did too. This is especially true given the fact that the Coronado expedition is the only reliable firsthand account of people living in the Caprock Canyonlands. All subsequent information for the region is based on primary observations of these people while they were roaming elsewhere or secondary accounts of their activities as described by other groups. While the Spanish were certainly aware of and recognized different Native American cultural groups, their observations usually record very few of the distinctive differences between the various Plains peoples. Many observations, such as the fact that the Teyas tattooed their bodies while the Querechos did not, are important but do not have much bearing on interpreting archeological information. Very few accounts provide specific information about where Plains groups lived while they were not at the Puebloan villages to trade.

The archeological evidence indicates that the canyonlands were an important home territory for at least one group, probably more. Several important Garza complex sites (that is, Bridwell, Floydada County Club, Montgomery, and Pete Creek) represent major residential or base camp locations where lots of people lived over long periods of time (probably several hundred years). The diversity of pottery and arrow points suggests that these sites may have been trade localities where one group lived but others came to visit periodically. Garza and Lott points are present at these sites, but they account for less than 10 percent of the arrow points in any one site, while the majority are Fresno (30–55 percent) and Washita-Harrell (33–52 percent) points. There are many possible explanations for this, but here are just a few. First, Garza peoples were merely periodic visitors to these sites, and it was people who used Fresno and Washita-Harrell points who lived at these locations most of the time. Second, Garza peoples were at these sites most of the time, but they also used Fresno and Washita-Harrell points in conjunction with Garza points. And third, these locations were originally Garza campsites early on, but they were used more intensively by later peoples.

Blakeslee: The documents do not say that the first barranca was situated at the edge of Cona, only that Cona extended for three days of travel in some unspecified direction(s).

Q: It has been proposed that the archeologically defined Garza complex represents the remains of the Teyas. As with the Tierra Blanca complex, does the Garza complex represent a distinct cultural group? Is the area of recognized Garza complex sites coextensive with what is known of the territory utilized by the Teyas?

Blakeslee: What we know about the Cona of the Teyas is that wherever it was, it extended three days travel, which doesn't correspond to either of the archeological complexes, both of which extend for far more than three days of travel. To make this part of the documentary evidence fit the assumption that the Teyas created the Garza complex is to assume in addition that Cona was just the territory of one Garza group within a larger territory. My reaction is that this is like adding cycles and epicycles to the orbits of the planets to make their motions fit the assumption that they move only in perfect circles.

Furthermore, we have the Querechos, if they are Tierra Blanca, having a lot of pottery from Pecos, but the people from Pecos calling them *takuquresh*—a name that implies they are allied with Keres, not Pecos. I don't think there is a good correlation here, either.

Finally, I have another set of reasons that has to do with the Jimmy Owens Site and the little we know about it. I'm confident that this is one of the major campsites of the Coronado expedition, which leads to questions of which one is it and where is the other one? But what I can't do (if this is the northern end of Garza territory) is to put the last camp to the south, as I have already said. I get a better fit if I assume that both the Querechos and the Teyas left archeological sites that we call Tierra Blanca.

Hughes: The trouble is that we don't know the extent of the Garza complex or the Tierra Blanca complex in detail. But it is the most probable thing we know now. The Coronado expedition likely passed through only part of the Garza territory; they didn't know about the rest of Teya territory. The documents give circumstantial clues: the Teyas were painted, and all through the plains the Jumanos were always painted. Also the Wichita, Pawnee, Caddoan people were all painted.

Boyd: Geographically, the location of Casteñeda's Teyas and the core territory of the Garza complex fit like fingers in a glove. If the Jimmy Owens Site in Blanco Canyon is one of Coronado's barranca campsites, it is located within but along the northeastern periphery of the core area defined for the Garza complex. I do not think that the Garza complex and Wheeler phase of southwestern Oklahoma are related, as has been suggested by some researchers.

Q: For how long after the 1540s are the Teyas identifiable in the historic and archeological record?

Boyd: In contrast to the Querechos, the Teyas are not as well documented in the ethnographic record, and there is much less agreement as to later connections. While many people think that Coronado's Teyas are the people later called Rayados and/or Jumanos, others do not. Unless substantial new discoveries of previously unknown ethnohistoric accounts are made, I doubt that there will ever be a widespread consensus tracing the Teyas through time or linking them with the archeological record.

Riley: I believe that the Teya became the Jumano, identified by the Spaniards beginning in the early 1580s and occupying the old Teya area in the Llano Estacado plus the Pecos Valley west of the Llano and extending south and east through the Toyah Basin and into the canyon country beyond. They continued to occupy at least parts of this area throughout the seventeenth century, although they were increasingly impacted by the Apache. As late as Juan Sabeata's time they were still an identifiable group. However, as Hickerson has pointed out, by the end of the seventeenth century, Apache were pushing out the last remnants of Jumano along the Pecos and Colorado drainages. In 1994, Hickerson suggested the possibility that the Jumano may have been one ethnic element in the Kiowa, those aberrant Tanoan-related speakers off to the east.

Q: Can anything be said with confidence about the extent and limits of the Teya territory? Specifically, how far north and south among the caprock canyons is Garza complex evidence found? Is there overlap (geographical and temporal) with Tierra Blanca sites? What about ethnohistorical evidence for the Teyas? What can we say with confidence about the location of Cona?

Hughes: I wish we knew more about the sites at the heads of the caprock canyons to the north, between Blanco Canyon and Palo Duro. There are sites with glaze polychrome ware at the heads of all the canyons on north of Blanco Canyon. Very little work has been in those canyons: Quitaque, Los Lingos, Tule. And there are all these glaze polychrome sites. Perhaps this is where Cona was.

Boyd: The seasonal migration model described for the Querechos is probably applicable for the Teyas. Trading at the pueblos in the fall and early winter, back to winter in the Caprock Canyonlands, then out across the Llano, canyonlands, and/or rolling plains to hunt and gather through the spring and summer. While their core area in the Caprock Canyonlands was relatively small (that is, limited to the Brazos and Colorado River drainages), the full geographic range of Garza peoples, as evidenced by the distribution of Garza and Lott points, was quite large. Garza points have been found as far southwest as the La Junta region of Texas and northern Chihuahua, as far west as Garnsey Springs in southeastern New Mexico, and eastward into southwestern Oklahoma. Thus, it appears that Garza peoples were roaming a vast area and were probably coming into contact and trading with groups all around them, although it is likely that their territory changed through time. The extent to which Garza peoples interacted and traded with peoples in the La Junta region or Wheeler phase peoples in southwestern Oklahoma is not well known.

The overall artifact assemblages described for Tierra Blanca and Garza both fit the ethnographic model of seasonal hunter-gatherer people who concentrated on bison hunting and part-time trading. Collectively, these two complexes cover a very large area of good bison-hunting range (that is, essentially all of the Texas Panhandle–Plains). Unfortunately, the total amount of archeological work in this area is limited, and the total number of known protohistoric sites is small. I suspect that many more protohistoric sites will eventually be found and that the core areas for both complexes will be enlarged.

Riley: A very good bet from the Spanish accounts is that the Teyas spent the winter months at La Junta and perhaps in the Toyah Basin to the north. This would explain the knowledge of Cabeza de Vaca given by Teyas to Coronado. The description of a Plainslike group with the stone boiling method of cooking and a discussion of the topography of the area by Cabeza de Vaca strongly suggests that he was describing the Teyas as of 1535. Six years later the Teyas gave news of him to Coronado.

Q: Were the Teyas likely of a single linguistic stock? What evidence supports the various possible linguistic affiliations?

Riley: That is likely, though the old argument of Scholes and Mera that the word Jumano referred to a variety of distinct tattooed or painted peoples cannot be discarded out of hand. From present evidence, however, it does seem likely that the Teyas-Jumano formed an identifiable group. The balance of evidence seems to make these peoples related to the Piro (that is, Tanoan), though the possibility that they might have been Caddoan speaking needs to be addressed. Apaches they weren't!

Hughes: I have a strong feeling that the Canadian breaks were for a while a refugium for Caddoan-speaking, western Plains Villagers from western Nebraska and Kansas moving southward away from the Querechos-Apaches and congregating in greater numbers southward in the Texas Panhandle. Beginning in about A.D. 1300 you get an enormous diversity of village traits in the Texas Panhandle. Then all of a sudden by A.D. 1450, nothing; the village stuff is gone. Here and there the village house sites are found with skeletons spread across the floor; they were never properly buried. Some of these Caddoan-speaking villagers were pushed south out of the Canadian drainage and in Coronado's time are known as the Teyas. And those scenes of violence in the Canadian breaks dating from the middle fifteenth century are evidence of the animosity between ancestral Querechos and Teyas referred to in the Coronado documents. That's how I see it.

Boyd: I suspect Coronado's Teyas were of a single linguistic stock, but that does not mean that all subsequent references to them positively relate to the same group. Teyas and Jumano may have at times been used as catchall terms that included people of similar cultures but different languages. There is little agreement as to what language the Teyas spoke, but various theories have been presented and warrant consideration (that is, Habicht-Mauche posits "Caddoan," and Hickerson, "Tanoan"). No single theory stands out as being the most likely. From an archeological perspective, the language they spoke is not nearly as important as whether they acted as and perceived themselves as one cultural group, distinct from all others.

Blakeslee: I do not believe there is any way to say whether we are dealing with one or several languages simply by looking at a named archeological complex. Nor can we say that some of the groups that created it were not habitually at war with others. Just before he died, the late Robert Stevenson was working in Virginia on the archeology of the Powhattan confederacy, the group to which Pocahontas belonged. He said that there was absolutely no difference in the archeology of that group and the villages of their sworn enemies. Closer to home, on the Plains, the Coalescent Tradition villages of the Dakotas include the remains of the Caddoan-speaking Arikaras and the Algonkian-speaking Cheyennes. And some Teton Dakota bands have traditions of having lived in Arikara villages and of having made Arikara-style pottery.

Q: What were the Teyas' relations with their neighbors? What evidence is there for trade or other peaceful interchange and also for hostility?

Hickerson: I've argued that the Teyas were a group of Jumanos and that the Jumanos were, in origin, Plains Tanoans. As such, they had both trade and kinship connections with the Pueblo Tanoans, especially the Piro. They traded widely on the Plains, dealing with Caddoan and other tribes. I think it's very likely that more than one language was in use in this trade sphere. Besides the sign language that was used in Texas, a Caddoan-based lingua franca is a strong possibility.

Boyd: While the Teyas maintained trade relations with outside groups (for example, select eastern pueblos and perhaps Caddoan peoples to the east), they are described as having been long-time enemies of the Querechos-Apaches. With the possible exception that the Bridwell site may have had a walled fortification enclosure (that is, Baugh proposes that a wooden palisade wall was present, but the evidence is far from conclusive), there is no archeological evidence for intercultural conflict among the Garza complex. However, this is an archeological sampling issue, because only one human burial (as yet unreported) is definitely attributed to the Garza complex, and other types of archeological evidence for violence are subtle. It is likely that intersocietal conflict was prevalent among the Garza culture. The Teyas equal Garza model would be substantially supported if some evidence of violence associated with Garza or Tierra Blanca complex burials were found.

Summary

With one exception, the panelists leaned toward the idea that the archeological Tierra Blanca and Garza complexes correlate with two culturally distinct peoples known from the documents of the Coronado expedition as Querechos and Teyas, respectively. Most likely, according to this thinking, the Querechos were Athapaskans, ancestral Apaches. The Teyas appear more enigmatic. Some panelists favored an eastern affiliation with the Caddo for them, and others saw a probable western affiliation with the Piro pueblos.

Importantly, Judith Habicht-Mauche pointed out that the complexes appear to be considerably more than just arbitrary groupings of slightly different artifact assemblages. Rather, she argued that the ceramic technology traditions apparent in the Tierra Blanca and Garza complexes point strongly to distinct cultures with different geographical and social origins.

The objections raised to correlation between archeological complexes and cultural groups recognized by sixteenth-century Europeans were principally cautionary, no alternative hypothesis being offered. Rather, researchers were admonished not to conclude hastily.

All panelists agreed that the thinness of the material evidence hampers drawing definitive and precise conclusions about the protohistoric cultural geography of the Texas Panhandle and South Plains and adjacent areas of unknown extent, all or parts of which may have been inhabited or exploited by the people responsible for what we know as the Tierra Blanca and Garza complexes.

Of immediate concern for study of the Coronado expedition and its encounters with native peoples of the region, most panelists agreed that in the 1540s there was probably a transition or boundary between territories used by Querechos–Tierra Blanca and Teyas-Garza somewhere in the ninety miles separating Palo Duro–Tule Canyons (perhaps a Tierra Blanca core area at certain seasons at the time) and Blanco Canyon (a corresponding core area of Garza peoples). The peripheral limits of the two territories are seen as even fuzzier. The Teyas-Garza may have ranged over much of west Texas and southeastern New Mexico and even east and northward into western Oklahoma. Meanwhile, the Querechos may have seasonally migrated across the Texas Panhandle, northeastern New Mexico, and adjacent areas in what is now Colorado, Kansas, and the Oklahoma Panhandle.

For most panelists, the Teya homeland known as Cona must have been on the eastern or southeastern margin of the Llano Estacado. As such, it would almost surely include the Jimmy Owens Site in Blanco Canyon. All of these possibilities, though, remain hypotheses hedged by caveats and cautions. The protohistoric Querechos and Teyas certainly deserve the kind of concerted study that would test these hypotheses and perhaps more confidently reveal the first Plains peoples directly affected by Old World natives.

ELEVEN

The War for the South Plains, 1500–1700

NANCY P. HICKERSON

SINCE THE BEGINNING OF RECORDED European history in North America, the South Plains, as the portion of the Llano Estacado lying south of the Texas Panhandle is known, have been a battleground in repeated conflicts involving Native Americans. In the sixteenth century, Spanish conquistadores witnessed the enmity between groups called "Querechos" (Apaches) and "Teyas" (Jumanos). Their narratives provide our earliest glimpse of a war that would continue for more than a century, affecting native peoples from New Mexico to the Texas coast. A second war began early in the eighteenth century when the Comanches entered the South Plains. They would displace the once dominant Apaches and hold sway, albeit briefly, as the premier native power in the region. Finally, in a third period of bloody war, the United States cavalry would defeat the Comanches and other tribes in a pan-regional conflict—the "Indian wars" of the nineteenth century—that opened the plains to Euro-American occupation.

In each of these wars, an invading population extinguished, displaced, or incorporated its predecessors. In each case, sweeping demographic, economic, and social changes were put in motion, not only in the South Plains but also in adjacent areas. In this chapter I examine the first and most obscure of these wars, looking to the identities and strategies of the winners and losers in a struggle that predated Spanish entry into the region (but in which Spanish interests would be much involved) and to an understanding of the outcome.

"Old Amerinds" of the Greater South Plains

In late prehistoric times, a vast expanse of arid to semiarid land, stretching from the South Plains to southern Texas and the Gulf coast, was thinly occupied by small groups of hunter-gatherers. A shared food-gathering adaptation, doubtless of great antiquity, characterized this huge region. The majority of the tribes, Karankawans, Coahuiltecans, and others, were constituted of nomadic or seminomadic bands that subsisted on wild foods such as nuts, berries, deer, shellfish, mescal roots, and prickly pear fruit, harvested according to season. As depicted in the *relación* of Cabeza de Vaca, contacts at food-harvesting sites were important occasions for social and economic exchanges between groups. Feuds were common, but conventions maintained peace during harvest periods, and traders had neutral status.[1]

Unlike other arid regions of North America, this one lay between two disparate areas of more complex agricultural societies. In the west, the Rio Grande and its eastern tributaries marked the frontier of the Oasis culture area of the Southwest, which had cultural ties to Mexico. In the east, the lower courses of several major rivers, from the Arkansas to the Trinity, constituted the westernmost extension of Mississippian civilization. Trade routes, which for the most part followed watercourses, crisscrossed the plains and provided links between agricultural and nonagricultural areas.

In the natural pastures of the South Plains, bison were a prime resource that attracted hunters from a wide radius. The Jumanos, a Tanoan people with ties of language and kinship to village populations in New Mexico and the Rio Grande valley, were widely known as bison hunters and were closely identified with this region.[2] In the seventeenth century, the wide-ranging trade contacts of the Jumanos would become the basis for an informal alliance of indigenous tribes as they confronted and attempted to stem the tide of Apache expansion in the South Plains.

Apache Genesis

The time, circumstances, and consequences of the arrival of the Apachean peoples in the Southwest and South Plains have been subjects of a long and convoluted discussion.[3] Most twentieth-century scholars have rejected or modified the views of pioneer researcher Adolph Bandelier, who evidently saw the Apaches as ubiquitous aggressors and instigators of warfare and other forms of violence. I would not, under any circumstances, wish to return outright to Bandelier's position. However, I find it difficult to conceive of the entry of the Apacheans into their historical territories as anything other than an invasion, and this invasion *did* involve violence.

Apachean is the southernmost branch of the Athapaskan language family, usually considered to be part of a larger Na-Dene superfamily or phylum. Linguistic, cultural, and genetic clues all indicate the Athapaskans to be descendants of one of two relatively recent migrations from Asia into North America, the other being the Inuit, or Eskimo-Aleut family. Prior to these late migrations, an autochthonous Native American population, speakers of the hundreds of different languages that Joseph Greenberg lumps together as *Amerind,*[4] had increased, dispersed, and differentiated over the course of roughly twenty millennia. As a consequence, the more habitable regions of the continent were already populated. Was there room for newcomers? And would newcomers be welcome?

It appears that both Inuits and Athapaskans found an initial niche on the North American continent, roughly two thousand to three thousand years ago, by dint of their ability to exploit underutilized (or marginal) environments. The Inuits, equipped with a specialized cold-weather technology, dispersed along the Arctic coast from Siberia to Greenland. The Athapaskans, from an early toehold in southern Alaska, spread both north and south along the cordillera of the Rocky Mountains. Richard Perry argued that the Athapaskans were, from the beginning, a mountain-adapted people.[5] He characterized their basic subsistence hunting strategy as a "mixed bag" that exploited the multiple ecological zones concentrated in the mountain environment. At times this strategy was supplemented by opportunistic big-game hunting in adjacent flatlands, typically employing the technique of the game drive.

In the tundra of northern Canada and in the Great Plains, the hunting of large herbivores (caribou and bison) made possible the expansion of Athapaskan territories. In intervening latitudes, similar sallies were doubtless made, with variable success; archeologists have suggested a number of sites as evidence of such occupancy.[6] In the south, as in the north, the Athapaskans would initially have established their bases in mountain locales before attempting inroads into the neighboring plains. The early Apaches probably made their way to mountainous areas in the Southwest in the late fourteenth or early fifteenth century and began to colonize the South Plains by the sixteenth. Their domain in the plains peaked in the late seventeenth century and began to flounder by the eighteenth.

Events, Times, and Places

Two mountain areas stand out as likely sites of early Apache occupancy adjacent to the South Plains. One of these is centered in the Sangre de Cristo range. It is likely that the "Querechos" of the Coronado era were based in or associated with these mountains.[7] Though it is less clearly documented, there is reason to suggest that another early Apache stronghold lay further to the south, in the Sacramento and/or Guadalupe Mountains. Precursors, respectively, of the Jicarilla and Mescalero Apaches, the mountain people increased and made their presence felt, scouring the neighboring hills and valleys and staking out hunting territories in the plains.

East of the Rio Grande, fertile areas and routes of travel were largely defined by streams and other water sources. The Canadian River provided a natural route between the northern pueblos of New Mexico and Quivira, the powerful Wichita confederacy, which lay beyond the confluence of the Canadian and Arkansas.[8] Farther south, a "water route" of springs and wells led from the eastern pueblos to the headwaters of the Brazos, Colorado, and other rivers in the Llano Estacado. The Río del Norte was the main highway from New Mexico to La Junta de los Ríos and other points south, while the Pecos inclined toward the upper Concho and Colorado. From the lower Pecos, Toyah Creek delineated a route through the Davis Mountains between the Pecos and La Junta de los Ríos.[9]

In the war for the South Plains, the Apache invaders were pitted against the earlier occupants—first and foremost, the Jumanos. These appear earliest as the "Teyas," whose expertise as hunters and guides in the plains environment is well attested in the narratives of the Coronado expedition.[10] Bandelier was the first modern historian to call attention to the frequent references to Jumanos (Xumanas, Humanas, etc.) in subsequent documents of the sixteenth and seventeenth centuries and to pose questions about their identity, territorial distribution, and decline.[11] They seem to have been everywhere, at La Junta, on the Pecos and the Colorado, in the eastern pueblos, on the Llano Estacado, and on the Arkansas, at the gateway to Quivira. Bandelier and a number of later scholars offered ingenious explanations for this ubiquity, from wide-ranging migration to the "lumping" of a number of different tribes under a generic name.[12] However, a coherent picture of this remarkable people begins to emerge only when they are considered in a regional historical context, and especially when juxtaposed with their rivals and long-time enemies, the Apaches.

The scattered geographical distribution of the Jumanos was, in large part, a function of their seasonal movements as hunters and of their related role as traders.[13] Historical references point to the existence of two core Jumano locations in the plains: a large settlement near the confluence of the Concho and Colorado Rivers and a number of rancherías located in canyons or barrancas along the eastern edge of the Llano Estacado (map 11.1).[14] At an earlier date, prior to the arrival of the Apaches, a similar Jumano base may have been located farther to the north, somewhere along the trail from the northern pueblos to Quivira.

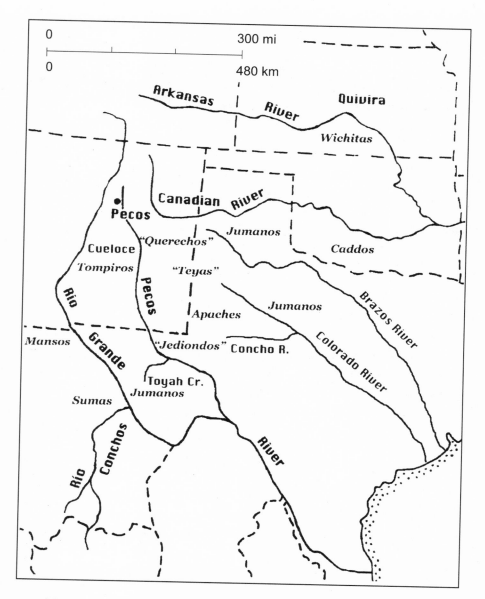

Map 11.1.   Culture groups and areas of the South Plains, circa 1500–1700.

These permanent Jumano bases would have had shifting populations as hunters and traders came and went, but they likely were maintained year-round. Their strategic location is obvious, because they sit astride the most important trade routes, defined by the Colorado, Brazos, and other river systems. In addition, the ranchería of the Jediondos (either Jumanos or Jumano allies),[15] was situated at a strategic point, the intersection of the Pecos and the trail linking La Junta with the upper Colorado. In 1580, a chain of Jumano rancherías lined La Junta trail. A century later, there is no mention of them, possibly because of their vulnerability to attack. As witnessed by Spanish observers, the war for the plains was fought on northern and southern fronts, with a focus on the trade routes.

The Northern Front

In the north, confrontations between Apaches and Jumanos may have begun in the foothills of the Sangre de Cristo range. The Apaches preempted territory, which they defended, and gradually extended their holdings. Apaches soon replaced Jumanos in trade at the northernmost pueblos of Taos and Picurís, exchanging meat and pelts for corn and other produce, as witnessed by Coronado and his followers. The more extensive the Apache occupancy of the plains to the east, the more effectively was a de facto blockade imposed on the pueblos of New Mexico. An individual village might be locked into a trade and/or raid relationship with an individual Apache band. Several decades of escalating Apache dominance of the plains effectively extended this relationship to the region as a whole. Thus, the Apache presence eventually ended the earlier flow of goods and artifacts, back and forth across the plains, in which the Jumanos had served as middlemen.

By Oñate's day, the Apache trade sphere extended from Taos to Pecos Pueblo. Farther south, the Tompiro province was home to a Jumano population and provided the main gateway for Jumano traders. This was still the case in the 1620s, but the Jumanos were being challenged in the Llano Estacado and may already have been losing control of the route between their rancherías and the Tompiros. In this period, too, the Apaches of the plains were at war with the Caddoan tribes and sometimes brought Wichita and Caddo prisoners to be sold as slaves in New Mexico.

During the 1620s, Jumanos from the plains repeatedly requested Spanish assistance, hoping to maintain their routes and territories. In 1629, a Jumano leader called Captain Tuerto was able to persuade fray Juan de Salas to bring a party of soldiers and clerics to visit a Jumano ranchería on the Llano Estacado. The Franciscans, however, declined to establish a permanent mission, as the

Indians had desired. Instead, they returned a year later and escorted a number of refugees to join those already present in the Tompiro province of New Mexico.[16]

By 1650, it appears that the Jumanos had been forced to abandon the Llano Estacado entirely. Spanish trading parties from New Mexico now made annual visits to the Colorado River location, which also was the objective of two military expeditions. In one case, in 1654, Spanish soldiers joined the Jumanos in attacking downstream tribes on the Colorado. The motive is unclear, but it may have been the elimination of an obstacle to trade and diplomacy directed toward the Caddo and other eastern tribes.[17]

At the same time, the Tompiro province had come under siege. Apaches began arriving for trade and were met with resistance by the resident Jumanos. Raids and attacks on mission churches followed, blamed on the "Seven Rivers" Apaches of the Sacramento Mountains region. Twenty years more, and the Tompiro province was in ruins. The Jumano population had "removed," under Franciscan auspices, reportedly to join the Piro and Manso missions near El Paso.[18]

The Southern Front

In 1580, the earliest Spanish explorers and prospectors were welcomed in large farming villages of the Julimes and Jumanos at La Junta de los Ríos. On the way north, however, the Spaniards were warned to beware of a people "of a different nation" who were "numerous, very brave, and warlike" (a likely reference to the Apaches based in the mountain ranges east of the Rio Grande).[19] In 1581, returning to La Junta by way of the Pecos River, the Espejo expedition encountered Jumano hunters on the lower Pecos near the mouth of Toyah Creek and visited the Jumano rancherías along the trail between the Pecos and La Junta.[20]

Following the Espejo expedition, we hear little news of La Junta and its eastern frontier for almost a century. In the aftermath of the Pueblo Revolt of 1680, a series of anti-Spanish uprisings swept through the Rio Grande valley below El Paso, and Apache raiders began to harass both Indian and Spanish settlements. At about the same time, church and government officials at El Paso received a series of appeals that must have had a familiar ring. The Jumanos and their friends were once more petitioning for help: shelter for displaced natives of the Rio Grande valley, who were streaming toward La Junta, support for the Jumanos, whose lands on the Colorado were now under siege, and military aid for defense of the hunting grounds and trade routes between the Rio Grande valley and central and eastern Texas.

Responding to the direct appeal of the Jumano leader Juan Sabeata, Captain Juan Domínguez de Mendoza and a company of New Mexican soldiers descended the Rio Grande in December 1683. En route, they repeatedly encountered displaced Suma Indians, who told of being driven from their lands by Apache attacks. Three priests had gone ahead, led by the custodian of the Franciscan order, fray Nicolás López. The priests first established missions at La Junta for the numerous refugees already gathered there. Then, two of their number joined the military party and a large escort of Jumanos and other Indians to follow the trail toward the upper Colorado, where they were to meet with representatives of more than thirty eastern tribes.

After Domínguez de Mendoza's party had crossed the Pecos, he described in his journal the constant apprehension of the Jumanos, their certainty that Apaches were nearby—probably kept at bay by the presence of the Spanish militia—and the repeated theft of horses, both Jumano and Spanish. However, the Indian leaders, who had reasoned that the Apaches were the common enemy of their tribes *and* the Spanish colonists, were frustrated in their hopes for an alliance with Spain. At El Paso, Governor Cruzate had been receptive to renewal of the Jumano trade, and the Franciscan clerics were eager to save Indian souls at La Junta and in the plains. But in Texas, the New Mexican militia, after enjoying a glorious bison hunt, paused to appraise the circling Apaches and beat a rapid retreat to El Paso.[21]

Juan Sabeata continued to lead trading expeditions from La Junta to the Caddo and other nations of eastern Texas for roughly another decade.[22] However, it is likely that the Jumano rancherías on the upper Colorado were abandoned by 1685 at the latest. Fray Alonso de Posada, writing in 1686, raised the possibility of resettling the Jumanos on this river, in connection with a proposal for developing the area as a defense against French inroads. The Jumanos, he suggested, would willingly "go and settle on the said river because it is their land which the Apacha nation took away from them and whom they hold as enemies."[23]

The developments that Posada advocated were never undertaken. Maps drawn after 1700 show the upper reaches of the Colorado and Brazos as Apache territory. From there, Apache bands that came to be called Lipans began to make raids on the new Spanish settlements and missions of eastern Texas and to press farther toward the coast.

Apache Success and Jumano Failure

I have outlined a picture of incremental but seemingly unstoppable Apache expansion, matched by Jumano retreats to the point that they were extinguished, at least as a named group. It remains to consider how and why this occurred. What was the secret of Apache success? It may be impossible to give a definite answer. So little is known of the particulars of this story that one can only attempt to discover and assess the factors that might have been critical. I briefly review the possibilities, considering what is known and what might have been.

1. Were the Apaches more skilled than the Jumanos in dealing with the South Plains environment? No. The Jumano culture developed in situ, out of the heritage of the Jornada Mogollon, and was indigenous to the South Plains.[24] From early to late, we read of their geographical knowledge, hunting prowess, and environmental savvy. It is hard to imagine that the sixteenth-century Apache newcomers could have rivaled the Jumanos' knowledge of the region and its resources.

2. Did the nature of their society give the Apaches an edge? Judging from their later historical descendants, the early Apacheans were probably a matrilocal people with either bilateral or matrilineal descent and with some occurrence of sororal polygyny. Neighboring households, usually related, would have constituted local bands. Beyond this level of organization, Apachean tribes typically have shown great flexibility, local groups combining, segmenting, shifting, and regrouping. Neighboring bands often cooperated in peaceful or warlike activities. Leadership was charismatic, and able hunters or warriors sometimes attracted large followings of individuals and families.

The social organization of historic Apachean cultures undoubtedly evolved in, and was well adapted to, a nomadic or seminomadic lifestyle. We get a glimpse of the nomadism of the seventeenth-century Apache Vaqueros as seen by fray Alonso de Benavides:

> I cannot refrain from telling one thing, somewhat incredible, howsoever ridiculous. And it is that when these Indians go to trade and traffic, the entire rancherías go, with their wives and children, who live in tents made of (the) skins of buffalo, very thin and tanned; and the tents they carry loaded on pack-trains of dogs . . . and the people carry their merchandise [thus] loaded, which they barter for cotton cloth and for other things.[25]

It would appear that Benavides found the nomadic culture of the Apaches strikingly different from that of other Indian traders who would have visited New Mexico during his tenure there, namely, the Jumanos.

As for the Jumanos: no recent historical people can be certainly identified as their direct descendants, to provide a model for inference about the organization of their society. But because I believe they were kin (as well as trading partners) of the Tanoan pueblo groups,[26] and they may have been ancestral to the Kiowa tribe, I surmise that a bilateral or weakly patrilineal organization prevailed, with patrilocal residence.

Early writers referred to Jumano leaders as "captains," suggesting that they had authority in relation to their own people and in dealings with outsiders. Males may have traveled, alone or in groups, as traders, guides, or warriors. Thus, fray Juan de Salas's party was led by Jumano guides and was met three days from the ranchería by ten Jumano captains. No women and children are mentioned at that point, although they are mentioned later in the description of the ranchería. In the 1680s, Juan Sabeata was known as a native "governor," with authority over the captains, or headmen, of several widely scattered bands (at La Junta, on the Pecos, and on the Colorado).[27]

Brief remarks by Castañeda and other early writers indicate that men, women, and children were in residence in the Jumano rancherías, while individuals and small groups arrived and departed (to accompany Coronado's party as guides, for example). If numbers of men were absent at any given time, the rancherías would have been vulnerable to surprise attack. When hostilities were anticipated, however, the women were taken to a safe place, presumably to the Tompiros or to other allies.

3. Did the Apaches have technological or other material advantages over their neighbors in the South Plains? Perhaps they did. Some unique technological components of Apache nomadism can be identified or inferred—perhaps most obviously, the light-weight and easily portable teepees that Coronado admired and that so captivated Vicente de Zaldívar that he had to have one of his own. The quality of Apache skin working was remarkable. Pack dogs carried the teepee covers and dragged the tent poles from one campsite to the next.

Both Apaches and Jumanos used dogs as beasts of burden. It is likely that the Apaches introduced the idea of dog traction, which may have developed earlier among northern Athapaskans.[28] It is also possible that the dogs that accompanied the Apaches into the Southwest were larger and/or stronger than the indigenous breeds.

Was Apache weaponry superior to that of the Jumanos and their neighbors? There is little to surmise on this question. If the archeological cultures can be clearly defined, then comparison may reveal significant differences. Early observers, at different times, characterized both Jumanos and Apaches as excellent archers. Luxán, the narrator of the Espejo expedition, characterized the Jumano bows as "Turkish, all reinforced and very strong, and the strings are made from the sinews of the buffalo."[29] Alonso de Posada observed that Apache warriors "never carry . . . more than bows and arrows, all carved and ornamented,

. . . carried in the Turkish manner, so thus distinguished from all the rest, one recognizes them on sight to be of that nation."[30] It appears likely that Apache military predominance had more to do with numbers and strategy than with weapons per se.

4. Were there important territorial or demographic variables? What explains the repeated references to large numbers of Apaches? The Apacheans were invaders who fought to gain territory and would then fight fiercely to retain possession and exclusive occupancy of that territory. Benavides indicated that the "Apaches de Navajo" were united in defense of their territory. On one occasion, they came to make war on the "Christian" Indians (of the Tewa pueblos) "in revenge for having entered upon their lands." Throughout their vast expanse, Benavides noted that each Apache household "has its recognized land" for farming.[31] According to Posada, writing fifty years later, the "Apacha" nation "possesses and is owner of all the plains of Cibola. The Indians of this nation are . . . the common enemy of all nations who live below the northern region. They have destroyed, ruined or driven most of them from their lands. This nation occupies and has its own lands and as such they defend them."[32]

In the plains, the Apache concept of exclusive territoriality may have been an innovation imposed in a region where bands and tribes were surely associated with traditional use and occupancy areas but did not claim exclusive access to major resources. It was evidently an awareness of the growing threat to their own subsistence and security that brought the indigenous tribes, under Jumano leadership, finally to seek Spanish assistance in resisting the Apache advances.

Numerical superiority may have given the Apaches an edge over the other occupants of the plains, while the presence of Spanish military forces and firearms secured the pueblos of New Mexico. A striking aspect of Benavides's *Memoriales* of 1630 and 1634 lies in its repeated allusions to vast numbers of Apaches. According to Benavides, the "huge Apacha nation" had "more people than all the nations of New Spain together, even including the Mexican."[33] Even granting that the missionary fathers tended to exaggerate the numbers of their target populations, it appears clear that the Apaches were seen as very numerous, surrounding and outnumbering the villagers of New Mexico, not to mention the scattered bands of nomads like the Jumanos.

One would assume that the first Athapaskans to enter the mountains of New Mexico were few, and that their numbers had increased over two, three, or more generations before we meet them in the historical record. But reproductive increase in situ may not be the only explanation for a rapid escalation of population that accompanied the Apaches' territorial expansion. The pioneer

Apaches were the southern vanguard of an Athapaskan continuum that extended through much of the cordillera of the Rockies. Once they were established in New Mexico, it may be that news of their secure mountain retreats and access to rich hunting grounds spread northward, from one band to the next, attracting more émigrés and precipitating a prehistoric land rush.[34]

5. What was the Jumanos' fatal flaw? Did their allies abandon them? The same features of Jumano spatial and social organization that facilitated their earlier success as hunters and traders—their wide-ranging travel, far-flung network of trade routes and rancherías, and extensive but remote links with trading partners—may also have constituted their Achilles' heel, the key to their vulnerability and ultimate decline. Battles may or may not have been fought when the Apaches first began to make inroads into the plains, but once they had gained a foothold, establishing a presence between the Jumano enclaves in the eastern pueblos and their distant rancherías in the plains, Apache victory seems almost inevitable. It might have been fairly easy to waylay travelers, ambush trading parties, prey on isolated camps, and blockade the pueblo ports of entry. Eventually the Jumanos' canyon strongholds were besieged (evidently the situation that brought fray Salas to the plains of Texas), and the inhabitants surrendered or fled; many may have died. At the end, as Bolton noted, bands of "Apaches Jumanes" could be found along the Rio Grande near La Junta.[35] Thus, some of the Jumanos, like the Sumas, Mansos, and others, were eventually assimilated into the ranks of their conquerors. But in the east, refugees and survivors of the war for the South Plains may also have joined the ranks of allies such as the Caddo and Wichita or may even have become the nucleus of new plains tribes such as the Kiowa.[36]

As to the network of "allies," it is clear that the Jumanos, as traders, had cordial relations with their wide network of trading partners. The impetus to form a binding alliance, however, may have come too late. It was only in the 1680s, when Juan Sabeata was able to rally the scattered Indian nations and to represent them in dealing with officials in New Mexico and Nueva Vizcaya, that the basis for an alliance emerged. Perhaps these nations were simply too widely dispersed for close cooperation to be possible, at least in pre-horse times. Also, the eastern bands and tribes might not have perceived the seriousness of the threat to their hunting grounds and other resources until it was too late for effective resistence.[37]

The South Plains War and the "Jumano Problem"

In earlier papers and a book dealing with the Jumanos, I attempted to explain the wide geographical distribution of these people as a function of their historically documented role as traders. It now seems obvious to me that a century or more of war should also be part of the explanation. War results in deaths, loss of territory, and captives, and war produces refugees. Where can refugees go? The Jumanos must have turned for assistance to related or allied communities—perhaps in some cases to the same communities where they had been accustomed to overwinter. Thus, after fray Salas's visit in 1639, refugees from the plains of Texas removed to the Tompiro region of New Mexico, settling near Cueloce, the port of entry for the Jumano trade. Forty years later, after a prolonged Apache siege of the Tompiros, the Jumanos again retreated, moving southward and joining, at least temporarily, the Piros and Mansos. These cases were reported by, and evidently involved the assistance or intervention of, Franciscan clerics. But they suggest a pattern that may also apply to earlier, undocumented population movements. I will briefly mention two possibilities that may merit further investigation.

First, in early colonial documents, the Tompiro pueblos appear to be unusual in the presence of two different population groups, Piro and Jumano. The two groups evidently spoke the same language (or closely related Tanoan dialects), but the Jumanos were distinguished by their painted facial and body ornamentation. They were often called "rayados" by the Spaniards. Of three Jumano pueblos, the largest was Cueloce, or "Las Humanas," situated at the extreme south of the Tompiro region.[38] In 1979 Gordon Vivian, who conducted extensive archeological research at this site, commented that ceramic and other evidence pointed to a late prehistoric wave of influence from a southern Jornada Mogollon tradition and suggested that this influence coincided with a population influx into the Tompiro region around A.D. 1400.[39] For roughly the same time frame, other archeologists have posited a large-scale depopulation, along with indications of warfare, in the mountains of southern New Mexico. Could the coincidence of these events reflect (1) the initial movement of Apaches into the Sacramento Mountains region, precipitating (2) the displacement of a Jornada (or Jumano) population that (3) subsequently relocated to the Tompiro pueblos?

Second, in 1601 Juan de Oñate's army, approaching Quivira, encountered a large group of people, a "gran población," on the banks of the Arkansas River. New Mexican Indians accompanying the army identified these people as Jumanos. Modern scholars have tended to discount this fact and generally assume that these so-called Jumanos were simply an outlying community of Wichitas. But among the Indians with Oñate were a substantial number from the Jumano pueblo of Cueloce. Perhaps their testimony should not be so casually discounted.[40]

Might this not be another case in which "real" Jumanos, having lost their land to their enemies, sought a place of refuge with friends and allies? In the *gran población* we may see the remnants of a Jumano band, perhaps the "Teyas" whose familiarity with the road to Quivira was evident when they served as Coronado's guides. As allies and trading partners of the Wichita people, the Teyas were, as Castañeda observed, accustomed to spending their winters "at the gates of Quivira."

Over time, these Jumano refugees (if such they were) would become culturally and linguistically assimilated, incorporated into the Wichita confederacy. But as much as a century later, New Mexicans regularly applied the name "Jumano" to the Taovayas (or Tawehash) division of the Wichitas, who may have retained both the emblematic body decoration and the penchant for trading of the earlier tribe. There could be, in these respects, a remarkable parallel to the situation of the Jumano enclave in the Tompiros.

Notes

1. Núñez Cabeza de Vaca, *Castaways,* especially 79–83.
2. The linguistic identity of the Jumanos has long been a subject of controversy. For the case for the Tanoan link and a historical perspective on the issue, see Nancy P. Hickerson, "The Linguistic Position of Jumano," *Journal of Anthropological Research* 44, no. 3 (1988): 311–26; and Nancy P. Hickerson, *The Jumanos: Hunters and Traders of the South Plains* (Austin: University of Texas Press, 1994), xi–xxviii.
3. *Apachean* includes the scattered Apache populations (Mescalero, Jicarilla, etc.), as well as the Navajos. All, with the possible exception of the Kiowa Apache, are considered to speak dialects of a single language. See Harry Hoijer, "The Chronology of the Athapaskan Languages," *International Journal of American Linguistics* 22, no. 4 (1956): 219–32.
4. Joseph H. Greenberg, *Language in the Americas* (Stanford, California: Stanford University Press, 1981).
5. Richard J. Perry, *Western Apache Heritage* (Austin: University of Texas Press, 1991).
6. For contrasting perspectives on Apachean origins and prehistory, see Richard J. Perry, "The Apachean Transition from the Subarctic to the Southwest," *Plains Anthropologist* 25 (1980): 279–96; Perry, *Western Apache Heritage;* and James H. Gunnerson and Dolores A. Gunnerson, "Apachean Culture: A Study in Unity and Diversity," in *Apachean Culture History and Ethnology,* eds. Keith H. Basso and Morris E. Opler (Tucson: University of Arizona Press, 1971), 7–27.
7. Dolores A. Gunnerson, in *The Jicarilla Apache* (De Kalb: Northern Illinois University Press, 1974), considers that the "Apaches of Quinia," present in the Sangre de Cristo Mountains in the 1620s, were ancestral to the Jicarilla Apaches.
8. The source of the word "Quivira" is unknown. Although it is usually considered synonymous with the historic Wichita, it may originally have had a broader significance, perhaps as an inclusive reference to the Mississippian agricultural societies.
9. The Jumanos and, later, the Apaches were probably familiar with most or all of the trails, springs, and lookout points that were later used by the Comanches, as detailed by Daniel J. Gelo, "Comanche Land and Ever Has Been: A Native Geography of the Nineteenth-Century Comancheria," *Southwest Historical Quarterly* 103, no. 3 (2000): 273–307.

10. Some scholars, including Gunnerson, *Jicarilla Apache,* have identified both Querechos and Teyas as Apachean; others believe the Teyas were Caddoan (e.g., Judith Habicht-Mauche, "Coronado's Querechos and Teyas in the Archeological Record of the Texas Panhandle," *Plains Anthropologist* 37 [1992]: 247–59).

11. Bandelier, *Final Report.*

12. See Frederick W. Hodge, "The Jumano Indians," *Proceedings of the American Antiquarian Society for 1900–1910,* n.s. 20 (1911): 249–68; Herbert E. Bolton, "The Jumano Indians in Texas, 1650–1771," *Texas Historical Association Quarterly* 15 (1911): 66–84; France V. Scholes and Harry P. Mera, "Some Aspects of the Jumano Problem," *Contributions to American Anthropology and History* 6, no. 34, Carnegie Institution of Washington Publication 523 (Washington, D.C., 1940); and J. Charles Kelley, "Jumano Indians," in *The Handbook of Texas,* eds. William P. Webb, H. Bailey Carroll, and Eldon S. Branda (Austin: Texas State Historical Society, 1952), 933–34, among others.

13. I have elsewhere suggested that the Jumanos had a primary role as bison hunters, moving seasonally from New Mexico to the plains of Texas, and subsequently became middlemen between their kinsmen in the pueblos and the eastern tribes, including the Caddo and Wichita. See Nancy P. Hickerson, "Jumano: The Missing Link in South Plains History," *Journal of the West* 29, no. 4 (1990): 5–12; and Hickerson, *Jumanos.*

14. The large settlement was visited by Ortega in 1632, by Domínguez de Mendoza's expedition in 1684, and possibly by Cabeza de Vaca in 1534. The rancherías were visited by Coronado's expedition in 1541 and by Salas in 1629.

15. The Jediondos were visited by the Domínguez de Mendoza expedition in 1684.

16. Recounted in Benavides's *Memoriales* of 1630. Fray Alonso de Benavides, "The Memorial of Fray Alonso de Benavides, 1630," trans. Mrs. Edward E. Ayer, *Land of Sunshine* 13 (1900) and 14 (1901); and fray Alonso de Benavides, *Fray Alonso de Benavides' Revised Memorial of 1634,* eds. Frederick W. Hodge, George P. Hammond, and Agapito Rey (Albuquerque: University of New Mexico Press, 1945).

17. Recounted in Posada's *Report* of 1686. Alonso de Posada, *Alonso de Posada Report, 1686,* ed. Alfred Barnaby Thomas (Pensacola, Florida: Perdido Bay Press, 1982).

18. Charles W. Hackett, ed., *Historical Documents Relating to New Mexico, Nueva Vizcaya, and Approaches Thereto, to 1773,* collected by Adolph F. Bandelier and Fanny R. Bandelier, Carnegie Institution of Washington Publications 330, Monograph Series 2 (Washington, D.C.: Carnegie Institution of Washington, 1926).

19. Hammond, and Rey, *Rediscovery of New Mexico,* 79.

20. Recounted in Herbert E. Bolton, ed., *Spanish Explorations in the Southwest, 1542–1706* (New York: Scribner, 1908); and Espejo, "Report of Antonio de Espejo."

21. For Domínguez de Mendoza's account of the expedition, see Bolton, *Spanish Explorations.*

22. Juan Sabeata's career is recounted by J. Charles Kelley, "Juan Sabeata and Diffusion in Aboriginal Texas," *American Anthropologist* 57 (1955): 981–95; and Hickerson, *Jumanos.* For insight into the Jumano situation in Nueva Vizcaya, see Hackett, *Historical Documents.*

23. Posada, *Alonso de Posada Report,* 57.

24. The late prehistoric Jornada focus was an eastern extension of the Mogollon, a major Southwestern cultural tradition. Bordering on arid and semiarid areas, it lacked the irrigation agriculture and substantial architecture of the nuclear Mogollon and incorporated a greater reliance on hunting and gathering.

25. Benavides, "Memorial," trans. Ayer, 45.

26. I base this suggestion in part on the Tanoan affiliation of the Kiowa language, as well as on cultural similarities and inferential historical connections. See Hickerson, "Linguistic Position of Jumano."

27. Hackett, *Historical Documents.*

28. In a recent history of dogs in the Americas, Marion Schwartz suggests that the use of "backpacking dogs" was brought to the South Plains by the Athapaskans but denies that this included the use of the travois. Schwartz probably assumes that the Jumanos-Teyas were Athapaskan. Marion Schwartz, *A History of Dogs in the Early Americas* (New Haven: Yale University Press, 1997).

29. Espejo, "Report of Antonio de Espejo," 159.

30. Posada, *Alonso de Posada Report,* 42.

31. Benavides, "Memorial," trans. Ayer, 438–41.

32. Posada, *Alonso de Posada Report,* 36.

33. Benavides, *Memorial,* eds. Hodge, Hammond, and Rey, 100.

34. This is, admittedly, a speculative suggestion. If deemed worthy of consideration, it has the virtue of explaining, at least in part, both the surprisingly large Apache population and the geographical discontinuity between northern and southern divisions of the Athapaskan family.

35. Bolton, "Jumano Indians," 66–68.

36. An argument for this possibility is developed in Nancy P. Hickerson, "Ethnogenesis in the South Plains: Jumano to Kiowa?" in *History, Power, and Identity: Ethnogenesis in the Americas,* ed. Jonathan Hill (Iowa City: University of Iowa Press, 1996), 71–89.

37. Some remnants of the indigenous tribes, dispossessed both by the eastern sweep of the Lipan Apaches and by the beginnings of European settlement in Texas, made up the so-called Ranchería Grande, a shifting mass of Indians that wandered between the Colorado and Brazos Rivers until roughly the mid-eighteenth century. See Herbert E. Bolton, *Texas in the Middle Eighteenth Century* (Berkeley: University of California Press, 1915).

38. The ruins of the great Jumano pueblo of Cueloce constitute the archeological site now known as Gran Quivira, part of the Salinas Pueblo Missions National Monument near Mountainair, New Mexico.

39. R. Gordon Vivian, *Gran Quivira: Excavations in a Seventeenth-Century Jumano Pueblo,* Archaeological Research Series no. 8 (U.S. National Park Service, 1979), 145–47.

40. Early in 1601, Vicente de Zaldívar led a punitive attack on the Jumano pueblo. At the end of a week-long siege, the adult men of the pueblo were given in servitude to Zaldívar's soldiers. Zaldívar and his troops then departed almost immediately on the expedition to Quivira, doubtless with the Jumano slaves in tow.

TWELVE

The Jimmy Owens Site:
New Perspectives on the Coronado Expedition

DONALD J. BLAKESLEE AND JAY C. BLAINE

IT HAS BEEN MORE THAN one hundred years since George Winship published translations of some documents of the Coronado expedition,[1] an event that initiated modern investigations of that epochal journey. In the ensuing century, numerous scholars have attempted to trace the route of the expedition. Some agreement has been achieved regarding the most easily identified portions of the route: the Zuni pueblos, the pueblos of the Rio Grande Valley, and the grass house villages of the Wichita Indians in central Kansas. For the Texas portion of the route, however, the documentary accounts are vague and sometimes mutually contradictory. As a result, many routes have been proposed, from several that never take Coronado south of the Canadian River to others that have him on the Conchas River, far to the south. Until now, there has been no material evidence to confirm the location of any of the camps on his Texas route.

In this chapter, we report work done at the Jimmy Owens Site (41FL81), with an emphasis on the problems the site presents to the archeologist. We review the evidence we believe demonstrates that the site was created by the expeditionary force of Francisco Vázquez de Coronado, and we discuss the data accumulated so far with regard to determining which of the army's two main camps this site might represent. We end with a brief description of plans for future work at the site.

Discovery of the Jimmy Owens Site

A series of symposia held in Amarillo, Texas; Lyons, Kansas; and Las Vegas, New Mexico, have brought together a wide range of people interested in the Coronado

route. In 1990, the late Margaret Harper of Canyon, Texas, organized the first symposium. After listening to the evidence presented there, the senior author of this
chapter concluded that just enough evidence might be available to enable delineation of the route—a judgment made on the basis of experience tracing the route
of the Mallet expedition of 1739, for which a seven-page document provides the
only written description.[2]

Out of the second and third symposia, there developed a loosely organized
set of people who continued to investigate the Texas portion of the route. They
included, besides Blakeslee, the late Billy Harrison, archeologist, Panhandle-
Plains Museum, Canyon, Texas; the late Al Schroeder, archeologist and ethnohistorian, National Park Service, Santa Fe; David Snow, archeologist, Museum
of New Mexico; the late Mildred Wedel, ethnohistorian, Smithsonian Institution;
the late Waldo Wedel, archeologist emeritus, Smithsonian Institution; numerous
local residents and amateur archeologists; and, among the other contributors to
this volume, Jay Blaine, Richard Flint, Shirley Cushing Flint, William Hartmann,
the late Jack Hughes, and Carroll Riley.

As our study of the problem proceeded, we developed a methodology that
involved several critical elements. The first was open debate; for every issue in
the overall problem, someone stepped forward as a devil's advocate, challenging the general consensus.[3] A second element was fieldwork. Grants from
Wichita State University and the Harrington Foundation enabled some of us to
travel across the parts of Texas specified in various hypotheses regarding the
route. Later, the Summerlee Foundation of Dallas supported two years of excavation and other work at the Jimmy Owens Site. Jack Hughes and Billy Harrison
contributed their vast knowledge of the local archeology, geology, vegetation,
and water holes. Blakeslee began a review of Indian trails, a study that has been
expanded enormously by Alvin Lynn, a local resident. We even traveled the
Panhandle in the same season that Vázquez de Coronado was there in order to
get the best possible sense of what his men had experienced.

The final element in our approach has been a critical reanalysis of all of the
previously proposed routes, an effort made relatively easy by the historiography
of Joseph Sánchez.[4] Some proposed routes were no more than assertions of
faith that Coronado had been in a certain region. Others used descriptions of
the landscape or the vegetation to support one hypothesis or another. What we
did was to take all of the documentary evidence as criteria by which to judge the
accuracy of the various hypotheses. This process led most of us to reject all of
the proposed routes except for the set that had Coronado's main camp somewhere between Yellow House Canyon on the south and Palo Duro Canyon on
the north.[5] Only this area fits the bulk of the documentary evidence.

During the fieldwork we received publicity in local newspapers. This led Nancy Marble, a member of the board of the Floyd County Historical Society, to contact us about an artifact in her museum. She had read an old newspaper account of the discovery of a chain mail gauntlet in the county, traced down the finder, and purchased the artifact for the Floyd County Historical Museum. She contacted Blakeslee, and he visited the site of the find, near a *playa* lake on the edge of Blanco Canyon. Blakeslee was given a guided tour of the canyon by the late Jimmy Owens, a local man who had been using a metal detector to find historic Comanche and Kiowa sites.

Owens promised to look for evidence of a Coronado camp, and eventually he found it. The first possible expedition artifact that he located was a possible iron crossbow bolthead, which he found in the canyon. Later, he found a copper bolthead in the canyon almost directly below the spot where the gauntlet had been found. This prompted archeological work over the Labor Day weekend of 1995, which uncovered another copper bolthead. Found by Ray Macha, it came from a spot over three miles from the first copper point and the gauntlet. In the next few months, Owens was able to delineate a large concentration of metal artifacts near Macha's find, and we now understand this to be the main camp of Coronado's expedition.

Investigation of the Site

The main concentration of Spanish metal artifacts covers an area about 350 by 200 meters in extent along the edge of a terrace of the White River in Blanco Canyon (map 12.1). Remnants of an Indian trail are visible on either side of the canyon, where it took advantage of natural gaps in the caprock. The site appears to be located where the trail crossed the river (which now flows only intermittently).

Today, the site is covered with mesquite scrub and short grasses. Within living memory, however, the water table was much higher, and the canyon floor supported tall grasses and was free of mesquite. When Coronado visited in 1541, the canyon would have been a green oasis in the midst of the high plains. The Spaniards' accounts of the canyons they visited describe groves of trees along the stream courses, including nut trees and mulberries. Other vegetation mentioned includes grapevines and currants.[6] All of the plants mentioned in the accounts once grew in Blanco Canyon and probably in all of the well-watered canyons along the eastern escarpment of the Llano Estacado.

Preliminary results from geomorphic investigations conducted by Rolfe Mandel of the University of Kansas indicate that historic farming upstream has changed the configuration of the landscape at the site. Today, the river terrace

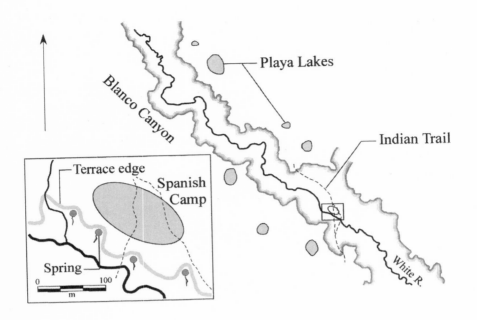

Map 12.1.   Location and apparent structure of the Jimmy Owens Site (41FL81).

that contains the site is approximately six feet above the level of the floodplain. At the time the site was occupied, however, the surface of the floodplain lay about eight feet below its present location. The paleosol that marks its former location is a *cienega* soil, which means that the floodplain was quite swampy. It is likely that a series of springs issued from the base of the terrace, and these would have provided readily accessible water for Coronado's men. The well-watered floodplain would have been fully capable of supporting the nut trees mentioned in the Coronado documents.

The Jimmy Owens Site presents the archeologist with some difficult problems, and finding solutions to them has shaped the course of our investigations. For example, the section of the canyon that contains the site is heavily infested with mesquite trees. When it became clear that the trees were preventing full coverage of the site with metal detectors and were making accurate mapping almost impossible, we began a program of mesquite clearing. We have used a "tree terminator" donated by the Chance Manufacturing Company of Wichita Falls and have had the occasional use of another loaned by Jim Doucette of Lockney, Texas. A large part of the clearing, however, has been done by hand and with chain saws.

Another consideration has been for the family that lives on the property and whose ranch encompasses the site. They are not named here because they wish to remain anonymous. They asked that we keep our crews small and our visits relatively short so that ranching activities would not be interrupted by our investigations. The family has offered us the best of West Texas hospitality on every visit and has made the extraordinary gesture of donating all of the collected materials to the local museum, and we have been happy to follow their wishes.

Once an area has been cleared, we use a team of metal detector surveyors to cover all of the ground surface to locate metal targets. These are flagged, and their approximate depth and nature (ferrous or other metal) are recorded from the metal detector readouts. The detectors generally provide excellent discrimination between ferrous and other kinds of metal but are less accurate in determining depth of burial. We have also found that soil moisture has a strong effect on the depth at which detectors will record small pieces of metal. Nevertheless, the use of metal detectors is far more cost efficient and far less destructive than most other techniques.

Once the metal detectors have found the targets in an area, we map in pin flags with a transit. This process is made possible by the fact that the bulk of the Coronado-era artifacts lie within 20 centimeters of the ground surface. This makes the use of metal detectors possible, because many of the metal artifacts are small, and metal detectors cannot locate those buried more than about 20 centimeters deep.

At the same time, however, the shallow burial of the 1541 ground surface has made interpretation of the resulting maps difficult. Coronado's expedition stayed at the site for a maximum of two weeks, but the canyon has been occupied at least intermittently for twelve thousand years. Artifacts from the whole span of the historic period, and perhaps some earlier artifacts as well, are intermingled in the 20-centimeter zone. Luckily, the site was never plowed, but the early use of the canyon by Comancheros and *pastores* and its more recent use by ranchers means that not all of the metal targets located by the metal detectors are associated with the Coronado expedition. Indeed, a minority of the metal artifacts excavated so far appears to have come from the expedition. The most common items excavated to date are fence staples, pieces of wire, bullets, buckshot, and pieces of tin cans.

Indeed, until our last visit to the site, in March 2000, we had an incorrect idea of the location of the upstream end of the Spanish camp. This fact reflects in part the presence of a historic trash dump associated with an old ranch headquarters. Objects from the dump have been spread widely by floods, and as one proceeds northwest across the site, the density of recent metal artifacts increases.

That density completely obscured the boundary of the camp until we initiated a new procedure.

In March 2000 we laid a 10-meter-wide transect across the long axis of the site. We then divided the transect into 10-meter squares, marking the corners with PVC pipe and running string around the boundaries of each square. The string is marked at 1-meter intervals, and we stretched two similarly marked cords across the squares between the marks. This gave us a corridor one meter wide that we could move across each square. We used metal detectors to mark every target in each corridor and then mapped them. To do so, we used a gadget that consists of a 1-meter square formed by small-diameter PVC pipe, with the pipe drilled every 10 centimeters to allow it to be strung into a set of 10-centimeter squares. We laid this device on top of the marked cords and mapped the targets quickly, with an accuracy of about 1 centimeter.

After we mapped each row, we used small tools to excavate each target. We then recorded the depth and identity of each metal item. The metal artifacts were then sorted into three categories: not Coronado-related, possibly Coronado-related, and definitely Coronado-related. Any Coronado-related and possibly Coronado-related objects were to be replaced by plastic beads so that there could be no confusion about the spots from which they derived.

We started the grid about 20 meters beyond what we thought was the site boundary and were able to complete 100 meters of coverage. As it turned out, we found only one possibly Coronado-related artifact in the 100-meter by 10-meter area covered. It is the tip of a square nail that was found 99.76 meters from the point of origin of the transect.

This transformed our image of the site, because the first 100 meters of coverage brought us very close to an area that we were excavating. This area encompasses a zone that has produced the majority of copper crossbow boltheads collected from the site and a considerable number of the kinds of nails that are associated with the Coronado expedition.

Previously, we had excavated a series of test pits across the mapped portions of the site in order to recover a sample of the material culture and to investigate patterns that emerged from the mapping. We have used shovels to scrape off the overburden and trowels to excavate the artifact-bearing zone. All fill has been passed through quarter-inch mesh screening.

Features uncovered to date include a post mold, several shallow basins, and traces of hearths. Bison bone associated with the features shows evidence of having lain on the ground surface for at least several months after deposition, and the same length of exposure to West Texas winds means that charcoal has been scarce. Indeed, to date we have uncovered only one (badly disturbed) hearth that we are certain is associated with Coronado. The few well-preserved hearths are all associated with later artifacts.

With only two exceptions, we have been unable to discern a clear pattern in the distribution of the metal targets, the metal objects excavated, or the features encountered. The metal targets, again, include a majority of items from later time periods. The features also appear to derive from a variety of time periods, and the artifacts likely to have come from the Coronado expedition are rather thinly scattered. This is why we began the transect across the site in which we are excavating every metal target. Although this process removes the metal artifacts from their context, the resulting map and the plastic beads used to replace the artifacts mean that the contexts of the Coronado-era artifacts can be recovered by block excavations in the future.

The two exceptions to the lack of pattern are widely separated in the site. We excavated a series of blocks near what we thought was the downstream end of the site, and these yielded a series of Coronado-related artifacts, mostly nails. The nails appeared to lie in three sets, each approximately 10 meters in width, and to be separated from one another by 10 meters. The scatters were so diffuse, however, that we were not absolutely certain that our results were not part of a random pattern.

At the other end of the site, near the end of the 100-by-10-meter transect, however, was a much clearer distribution. In this area, a dirt road crosses the site, and it was in this vicinity that Jimmy Owens and Ray Macha found the first crossbow bolthead from the main camp. Subsequently, Owens and Roland Adams used metal detectors to collect sixteen crossbow boltheads (with the permission of the landowner) before we had the opportunity to convince them that uncontrolled removal was destroying evidence. We returned to this spot and initiated a block excavation at the edge of the road where erosion had exposed a few pieces of burned caliche. We have continued to expand this block excavation and have uncovered what is, for this site, a dense concentration of artifacts.

The complex uncovered so far includes one badly disturbed hearth that is surrounded by a pattern of bone residue (fig. 12.1). Nearest to the hearth are some very small fragments of bone. Outside of these is a relatively sterile area, but this is surrounded by a third zone that contains relatively large fragments identifiable as bison bone. We interpret the sterile zone as the place where men squatted or sat around the fire, tossing bones over their shoulders when they had finished eating.

Adjacent to this pattern, on the side toward the river, we have uncovered a concentration of distinctive nails. None of the nails in this concentration shows any sign of use as a horseshoe nail, and they may have been used to construct

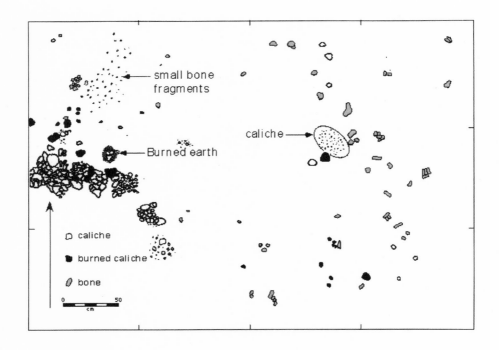

Figure 12.1. Hearth remnant and associated animal bone in block excavation at the Jimmy Owens Site (41FL81).

temporary shelters. Also in this general area, but unfortunately coming from the dirt road, is one copper crossbow bolthead. This specimen was somehow missed when Owens and Adams first investigated the site with their metal detectors.

Evidence for a Coronado Relationship

The Jimmy Owens Site stands out from other sites in the region that yield metal artifacts. First, there is simply its immense size. No other early historic campsite in West Texas, up to and including those of the Comanchero era, is as large as the Jimmy Owens Site. This probably reflects the fact that no other Spanish expedition to this part of Texas was ever as large as Coronado's.

A more direct form of evidence of the identity of the site consists of the copper crossbow boltheads. Of all of the land expeditions into the American Southwest, only the Coronado expedition is known to have carried crossbows.[7] In all of New Mexico, fewer than fifteen such objects had been reported prior to our research, all of which have come from sites known to have been or likely to have been visited by Coronado. A recent study of the boltheads (see chapter 14) showed that some of those from the Jimmy Owens Site were so similar to boltheads from sites such as Hawikuh and Kuaua that it is likely they were manufactured by the same persons.

The distribution of the copper boltheads is such that they can be considered horizon markers for the first half of the sixteenth century in the American Southwest. Crossbows were being replaced by firearms during that half-century, as is evidenced by the arquebuses that Coronado's men also carried. By the time of Oñate's colonizing of New Mexico, crossbows appear no longer to have been in use. If they had, New Mexico should have yielded many more of them, and from a much wider variety of sites.

Another potential horizon marker is a variety of nail that is the most common at the site (fig. 12.2). The present nail sample includes at least four different hand-wrought types. The variety that is most common is found in both used, or distorted, and apparently unused condition. In the experience of the junior author, this type is quite unusual when compared with the general run of wrought-iron nails from English, French, and Spanish sites of colonial times.

A rather unusual group of characteristics defines the head form of these nails. As viewed from above, the subrectangular head displays two facets. A central crowning ridge, like that on a gabled roof, is formed where the two facets meet. What sets these nails apart from most that we have seen in the literature is the fact that the underside "eaves" are also angled, typically between 140 and 160 degrees. Similar nails have been found in New Mexico in a sixteenth-century campsite that Bradley Vierra argues has a Coronado affiliation.[8] They also show up in the Martin Site, associated with the Soto expedition and excavated by B. Calvin Jones and Charles R. Ewen, and in sixteenth-century sites in Panama (see chapter 15).[9] This style of nail does not appear to have survived the sixteenth century, making it another horizon marker.

Unused specimens of these nails suggest that the downward slope of the lateral undersides were designed to have a clasping function, a use that would have been enhanced when the ends of the head penetrated the surface into which the nail was driven. It is also possible that the angled underside was intended to fit a rounded surface of small diameter. It is probable that the blacksmith needed a special nail heading device in order to produce this form. At any rate, compared with the vast majority of hand-wrought nails, these clearly are a special case. Production would have been more labor intensive and thus of higher cost than production of the ordinary nail types. The justification for this cost appears to be that the nails met some special need.

Their presence in large numbers at the Jimmy Owens Site (and the Martin

Figure 12.2. Sixteenth-century nail in situ at the Jimmy Owens Site (41FL81).

Site) raises several questions. First, what were they used for? The expedition depended strongly on horse transport. Shoeing the Spanish horse or mule of the period typically called for thirty-two horseshoe nails per beast for each complete shoeing event. We are not aware of any other needs that would have been known in advance that would have required nails in such large numbers.

Parts of typical Spanish-style horseshoes are also found at the Jimmy Owens Site. One still contained such a nail in articulation, and other nails of the type in question show wear and other modification consistent with such use. The heads of some nails are almost worn away, shanks are clinched, and tips have been snipped off, all clear evidence of use as horseshoe nails. This is especially puzzling because the head and uppermost shank configuration of these nails appear quite unsuitable for horseshoeing, although their lower shank width, thickness, and length are suitable. Ewen and Hann and Vierra offer other reasons for doubting that this type of nail was intended for horseshoeing,[10] but it is clear that some of them saw such use at the Jimmy Owens Site.

If these nails were made to be used in horseshoes, we cannot explain the angled form of the underside of the heads. One one hand, if the soft iron nails were hammered hard enough, the head would flatten out against the horseshoe. In that case, there would be no obvious reason for angling the underside in the first place. On the other hand, if the nails were not hammered hard enough to flatten the heads, the stresses produced by the horse's walking would eventually flatten them—something that can be seen on well-worn specimens. In this case, the flattening of the nail heads would loosen the horseshoe.

To compound the situation, typical Spanish horseshoe nails are also present in the Jimmy Owens Site collection, but in smaller numbers, and some of them appear unused. Although these specimens appear to be similar in age to the more common type, as judged from the extent of corrosion, they might derive from later use of the site by Apaches, Comanches, Kiowas, Comancheros, and pastores.

Possibly the bifaceted-head nails were an early experiment in horseshoeing with the wide and flat-branched Spanish horseshoes. Because of the nail shank configuration, the long axis of the head would position across the long axis of the shoe branches and thus could have contributed to better traction. A perhaps more likely scenario is use of the bifaceted-head nails to supplement a decreasing supply of typical Spanish horseshoe nails. This speculation, however, does not resolve the questions of their original purpose and why Coronado's men carried them in such large numbers. Whatever their purpose, the fact that use of these nails did not survive the sixteenth century means that they help to "nail" the identity of the site.

Other artifacts from the site that suggest a sixteenth-century date are varied. Most common are pieces of horse gear, including horseshoes, bits, and fragments of harness. A sword belt chafe and a possible pack saddle fragment are among the more interesting ones.

Interpretation

A 1992 National Park Service study concluded that "the historical, ethnographic and archeological evidence is at present too fragmentary and vague to confidently identify Coronado's route between known sites."[11] The Jimmy Owens Site, however, has already contributed significantly to our understanding of the route the expedition followed across Texas. It narrows the range of possibilities considerably. When we are able to identify which of Coronado's campsites it represents, much of the route should become clear (map 12.2). To clarify this issue, a brief review of the Texas portion of the *entrada* is in order.

After a dismal winter spent fighting the natives of Tiguex, Coronado went east onto the plains to investigate a place reported to have gold. In doing so, he passed through Pecos Pueblo and crossed at least one major river. Eventually, he came to the buffalo plains and met two camps of people he called Querechos. He wandered lost for a while on the featureless high plains before coming to a large canyon in which he found a camp of people he called Teyas.

After exploring the Teya country from this base camp, Coronado separated his expedition from his new hosts and left the bulk of his contingent in another canyon, taking a party of only thirty men northward to what is now Kansas. After thirty days of travel, he reached the Arkansas River in southwestern Kansas and followed its north bank into the land he called Quivira. After exploring this region

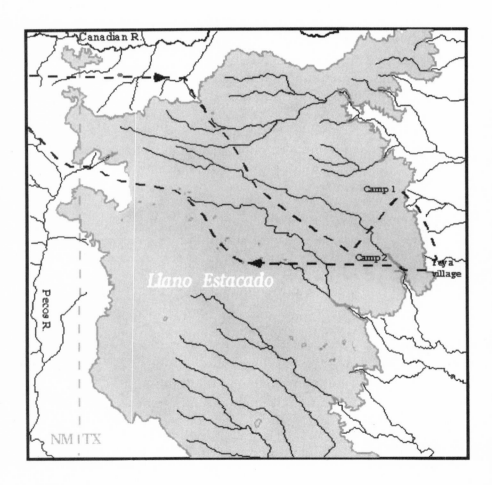

Map 12.2. The Texas portion of the Coronado route, using the assumption that the Jimmy Owens Site is the second major camp.

THE JIMMY OWENS SITE

and finding no gold, he returned to his main camp at Tiguex. The main group had returned there previously after spending two weeks hunting bison from the camp in the second canyon. Their return trip was relatively rapid, and it is likely that they never spent more than a single night in any spot during that trip.

Thus there are only two places in Texas where the expedition spent more than a day or so, and both of them are in canyons. The records suggest that the archeological sites produced by the two camps should look quite different from one another. In the first camp, there was a village of Teyas, probably an encampment of teepees. The records do not tell whether Coronado camped immediately adjacent to the Teyas or at some distance from them, nor do they specify how long his party remained in this spot. While they were there, however, the Spaniards were hit by a severe thunderstorm, with hail that broke every pot in camp and stampeded the horse herd. Few animals were lost, however, because they were hemmed in by the canyon walls.

Teya guides led Coronado through their country and one day's travel past the last village to a second, empty canyon, where Coronado left the main group. This canyon was described as larger than the first, approximately one league (2.5 miles) across. Each day the men rode out from the canyon to hunt bison on the plains above, and every day some of the men became lost. To help the lost men find the camp, the Spaniards blew trumpets, lit bonfires, and fired guns.

These documentary clues suggest the following distinctions between the two campsites: The first camp should be in the smaller of two canyons and should contain two concentrations of sixteenth-century pottery, reflecting the vessels in the Teya Indian and Spanish camps, respectively. The Teya camp should have some of the trade goods that Coronado is likely to have carried, such as brass bells and Nueva Cádiz beads. The second camp should be in a canyon a league wide, should have far less pottery than the first camp, and should instead have evidence of extensive bison hunting.

To date, the Jimmy Owens Site has yielded both bison bone and pottery. The pottery is badly broken, perhaps the result of the hailstorm. However, the bison bone is also highly fractured and deeply weathered, evidence that the materials left behind by the Spaniards lay on the surface for at least several months. Hence breakage and scattering of the pottery cannot be considered conclusive evidence that this was the first camp. Furthermore, not all of the pottery found so far is associated with the campsite. Indeed, the surface finds reported by Blakeslee, Flint, and Hughes have turned out not to be in association with the main camp.[12] To date, our excavations have uncovered only two concentrations of broken pottery of types that could have been in use in 1541, and each concentration contains sherds from only a single vessel.

Evidence suggesting that the Jimmy Owens Site is the second camp comes from its context. Before his death, Owens located three scatters of early Spanish material upstream from the main concentration. One of these includes the area where the first copper crossbow bolthead was found, near a spot that yielded a piece of chain mail and below the spot where the chain mail gauntlet was found. He also found a few of the distinctive nails in this location. This spot lies about three miles up the canyon from the main concentration of metal artifacts. Above it are two more spots that have yielded a few of the nails, the uppermost of which is 5.5 miles above the main camp.

These apparent outposts all occur at places where there are natural breaks in the caprock, breaks that were used as Indian trails. The three artifact clusters, moreover, are located in the canyon, near the river, at the only spots where one can enter or leave the canyon on horseback. Downstream from the Jimmy Owens Site, there are no natural breaks in the caprock until one reaches the spot where the modern highway crosses the canyon. Just below the modern highway, on the north rim of the canyon, is a well-preserved trail, but we have not yet had a chance to search in this relatively heavily used area for Coronado-related material.

Also in the canyon are several aboriginal sites worthy of consideration. A short distance above the Jimmy Owens Site is the Montgomery Site. Much farther up the canyon is the Country Club Site, and at a similar distance downstream is the Bridwell Site. All three are assigned to the Garza complex and should date to the Coronado era.

If Blanco Canyon is the first canyon visited by Coronado, then we would expect to find some trade goods in one of the other sites in the area, which would be the remains of the Teya village. No such artifacts have been reported from any of the sites in question. If Blanco Canyon is the second canyon visited, then we have to make the assumption that the canyon happened not to be occupied by Indians in 1541, even though they camped there in other years.

If it is the second canyon, however, the fact that men got lost while hunting bison might explain the presence of the outposts. In order to guide the hunters back to camp, their companions lit bonfires. To be visible to the lost hunters, the fires would have to have been on the canyon rim, and to be useful, they should have been placed at spots where the horsemen could get back into the canyon. The scatters of nails might reflect the construction of lean-tos to shelter the men who were sent out to gather the wood for and to man the bonfires.

The trail that enters the canyon downstream from the Jimmy Owens Site does so at a spot in the canyon that is approximately a league wide. This trail used to be the buggy trail that ran to the canyon from Roaring Spring.[13] Roaring Spring and the Mott Camp (a major cottonwood grove with good water that is upstream from Roaring Spring) are both good candidates for the site of the last Teya village through which Coronado passed, but both have been used heavily in recent years, making location of diagnostic artifacts difficult.

If Blanco Canyon is the last canyon visited by Coronado, then the first canyon must lie to the north. Candidates are numerous, because the escarpment is dissected by many smaller canyons in this region. If Blanco Canyon is the first canyon visited, then a larger canyon has to be the site of the second camp. Only Tule Canyon and Yellow House Canyon fit the bill. Both could be reached in four days of travel from Blanco Canyon (three days in Teya country and one day beyond), and both are larger than Blanco Canyon.

It may well be that we cannot determine the identity of the Jimmy Owens Site with any certainty until the second camp is found. Once this is done, however, the major outlines of the Coronado route across Texas will become clear.

Future Work

With every site, there comes the question of how much further work is justified. To date, we have collected enough diagnostic material culture to determine to our satisfaction that this is a site of the Coronado expedition. We have not yet resolved to everyone's satisfaction the question of which major camp it is, and the answer may require finding the other major camp. We have also been unable to identify the remains left by the Mexican Indians who made up much of Coronado's armed force. We had hoped to find pieces of obsidian from central Mexico and perhaps some pottery from their homeland as well.

This has not happened. Instead, all of the identifiable flaked stone from the site, which is not plentiful, is from relatively local sources: Edwards Plateau chert, Alibates chert, and Tecovas jasper. There are two possibilities to explain this. Either we have not found the Mexican Indian portion of the camp or, by the time they had arrived in Blanco Canyon, the Mexican Indians had used up all of the chipped stone they had started out with and had replaced it with materials obtained from local people.

Another potential goal is to delineate the internal arrangement of the camp. Our recent results suggest that it had at least one definite boundary, and some simple calculations indicate that fifteen hundred people could have camped within the boundaries of the main concentration of artifacts. We plan to continue the transect across the site to determine where other concentrations of artifacts lie. We also plan to use a magnetometer and a resistivity meter across the same transect after the metal targets have been removed to search for subtler features such as hearths and pits.

The landowners have donated all of the material from the site to the Floyd County Historical Museum. Some of the artifacts are already on display, and plans are under way to expand the museum so that the materials from the Jimmy Owens Site can be used to educate the public and to draw heritage tourism to the region.

Notes

We are grateful to Wichita State University for a seed grant, to the Harrington Foundation for support of the background research, and to the Summerlee Foundation of Dallas for the funding that has allowed two years of survey and excavations at the Jimmy Owens Site. None of the work would have been as fruitful and as enjoyable as it has been, however, without the support and hospitality of the good people of Floyd County.

1. Winship, *Coronado Expedition.*
2. Blakeslee, *Along Ancient Trails,* 215–25.
3. Blakeslee, Flint, and Hughes, "*Una Barranca Grande,*" 370–83; see also chapter 10, this volume.
4. Joseph P. Sánchez, "A Historiography of the Expedition of Francisco Vázquez de Coronado: General Comments," in Flint and Flint, *Coronado Expedition to Tierra Nueva,* 31–35; Joseph P. Sánchez, "A Historiography of the Expedition of Francisco Vázquez de Coronado: Compostela to Cíbola," in Flint and Flint, *Coronado Expedition to Tierra Nueva,* 138–48; Joseph P. Sánchez, "A Historiography of the Expedition of Francisco Vázquez de Coronado: Cíbola to Río de Çicuye," in Flint and Flint, *Coronado Expedition to Tierra Nueva,* 215–24; and Joseph P. Sánchez, "A Historiography of the Expedition of Francisco Vázquez de Coronado: Río de Çicuye to Quivira," in Flint and Flint, *Coronado Expedition to Tierra Nueva,* 281–301.
5. Donald J. Blakeslee, "Which Barrancas? Narrowing the Possibilities," in Flint and Flint, *Coronado Expedition to Tierra Nueva,* 302–19.
6. Blakeslee, "Which Barrancas?" 308.
7. Rhodes, "Coronado Fought Here," 44–56; see also chapter 14, this volume.
8. Vierra, "Spanish Campsite."
9. Charles R. Ewen and John H. Hann, *Hernando de Soto among the Apalachee: The Archaeology of the First Winter Encampment* (Gainesville: University Presses of Florida, 1998), 82–84.
10. Ewen and Hann, *Hernando de Soto,* 83; Vierra is cited in Ewen and Hann, *Hernando de Soto,* 84.
11. U.S. Department of the Interior, National Park Service, *Coronado Expedition: Arizona/New Mexico/Texas/Oklahoma/Kansas (March 1992),* National Trail Study and Environmental Assessment (Denver, 1992), 13.
12. Blakeslee, Flint, and Hughes, "*Una Barranca Grande,*" 370–83.
13. Georgia Mae Erickson, personal communication, 1999.

THIRTEEN

First Arrivals: *Coronado, Hank Smith,* and the Old Springs of the Llano Estacado

JOHN MILLER MORRIS

The world we now view from the literate West—the vistas of time, the land and the seas, the heavenly bodies and our own bodies, the plants and animals, history and human societies past and present—had to be opened for us by countless Columbuses.

—Daniel J. Boorstin, *The Discoverers*

THERE IS A PREVAILING DESIRE for *wonder* guiding all first arrivals—a psychological curiosity about "the other side of the mountain" that primes us for discovery. This curiosity is probably primordial, ingrained at some deep level within our pattern-seeking and symbol-mongering species. New or unexploited habitats once equated with improved resources for hunters and gatherers. Long before worker bees settled into the pollution domes of metropolitan habitats, carpooling children to local "discovery centers," men, women, and children alike roamed their worlds. Indeed, the predominant history of humanity is one epic journey of migration out of Africa. Finding a wondrous new land, such as Australia, Hawaii, the Valley of Mexico, or the Great Plains, is to see a privately beautiful world opening before keenly territorial eyes. Later arrivals see the same geomorphology and scenes, but the thrill of discovery may not be as keen. To be a *first arrival* is to enjoy the paramount feelings of pure discovery—and first claim.

Consider the southern High Plains, or Llano Estacado region. Within the last hundred years the very meaning of being "first" on these shortgrass plains has altered radically. Some portions of these plains, such as Blackwater Draw and Yellow House Canyon, show human time lines some threefold greater than once imagined possible. Over thirteen millennia, various "first" arrivals have claimed the eastern escarpment canyons and surrounding plains of the Llano Estacado. All of the newcomers used its resources, wove the land into their myths, knowledge, and history, and claimed from it various rights of discovery and territorial ownership. One of the foremost rights claimed was the reward of appropriation—especially the acquisition associated with being "first." It is this sense of "firstness" linked to the southern High Plains (if not to the Greater Southwest) that I find intriguing among our own perceptions today.

The Coronado expedition of 1540–42, for example, was an embarrassing blunder and an expensive investment failure in its day. Worse, alleged violations of "human rights" tainted the entire enterprise, leading to the title *Great Cruelties* for historian Richard Flint's recent study of the aftermath documentation. However that may be, more than three centuries later a group of men discovered the Coronado expedition and gave it a new significance.

By the close of the nineteenth century, scholars such as Henri Ternaux-Compans, Joaquin Garcia Icazbalceta, and George Parker Winship had resurrected Francisco Vázquez de Coronado from the dustbin of history. By 1940, American writers and artists had created an entire romantic horizon for "the first Europeans," that is, the first "white men" to visit the Pueblo peoples, or the Grand Canyon, or the Great Plains. Americans learned to admire the expedition, not for its "cruelties" but for the mantle of "discovery" that now shrouded the *entrada* of Vázquez de Coronado. Soon the final name of a formerly disgraced leader adorned countless Southwestern motels, restaurants, tourist courts, hotel suites, streets, shops, theaters, and local schools. The very name was a sign of promise.

The epic-scale Coronado expedition of 1540–42 may have set out for gold (wealth that lay hidden in nearby mountains along much of the route), but its members found something else—new lands. Without gold, of course, the expedition was judged a failure in its day. But as time slipped by, members of the expedition such as Juan Jaramillo remembered that they had found something precious after all—new and fertile lands, not unlike the best lands of Spain. Moreover, they recognized and conceived of themselves as "discoverers." Like Lewis and Clark, Coronado's conquistadores felt the emotional release associated with first arrivals, the elucidation of being the first people of their culture to see certain lands and climes.

Fortunately, those perceiving discovery often are stirred to recall or record the memorable experience. Whether in songs, oral history, diaries, chronicles, letters, or narratives, first arrivals often share their thoughts, thrills, and claims later in life. One of the greatest chroniclers of the sixteenth century, Pedro de Castañeda, epitomized this recognition of discovery. Castañeda not only felt "the wonder" but devoted a significant share of his early 1560s narrative to the *cosas señaladas,* the "wondrous things," he saw as a Coronado expedition member. Writing his account "for all those who are by nature inquisitive," Castañeda promised: "In it will be found things difficult to believe, indeed. All of which, or most of them, I have seen with my own eyes."[1] Significantly, almost a quarter of his narrative is devoted to the mysterious plains country discovered in 1540–42.

The emotional claim of landscapes on memory and soul tugs at us no less than it did Castañeda. Many Americans feel a historic connection to discovery, now often abbreviated as a compass point—"the West." The prolific author and screenwriter Will Henry tried to capture the feeling of the West in a May 1983 letter:

> I saw the West early enough in the present century (1930) and when I was young enough (18) to behold it all pristine as a vision not alone larger than life, but hauntingly more precious. . . . [T]he West was something far, and mysteriously more, than simply its history. It was a *private world* for me. I alone rode it in a time and to a distance known to no other horseman than myself. . . . O, Dear Lord, how it rooted me. The West was for me another space. It lay beyond the normal space that others saw.[2]

We can and should celebrate all newcomers to the southern High Plains. Indeed, a synergy may be emerging from a comparative study of three such "first arrivals": Paleolithic frontiersmen, European explorers of the mid-sixteenth century, and Anglo-American pioneers of the nineteenth century. Even these arrivals are only part of a much longer migration of species, a chain of discovery and introductions from Eurasia to the Americas reaching back some 33 million years. As diachronic loci though, two drainage systems of the southern High Plains, White River and Yellow House Draw, can serve as examples. Yellow House Draw shows a long chain of human occupation, and Blanco Canyon on the White River has yielded archeological evidence most recently associated with Coronado's arrival in Texas. From a postmodern perspective, of course, the plains and canyons of Lubbock, Floyd, Crosby, and nearby counties have seen many first arrivals, most recently a wave of Hispanic migration from Mexico to the Great Plains. Indeed, one can argue that the condition or state of being "first" is an ongoing human process, for all of us, in every age, and especially for youth.

Eurasian First Arrivals

Francisco Vázquez de Coronado and his cohorts were certainly not the first people of Eurasian descent to witness the glories of Blanco Canyon. A shadowy people known as the "pre-Clovis" may have been the first human arrivals in North America. Controversy swirls around them, but if they existed, they likely arrived some 18,000 to 24,000 years ago, possibly earlier along the Pacific Ocean coasts. Researchers announced in April 2000, for instance, that the Cactus Hill Site, forty-five miles south of Richmond, Virginia, was yielding apparent human tools and charred bone dating back 15,000 to 17,000 years ago. Artifacts from Sandia Cave near Albuquerque were once posited as precursors. As yet, though, there is no comparable evidence of any pre-Clovis people sojourning on the High Plains. Archeologists are still busy at the Lubbock Lake Landmark Site in Yellow House Canyon, a logical place to find the pre-Clovis if they ever visited the plains.[3] And there are mysteries still unfathomed around the forgotten springs of the Llano Estacado. Nevertheless, the presence (or rather absence) of pre-Clovis people on the High Plains remains only a tantalizer. Pre-Clovis aside, who were the authentic "first arrivals," the first and undoubted *Homo sapiens sapiens,* in the Southwest?

Answers to that question came from the ancient headwaters and upland marshes that once drained into Yellow House Canyon. In the early 1930s, as dust-bowl winds deflated the Texas–New Mexico plains, two amateur artifact hunters made a historic discovery. At a recent gravel pit seven miles north of Portales and fourteen miles southwest of Clovis, New Mexico, they found unusual fluted projectile points and bones of extinct fauna. The site sat in an ancient depression, probably a spring-fed pond that once drained southward into Blackwater Draw, itself a remote upper drainage of the Brazos River. Careful excavations by Edgar B. Howard and John L. Cotter in 1933–37 revealed a magnificent Paleoindian presence around the ancient wetlands of upper Blackwater Draw. (Blackwater Draw merges downstream with Yellow House Draw, just upstream of modern Lubbock, to form the North Fork Double Mountain Fork of the Brazos River.) The fluted Clovis points emerging from the Blackwater Draw Formation are now dated back some thirteen thousand years. Indeed, the "Clovis Gravel Site" soon became famous, a type locality that replaced the 1920s Folsom Man with the 1930s Clovis Man as the first *indisputable* human arrival in North America.

Clovis frontiersmen appeared on a verdant southern High Plains savanna about 11,200 B.P. (corrected to 13,200 years ago). At the end of the last ice age the Llano was blessed for a spell with good rainfall, leading to abundant playas and numerous active springs in the draws, stream channels, and canyons of the Llano Estacado. A mosaic of ponds, upland marshes, and remnant ice-age lakes further maintained a megafauna epitomized by the mammoth. Clovis bands apparently frequented certain portions of the High Plains. Their artifacts are often correlated with ancient springs feeding the draws or with playa lake sites.[4]

Like European arrivals in the sixteenth century, the Clovis people likely hunted on the uplands and frequented the watercourses, including the discharge springs of downstream Blanco and Yellow House Canyons. Juan Jaramillo noted that Coronado's expedition traveled—not unlike a highly mobile Clovis band— "along the waters found in the cattle country."[5] Indeed, if the draws and former wetlands of the southern High Plains have given the world glorious evidence of the Eurasian pioneers, they now show promise of doing the same for the Spanish. Of curious interest in this regard is the clustering of Clovis sites in the Southwest along two otherwise unrelated watercourses—Blackwater Draw and the San Pedro River in Arizona—both possible corridors for the Coronado expedition as well.

Clovis bands were apparently fond of the springs, large playas, and marshes of the region. Their bone and stone technologies suggest a sophisticated people rapidly exploiting New World resources at the end of the Pleistocene. At Blackwater Draw, Lubbock Lake Landmark, Miami, and other places, the Clovis may have demonstrated *ecological release,* a biological "manifest destiny" of sorts. As technology-wielding predators, the Clovis likely "exploded" in the New World, expanding rapidly in an environment unadapted to the newcomers' ways. Thus, the Clovis lived well off big game, ate lots of turtles, too, it seems, and hunted and gathered around springs and playas.

These first known arrivals frequented Yellow House, Blanco, and related canyons because these springlands (local areas with an abundance of springs) offered significant advantages. The water was purer, with fewer polluting admixtures from man and beast. Nearby plant food resources were often excellent: berries, nuts, grapes, herbs, and the like. Springs and marshes were also excellent ambush sites for larger game. Trees and plants offered concealment for human hunters, while boggy ground mired big beasts such as the preferred woolly mammoth. Concealment, surprise, and boggy terrain gave the Clovis pioneers better odds in attacking larger animals. It seems likely that the first Clovis people in the region, perhaps enterprising bands moving in to harvest animals in refugia left over from a prior drought, not only worked the uplands but also headed straight for the springlands of Blanco, Yellow House, and nearby canyons and draws.

Their arrival was quite likely bad news for the mammoths. For years a conceptual pendulum has swung between two theories about the demise of mammoths: climate change versus human hunting pressure. Both viewpoints are argued ably by scientists. What is clear is that a major episode of extinction struck the North American plains, and it eliminated many former species of Blanco and Yellow House Canyons. Some three-fourths of the megafauna died out, an unusually high percentage. "By the end of the Clovis occupation," comments

Vance Holliday, "most of the megafauna was gone."[6] Climatologists have new evidence that climate change may be rather sudden (if not catastrophic to some creatures and habitats). But in a larger and global context, it looks increasingly as if human migration into new habitats leads to overhunting and high rates of species extinction.

From 11,200 B.P. to 10,900 B.P. (13,200 to 12,900 years ago), the Eurasian pioneers of Yellow House and Blanco Canyons may have devastated the local megafauna. If so, then the Clovis first arrivals altered the biology of the High Plains far more than any subsequent group—at least until the European Americans arrived in the 1870s–80s. Paul Martin overstated this idea in his (much-debated) "Blitzkrieg" theory of Pleistocene overkill, but the core idea of a human-induced extinction episode is once again considered seriously. Clovis points do fade away around 10,900 B.P., suggesting that these first arrivals lasted a mere three centuries or so on the plains. Folsom points then appear around 10,800 B.P.—for example, at the Plainview Site upstream from Blanco Canyon. The Folsom people were named for a 1908 type locality discovered by George McJunkin, a cowboy near Folsom, New Mexico. (Like Esteban de Dorantes, McJunkin was of African descent and raised in slavery; both rose in life, were the first to see something important, and pointed the way for others to follow.) Folsom Man, too, appropriated the adjacent plains, draws, and escarpment canyons.

The remaining fauna, such as the giant bison (*Bison antiquus*), adapted to climate shifts if not to lasting human predators. Giant bison, for instance, diminished in size and likely developed strong herd behavior as an adaptive response. Eventually this elaborated herd behavior triumphed as tens of millions of bison became the keystone species of the Great Plains ecosystem. The immense size of the herds and their obvious group behavior certainly intrigued Coronado's men in the spring of 1541. Castañeda reported Spanish astonishment as one stampeding bison herd plunged into a small draw, filling it with their writhing bodies (and drawing several Spanish horses into the melee) until the other bison could cross over. Yet the Plainview archeological site suggests that Folsom people may have benefited from similar (if not induced) stampede kill sites in the local stream channels and draws. What struck the Spaniards as unusual or "wild" about the bison may in fact have reflected a pattern of coevolution between bison and the first humans. "The herding behavior of the bison," Tim Flannery remarks, "first arose as an adaptation to avoid the human predator, and this strategy protected these species for at least 13,000 years."[7]

In Blanco and Yellow House Canyons, the Clovis mammoth hunters and Folsom bison "wranglers" soon gave way to a long, complex, and still-debated series of arrival cultures. The advent of the Holocene, the great desiccation of the High Plains, with enormous dust storms and droughts, altered Paleoindian and Archaic habitats and populations in ways about which we can only gather data and speculate. However, the "big drying" naturally emphasized the importance of large playas, saline lakes, and Ogallala Aquifer discharge springs in the canyons. These watered and favored places attracted all, including bison and their completely dependent human and canine predators. Climatic shifts, habitat changes, population migrations, warfare, and captivity shaped a panoramic tableau of newcomers for the caprock canyons. The more recent the arrivals were (like the Teyas and Querechos observed in the sixteenth century, or the equestrian Comanche and Kiowa "pioneers" of the early eighteenth century), the more we understand their population flows into and out of the plains and canyons.

Curiously, while Coronado's men claimed the privileges of "first arrivals," an even larger demographic group was noting their passage, a group also relatively new to the Southwest—namely, the flat-faced Na-Dene migrants. The Nadene, specialists in colonizing marginal lands, were part of the second human wave that arrived in North America from Eurasia. Some nine thousand years ago they settled the forested coasts of western Canada. Highly adaptable, some Na-Dene eventually crossed the mountains to exploit the upper Great Plains. These Athapaskan people adapted to the world's largest grassland, followed and exploited its herds, and eventually migrated southward. After 1300 A.D., southern Athapaskan bands filtered into the northern plains and plateaus of the Southwest. Eastern Na-Dene frontiersmen became the Apaches of history, while western bands became the enduring Navajo.

Although the accounts of the Coronado expedition failed to mention the Navajo, Carroll L. Riley at least believes Navajo bands saw or soon heard of the conquistadores. In the spring of 1541, the Coronado expedition did encounter the roving eastern Na-Dene on the southern High Plains. They called them Querechos, admired their command of sign language, considered them a "good people," and recognized their ethnic singularity. Pedro de Castañeda's extensive comments on the Querecho provide invaluable insights into their Eurasian heritage, such as their use of the dog travois. In this sense, study of the Coronado expedition tells us much about other newcomers, too.

Spanish First Arrivals

The Coronado expedition has a palpable sense of "firstness" connected with it. For many parts of the United States it is a beginning itself, a divide between so-called prehistory and history. The history of the expedition itself has grown larger, both in the imagination and in the scholarship. For the first time, it is acknowledged, Europeans tramped over a great deal of the Southwest and Great Plains. The expedition's geographic scale was indeed vast, a swath of Spanish exploration stretching from Alarcón's fleet on the Colorado River to Coronado's captains on the High Plains of Texas, and on to the captain general himself among the Wichita and Pawnee of Kansas. In scope it was a magnificent panorama of discovery.

The expedition's contribution to North American geography was immense, advancing knowledge especially of the Great Plains. If the discoveries and names were wildly misplaced on the published maps of cartographers in the Old World, it was not the fault of Coronado, who apparently ordered the production of records and even maps. In composition his entrada was surprisingly multicultural. It thus introduced various ethnic groups to the "northern mysteries," including Mesoamericans, Afro-Iberians, and Europeans (Spanish and Portuguese, of course, but also the first French, Italian, German, and English speakers). Under Viceroy Mendoza's strictures, the expedition fostered a strong religious component. Not only did Coronado's friars bring Christianity for the first time into newly discovered realms, but several of them stayed behind as martyrs for the faith.[8]

Undermining the reality of these Spanish first arrivals in modern eyes, however, has been a large disconnection between their past and our present. Great uncertainties and convoluted debates surround the actual 1540–42 exploration routes. The question of where Coronado went and what he saw is not only important but has led to almost a century and a half of contention. In a 1992 study that rejected a proposed "Coronado National Trail," the National Park Service pointed to all the uncertainties and labeled large areas of Coronado's travels as falling into a "Zone of Uncertainty." The largest such zone of all the uncertainties, regretfully, was the southern High Plains.[9]

Coronado's route across the flat plains of Texas and New Mexico has taken numerous and erratic paths. Some scholars argue that he never encountered the southern High Plains, and some Texas scholars are reluctant to share Quivira with any other state but Texas. In 1869, the U.S. Army officer James H. Simpson first attempted to map the Coronado expedition against the geography of the United States. On his map of the expedition route, Simpson marched the outbound expedition northward from Cicuye (Pecos Pueblo), along grassy plains bordering the Front Range, into modern Colorado, and then suddenly eastward toward the Great Plains.[10] He did not locate or discuss the barrancas or canyons at all. These features would emerge and figure prominently in later deductions about the route. Simpson did note Castañeda's report of salt deposits, and he projected a return route for the main army that crossed the northwest corner of the Llano Estacado to reach the Portales Valley and Pecos River.

In the early 1900s, scholars such as George P. Winship and Frederick W. Hodge turned the expedition far southward, especially to the Concho River and Colorado River watershed. By the late 1920s and 1930s, most scholars recognized the critical role of the mysterious barrancas in locating the expedition. This attention to the "deep ravines" tended to reorient the expedition toward the greatest of the escarpment canyons, namely, scenic Palo Duro Canyon. The eminent borderlands historian Herbert E. Bolton convinced many Americans in the 1940s and 1950s that Coronado encountered Tule Canyon and relocated to Palo Duro Canyon, the "deep barranca" spoken of by Castañeda. Bolton thus placed the expedition on the Prairie Dog Town Fork of the Red River watershed.[11] The reputed connection of Coronado to Palo Duro Canyon was popular with the public and was celebrated in local art and tourism and at Palo Duro State Park. Although overshadowed by Bolton's hypothesis, a third major routing possibility was championed by the West Texas historian William C. Holden, who pointed, significantly, at the escarpment canyons of the Brazos River, especially Blanco and Yellow House Canyons.

The discovery of crossbow boltheads at the Jimmy Owens Site in the 1990s suddenly challenged routes either north or south of the Brazos River watershed. Suddenly, Blanco Canyon looked like a much better bet for a conquistador campsite than Palo Duro Canyon. The shift in attention from Palo Duro to Blanco had taken half a century, but for the first time a particular place for the expedition suddenly materialized out of the official "zone of uncertainty." Recently, the state of Texas dedicated a historical marker to acknowledge the significance of the Jimmy Owens Site.

The key place has proven to be the middle stretch of Blanco Canyon, in southern Floyd County, where a large number of crossbow boltheads have surfaced. Castañeda's description of this "deep barranca" has often been quoted— but, problematically, in a way that describes most of the escarpment canyons of the Llano and even ravines and watersheds farther away. Nevertheless, his remarks on the second barranca's width (one league), timber, grapevines, and fruits are in remarkable accordance with the geography of Blanco Canyon in the sixteenth century.[12] His narrative suggests that the expedition had identified a favored native landscape, called Cona, and simply relocated there.

Cona was an important place for the Coronado expedition. Like other new arrivals, the Spaniards likely congregated and camped around its springs, in this case the waters of Blanco Canyon. Why go to the springs? For one thing, Spanish domesticated animals relied on regular watering. Castañeda himself extolled Cona's human advantages: flowing water, campsites, woodlands (*arboledas*), grape arbors, fruits and nuts, and landscape features happily contrasting with the flat, disorienting plains on either side. Perhaps the springs of Blanco Canyon also blunted the transmission of waterborne diseases among the Europeans themselves. In any event, the discharge springs in the canyons made an impression on Castañeda, who noted that regular bison trails led down to the water below the flat surrounding plains.[13]

Stirred by their own past, the Spaniards looked into the pasts of the new lands and peoples they met. The fortress ruins of Chichilticale generated speculation and inquiry into its history and abandonment. And just as twentieth-century people reflect on the arrival of conquistadores, so the Renaissance Spaniards even speculated on ethnogenesis, including the arrival of Native Americans into the Southwest. Pedro de Castañeda's intuition held that the civilized Pueblo people of New Mexico had once been newcomers—immigrants from a distant Eurasia, now living in the New World. Castañeda wrote that "they must have come from that region of greater India, the coast of which lies on the west of this land."[14] Although aware of shortfalls in his geography, or "cosmography," Castañeda boldly rejected the widely assumed notion of a "Strait of Anian" or Northwest Passage across the new continent. He thus believed North America was linked in its northern latitudes to "greater India" (Eurasia).

Without knowledge of the Bering Sea, of course, Castañeda was missing a key piece of the puzzle. Yet modern science has only vastly refined his prescientific view—namely, that the ancestors of the Zuni and Tiwa, among others, had left Asia, bridged northern latitudes with culture and technology ("crossing the cordilleras," as he remarked), and then drifted southward, "settling where it seemed most suitable to them." Science allows us to extend the time frame, factor in changing climate, and lower and raise sea levels. Then the Pleistocene plains of "Beringia" emerge from a watery grave and do link Eurasia with North America. We have a million reductionistic details to add to Castañeda's hypothesis, but could he hear their broad outline today, he might wink and say, "I supposed much the same in the 1560s."

The very diversity of native cultures seen by the Coronado expedition suggests the long aftermath of "ecological release" often associated with first arrivals. Newcomers from Eurasia to North America, whether grizzly bears, sloths, or humans, can experience an explosion in numbers and diversity—over time, even an acceleration of speciation as geographically isolated populations adapt to different regions and become subspecies. This release occurs in part because newcomers have few rivals and the existing fauna is unable to process proper responses. This slowness to respond to dangerous new arrivals allows omnivores, in particular, to seize advantages and exploit rich new resources. Pedro de Castañeda foreshadowed the hunting advantages accruing to first arrivals when he observed that rabbits of the Great Plains paid no attention to men on horseback. Neither their genetics nor learned behavior told the rabbits to flee from ungulates—but men on foot triggered the usual flight response.

The ecological release experienced by the Spaniards in New Spain was dramatic, in some ways like that of the Clovis people on the High Plains. But Spanish "guns, germs, and steel," to borrow Jared Diamond's trilogy of fate,[15] did not collapse the megafauna so much as they collapsed the diversity of human cultures. Spanish cultural and religious influences fostered a universalism. Significantly, though, all kinds of portmanteau creatures also arrived with the first Europeans. The return of the horse to the land of its origin, the mid-continental grasslands of North America, was momentous.

The species had started on the Great Plains, migrated to Eurasia, experienced ecological release on the Eurasian plains, and been domesticated during the middle Neolithic. Once, domesticated horses spread to Africa and Europe. North America's own species of horses had succumbed to extinction around eighteen thousand years ago. Coronado's men likely brought a fair number of "Barb," or North African, horses with them. Contrary to some popular opinion, it is unlikely that Coronado's Barbs escaped in sufficient numbers to put the tribes on horseback, much less to breed the large herds of mustangs that eventually arose in the West. Nevertheless, as Castañeda noted, the mere appearance of armed men on horseback was useful for Spanish intimidation and subordination of native tribes. As a brave people, the Teya (Garza complex) natives of Blanco Canyon must have seen the inherent possibilities in horses for the plains.

The major risk associated with Spanish arrivals on the plains was their transmission of virulent Old World diseases to local tribes. New arrivals who bring other, multiplying new arrivals with them (horses, smallpox, syphilis) can be dangerous indeed. Epidemics and immense biological terrors often followed in the wake of Spanish warfare, expeditions, settlements, and, especially, missions. Given the large scale of Coronado's expedition, its diverse hosts (germ-laden Europeans and native allies from central Mexico), the possible escape or capture of various animals, and even plant or weed seeds sown along the route of the expedition, the possibility of some biological transmissions exists.

No obvious epidemiological damage, however, can be associated with the Coronado expedition. In his book *Rio del Norte,* Carroll L. Riley assesses disease transmission by the Coronado expedition as "possible" but lacking in evidence. Riley notes that the traditional European childhood diseases were most likely absent from the start. The possibilities for transmitting syphilis and yaws were greater, and some New World Spanish lice apparently harbored the Rickettsia microorganism causing typhus.[16] Considering that associated parasites, bacteria, gut organisms, and so on actually outnumber human cells in our bodies, the transmission of even low-level European germs cannot be taken lightly.

Alfred W. Crosby has written brilliantly about the general process of "ecological imperialism," that is, the biological and social issues associated with the movement of people and their domesticated plants and animals from the Old World to the New.[17] In a telling passage, Castañeda marveled that the Castilian chicken had arrived before the conquistadores in the province of Suya, a Ópata locale in the upper Sonora Valley. "We could not understand how they had passed through so much hostile territory," he commented.[18] Did microorganisms, perhaps even a species-crossing strain of influenza, travel with the chickens of Suya as well? In some cases Spanish animals accompanying expeditions escaped or circulated elsewhere. Fray Juan de Padilla certainly carried a domesticated menagerie with him to Kansas. Hernando de Soto and other explorers of "La Florida" eventually lost enough pigs to spawn the feral razorbacks of the Southeast. Because the Spaniards spent the greatest amount of time among the Ópata and Puebloans, these populations experienced the greatest opportunities and risks. But Spanish sojourns among the Teyas of Blanco Canyon and the Wichitas of the Arkansas River may have introduced an initial "ecological imperialism" there as well.

Old World diseases would soon devastate, depopulate, and even destroy the diverse human cultures encountered on the first leg of the Coronado expedition. Native societies proximate to New Galicia, such as the Taracahitan-speaking tribes, would suffer severe epidemics from 1540 to 1600. Even the more distant Serrana province was soon devastated. With little understanding of genetics, immunity, or germ theory, the European arrivals from the Old World unknowingly brought a cascade of pathogens for ecological release. Natives themselves likely passed these invisible new arrivals along their trade routes. Tribes that had once welcomed Cabeza de Vaca as a great healer eventually learned to fear a common means of respiratory transmission: the "Spanish breath."

If the natives of Blanco and Yellow House Canyons avoided horrible contagion in their 1541 refugia, it was largely because Coronado and the Spaniards chose not to stay in the area for long. By the time the next large Spanish expedition appeared in Blanco Canyon, some drastic changes had taken place in ethnicity and population size. The descendants of the former Teyas and Querechos were elsewhere; Blanco and Yellow House Canyons now belonged to the Comanchería. After enduring a terrible dust storm on May 18, 1808, "which made it look like the end of the world," Francisco Amangual and two hundred Spanish soldiers arrived on May 19 at Blanco Canyon. They found that day:

an extensive valley covered with trees in a canyon that is formed by a little caprock to the west; the trees are found at the foot of the caprock; at the bottom of the canyon there is a creek with white sand and clear, fresh, running water [*agua corriente*]; it flows from northwest to southeast, and comes from a point in the valley formed by yesterday's hills in the west.[19]

Amangual's men marched up Blanco Canyon in a show of force, but few people were there to be impressed. His force certainly did not find Castañeda's "Cona" with its populous rancherías and bean plots stretching for three days' journey. For the past three days, in fact, Amangual had complained in his diary of problems with his guides, "because the guides we had, had become gravely ill." In his May 20 diary entry, written in Blanco Canyon, Amangual recorded "nothing more unusual" than leaving behind "the sick Indian woman" at a small nearby Comanche camp—"because she became worse."[20]

American First Arrivals

In the last quarter of the nineteenth century, the most intense "ecological release" since the Clovis era took place on the southern High Plains. The new arrivals were Americans, a diverse group of westering folk whose country acquired the land in a war with Mexico. The Americans explored the Llano Estacado in the 1840s and 1850s and then returned with an army of conquest in 1875. Their initial shock wave removed the last of the tribes in ways that now eerily resemble "ethnic cleansing." It also turned the bison herds into industrial commodities and fostered a major expansion of Anglo cattle ranching and pioneering ventures. As early as 1878 the colorful Englishman and ex-bison hunter Frank Collinson drove a large herd of domesticated cattle into newly vacant Blanco Canyon pastures. Collinson worked for Anglo interests in New Mexico that intended to find the best parts of this last "open range." He was part of that generation of first arrivals, the pioneer cattlemen, who found the geography, especially the springs of the caprock canyons, most appealing. There were good reasons, perhaps, for the first American arrivals in Blanco Canyon to camp where the Spaniards had been before.

Like Coronado before him, Collinson was traveling eastward into the High Plains. He had been engaged to move Jingle Bob cattle from John Chisum's herds near Fort Sumner, New Mexico, to buyers in northwest Texas. As related in his book, *Life in the Saddle,* Collinson simply followed the old Cibolero Trail across the Llano.[21] This trail ran past Portales Spring, upper Yellow House Draw, Spring Lake, and Running Water Draw and then down into Blanco Canyon. (In turning back to Tiguex, Coronado's main expedition and herds had recrossed the plains using much the same prehistoric corridor of travel). Other trails and branches crossed the plains to Yellow House, Tule, and Palo Duro Canyons. Caprock canyons like Blanco and Las Lénguas (where Collinson's herd finally ended up) were favored by the Anglo wave of arrivals for a basic reason. The energetic discharge springs made the escarpment canyons better than the regions on either side—at least for stock raising.

The High Plains to the west, Frank Collinson argued, had a problem. The grasslands there might be fair, but rainfall seemed less frequent or certain. Too often, playas were few or ran dry in late summer, when the rancher's cattle and pocketbook were suddenly threatened. The extensive and rolling plains east of the caprock had an environmental problem, too. Their streams and rivers ran through old Permian "redbeds," formations laced with gypsum, brine springs, and the like, all flavoring the water with bitter, salty tastes for humans and domesticated beasts. With the hardy bison being hunted to near extinction, the replacement ruminants, cattle and horses, needed closer access to good water. In dry years, Collinson thought, this proximity was critical. Grass was not the limiting factor; it was proximity to unfailing water that was necessary for domesticated stock.

The first cattlemen thus followed a spatial logic. They found the plains on either side of the caprock to be interesting but not necessarily the most compelling places to live or make a living. Charles Goodnight acted accordingly when he trailed a herd of cattle into Palo Duro Canyon in the fall of 1876. Goodnight and his investor, John Adair, soon appropriated the spring-fed canyons of the Prairie Dog Town Fork for their JA ranching empire. As an 1876 bison hunter, Frank Collinson had "discovered" and named Roaring Springs in Motley County.

In 1879, after resting and fattening his cattle herd in Blanco Canyon, Collinson pushed on to the waters of Las Lenguas Canyon. This spring-fed caprock locale had seen versions of cattlemen before. New Mexican comancheros had traveled to Las Lenguas for many prior decades to buy stolen livestock held by Comanches. (An equally notorious comanchero trading site was Cañon del Rescate, or Ransom Canyon, on lower Yellow House Canyon.) For Collinson, the pastures of Las Lenguas were perfect. "The Cap Rock was on the west," he wrote of his arrival, "and the water was the finest in Texas."[22] When rustlers and outlaws moved into the region (presumably to pick up where the comancheros had left off), the Texas Rangers were not far behind. Captain G. W. Arrington rode into Blanco Canyon in September 1879. His company established "Camp Roberts" on a spring-fed stretch of Running Water Draw above the mouth of the canyon. Caprock springs were obvious assets to Frank Collinson and Captain Arrington. Permanent water was best.

Hank Smith was another arrival in the eastern canyonlands. He was born Heinrich Schmitt, his parents' eleventh child, in Rossbrun, Bavaria, in the summer of 1836, not long after the Battle of San Jacinto.[23] His father died when he was twelve, and in 1851 Heinrich and two older sisters immigrated to the United States. In 1854 Heinrich Schmitt, a youth of eighteen or so, joined a wagon train and traveled down and back along the Santa Fe Trail. He worked as a surveyor's assistant on the Missouri River in 1855–56. In 1857 he was a bullwhacker who showed up at Fort Laramie in Wyoming. Later that year he made it all the way to San Bernardino, California. Around this time he began to use an anglicized name: Heinrich became Henry (or the affectionate diminutive, Hank), and Schmitt became Smith. Because everyone in the West customarily flaunted a middle name or initial, he adopted the popular "Clay" for a middle name. Thus appeared the anglicized creation Henry C. ("Hank") Smith.

Hank Smith, the beloved idol of Crosby County, bears some similarities to Francisco Vázquez de Coronado. Both men traveled from Europe to North America as youths, and both found destiny in following stars to the southwestern frontiers of North America. Like Coronado, Hank Smith was lured to the Southwest by a desire for wealth. Indeed, Smith prospected for gold in California and Arizona—surely a more sensible geographical alternative than El Turco's Quivira. Smith also saw military service, fighting under the Confederate flag back east.

Hank Smith moved to Texas after the Civil War. Starting as a government contractor in El Paso and then moving on to Fort Griffin, he married a Texas girl of Scottish birth, Elizabeth Boyle, at Fort Griffin in 1874. At Fort Griffin, Smith made money—the U.S. Army was a primary source of development capital on the West Texas frontier. The couple had children and was doing fine until a heavy investment by Hank Smith—like Coronado's investment in a profitless expedition—turned troublesome. Smith had loaned money and built a nice rock house for a speculative cattle ranch in Blanco Canyon in distant Crosby County. But the speculation had failed, and the owner fled the ranch to escape creditors.

There was nothing to do but salvage the indebtedness, so Hank Smith acquired a Blanco Canyon ranch in partial payment. He and his family arrived in November 1878, determined to reverse their financial misfortunes. When the Smiths arrived at the Rock House, a home he called "Mount Blanco," they were to all intents and purposes "the first permanent settlers in the county." What can we learn from this German-American as a first arrival? That is, when the Smiths came to Blanco Canyon, what features and sites there attracted them? The choices might say something about other arrivals, possibly even the Coronado entrada.

Hank Smith wrote eloquently about their locational decisions in late 1878. His remarks bear quoting because they testify to the springland nature of Blanco Canyon:

> Our party arrived here from Fort Griffin, November 1st, in good health and good spirits. Mount Blanco is situated in Canyon Blanco, and a most beautiful place it is, *being the Yosemite of Texas*. The canyon is about thirty miles long and freshly watered by numerous lakes of pure fresh water; *and one cannot travel a half-mile without seeing a good spring*. One of the best water powers in the state is at Silver Falls, at the mouth of the canyon, they fall about twenty feet. We are located near the center of the main canyon, at the mouth of Crawfish Canyon which is three or four miles wide, a fine stream of living water passes through it, being the head water of the Salt Fork of the Brazos River.[24]

After reading W. Hubert Curry's book, *Sun Rising on the West: The Saga of Henry Clay and Elizabeth Smith,* one notes similarities in the canyon experiences of the Smith family and those of Coronado's men. Both gathered locally abundant plant foods like plums, currants, and grapes, and both encountered bison in the canyons. Both arrivals also had to contend with destructive hailstorms. Pedro de Castañeda's account of a battering hailstorm in the spring of 1541 is a familiar piece of history.[25] It can be compared with a less well-known account by a Miss Leona Leonard, a school pupil writing some three and a half centuries later: "On a seemingly normal spring afternoon such a storm hit our little one-room Mount Blanco schoolhouse, in 1897. Almost without warning the thunder was roaring, lightning flashing, wind blowing, and baseball-size hailstones were shattering glass over the room."[26]

Like all the first arrivals, Hank Smith was interested in the water, game, and grass resources of the new land. As a former teamster, he took special interest in identifying and utilizing the Ogallala discharge springs. He was never the devoted livestock man that, say, Charles Goodnight was, but he proved active as a vanguard for American "ecological imperialism." Like the early Spaniards, he did not share the typical Anglo rancher's antipathy toward sheep. Indeed, Hank Smith assembled large flocks of sheep that grazed up and down the new lands. By the 1880s he had enough mutton in Blanco Canyon and downstream to keep a large entrada well supplied. Like the Spanish chronicler from Nájera, he also had an abiding interest in geography. He read government reports on the new country, served as an official weather observer, experimented with trees and cultivated varieties, and took a lively, even scholarly interest in natural history. He was naturally drawn to those innate curiosities of the eastern caprock canyons—the old springs of the Llano Estacado.

Other arrivals soon joined Smith and Collinson in settling the caprock springlands. That is, if first comers prospered in proximity to sure and permanent waters, other settlers were soon equally astute. One important newcomer was George Washington Singer, who left Ohio in 1879 for the raw Quaker colony on the High Plains at Estacado. Around 1881 Singer relocated his family to Yellow House Canyon. As the first settler he got to make the choice for a home place. Interestingly, he picked a spring-fed site virtually on top of the Lubbock Lake Landmark of later archeological renown. Did Clovis hunters and Quaker merchants have similar tastes in settlement sites? There Singer built a one-room store—never locked—and settled in as a pioneer merchant. Bearded and fond of his buffalo gun, Singer also opened a post office in June 1884. He called his store and post office "Lubbock, Texas," the foundation of today's great plains city.

Yellow House Canyon, like nearby Blanco, yielded stone for building material and timber for construction, fence posts, and fuel. Its main springs attracted travelers and their converging trails, provided fair shelter from winter winds, and offered shady respites from summer heat. In short, escarpment waters provided a favored ecotone, rich in wild foods and game animals, because sure water draws deer, bison, wildfowl, antelope, bear, and turkey. Food, fuel, water, shelter, and beauty—are not these some of the essentials of a good life? Springs could even be harnessed for power. Their cold, constant-temperature waters were excellent for food preservation, such as chilling milk and butter. Many early ranches constructed "spring houses" over them, as was done on the famed Spur Ranch, for example.

Hank Smith may not have been the first European to utilize the Blanco Canyon springs, but he was possibly the first to consider their natural history. Smith's experience as a gold miner had opened his eyes to geology. In examining nearby springs, he also noticed quantities of a fine sand emanating along with the waters. In considering the origins of the "water powers" of Blanco Canyon, he thought the locally abundant springs were mere heralds of an enormous and untapped underground river. Theoretically, this subterranean river began on the slopes of the Rocky Mountains, where melting snow poured into underground fissures. These underground streams then formed an immense sheet of water flowing southeastward beneath the plains.

Because the supply was renewable, the underground resource seemed inexhaustible. Where Spanish captains had dreamed of gold, American entrepreneurs now saw Quivira in an endless and powerful amount of "artesian water." Quoting an 1880 report by a self-styled (and possibly fictitious) expert named Captain Livermore, Hank Smith proposed that Blanco Canyon's vast underground river be harnessed for a new age. By confining and developing its artesian pressure, mankind could even water the vast plains above. It was a beautiful and common myth of the day, and a belief—like Quivira—that persisted for a long time.

The true origin of the "water powers" of Blanco and Yellow House Canyons was recognizable in the early 1900s. Beneath the level plains were immense deposits of porous sand and gravel above an impermeable or "redbed" stratum. Filled by ancient rains, the deposits contained hundreds of millions of acre-feet of water, enough to transform the plains above through irrigation. The "Shallow-water Belt," or Ogallala Aquifer, underlay a considerable portion of the southern High Plains. In 1879 Hank Smith had tapped it fortuitously in digging a High Plains well for the Quakers at Estacado. Around 1910 big irrigation wells appeared on Running Water Draw at Plainview and vicinity. They were pumped continuously by land promoters, mostly to impress trainloads of the latest new arrivals—Midwestern land seekers looking for good farms at cheap prices. At Plainview, some wells pumped water merely to maintain an artificial "pleasure lake," an environmental challenge thrown down on the level plains by humankind.

Residents of Floyd and Crosby counties took a lively interest in their springs; some even noticed a gradual change under way. As a boy growing up at Mount Blanco, A. L. "Flukie" Smith, son of Bob Smith, remembered in particular one big, so-called artesian spring: "What I remember about it is that I've seen Dad and a bunch tie weights on lariat ropes and let down as many lariats as they had. They would let down four or five lariat ropes tied together, and the water would be boiling up out of the ground. The last time I was there it had gotten much weaker."[27]

But where is this old artesian spring, famed among the early settlers and first arrivals? The answer can be found in an early published letter of Hank Smith's:

About four miles above Mount Blanco [proximate to the Montgomery Ranch in Floyd County] is the largest of them [the springs]. This spring really being the main source of White River. The water constantly boils out of this spring, but bubbles and flounders in the basin. A mile or so below this spring is another, and near the mouth of Crawfish are two more [springs], smaller than the first spring but in all characteristics the same.[28]

Students of the Coronado expedition may find it interesting that the first Anglo arrivals in Blanco Canyon settled below the prominent, reputedly artesian spring on the old Montgomery Ranch. Had Coronado's men followed a similar logic and impulse, they might equally have camped near or downstream from the main spring on the ranch. In Gunnar Brune's fascinating volume *Springs of Texas,* the "Montgomery Springs" are described as major discharge springs from the

Ogallala Aquifer located just north of the Crosby County line.[29] The springs take their name from Thomas Montgomery, a cattleman who settled nearby in 1887.

Massie Springs was further up the canyon, about seven miles southwest of Floydada. Just downstream of Massie Springs is an excellent Folsom site at Floydada Country Club. On an 1875 map, these springs are labeled as being the "Head of Running Water," that is, the source of the downstream White River. Of course from the older Hispanic perspective, what really made the waters *run* in Running Water Draw—the *agua corriente* of the historic Ciboleros—was the motive energy contributed by all the discharge springs.

Other important springs lay downstream in Crosby County. Indeed, Crosby County's portion of Blanco Canyon and its escarpment coastline constituted a major springland. There was Dewey Springs, and the old beaver dam forming Dewey Lake. On the nearby terrace Captain Arrington's Texas Rangers had built Camp Roberts, a site now located just above the Camp Rio Blanco Girl Scout Camp. There was also Silver Falls Springs, with its luxuriant grapevines, and Ericson Springs, C Bar Springs, Wilson Springs, L7 Springs, and Cottonwood Springs—all formerly contributing to a strong baseflow of the White River.[30] To say the least, Blanco Canyon was once rich in springs. In 1887 the rancher Robert Tilford journeyed up the canyon from Smith's Rock House to Buck Allen's place. Tilford wrote: "Upon my trip up White River from the House to Buck Allen's, I counted over 100 springs that are flowing and on my trip south I ceased to count after I had gone over 123."[31]

Irrigation pumping on the High Plains above depleted the reservoir pressure for the canyon discharge springs. By the middle of the last century, few of the former springs counted by Tilford were in evidence. Gunnar Brune quotes Monte Williams as saying that Montgomery Springs "ceased flowing about 1948." Massie Springs stopped flowing around 1945.[32] Most of the old springs of Blanco and Yellow House are memories now, buried in rubble, choked with sand, even their sites half lost to time and memory. Perhaps a future archeologist will dig out the big discharge springs and discover, a layer or two beneath the lead weights and lost lariats, an errant sword hilt or horseshoe from the sixteenth century.

The old caprock springlands are very worthy of study. First arrivals of all kinds—Pedro de Castañeda, Francisco Vázquez de Coronado, Francisco Amangual, Frank Collinson, G. W. Arrington, and Hank Smith, to name only a few sojourners at Blanco Canyon—depended on their healthful waters and favored campsites. Sojourners such as Pedro de Castañeda and Hank Smith were even kindred personalities in many ways; both joined armies, chased rainbows, showed an interest in natural history, and wrote of their travels. Countless if nameless other travelers—comancheros, Ciboleros, pastores, army soldiers, Texas Rangers, and Anglo-American settlers—also watered their stock, camped nearby, and pursued lives of historical purpose and utility.

Sadly, the historic springs of Blanco and Yellow House Canyons may never again "boil" with copious draughts of cool water. Thousands of High Plains irrigation wells dictate otherwise. But in their environs and stratigraphy we find evidence of the first arrivals: perhaps the shadowy pre-Clovis people, certainly the intrepid Clovis and Folsom, equally the skillful Archaic peoples, the prehistoric Teyas and Querechos, and the historic Comanches and Kiowas. They certainly show tracks of the most recent arrivals as well—the American cowboys, ranchers, settlers, farmers, and promoters who used these favored places. In our own time there are other newcomers to the region: post–Vietnam War refugees from Asia, legal and illegal migrants from Mexico, and urban-transplanted Yankees and Midwesterners. Invasive species such as armadillos, Johnson grass, tumbleweeds, and boll weevils have colonized the land as well.

For 132 centuries the grassy plains and watered canyons of the Southwest have cradled dreams and crafted legends of "pioneers"—those arrivals first with God and earth. Periodically, it seems, climate or human agency subtracts old pioneers and stocks some new ones. Many of the twenty-first-century's auguries may prove challenging for the current settlers of the High Plains. Global warming, endangered species, agribusiness corporations, bioengineering, pollution, prolific crop diseases and acquired resistance, erosion, and looming groundwater depletion are all set against a backdrop of aging rural demographics, globalized markets, high capital costs, and largely declining county populations.

Perhaps the biggest challenge for a twenty-first-century frontier people on the Llano is to develop sustainability paradigms—something more than stabbing the last mammoth, infecting the last native, shooting the last bison, or pumping the last gallon of Ogallala water. As the Clovis people discovered, there may be a limit to the taking of mammoths, or as Coronado learned, a limit to finding gold. Or perhaps "sustainability" itself is our modern Quivira, a mythic belief in a land of abundance, wealth, and bioregional harmony. El Turco claimed Quivira was "mas allá"—farther on—and the same might be said for agrarian sustainability. Whether the arrivals are Clovis hunters, Spanish conquistadores, or American farmers, maintaining a populous culture on the southern High Plains has never been easy—at least in the long term. And without the old springs of Blanco and Yellow House Canyons, sustainability may prove harder than the massive release of technology and organisms that changed the land. At the moment, one nagging question for the Llano Estacado is not who was first to arrive, but rather, who will be the last family farmer or rancher left?

Notes

1. Hammond and Rey, *Narratives,* 193.
2. Dale L. Walker, "'Dear Soapy' Letters from Will Henry," *Roundup Magazine* 7, no. 4 (2000): 12.
3. For two important studies of Lubbock Lake Landmark, see Eileen Johnson, ed., *Lubbock Lake: Late Quaternary Studies on the Southern High Plains* (College Station: Texas A&M University Press, 1987); and Craig C. Black, ed., "History and Prehistory of the Lubbock Lake Site," *Museum Journal* 15 (Lubbock: West Texas Museum Association, 1974).
4. Vance T. Holliday, *Paleoindian Geoarchaeology of the Southern High Plains* (Austin: University of Texas Press, 1997).
5. Hammond and Rey, *Narratives,* 301.
6. Holliday, *Paleoindian Geoarchaeology,* 179.
7. Tim Flannery, *The Eternal Frontier: An Ecological History of North America and Its Peoples* (New York: Atlantic Monthly Press, 2001), 224–27.
8. See Fr. Angélico Chávez, *Coronado's Friars* (Washington, D.C.: Academy of American Franciscan History, 1968).
9. U.S. Department of the Interior, National Park Service, *Coronado Expedition,* maps 15–16.
10. Simpson, "Coronado's March," map insert before page 309.
11. Bolton, *Coronado,* 261–71, and see map, 412.
12. For a detailed study of Castañeda and Blanco Canyon, see Morris, *El Llano Estacado,* 75–93.
13. See Castañeda's Spanish text in Winship, *Coronado Expedition,* 168; compare the Spanish to the English mistranslation in Hammond and Rey, *Narratives,* 261.
14. Hammond and Rey, *Narratives,* 259.
15. Jared Diamond, *Guns, Germs, and Steel: The Fates of Human Societies* (New York: W. W. Norton, 1997).
16. Riley, *Rio del Norte,* 222–24.
17. Alfred W. Crosby, *Ecological Imperialism: The Biological Expansion of Europe, 900–1900* (New York: Cambridge University Press, 1986).
18. Hammond and Rey, *Narratives,* 251.
19. Loomis and Nasatir, *Pedro Vial,* 489–90.
20. Loomis and Nasatir, *Pedro Vial,* 492.
21. Frank Collinson, *Life in the Saddle* (Norman: University of Oklahoma Press, 1963), 119–20.
22. Collinson, *Life in the Saddle,* 121.
23. An excellent biography of Heinrich Schmitt is in W. Hubert Curry's *Sun Rising on the West: The Saga of Henry Clay and Elizabeth Smith* (Crosbyton, Texas: Quality Printers and Typographers, 1979).
24. From Smith's letter of December 6, 1878, published in Fort Griffin's newspaper, *The Frontier Echo,* reproduced in Curry, *Sun Rising,* 161.
25. Hammond and Rey, *Narratives,* 238.
26. Curry, *Sun Rising,* 194.
27. Curry, *Sun Rising,* 199.
28. Curry, *Sun Rising,* 197.
29. Gunnar Brune, *Springs of Texas* (Fort Worth: Branch-Smith, 1981), 184.
30. See the individual spring entries in Brune, *Springs of Texas,* 142–44.
31. Brune, *Springs of Texas,* 143.
32. Brune, *Springs of Texas,* 184.

FOURTEEN

Spanish Crossbow Boltheads of Sixteenth-Century North America: A Comparative Analysis

FRANK R. GAGNÉ JR.

THE CROSSBOW WAS THE BACKBONE of Francisco Vázquez de Coronado's artillery-type weapons. The gunpowder firearm's recent arrival on the European battlefield was impressive, but technological improvements to ensure its reliability were yet to be incorporated. The gun of 1540 was unreliable, and its use depend-ent upon the weather and other variables. The crossbow, on the other hand, had been battle-tested for centuries and was highly reliable. When Coronado's army went north, so did the common crossbow, ensuring its place in American history.

The crossbow is usually thought of along with castles, knights, and medieval times. What is often forgotten is that when Coronado went north, the transition from Middle Ages to Renaissance was under way in Spain, and a very different cos-mos existed for all. Just as sixteenth-century Europe and that of today are vastly different, so were the European and American worlds of the sixteenth century. From the Old World came weapons of destruction that could not be fathomed. Such was the crossbow that shot from the mists of antiquity and into the Americas.

During medieval times the crossbow was introduced and developed as such a lethal weapon that a papal bull issued by Pope Innocent II in 1139 forbade its use. The pope denounced the crossbow as "hateful to God and unfit for Christians" because it proved so lethal to knights on crusades. Later this edict was modified so that Christians were permitted to use crossbows against their Muslim enemies. Shortly thereafter, Christians began using them freely against one another as well. The knight now had to fear even a peasant on the ground, not just another knight. By 1370 the European crossbow came equipped with an iron bow. The crossbow was the most powerful weapon of war for the next century, until gunpowder firearms began replacing it in 1460–70.

The crossbow had been used in China for perhaps two thousand years, and Europeans felt the sting of its power and accuracy during the Crusades against the Muslims. In both Europe and Asia, the need for armor-penetrating capability had given rise to metals that were far superior in penetrating power than was stone. As medieval armor improved, so did the crossbow's ability to penetrate it. Projectile points made from iron that could be fired with sufficient velocity and force could penetrate iron armor. The English long bow and the firearm were less powerful but also capable of stopping an armored knight.

The documentary record clearly shows that both the Soto and Coronado expeditions made use of the crossbow. Crossbow boltheads (dart points) have been discovered at sites associated with both *entradas*. History also records the earlier use of crossbows in the Americas by Hernán Cortés, Francisco Pizarro, and others. Of special interest is their use by the force led by Cortés during the conquest of Tenochtitlán (later Mexico City) in 1521. Spanish mercantalist prohibition of the mining of iron in the Americas necessitated importation of this metal from Europe. In Mexico, because of the resulting iron shortage, Spaniards used copper as a substitute for iron where possible. Experienced indigenous craftsmen were able to work native gold, silver, and copper in Mexico.[1] The copper crossbow bolthead was found to be sufficiently lethal when used against hide and cotton armors.[2] Cortés recognized this and used copper boltheads during many of his assaults. From native settlements around Tenochtitlán, he requisitioned and received delivery of eight thousand boltheads in a span of eight days. Native artisans successfully accomplished the feat.[3]

Less than twenty years later, Francisco Vázquez de Coronado took advantage of the same native technology. Crossbows were still in use in his time, although they were soon to be replaced by firearms. According to the expedition's muster role, nineteen crossbows and twenty-two gunpowder firearms went north with Vázquez de Coronado,[4] but by the time of Juan de Oñate's colonizing expedition of 1598, the crossbow was absent from the muster of weapons. Only two other sixteenth-century entradas into the Southwest may have used crossbows: the Chamuscado-Rodríguez-López and Espejo-Luxán expeditions. Neither of these two parties reached as far east and north as the Panhandle of Texas.[5]

Therefore, in the Southwest the presence of crossbow boltheads indicates a time window of 1540 to no later than the 1580s. Boltheads can help identify sites that are specific to that interval, and copper boltheads found outside New Mexico should be diagnostic of the Coronado expedition. The historical documentation shows the Coronado entrada to have been the first and probably the last to have carried an appreciable number of crossbows into the Texas Panhandle, Oklahoma, and southern Kansas. This fact allows boltheads to be used as unique horizon markers in the archeological record in this region. The presence of boltheads permits relative dating of artifacts in association with them. It appears that the crossbow boltheads offer a new opportunity for identifying sites along Vázquez de Coronado's route.

Nearly ten years ago a National Park Service study concluded that "the [Coronado expedition's] route is not sufficiently known at this time" to enable researchers to find and establish the trail.[6] The identification of the Jimmy Owens Site (41FL81) in Floyd County, Texas, as a location visited by the Coronado expedition alters this situation. It raises a number of questions and a working hypothesis that was tested during my study of American crossbow boltheads of the early Spanish colonial period.

Simply put, boltheads from Texas were compared with other boltheads from the Americas. Morphological and dimensional similarities and differences were noted. From the resulting data, answers to the following research questions were made with reasonable assurance of accuracy. (1) Could crossbow boltheads be used for relative archeological dating? (2) Could they significantly help to identify early historic sites? (3) Did evidence from the Jimmy Owens Site support or refute its status as a Coronado expedition campsite? (4) Could the use of ferrous and nonferrous metals in protohistoric boltheads and other tools assist in identifying the social, economic, and political groups making up the Coronado and Soto expeditions? (5) How should the data on boltheads be organized?

Boltheads Examined for This Study

To answer these questions, I examined a total of fifty-six crossbow boltheads from known sixteenth-century Spanish archeological sites (table 14.1). The sites selected for study are, with three exceptions, known campsites used by Francisco Vázquez de Coronado during his entrada into the Southwest in 1540–42. The exceptions are sites in Florida and the Caribbean. All boltheads studied are dated to the same period, circa 1540–60.

All points were compared with those collected archeologically from the Jimmy Owens Site. The full assemblages of cultural material from known Coronado expedition sites are similar to what has been excavated at the Jimmy Owens Site, but this study focused only on the crossbow boltheads.

Twenty-four of the boltheads—the largest individual assemblage examined—are from the Jimmy Owens Site. They are morphologically and stylistically indistinguishable from the other boltheads previously associated with the Coronado expedition.

In addition, I examined the crossbow boltheads associated with excavation

Table 14.1

Summary of the Sample of Crossbow Boltheads

Site	Number of Boltheads	Provenience	Examined?
Southwest			
Jimmy Owens Site	24	TX	Yes
Hawikuh	4	NM	Yes
Kuaua	1	NM	No
Bandelier's Puaray/Santiago	5	NM	Yes
Near Santiago	19	NM	Yes
Galisteo Basin	1	NM	Yes
Pecos Pueblo	2?	NM	No
Southeast			
Martin Site	1	FL	Yes
Emanuel Point	1	FL	Yes
Santa Elena	5	SC	No
Puerto Real	1	Dom Rep	Yes
Total examined	56		

of the ancestral Zuni pueblo of Hawikuh, located in west-central New Mexico near the Arizona border. The National Museum of the American Indian of the Smithsonian Institution made available the boltheads and other material culture items from Hawikuh. These artifacts, the first crossbow boltheads found in North America, were collected by the Hendricks-Hodge Expedition of 1917–23, which focused on two historic villages, Hawikuh and Kechipawan. Of the five putative boltheads housed at the National Museum of the American Indian, I considered only four to be genuine boltheads. The fifth, specimen number /3976, was determined not to be a bolthead and was excluded from the study.

Boltheads from the site of Kuaua and from the site that Adolph Bandelier called Puaray, both in the central Rio Grande valley, are also thought to have been associated with the Coronado expedition. Puaray, now generally known as Santiago Pueblo (LA 326), is located nearly opposite present-day Bernalillo, New Mexico, on the west side of the Rio Grande. It was one of many Tiguex villages visited by the Coronado entrada in 1540–42. By the early 1600s, the village had been abandoned. Marjorie Ferguson Tichy, who excavated the site, reported objects that she called "pen-points," along with the remains of a human "buried with a copper pen-point(?)."[7] The point was said to be lodged in the individual's sternum. These objects plus one from Kuaua collected by Bandelier, since identified as crossbow boltheads, are now in the collection of the Palace of the Governors, Museum of New Mexico, in Santa Fe. Five of them were inspected and included in this study.

I also examined a private collection of boltheads from near Santiago Pueblo, owned by Dee Brecheisen (see fig. 15.3). This collection made up the second largest population of boltheads known to exist, nineteen. A single bolthead from the Galisteo Basin was also made available from the private collection of Forest Fenn in Santa Fe.

The 1915–25 excavation of Pecos Pueblo near Pecos, New Mexico, produced a copper object that Alfred Kidder, in his report on the 344 iron and copper objects found at Pecos, described as "an arrow-point with base bent to enclose the shaft."[8] Later excavations at Pecos uncovered two additional pieces of copper described as arrow points, both similar to the basic form of a crossbow bolthead before the ferrule is completed.[9]

Not all archeologists agreed with Kidder's artifact identifications of the 1930s. In 1939, Tichy maintained that "judging from their size, the artifacts were pen points when the two sets of artifacts were compared."[10] Even Kidder had doubts, placing a question mark after his identification of an object he labeled "Projectile point (?) of sheet copper." The photograph of the object, however, leaves no doubt that it was a bolthead very similar to the others included in this study.[11] This and another possible bolthead were evidently once curated in the Kidder-Pecos collection at the Peabody Foundation, Phillips Academy, Andover, Massachusetts. Because they have not been located, the bolthead(s) from Pecos were not examined for this study.

In addition to artifacts from Southwestern sites, I examined boltheads associated with Spanish expeditions in the southeastern United States. The sample included one bolthead associated with Hernando de Soto's winter camp, the Martin Site in Tallahassee, Florida (made available by Roger C. Smith, Bureau of Archeological Research), and a bolthead from a Spanish galleon of the 1559 Tristán de Luna fleet (Emanuel Point, Pensacola Bay). John Bratten, of the University of West Florida Archaeology Institute at Pensacola, had recently recovered the latter bolthead. A single bolthead from Puerto Real, in the Dominican Republic (Hispaniola), was also examined. The Puerto Real site was abandoned in 1578. The settlement of Santa Elena, South Carolina (1566–87), was established in an effort to protect homebound Spanish fleets and to check French incursion into territories in eastern North America claimed by Spain. The crossbow boltheads recovered from Santa Elena have been subjected to a variety of conservation procedures and were not included in this study.

Methods

Forty-one of the total population of fifty-six boltheads examined were selected for quantitative statistical analysis. When reviewing the statistical analysis, it is imperative to remember the size of the population being subjected to analysis, because it is, in an absolute sense, quite small, though it includes the lion's share of boltheads from locations thought to have been visited by the Coronado expedition. The population size is, however, sufficient for production of morphological scattergrams. Relative distance matrices were produced in order to examine potential variation among bolthead classes, and canonical axes were identified in order to elucidate the specific nature of the variation.

Identical measurement techniques for attribute analysis were applied to all of the crossbow boltheads examined in this study. Measurements were taken using an electronic digital caliper and an Oahaus electronic digital scale. For each bolthead, I recorded the provenience and made a number of discrete quantitative observations (fig. 14.1). Seven separate measurements were recorded for each specimen, except when the condition of a specimen precluded one or more of them. Because the digital caliper is sensitive to 0.01 millimeter, a false accuracy must also be immediately acknowledged. This is especially true of the bolthead attributes subjected to measurements for which no clear demarcation can be established. Such is the case with point length and ferrule length. Sometimes these two somewhat arbitrary numbers—representing, respectively, the distance from a bolthead's point to the top of its ferrule and the distance from there to the blunt end of the bolthead—do not add up to its total length. This is due

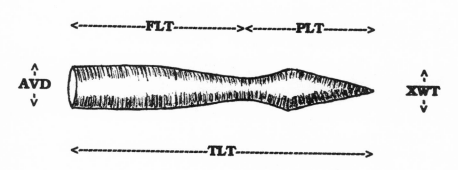

Figure 14.1. Diagram of a crossbow bolthead from Hawikuh, showing some of the measurements taken for each bolthead in the sample. Key: AVD, average ferrule diameter; FLT, total ferrule length; PLT, total point length; XWT, maximum width of point; TLT, total length. Drawing by Richard Flint.

to differences in interpretations of the demarcation point (the location at which the point ends and the ferrule begins). Ferrule thickness is also subject to wide variation throughout its length and therefore cannot be taken as a critical measurement. Instead, it is considered to be a "spot measurement."

It is my position that measurements should be accepted to an accuracy of no more than 0.1 millimeter, even though I report the measurements to two decimal places, as indicated on the electronic caliper, with no attempt to round them off (table 14.2). If a greater accuracy is needed at a future date, digital photographs of the boltheads are available for study. Digital photos allow measurements to be made to the pixel if needed, and with far greater accuracy through use of temporary markers that do not affect the boltheads themselves.

The selection of measurements to be taken was based on an article published by Bruce T. Ellis in 1957.[12] The Palace of the Governors of the Museum of New Mexico in Santa Fe made the Ellis assemblage of five copper crossbow boltheads available for my inspection. This group was used as a control for measurement analysis and for understanding the terms Ellis used in his report. The remaining bolthead of the six Ellis studied is presumed lost.

Ellis established the descriptive terminology of "solid, sheet, and triangular" and even offered an example of how he thought Coronado expedition personnel had fabricated the boltheads. His terminology was readily applicable to the assemblages I examined. Ellis recorded three attributes: point length, point width, and point angle. To these I added weight, overall length, ferrule thickness, and ferrule length. The terms Ellis used to describe preforms, or blanks, of either sheet- or block-style points are also employed. My intent was to build upon what he had reported.

The boltheads analyzed were identified as having two shapes: diamond and triangular. Dimensionally the boltheads were either solid (block) or flat (sheet). These attributes allowed four basic types of boltheads to be identified: cone, solid diamond, solid triangle, and flat triangle. Within the triangle class, two subtypes were noted: triangular proper (essentially equilateral) and triangular oblique (one side longer than the other). Additionally, boltheads without a restricted neck and made from solid stock were classed as short block and may be described as oblique or triangular proper.

Results

Table 14.2 displays the data recorded for all forty-one boltheads selected for quantitative analysis. The first three columns record codes identifying the individual boltheads and the sites from which they were collected or repositories where they reside (41FL81 is the Jimmy Owens Site, SANLA refers to the point found at San Lazaro Pueblo, UNPVT refers to the private collections, NMAIS is the National Museum of the American Indian, and PALGV is the Palace of the Governors). The "form" column classifies each item as either flat (F) or solid (S), which reflects whether the stock from which the bolthead was manufactured was a sheet (flat) or a block (solid).

The "shape" column identifies each bolthead as diamond shaped (D), triangular proper (T), or triangular oblique (O). The "fold" column records how the ferrule of each bolthead was formed. With the point tip positioned away from the viewer, the fold is either right-over-left (1), left-over-right (2), or indeterminate (3). Color was recorded as light (L), dark (D), or shiny (S), without aid of a color chart. Weight was recorded in grams. Point angle (PTA) was recorded in degrees from photographs of the boltheads using a simple protractor.

Total length (TLT) is the maximum distance in millimeters from the point

Table 14.2

Metric and Nonmetric Observations for Sample Crossbow Bolthead Specimens

Site	Catalog	FRGKey	Form	Shape	Fold	Color	Wt	PTA	TLT	PLT	FLT	FTH	XWT	AVD
41FL81 JOP		FRG001	S	D	2	D	7.00	28	47.98	24.18	24.00	0.7	6.70	9.4
41FL81 JOP		FRG002	F	D	2	L	2.90	30	29.13	11.36	18.90	0.6	7.40	7.9
41FL81 JOP		FRG003	S	T	1	D	3.85	30	37.54	13.40	23.50	0.5	6.80	8.0
41FL81 JOP		FRG004	F	D	2	D	5.05	40	41.90	11.43	28.00	0.7	8.30	9.0
41FL81 JOP		FRG005	F	D	2	D	4.20	30	48.60	15.00	28.00	0.8	7.90	
41FL81 WSU		FRG006	S	D	3	D	6.28	28	50.20	13.50	29.50	0.6	6.00	8.5
41FL81 WSU		FRG007	S	O	3	D	4.23	18	30.00	12.00	16.00	0.6	7.70	7.5
41FL81 WSU		FRG008	F	D	3	D	4.20	45	38.70	10.00	32.00	0.7	7.60	8.0
41FL81 WSU		FRG010	S	O	2	D	4.11	28	36.10	20.00	19.00	0.6	6.30	8.5
41FL81 FDA		FRG111	S	D	3	D	6.05	28	46.80	18.40	28.00	0.8	6.87	7.0
41FL81 FDA		FRG112	S	T	3	D	3.85	30	31.30	17.30	14.00	0.7	8.27	8.0
41FL81 FDA		FRG113	S	O	3	D	4.95	30	34.13	18.90	14.60	0.7	7.68	8.5
41FL81 FDA		FRG114	S	T	3	S	5.10	32	34.75	16.00	18.00	0.6	8.00	9.9
41FL81 FDA		FRG115	S	T	2	D	5.25	30	31.63	18.00	13.60	0.8	6.00	8.3
41FL81 FDA		FRG116	S	O	1	D	4.65	28	37.58	19.00	18.50	0.6	7.80	8.0
41FL81 FDA		FRG117	S	T	3	D	2.50	30	33.55	13.67	19.80	0.7	6.30	8.5
41FL81 FDA		FRG118	S	T	1	D	4.10	34	38.16	17.00	21.00	0.8	7.30	9.0
41FL81 FDA		FRG119	S	T	1	S	5.05	28	37.75	18.60	19.00	0.9	6.75	6.0
41FL81 FDA		FRG120	S	O	3	D	3.90	30	31.37	14.60	17.00	0.7	7.65	8.0
41FL81 FDA		FRG122	S	O	1	D	2.90	30	33.91	17.61	16.00	0.7	7.20	8.0
41FL81 FDA		FRG123	S	O	3	D	4.50	30	31.68	14.90	16.80	0.5	8.00	8.0
41FL81 FDA		FRG124	F	D	2	D	7.05	35	39.78	17.00	22.00	0.6	8.55	8.0
SANLA FFP		FRG125	F	T	2	L	3.90	30	38.01	11.90	27.69	0.5	7.27	7.0
UNPVT CFF		FRG127	F	D	1	L	3.90	42	39.03	14.00	25.50	0.6	10.70	
UNPVT CFF		FRG128	F	D	2	L	4.05	40	43.82	16.00	27.00	0.7	9.34	7.0
UNPVT CFF		FRG131	S	T	2	D	3.40	30	29.36	18.00	13.00	0.8	7.68	7.0
UNPVT CFF		FRG135	F	D	2	D	3.85	32	35.59	14.46	18.18	0.6	8.40	
UNPVT CFF		FRG136	S	D	1	D	5.86	26	38.75	17.00	21.19	0.8	6.57	8.0
UNPVT CFF		FRG137	S	D	1	D	4.20	22	40.00	13.63	21.81	0.8	5.14	7.0
UNPVT CFF		FRG139	S	D	1	D	5.50	28	44.17	12.79	21.50	0.6	6.25	9.0
UNPVT CFF		FRG140	S	D	1	D	11.40	30	55.41	25.00	30.00	1.0	8.17	10.0
UNPVT CFF		FRG141	S	D	2	D	10.90	30	57.95	21.00	36.00		8.70	10.9
UNPVT CFF		FRG143	F	D	2	D	3.00	40	42.62	13.93	28.00	0.6	6.60	7.0
NMAIS HA12-4536		FRG145	S	D	3	D	5.29	22	48.85	22.35	25.67	0.7	6.23	7.6
NMAIS HA12-4945		FRG146	S	O	1	D	3.23	30	34.25	14.30	20.00	0.7	9.56	9.0
NMAIS HA08-6602		FRG147	S	O	2	D	2.51	30	26.36	8.50	20.40	0.7		8.2
PALGV 6A-992845A		FRG150	S	D	1	D	5.10	25	48.91	21.90	29.14	0.9	6.26	8.8
PALGV 6B-492845B		FRG151	F	D	2	D	4.40	40	46.89	14.48	30.50	0.8	8.02	10.3
PALGV 6C-492845C		FRG152	F	D	1	D	4.45	30	41.91	19.70	24.75	1.0	9.70	7.6
PALGV 6D-492845D		FRG153	F	D	3	D	3.75	30	39.15	13.98	25.25	0.7	6.93	7.8
PALGV 6E-992845E		FRG149	S	T	2	D	3.70	30	34.38	19.57	15.00	0.3	7.49	7.5

tip to the distal end of each specimen. Point length (PLT) was measured in millimeters from the point tip to a line judged to represent the intersection of the point head and the ferrule. Total ferrule length (FLT) was measured in millimeters from the same point, the head-ferrule intersection, to the extremity of the distal end of the ferrule. Ferrule thickness (FTH) is a spot measurement in millimeters of the thickness of the metal forming the ferrule near its distal end. The maximum point width (XWT) represents the greatest width in millimeters of the point portion of the bolthead, regardless of where this occurs along its length. The final column in table 14.1 records the average diameter of the ferrule portion of each item (AVD). In many specimens the ferrules had been flattened, and in those cases a string was wrapped around the ferrule and the diameter of a circle with that circumference was calculated.

The data resulting from my examination of the forty-one boltheads were fed into the Statistical Analysis System (SAS) program. The scattergram of bolthead types that resulted indicates the clustering of block, short block, and sheet types (fig. 14.2), with the cone type (not shown in fig. 14.2) an exception. The classification of the boltheads recognizes the sheet and solid block types with the subdivision of the triangular types of either. The data on type determination (sheet, short block, and block) were subjected to canonical axis analysis, which revealed three distinct clusters, supporting the existence of a true typological division.

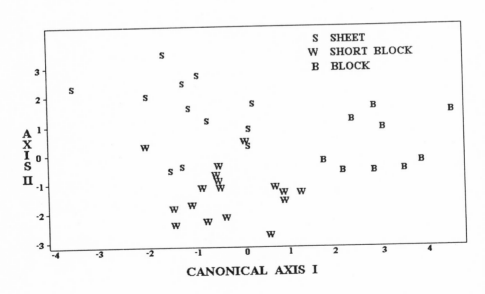

Figure 14.2. Scattergram of bolthead types.

The boltheads from sites known to have been associated with the Coronado expedition across New Mexico showed the same typology as those from the Jimmy Owens Site in Texas. In addition, specific attributes such as point length and ferrule length or even thickness were virtually indistinguishable between the New Mexico and Texas points. Some of the results were overwhelmingly convincing.

Boltheads recovered from geographically dispersed sites throughout the Southwest are so similar in morphology and size as to be all but indistinguishable. As but one instance, table 14.3 provides measurement data for three solid, diamond-tipped boltheads with constricted necks, one from Santiago Pueblo, one from the Jimmy Owens Site, and one from Hawikuh. All recorded dimensions of the three are startlingly close. They are so similar to one another that they could well be the "signature" of a single metalsmith. The smith might have been present at Hawikuh, the Bernalillo area, and Blanco Canyon. Alternatively, the three specimens might have been made by someone in Mexico and carried to and lost or expended at the three Southwestern sites by members of the Coronado expedition. These similarities are also true of the short block group and the sheet type group. Again, the similarities between the Southwestern assemblages are striking. Sheet-type boltheads are present at all known sites associated with Coronado in New Mexico and at the Jimmy Owens Site. The sheet-type bolthead from the Jimmy Owens Site, when compared with those from the other known Coronado expedition sites, is strikingly similar in attribute measurements. This is also true of the short block type, which is differentiated from the solid bolthead by the absence of a restricted neck.

Meanwhile, the boltheads from the Southeast share few of the attributes common to those from the Southwest. The boltheads from the Southeast are more robust and, most significantly, made from iron. Those from Puerto Real and the Emanuel Point shipwreck are similar to each other but are quite different from the one from the Martin Site.

Table 14.3

Comparison of Crossbow Boltheads from Three Sites

| | | Point | | Ferrule |
| | Length | Length | Point Width | Thickness |
Artifact	(mm)	(mm)	(mm)	(mm)
Private 14 Santiago	44.17	12.79	6.25	0.62
12/4563 Hawikuh	48.85	14.25	6.20	0.48–0.63
Frg-006 Jimmy Owens	50.20	13.50	6.00	0.60
Average	47.74	13.55	6.15	0.62

Judging from drawings, the boltheads from Santa Elena in South Carolina resemble those from Puerto Real and Emanuel Point more closely than they do the single example from the Martin Site. An unknown amount of this difference could be the result of corrosion, because only the Martin point has been cleaned and stabilized. The boltheads from the Southeast are morphologically quite different from the Southwestern ones, including those from the Jimmy Owens Site.

Conclusion

This limited study has shown that the boltheads found at the Jimmy Owens Site are indistinguishable from boltheads from the other known Coronado expedition archeological sites in the Southwest. Two bolthead types, block and sheet boltheads, have been recovered from both areas. Morphologically the two styles represent two different manufacturing processes. The block type appears more difficult to produce than the sheet type, requiring, as it does, hammer shaping of the point. Some of this apparent difficulty would have been eliminated, though, by using a shop aid or molding device.

All known Southwestern sites with crossbow boltheads have been associated with the Coronado expedition. All but one of the Southwestern boltheads are made of copper. The exception is a ferruled iron point from the Jimmy Owens Site. The virtual absence of iron points in the West cannot be explained by their having disappeared because of rusting. Instead, copper was the material of choice or necessity for the Coronado expedition, most likely the result of an iron shortage in Mexico, the expedition's place of origin.

The question of the source of the copper is yet to be addressed. I had hoped that trace metal analysis of the copper in the boltheads examined in this study could be conducted to determine at least whether it came from European or American sources. But an arrangement by which the analysis was to be done has not been concluded. I hope this question can be addressed in the near future.

We know that no sixteenth-century Spanish entrada other than the Coronado expedition was in the area of the Texas Panhandle with crossbows in significant numbers. The first assumption, then, must be that the assemblage of boltheads found at the Jimmy Owens Site derives from the Coronado expedition. Because the archeological record gives no indication of caching of the boltheads, secondary deposition may be eliminated as well. The wide disbursement of boltheads across the Jimmy Owens Site is not typical of future intended retrieval. This indicates that the boltheads were either used in the area or lost inadvertently.

One suggestion has been that a bag of boltheads was spilled during transportation—perhaps strewn about as horses bolted during a hailstorm reported by one of the chroniclers[13]—which might account for the concentration of boltheads south and west of the site's datum marker. Another remotely possible explanation for the scatter of boltheads is friendly competition or practice firing at a jackrabbit or some other target by a few of Vázquez de Coronado's crossbowmen. Such apparently reckless and knowing abandonment of metal, similar to that suggested by the concentration of more than two hundred sixteenth-century nails at the Jimmy Owens Site, presents the appearance of a group that is "going home" and no longer needs the metal to drive the expedition farther.[14] Because metal detectors removed many of the boltheads without thorough professional excavation, there is little information on their association with other artifacts. Explanations for the concentration of boltheads are still debated as excavations continue at the site.

The Spaniards could have made boltheads at any time from iron, but in the case of the Coronado expedition, they apparently did not do so. The dearth of iron points in Southwestern assemblages may indicate that a supply of copper boltheads was still available and considered sufficient. The copper boltheads could have easily been made in Mexico with either local or European raw material, or they could have been manufactured on the trail, with their individuality representing the work of different artisans associated with the entrada. The common features and measurements of some of the boltheads have permitted the stylistic grouping of boltheads that are quite similar despite being found great geographical distances apart.

These signature objects allow for the observation of movement by the expedition over time and space. Evidence of postmanufacture alternative usage of boltheads is seen in the conversion of several of them into clasps and awls. Clasps could have been used for heavy robes or attached to leather thongs and used as tie-downs. Evidence that this latter use may have occurred is seen in the inner arc of one of the two bent points, which is polished from wear. One of the bent points is from New Mexico and the other from Texas, again indicating the probability that the boltheads from both areas derive from a single source of users. The New Mexico point, however, lacks any polished arch and may be the result of impact and not remanufacture. Other boltheads from New Mexico show evidence of having been used as awls.

There can be little doubt that the copper crossbow boltheads recovered from the Jimmy Owens Site were manufactured and used by the same people who manufactured and used the nearly indistinguishable boltheads recovered at New Mexico archeological sites. Some of the boltheads from different sites are so similar to one another that I am confident in suggesting that they were made by the same person. That evidence, together with the recovery of hundreds of other sixteenth-century objects at the Jimmy Owens Site, makes the conclusion all but inescapable that the site represents an encampment of the Coronado expedition during the late spring or early summer of 1541. Identification of this campsite puts an important dot on the map of the expedition's route and significantly narrows the route possibilities across the Texas Panhandle and northward to Kansas.

Notes

1. Bernal Díaz del Castillo, *The Discovery and Conquest of Mexico, 1517–1521,* ed. Genaro García, trans. Alfred P. Maudslay (New York: Farrar, Straus and Cudahy, 1927), 28.
2. Arthur Woodward to Bruce T. Ellis, 1956, in Bruce T. Ellis, "Crossbow Boltheads from Historic Pueblo Sites," *El Palacio* 64, nos. 7–8 (1957): 211.
3. Díaz del Castillo, *Discovery and Conquest,* 391.
4. Cuevas, "Muster Roll."
5. Weber, *Spanish Frontier,* 66.
6. U.S. Department of the Interior, National Park Service, *Coronado Expedition.*
7. Marjorie Ferguson Tichy, "The Archaeology of Puaray," *El Palacio* 46, no. 7 (1939): 145–46.
8. Alfred V. Kidder, *The Artifacts of Pecos* (New Haven: Yale University Press, 1932), 305–8.
9. Rhodes, "Coronado Fought Here," 51.
10. Tichy, "Archaeology of Puaray," 146.
11. Kidder, *Artifacts of Pecos,* 307.
12. Woodward in Ellis, "Crossbow Boltheads," 209–14.
13. See Castañeda, *Relación,* Primera Parte, Capítulo 20, fol. 85r–86r, in Flint and Flint, *"They Were Not Familiar."*
14. By 1541 the Coronado expedition had major resupply problems. Clothing, for example, was critically short. Nor is there any evidence that exotic but culturally necessary foodstuffs such as wine and oil were getting through. As for metal, eruption of the Mixtón war in Jalisco in 1540 diverted most resources in Nueva España. The Mixtón war was a major uprising, involving tens of thousands of Mexican West Coast natives. Without doubt, the safety of the viceroyalty was in peril. Viceroy Mendoza finally had to lead a force of some twenty thousand in person to put down the revolt, after two earlier disastrous failures (during one of which Pedro de Alvarado died). The Mixtón war was the reason a second attempt to resupply the Coronado expedition by ship (under Hernando de Alarcón, like the first attempt) was scuttled. Not only was resupply iffy, but awaiting the expedition's return to the Rio Grande was an openly hostile Pueblo world. To imagine that in Blanco Canyon members of the expedition were squandering metal resources that they knew to be virtually irreplaceable strains credulity.—Eds.

FIFTEEN

Looking at a Mule Shoe: Sixteenth-Century Spanish Artifacts in Panama

DEE BRECHEISEN

I AM A RETIRED PILOT—both a fighter pilot with the U.S. Air Force and the New Mexico Air National Guard and a commercial airline pilot. In my capacity as a fighter pilot I had the opportunity to spend two weeks a year, for about ten years, in the Republic of Panama, where I heard stories about early Spanish coins and artifacts found along the Camino Real, which runs across the Isthmus of Panama. I became acquainted with several Canal Zone employees who offered to take me along on their treasure-hunting expeditions. On my first trip, I was happy to find several seventeenth-century coins, items of jewelry, and many iron artifacts, including a "goat's-foot" lever for cocking a crossbow. Few of the locals were interested in iron items, so I was able to keep all of those.

By this time in my life I had developed an interest in Spanish colonial history in the Southwest and had metal-detected on several early Spanish sites in New Mexico when I could obtain permission. I also had a fairly extensive library on the subject and therefore could identify many of the artifacts we found in Panama.

In reading the published material on Coronado expedition campsites,[1] I noticed reference to a distinctive type of "caret-head" carpenter's nail. I have found this same type of nail in Panama, singly and in mule shoes. The majority of mule shoe nails I have seen in Panama are different from the "caret-head," having a much higher head with a diamond-shaped profile. On the sites where artifacts indicated only the earliest colonial occupation, however, the nails in mule shoes were all of the caret-head type. Hoping to help determine a possible use of this type of nail, I took a mule shoe (one of many) I had found in Panama with embedded caret-head nails to the Jimmy Owens Site in 1999, explaining its origin and giving it to Donald Blakeslee, director of the ongoing archeological work there.

In this chapter I present information about an extremely important Spanish colonial trail in Panama and artifacts recovered along it. Those objects may assist in identifying artifacts associated with Coronado expedition campsites and help determine which other objects might reasonably be expected in those sites.

Panama

The first European to visit Panama was Rodrigo de Bastidas, in 1501. Columbus more thoroughly explored Panama's north coast on his fourth and last voyage to the Americas in 1502–3, making an unsuccessful attempt at establishing a settlement at the mouth of the Río Belén. He was impressed with the native population, because their society was much more advanced than those of the Caribbean Islands. And much to the Spaniards' delight, the natives of Panama had lots of gold:

> With the exception of the Chibcha craftsmen of Columbia, the ancient Panamanians were the most advanced craftsmen of gold in the Americas. The objects, some pounded into thin sheets and then shaped, others cast into zoomorphic figures, were probably used for jewelry. Spanish chroniclers report that even commoners wore gold bracelets, earrings, and nose rings. Members of the nobility wore even more, including headbands, necklaces, and large thinly pounded discs, which they wore on their chest. Noble women used gold bars as breast supports.[2]

The natives placed little value on gold as metal; the value was in the object it was fashioned into. Not surprisingly, conflict continually erupted as the Spaniards searched out and melted down gold objects. Gonzalo Fernández de Oviedo y Valdéz, royal chronicler of the Indies, reported that the Spanish governor of Castilla del Oro (Panama), Pedro Árias de Ávila (better known as Pedrarias), in his pursuit of gold, sent 2 million Indians on their journey of death between 1514 and 1531.[3] At one point, in retaliation, natives poured molten gold down the throats of captive Spaniards, saying, "Christians! Take your fill of gold!" By 1532, most of the region's Indian population was gone.[4]

It was from a mountaintop in central Panama in 1513 that Balboa got the first European view of the Pacific Ocean. The Spanish towns of Panama, on the south coast, and Nombre de Dios, on the north coast, were founded in 1519 as bases for exploring the newly discovered Pacific Ocean (map 15.1). After the

Spanish conquest of Peru in 1531, Panama became the transit point for the gold and silver found in Peru. The bullion arrived at Panama City on the south (Pacific) coast and crossed Panama to Nombre de Dios on the Atlantic or Caribbean coast. It is estimated that the royal treasure shipped through Panama from Peru from 1551 to 1739 was 112,110,000 *pesos ensayados* and that the registered private silver shipped through Panama from 1531 to 1660 was 278,272,000 pesos ensayados.[5]

The Isthmus of Panama proved to be an unhealthy place for Spaniards.

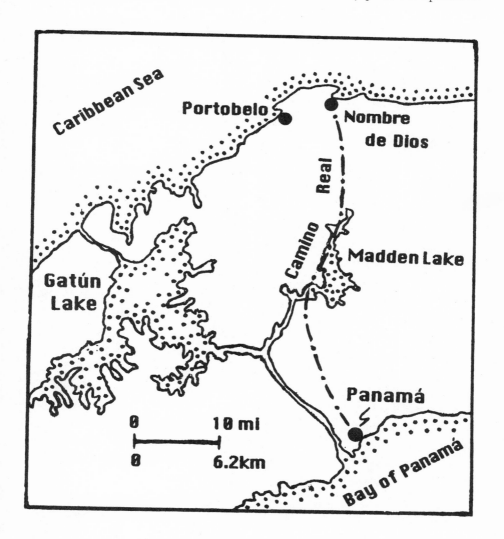

Map 15.1. The route of the Camino Real across Panama. Map by Richard Flint.

Average rainfall on the Atlantic side is 130 inches per year, and on the Pacific side, 70 inches per year.[6] Church records indicate that 46,000 people died at Nombre de Dios from 1519 to 1588 (approximately 666 per year). Early seventeenth-century descriptions of Panama tend to paint a dismal picture of the place: "The climate is very hot. The winds from January to June are strong, but they are sickly due to their high humidity. It is so humid here that it rains all year long, and owing to this the country is very sickly, suffering from fevers and bloody hemorrhages, which are a great problem."[7]

The Camino Real

Transportation across Panama took place on a series of roads that were cleared early in the sixteenth century. After the discovery of silver in Peru, these roads, little more than partially paved paths, together became one of the most important commercial routes in the Spanish New World.[8]

Two main routes were used. The first went from Panama City to Venta de Cruces, then via the Río Chagres on small boats to its mouth at San Lorenzo. From there travelers went via ship to Nombre de Dios and later Portobelo. This route was called Las Cruces Trail. Transit across it took between one and two weeks, depending on the level of the river. Las Cruces Trail was used until replaced by the Panama railroad in 1850.

The other route went from Panama City to Venta de Chagres, then up the Río Boquerón to the continental divide, and finally down to Nombre de Dios or Portobelo. This was the route known as the Camino Real. It was used extensively from 1531 until about 1740 and was abandoned by 1826. By 1600 the port of Portobelo had replaced Nombre de Dios as the northern terminus of the trail. This all-land route was preferred over the land-and-water route after pirates became a problem. Goods transported over the Camino Real were targeted by escaped slaves, called *cimarrones,* who were eager to share the wealth of the king. It was on the midsection of the Camino Real, in the area now periodically covered by Madden Lake (map 15.1), that most of my artifact collecting took place.

The primary purpose of the Camino Real was transportation of Peruvian silver to the northern coast to be exchanged for manufactured goods from Europe. These goods were in turn taken back across Panama for shipping to Peru. Pack mules were exclusively used for this task.

This exchange of goods for silver was formalized at fairs, as they were called, which took place every year that a fleet arrived from Spain for over two hundred years. Supplying silver for a fair required that approximately one thousand mules make three eighteen-league trips across the isthmus. The average mule train consisted of about fifty mules, handled by twenty-four black slaves, with an armed escort. The mules could carry about two hundred pounds each. Because mules were not raised in Panama, an average of one thousand per year was imported from El Salvador, Nicaragua, or Honduras. This suggests a rather high mortality rate for mules in colonial Panama. And indeed, often I have found four whole mule shoes in close proximity, which seem to have come from a single dead animal. This would indicate that crossing the isthmus was strenuous, even for mules. The records show that a mule required forty shoes for each fair season.[9] Little wonder, then, that along the remains of the trail there is, even today, an abundant supply of broken, worn-out mule shoes.

The Camino Real had several inns, or *ventas,* spaced along its length, which were used for overnight stops. Most sat on flat-topped hills, close to the trail. However, we have found artifacts on other small hilltops, now islands in Madden Lake, that seem to have been campsites. It is on and near these ventas and camps that most of the artifacts I discuss here have been found.

Along the Camino Real in Panama I have found a wide variety of Spanish colonial artifacts, including an anvil, bells, balls, buttons, beads, bottles, buckles, brass tacks, coins, candlesticks, clyster pumps, Chinese porcelain, crosses, gun parts, a goat's-foot lever, solid iron machetes, medallions, Majolica, mule shoes, lance points, nails, spikes, silver slugs, spurs, sword parts, stirrups, thimbles, tools, weight cups, and many unidentified fragments. Because today most of the Camino Real area is under water the greater part of the year, iron artifacts are in poor condition.

Madden Lake Campsite

In my experience, one small campsite in particular proved interesting. The objects on the site, which lies directly adjacent to the Camino Real within Madden Lake, appear to be exclusively from the sixteenth century. Briefly, the following artifacts have been collected from this campsite:

1. Several whole mule shoes, mule shoe fragments, and nails (fig. 15.1). There appears to be no difference between sixteenth-century and later mule shoes. However, the ones we found at this campsite invariably contained caret-head nails. Isolated individual nails from the site were also consistently of the caret-head type.
2. Coins. The coins on this site, which were silver one- and two-real denominations, all dated from the reign of Carlos and Juana and were minted in Mexico City between 1536 and 1556.[10]

Figure 15.1. Mule shoe with nails, Madden Lake, Panama, found by Dee Brecheisen. Photo by Richard Flint.

3. Silver. Several pieces of silver were found that appear to be from a puddle of silver poured into a depression in the earth. They were then broken into small pieces that were stamped, presumably by the assayer. The markings of these slugs are not legible enough to identify their place or exact date of origin. Frank Sedwick, a Florida dealer in early Spanish coins, however, thinks they date from very early in the colonial period and were possibly used before mints were established in the New World. Some coins dating from the reign of Fernando and Isabel have also been found in the vicinity of this campsite.

4. One small bell. It appears to be a one-piece construction of brass or copper. It is 1.5 inches high and 1.25 inches in horizontal diameter.

5. One fragment of a Nueva Cádiz bead, dark blue in color and approximately three-eighths inch in diameter. Nueva Cádiz beads are thought to have been produced and traded between 1500 and 1550.[11]

6. Two fragmentary socket-based iron lance points (?), each approximately 10 inches long with a 90-degree bend at the midpoint of the blade.
7. One fragment of blue on white porcelain, which appears to be of Chinese manufacture.
8. An assortment of lead shot of various diameters.
9. Two small spearhead-shaped brass objects with gold plating and fancy designs (1.5 by 0.5 inches). My best guess is that these are some type of clothes hook.[12]

Artifacts from Other Sites in Panama

The remainder of this discussion of artifacts from Panama deals with objects found at campsites that appear to have been used from the sixteenth to the eighteenth centuries. The following list does not cover all artifacts found along the Camino Real in Panama, but only those I have selected as most relevant and interesting.

1. Goat's-foot lever. Two fragmentary specimens were found near a small hilltop ruin. Associated with them were a large quantity of mule shoes, nails, and coins from the mid-sixteenth century.
2. Brass tacks. They are found near the ventas and camps in relatively large quantities and in assorted sizes and shapes.
3. Jet beads and ring. Very few of these items have been found. I know of only one ring, and it was located in a camp that contained some of the earliest coins. It may be worth noting that jet rings were brought to New Mexico by Oñate in 1598.[13]
4. Buttons and an aglet. I purchased one aglet, or metal lace tip, but have never found one in situ in Panama. This example is made from silver. Buttons are fairly common and of various shapes and construction:
   a. Cast, one-piece silver, ranging from flat to dome shaped
   b. Cast, one-piece brass, solid or open back and dome shaped; usually gold plated with decorations
   c. Plain stamped sheet silver, dome shaped with covered base and attached eye. None of the buttons is identical to the "ball buttons" found at Santa Elena, South Carolina.[14] Buttons range in size from 8 to 16 millimeters in diameter.
5. Mule bells and fragments. These artifacts are quite common. Most are made of cast white metal and measure 4–5 inches high, with a holed rectangular extension on top for attachment. Bases average 2.5–3.0 inches. Judging by the number of bell fragments, it would appear that all or nearly all mules wore bells.

6. Shot for firearms. This, too, is common, most being unfired. It ranges in diameter from 0.35 to 0.89 inches.

7. Clyster pump. An interesting item that must have been widely used. Fragments appear quite often, but the only whole specimen I have seen is a hollow cylinder, 10 inches long and 2 inches in diameter, with a rib-reinforced exterior. The top is locked by a twisting motion. This example, which I purchased, is missing the spout. The plunger has a space for gasket material and is missing the handle. Fragmentary specimens indicate other sizes of 1.6 and 1.25 inches in diameter.

Ernie Richards, editor of the newsletter *Plus Ultra,* told me, "If I'm not mistaken, the object . . . is the cylinder section of something we also find on shipwrecks. The instrument is called a 'clyster pump' and it was used to give people enemas in order to relieve constipation . . . which was a common health problem in the colonial period. Concoctions such as chemical salts (and even soapy water) were administered into the patient rectally, and relief was soon to follow, hopefully."[15] Fragments of clyster pumps have been found at some early New Mexico mission sites and are common on all Spanish colonial sites I am acquainted with, both in the Southwest and in Panama.

8. Crosses and medallions. These appear frequently near the large town sites. There must have been a large variety of them, because I have never seen two that were identical. Most of the crosses and all the medallions I have found have the top eyelet rotated 90 degrees from the plane of the cross or medal. Most are made of brass, but a few are of silver or gold. Crosses range in size from 3 by 2 inches to 1.0 by 0.75 inches. Medallions are oval, heart shaped, and elongated octagonal.

9. Buckles. These are mostly brass, although iron ones are found badly deteriorated. The brass buckles might have been used in clothing. They range in size from 3 by 2 inches to 2 by 1 inches.

10. Weight sets. These are the type that look like small, tapered, handleless cups that nest one inside the others, each having a specific weight. They were used in transactions to determine the weight of silver slugs and coins. Coins were often underweighted at the mint and were also frequently shaved by unscrupulous colonists. The outside cup in my reconstructed set (?) is 2 inches wide at the top and 1.4 inches high. The base is 1.45 inches wide.

11. Spurs. I have found both brass and iron spurs. Judging from their size and shape, the ones I have found appear to be from the later period. They are plain and have small rowels.

12. Stirrups. Most of the ones I am familiar with from Panama are of cast brass, approximately 6 inches high. The bases arch up in the center with cutout

designs and measure 5.0 by 4.5 inches. Decorations are usually present on the bases and triangular-shaped sides.

Comparing Artifacts

Some comparisons can be made between artifacts from known Coronado expedition sites and those from early historic sites in Panama. Interestingly, the mule shoes found in both places are identical for all practical purposes. Moreover, caret-head nails were definitely used to attach mule shoes in Panama in the sixteenth century. Such nails have been found in the Coronado expedition's campsites, and I believe it is safe to assume they were used for the same purpose there.

Large quantities of lead balls (shot) have been found in both Panama and at Santiago Pueblo (LA 326) in New Mexico (fig. 15.2). They appear to be identical, except for an oversized one from Santiago. It is 1.02 inches in diameter and weighs 3.26 troy ounces. It is the largest piece of shot I have ever seen. Could this have been used in the small cannon that Coronado left at Zia Pueblo when the expedition headed east in 1541?[16] Also found at Santiago were about twenty pieces of fired shot that appear to have impacted adobe. They include two pewter

Figure 15.2. Lead shot from Santiago Pueblo, New Mexico (LA 326), found by Dee Brecheisen. Photo by Richard Flint.

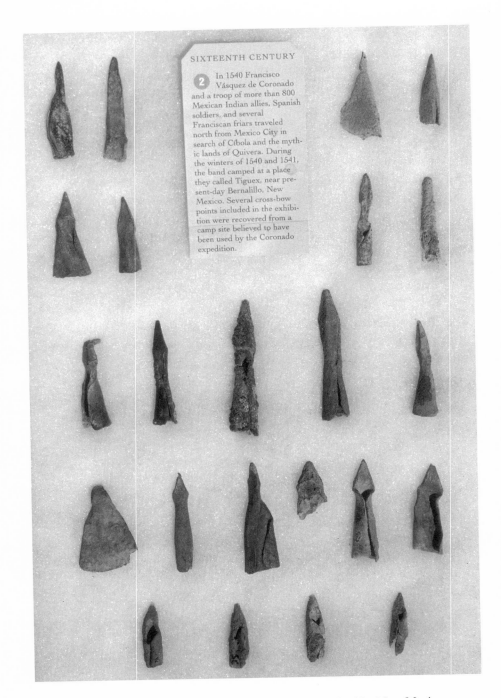

SIXTEENTH CENTURY

2 In 1540 Francisco Vásquez de Coronado and a troop of more than 800 Mexican Indian allies, Spanish soldiers, and several Franciscan friars traveled north from Mexico City in search of Cíbola and the mythic lands of Quivera. During the winters of 1540 and 1541, the band camped at a place they called Tiguex, near present-day Bernalillo, New Mexico. Several cross-bow points included in the exhibition were recovered from a camp site believed to have been used by the Coronado expedition.

Figure 15.3. Crossbow boltheads from Santiago Pueblo, New Mexico (LA 326), found by Dee Brecheisen. Photo by Dee Brecheisen.

or white metal balls. To explore the impact these balls underwent, I fired similar balls into adobe, which resulted in flattening very similar to that on the shot from Santiago. Santiago Pueblo has a much higher incidence of impacted bullets than other New Mexico sites with which I am familiar. I believe this is significant and may confirm Santiago as a site of violent conflict between the Coronado expedition and Pueblo Indians of the Rio Grande. That no shot has been reported from the Jimmy Owens Site seems unusual. It is my experience that shot is the most common object dropped at a campsite.

The Coronado expedition seems to have left crossbow boltheads wherever it camped or fought. Indeed, they may be diagnostic of the Coronado expedition.[17] Crossbow boltheads have been found in New Mexico at Hawikuh, Santiago Pueblo, San Cristóbal, and Pecos Pueblo and in Texas at Blanco Canyon. To my knowledge none, of either copper or iron, has been found in Panama. I have, however, seen two goat's-foot levers from Panama, which may indicate that crossbows were in use there, as one would expect them to have been.

Among the items carried by the Coronado expedition for trade with native people were "paternosters" and "jingle bells."[18] It has been suggested that these included Nueva Cádiz beads and Clarksdale bells, which date from the period.[19] Nueva Cádiz beads have been found in Panama, but none so far in Coronado sites, though a single such bead that may have derived from the Coronado expedition was found in southwestern Oklahoma.[20] Two fragmentary specimens of Clarksdale bells were found at Santiago Pueblo, but none, to my knowledge, has been discovered in Panama.

The following is my speculation about what other items might be found in a Coronado expedition campsite: coins or silver slugs, jet rings and beads, brass mule harness rings, clothing hooks (two have come from Santiago, small and of iron, but no large fancy ones like those found in Panama), Chinese porcelain, chain mail (fragments of chain mail were found at Santiago, the individual rings of three different sizes; no chain mail, to my knowledge, has been found in Panama), buttons (one was found at Santiago, cast in one piece of white metal, 0.5 inches in diameter, flat with crosshatch decoration on top; buttons are found in Panama, but none identical to those at Santiago), religious items, and possibly copper loops.

There has been much speculation over whether Santiago Pueblo is the Alcanfor or Coofor mentioned in the sixteenth-century documents of the Coronado expedition, site of the expedition's winter camp, or whether it might be Moho, one of the pueblos besieged by the expedition for about fifty days. I think it is Moho, for the following reasons: (1) The large number of crossbow boltheads likely indicates some sort of offensive military activity. Some of the boltheads show impact damage, and one was reportedly found in a burial. (2) Many balls flattened by impact could mean gunfire directed toward the pueblo. (3) The location of another pueblo, Kuaua, somewhat more than the half league above Moho reported by Castañeda corresponds to his description. And (4) the presence of a Coronado-era campsite nearby is convincing.

Notes

1. Bradley J. Vierra, ed., *A Sixteenth-Century Spanish Campsite in the Tiguex Province,* Laboratory of Anthropology Note 475 (Santa Fe: Museum of New Mexico, 1989); Flint and Flint, *Coronado Expedition to Tierra Nueva.*
2. Christopher Ward, *Imperial Panama: Commerce and Conflict in Isthmian America, 1550–1800* (Albuquerque: University of New Mexico Press, 1993), 42–43.
3. Charles Loftus Grant Anderson, *Old Panama and Castillo del Oro* (New York: North River Press, 1944), 233.
4. Anderson, *Old Panama,* 130, 233.
5. Ward, *Imperial Panama,* 8–9.
6. Roland D. Hussey, "Spanish Colonial Trails in Panama," *Revista de Historia de America* 6 (1939): 49.
7. Ward, *Imperial Panama,* 29.
8. Ward, *Imperial Panama,* 55.
9. Ward, *Imperial Panama,* 61, 63, 231.
10. Frank Sedwick, *The Practical Book of Cobs,* 2d ed. (Maitland, Florida: Frank Sedwick, 1990), 6, 94.
11. Marvin T. Smith and Mary Elizabeth Good, *Early Sixteenth-Century Glass Trade Beads in the Spanish Colonial Trade* (Greenwood, Mississippi: Cottonlandia Museum Publications, 1982), 11. See also Diane Lee Rhodes, "Coronado's American Legacy: An Overview of Possible Entrada Artifacts and Site Types and a Discussion of Texas Sites," *Bulletin of the Texas Archeological Society* 63 (1992): 27–51.
12. Stanley South, Russell K. Skowronek, and Richard E. Johnson, *Spanish Artifacts from Santa Elena,* Occasional Papers of the South Carolina Institute of Archeology and Anthropology, Anthropological Studies no. 7 (Columbia: University of South Carolina, 1988), 128–29.
13. Hammond and Rey, *Oñate,* 2:220–22.
14. South, Skowronek, and Johnson, *Santa Elena,* 134.
15. Ernie Richards to Dee Brecheisen, personal communication, March 5, 1994.
16. Richard Flint to Dee Brecheisen, personal communication, February 2000.
17. Vierra, *Spanish Campsite,* 218, 227; and chapter 14, this volume.
18. Hammond and Rey, *Narratives,* 217.
19. Rhodes, "Coronado's American Legacy," 35. See also Flint, "Pattern of Coronado Expedition," 222.
20. Byron Sudbury, "A Sixteenth-Century Spanish Colonial Trade Bead from Western Oklahoma," *Bulletin of the Oklahoma Anthropological Society* 33 (1984): 31–36.

SIXTEEN

Mapping, Measuring, and Naming Cultural Spaces in Castañeda's *Relación de la jornada de Cíbola*

MAUREEN AHERN

THE EXPEDITION THAT Francisco Vázquez de Coronado led beyond the northern frontiers of New Spain from 1540 to 1542 in search of the Seven Cities of Cíbola provided some of the earliest geographical knowledge about western North America and its indigenous peoples. Pedro de Castañeda de Náçera's account of that expedition's itinerary to Cíbola and Quivira was part of the sixteenth-century endeavor to make epistemological meaning out of American space. It "sought to define and describe a New World that was a missing part of the cosmos," as Barbara Mundy put it in her study *The Mapping of New Spain*.[1]

Although Ptolemy's 1406 and 1475 translated and published *Geography* had posited a geometrical system for measuring and mapping the entire globe,[2] it conceived of only three continents and thought the earth was three-quarters of its actual size.[3] When the Italian cartographer Pietro Coppo drew a world map in 1528 (map 16.1) and Hernán Cortés's pilots traced the first map of the northwest coast of what is now mainland Mexico in 1535 (map 16.2), the crucial relationships of longitude had still not been determined and the land masses of the new continents were still conceived of as islands or only faint, partial contours. "The New World still stood outside the known order of things," in Mundy's words.[4]

As Europeans began to explore North America, cartographers had to struggle to integrate their revolutionary information in a consistent map of the world.[5] The *relaciones,* or narratives of firsthand observations, by members of the Spanish expeditions beyond the northern frontiers of either Mexica or Spanish conquests were the basis of the Padrón Real, the official Spanish map compiled, continually updated, and kept secret by the cosmographers at the Casa de Contratación

Map 16.1. World map by Pietro Coppo, Venice, 1528. The area between Europe and Cimpagno (Japan) is shown as islands. Reproduced with permission of The British Library, London, BL G.7292.

in Sevilla. Carlos V's and Felipe II's royal cosmographers knew it was politically crucial to find accurate longitude lines and the precise distances for measuring that would finally establish them. Castañeda's participant account of the Coronado expedition's journey into the interior of North America was a key part of that same enterprise.

From the walled Zuni pueblo of Hawikuh or perhaps Kiakima,[6] in the final quarter of 1540, Vázquez de Coronado sent his captains on a great circle of inland exploration that ranged from the Pacific Ocean to central Kansas (map 16.3).[7] In just two years his captains' explorations produced information that transformed the geography of North America from the medieval island imagery of Columbus to that of a new continent about to appear on maps, where the toponyms Cíbola, Acoma, Tiguex, Cicuique, and Quivira configured new political and cultural spaces. In the imagination of New Spain, Quivira displaced Cíbola as frontier and object of mythic quest.[8]

Although various accounts were dispatched during the expedition, the most complete narrative of where it went and what it encountered was not written

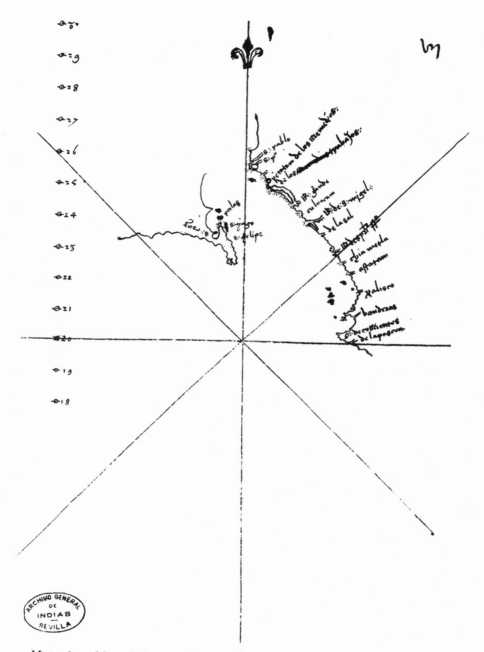

Map 16.2. Map of "la nueva Tierra de Santa Cruz de la California," discovered by Hernán Cortés, May 3, 1535. Earliest known map showing any part of the northwest coast of Mexico. Reproduced with permission of Spain's Ministerio de Educación, Cultura y Deporte. Archivo General de Indias, MP-México 6.

until around 1563, some twenty years after the events took place, by Pedro de Castañeda de Náçera, a member of the expedition.[9] Part 1 of his *Relación de la jornada de Cíbola* describes the chronological events along the various routes taken, whereas Part 3 narrates the winter encampment at Tiguex in 1541 and the return to New Spain in the spring of 1542. Between these two segments of historical action is positioned Part 2, to which no critical attention has been paid.

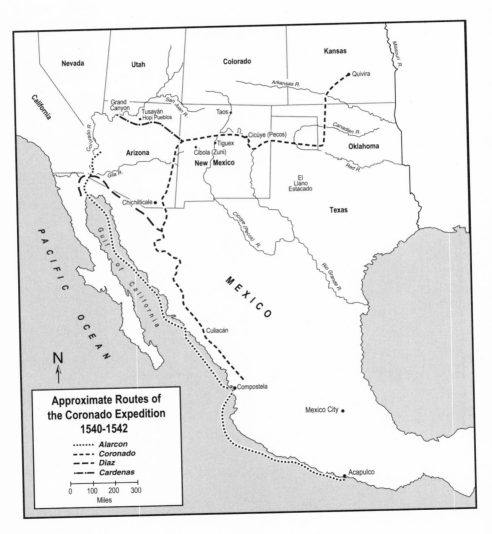

Map 16.3. Approximate routes of the Coronado expedition, 1540–42.
Map by Ron McClean, Office of Information Technology, Ohio State University.

It is an itinerary in eight chapters that traces territories, measures distances, and names places as it maps cultural spaces.[10]

It is my hypothesis that the ethnographic itinerary that makes up the "Segunda Parte en que se trata de los pueblos prouinçias de altos y de sus ritos y costumbres . . . ," as the original title of Part 2 appears in George Parker Winship's transcription,[11] constitutes the narrative pivot upon which the *Relación de la jornada de Cíbola* turns as it realizes the cultural and spatial configuration of a "new" *norte* and a "new" frontier, forming an intersection where the text must confront the terrain.

In this essay I examine the relationship of that segment of Castañeda's discourse to the early cartography of North America—in particular, to that of New Spain and New Mexico.[12] How did Castañeda understand and envision these spaces, and how does he represent them? How are his operations encoded, and what is their significance for our understanding of the radical transformations that were taking place in the conceptualization of North American frontiers and territories in the mid-sixteenth century? What roles do the processes of naming and measuring play in this discourse?

Mapping: Space and Projection in a Singular Prologue

Although our understanding of the map that informs this analysis is the modern one formulated by John Harley and David Woodward—that of "graphic representations that facilitate a spatial understanding of things, concepts, conditions, processes, or events in the human world"[13]—it does not essentially counter the concepts that governed the writing of the *Relación,* for "European maps of the sixteenth century were rooted in a spatial understanding of the human world."[14]

Castañeda conditions the reader's access to the space of the itinerary through the dramatic closure of Part 1, in which the final paragraph refers to the news that Coronado has brought back from Quivira about "large settlements and mighty rivers," a country much like Spain in fruits, vegetation, and climate, and the suspicion that gold existed there.[15] A tantalizing image of Quivira is suspended before the reader's eyes even before the itinerary begins.

Part 2 proper opens with an unusual prologue in which Castañeda declares the need to offer his readers "satisfacción" for any doubts caused by the "contradictory information of the existence of such widespread fame of fabulous treasure, yet no memory or appearance of having found it; of finding vast wilderness instead of settlements, towns instead of cities."[16] This initial disclosure of the discrepancies between what was anticipated and what was found reveals the narrator's awareness of the deficiencies of language before the terrain that confronts him. The narrative tack of alerting his reader to the doubts that assail him about his own text serves as a powerful builder of the reader's trust. Castañeda was writing with full hindsight of the negative reception that the expedition had received upon its return to Mexico some twenty years earlier, and he cautions his readers that *La jornada de Cíbola* contains matter for serious thought:

> It will give them cause to reflect upon and consider the uncertainties of this life. To please the readers I will give a detailed account of all the inhabited territory that was discovered and explored on this expedition, together with some of the customs and ceremonies based on what we managed to observe. I will also state the location of every province in order that one may thus be able to understand in what direction La Florida lies, where the greater India is situated, and how this land of New Spain is part of a [continuous) mainland with Peru, as well as with greater India or China. There is no strait in this region that divides it. On the contrary, the land is so wide that it contains vast uninhabited areas between the two seas.[17]

From this initial textual survey the addressee may proceed to spatially configure the geography of Quivira, bearing in mind that "La Florida" was a term roughly synonymous with the entire land mass northeast of Mexico. Neither is there a strait, the narrator clarifies, implicitly anticipating a query about the elusive Strait of Anian. Castañeda's detailed compendium of the known points of the western hemisphere of his time affirms that everything from New Spain to the land north of La Florida, or Terranova (Newfoundland), and south to Peru is continuous mainland connected to Greater India.[18]

Yet this same passage also demonstrates how successful Spain's Casa de Contratación had become at blocking the dissemination of important new geographic information gained by its pilots and explorers. The voyages of Cabrillo and Ferrer in 1542–43, which covered twelve hundred miles north along the Pacific coast to 42 degrees latitude, had "provided evidence to Spanish cartographers that Asia and North America were two separate continents . . . and added to the growing doubts that a strait existed through North America."[19]

On this point, Castañeda's information about the geographical relationship between Asia and North America lagged far behind that of the mapmakers. Although his narrative does not reflect all the changes in knowledge that were occurring at the time he was writing, the map drawn in 1542 by the royal Spanish cosmographer, Alonso de Santa Cruz, and carefully guarded from foreign eyes showed, in the extreme upper edge, castles for "la sept cibdad" and the caption "Tierra que envio a descubrir don Antonio de Mendoza."[20] During the same period Italian maps copied from captured official Spanish charts or manuscript maps also contained them. Giovanni Battista Ramusio incorporated the principal place names from Coronado's letter to Mendoza that he published in volume 3 of his *Navigationi et viaggi* (1556). Bolognino Zaltieri's map of the same year also contained a large number of Coronado place names and separated the American continent from Asia (map 16.4).[21]

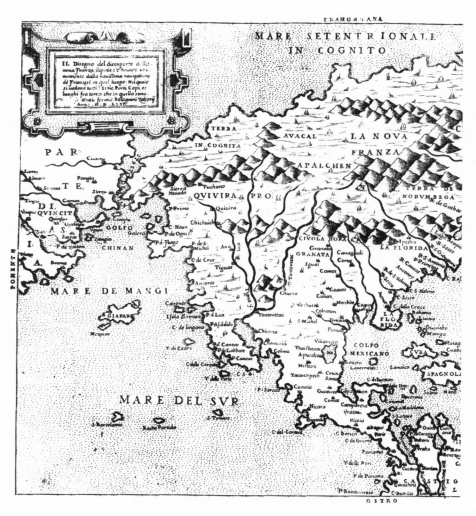

Map 16.4. "Il Disegno del Discoperto della Nova Franza," by Bolognino Zaltieri, 1556. This map contains a large number of Coronado place names and separates the American continent from Asia. Photo and permission courtesy of the Edward E. Ayer Collection, Newberry Library, Chicago.

Charles Polzer pointed out that historians and geographers alike have often despaired that Castañeda's discourse leaves much open for interpretation, vacillating as it does between macrolanguage and microdescriptions.[22] Yet in writing this way, Castañeda followed Ptolemy's early distinction between chorographic and geographic maps, which was influential at this time. Part 2 of his *relación* places the regional geography of Cíbola and Quivira within the larger frame of North America, then zooms in to a closer "view" of each point on the route, halting in each chapter of the itinerary to survey a panorama of the settlement and its human and material features. In this way, the narrative perspective combines topography as well as pictorial and human scenes, or chorography.[23]

Measuring: From Culiacán and Petatlán

The eight chapters of Part 2 that compose the itinerary are organized according to spatial segments that run along a north-south axis, those being the directions that late Renaissance cartography marked as its cardinal points, in contrast to the Amerindian cardinal points defined by the east-west course of the sun.[24] The lands beyond Culiacán are depicted as a continuous geographic expanse in which distances are measured in number of leagues from the imperial hub, Mexico City. Castañeda describes Baja California as peninsular, in terms of the length and width (in leagues) of the Gulf of California from the delta of the "río del tiçon," or Colorado River, to the tip of Baja.[25] Although the image of Baja California as an island appeared on some maps of New Spain well into the eighteenth century,[26] in 1563 Castañeda described it accurately, as Fernando de Alarcón had already done in his report on the maritime vanguard of 1540.[27]

Advancing from Petatlán to the Señora (Sonora) Valley, "thickly settled with comely people" (muy poblado de gente muy dispuesta), Castañeda naturalizes the territory he surveys into Spanish geography as "provincias" (provinces) and "poblados" (settlements), terms that from the onset invite settlement, in contrast to the "despoblado," or wilderness, that lies ahead. At Suya or Corazones the narrator anticipates the massacre of Coronado's base camp, as, he tells us in the narrative future, "will be seen further on" (como se bera adelante)—that is, in Part 3. At Corazones, for a long narrative moment, present and future merge.[28]

Measurements of distances were crucial information to send back to the cosmographers in Sevilla. Although according to royal decrees, or *ordenanzas,* all exploration parties were required to submit written reports of their journeys and routes upon return, nothing complete had been compiled for this one.

By the 1560s the Ibarra clan had begun to claim jurisdiction over territories that Coronado had traversed, and the English were penetrating the northern seas.

Castañeda wrote in order to set down a record of territory seen and therefore "known" only to the members of the Coronado expedition as a way of keeping Cíbola and Quivira alive in the political imagination of the viceroyalty for future settlement. He also wrote to make it "real" for Spanish cartographers, whose charts would integrate these northern expanses into the Spanish imperial world, setting the stage for their settlement and thus individual possession. In other words, this textual operation enacts the classic rhetoric of surveillance that so characterizes colonial discourse.[29]

Even at an early textual juncture, the discursive strategy of the itinerary is evident. Over the military and chronological events of the expedition from Culiacán to Quivira and the return to Cicuique (Pecos) told in Part 1, the narrator superimposes the linear geometric grid of Part 2, producing a montage on a north-south axis that is measured in numbers of leagues, identified by indigenous or bilingual toponyms, and divided according to the names of the ethnic groups that inhabited each segment. To the naming of each territory he adds brief comments about housing, clothing, language, sexual practices, food, and landscape that serve in their empirical qualities as an ethnographic gloss to the narrative of remarkable and violent action told in Parts 1 and 3.

In this way the two segments—the social and political configuration of Cíbola and the topographic measurement of its cultural spaces—function in narrative tandem, locating events and reinforcing the natural context in which they occur as the narrator moves back and forth between them. Through this strategy he is able to make precise references to a large number of places, peoples, and events that, prior to the Coronado expedition, had been ephemeral orality in the mouths of Núñez Cabeza de Vaca and fray Marcos de Niza and their Indian guides, or at best empty spaces on maps such as the one drawn by Battiste Agnese.[30] Cíbola and Quivira were regions of the globe that needed to be placed under the rational power of measurement and mapping because Spanish authorities in Madrid and Sevilla still conceived of them as the mythical places of the seven cities inherited from medieval lore, as seen on the Joan Martines map of 1587.[31] Twenty years earlier, fray Bartolomé de las Casas had written, "En las cartas de marear que los tiempos pasados se hacían, se pintaban algunas islas por aquellos mares . . . especialmente la isla que decían Antilla . . . , ésta estimaban los portugueses que sea la isla de las Siete ciudades, cuya fama y apetito ha llegado hasta nos y a muchos ha hecho por su codicia devariar y gastar muchos dineros sin provecho."[32] Even before that, these spaces were depicted as empty or blank or were known to those born in Mexico as the territory of the Chichimecas. Of course this so-called blank or empty space was only so for Europeans,[33] because the northern land mass had long existed in central Mexican cosmology as Aztlán, site of the seven caves of origin. It was also the world of the four cardinal points, infused with symbolic valence for the Pueblo Indians. Indeed, for at least a century before Spanish contact, Cíbola had been the destination of central Mexican merchants and traders traveling along a well-known trade route.[34]

Naming and Translating: Chichilticale and the Despoblado

As the expedition traveled out of the sphere of the Spaniards and their Tlatelolca and Mexica allies and into the vast northern expanses of desert, plateau, and plains peoples, the *Relación* illustrates how "naming is at the heart of mapping," as many cartographers have pointed out.[35] With translation, it becomes Castañeda's major rhetorical operation.

The abandoned great house, or "casa grande," that marked the beginning of the despoblado served as a major landmark on the trade route north. When Castañeda identified it by the Nahuatl designation *chichilticale,* he immediately explained in Spanish, "Era de tierra colorada o bermeja" (it was built of red ochre earth). That is, he added the explanation in Spanish without indicating that *chichilticale* was the equivalent of "red house," from the colonial Nahuatl form *chichiltic* for "something red" and *calli* for "house or structure."[36] Clearly, he assumed that his readers knew sufficient Nahuatl to infer the semantic relationship.

Perhaps as many as thirteen hundred Indian allies from central and western Mexico constituted the majority of Coronado's huge armed force of at least seventeen hundred men,[37] among them the guides who were reporting and inventing place names as they scouted. Some were Tlatelolcans whose departure in 1539 for "Tierra Nueva" was recorded as a major event in their own annals for the years 8 Acatl (1539) and 9 Técpatl (1540).[38] Spanish custom followed Roman colonization practices of renaming conquered territories, and in New Spain, Spaniards followed a similar Mexica imperial practice.[39] Composite Nahuatl and Spanish-language toponyms encoded layers of imperial meanings as they created new territorial identities in a partial erasure and rewriting of coexisting markers. In this way the northern frontier joined the geography of *Las Indias occidentales* through the double filter of Mexica and Spanish imperial signs.

These volatile referents through which the Coronado enterprise invented a "new" topography by suppressing older regional identities and features affected the relationship between topography and language. They may be read as instances in which the text stumbles or hesitates before the terrain, as though the new features to be reported were perceived as so remote or strange that in order to naturalize them into Spanish writing, they first had to pass through the familiar indigenous filter of Nahuatl.

As the language of the Mexica conquerors, Nahuatl was the lingua franca throughout central Mexico and the language of literacy taught by the Franciscans in their schools.[40] For Coronado's soldiers, Nahuatl speakers had been their military allies for the past twenty years and frequently were their servants, wives, or children. On the road to Cíbola they were fellow travelers in a hostile and unknown north that leveled and homogenized languages as well as men. Although many regional toponyms endured (e.g., Axa and Acu)—particularly those in the territories of the Zuni, Hopi, and Tiwa pueblos, where everything sounded as "new" to the Nahuatl- and Pima-speaking guides as to the Spaniards—peoples and places often underwent multiple renamings.

This process not only erased the landscape created by indigenous toponyms but also displaced ethnicities by using place names often received from enemy groups. The main Zuni pueblo, originally named Hawikuh, is rebaptized Cíbola, perhaps from an Ópata word meaning "Zuni."[41] Then it is renamed Granada for the native city of Viceroy Mendoza and turns up as "Nova Granada" or "Granata Nova," coexisting on Italian maps well into the next century, as on the Zaltieri map of 1556 (map 16.4) and on Cornelis Van Wytfliet's map of "Granata Nova et California (1597)," the first regional map of New Mexico, Sonora, and California.[42] These triple modalities of toponyms derived from regional languages as well as from Nahuatl or Spanish pass onto the map that Ramusio included in volume 3 of his widely distributed *Navigationi et viaggi,* published in Venice in 1556. Soon afterward, Abraham Ortelius's highly influential "Typus Orbis Terrarum" of 1564 incorporated place names from the Coronado expedition. It was the first map to show the full outlines of North America.

Embodying Cíbola: "Llevando el norte sobre el ojo isquierdo"

As Castañeda records how the vanguard party rode through the pine and oak forests of east-central Arizona to reach Cíbola, he instructs his readers that "siempre se ba subiendo la tierra hasta llegar a çibola que son ochenta leguas la uia del norte y hasta llegar alli desde culiacan se auia caminado lleuando el norte sobre el ojo isquierdo" (the land rises gradually until one reaches Cíbola, which is eighty leagues, sighting the way north over the left eye).[43]

This empirical locating by the careful counting of leagues anchors the text, tying its telling into a numerical reality that will serve as an explicit itinerary for any reader who wishes to find the way back to Cíbola and Quivira. Undoubtedly the precise calculation of leagues created the illusion of a concrete place in a terrain that Vázquez de Coronado had already qualified as "a sea so vast it had no limits,"[44] and that fray Marcos de Niza had certified as containing "seven golden cities."[45] Firsthand written observations of surveillance in the field were valuable complements to the precise mathematical calculations made with instruments, not only in terms of placing the new territory on the Padrón Real (official map) but also for the purpose of enhancing belief in the eyes of the addressee—in Castañeda's case, perhaps doctor Alonso Zorita.[46] Quantifying and measuring are also ways to translate the other. François Hartog, in his discussion of a "rhetoric of otherness" on the ancient frontier of the Scythians, pointed out that evaluative measuring is a necessary operation to translate the telling of extraordinary or marvelous events, or *thoma,* into the idiom of the world to which they are recounted.[47] In Castañeda's *Relación,* the events narrated in Parts 1 and 3 constitute sets of *thoma,* and Part 2 provides their anchor, fastening tight their empirical verification by constant measurements and pragmatic information.

The letter that Coronado wrote to Viceroy Mendoza on April 20, 1541, in which he described the route to Quivira, never reached Mexico City; the map that he enclosed with it has never been found. In 1563 there still existed no precise map of Cíbola or Quivira, nor a complete report of the expedition's itinerary or events. Therefore, the report written by Castañeda, as an eyewitness and participant in the events, required concision and accuracy, for it had to stand in lieu of that map in the immediate present as well as provide the basis for an official one in the future. On the northern frontier of New Spain, the relación or written report preceded the map, assuming a normative role in establishing a spatial order for resolving the articulation of the territory traveled, its alterity, and, above all, its future place in universal cosmography.

"A journey is above all about finding one's way . . . and an itinerary is how to do that."[48] At this point in the expedition, the narrator-traveler takes us literally by the hand, and as we travel north, he textually surveys, league by league, all that is seen and traversed, placing before us a measured and annotated itinerary that functions in much the same way our American Automobile Association "Triptik" map does for the same route today: 250 miles from Naco to Springerville; 85 miles from St. Johns to the Zuni reservation; flash floods on route 53; free campsites and drinking water at El Moro.[49] Castañeda's precise tally of the segments in leagues imparts the sensation of being on that trail, keeping the count between the poles of departure and arrival that generate the tension of the telling of any journey.[50]

Moreover, "llevando el norte sobre el ojo izquierdo" draws Cíbola, that mirage of so many decades of hearsay in New Spain, palpably near and corporally reachable via a cardinal point that is positioned over the left eye of the traveler. The textual direction stretches out a metaphorical hand to center Cíbola over the reader's line of vision, as it was within the writer's. The combination of geometric referents with references to the human body in the conceptualization of this cardinal direction reveals toponymies in the process of change. The human body as a personal referent that belonged to a much more ancient and universal code is now enunciated in the same phrase as the geometric one of eighty leagues on the route north.[51]

Once more the terrain challenges language, forcing it to seize various codes in order to write it. "American space both encourages and defeats the imagination; it encourages and defeats the linguistic structures through which the imagination expresses itself."[52] The textualization of the road to Cíbola requires two nonlinguistic codes—the mathematical one of counting leagues and the corporal one of locating the cardinal point in the narrating subject's body. At the *Relación's* most crucial point, the measurement of the exact distance to the desired Cíbola, Castañeda embodies his route. The narrating subject himself becomes the mobile point of reference to the space his progress marks and his discourse records.

Cíbola Humanscapes

Castañeda's depictions of the "provincia" of Cíbola (Zuni) begin with the architectural environment: how the pueblo is constructed, of what materials, the layout of its levels and plazas, and the number of its inhabitants. Then focus shifts to the small details of the humanscape: priests calling people to prayer on the terraces at dawn; dress, hairstyles, and sexual and marriage practices. Thus, our first view is from the Euclidean perspective of the structural grid, followed by a humanscape of pueblo activity, as if the eye scanned onto the terraces from a nearby elevation. At Tiguex there is division of labor and gender roles: "the houses belong to the women, the ovens to the men." Men weave, women raise the children and cook. A man plays a flute to which the women keep time with their grinding stones and sing. They keep large flocks of domestic turkeys and cultivate maize. For the observation that women go nude until marriage, the narrator declares that his source of information was "one of our Indians who had been a captive among these people for a year" (de un indio de los nuestros que auia estado un año catibo entre ellos), whom he personally questioned.[53] Here, as is frequent throughout the text, the careful identification of a local eyewitness informant serves to strengthen the credibility of the narrator's accuracy. Reliance on the testimony of eyewitnesses and participants was one of the principal elements of the Spanish concept of "historical truth" at this time. It held special significance for the audience of readers and authorities in far-off Mexico City and Madrid, who would never "see" for themselves these lands that they sought to exploit.

Castañeda's words made the humanscape of Cíbola "visible," drawing on it real figures that fleshed out the nebulous mythic landscapes fray Marcos had proclaimed. Nonetheless, Castañeda blurs the ethnic distinctions between the Zuni and the Hopi, lumping them together, as he also misses the ritual functions of their kivas.[54] But the place names for these settlements—Cíbola, Cicuye (Pecos), Maçaque, Acuco (Acoma), Tusayán, Tiguex—soon found their way onto Italian copies of Spanish maps of the region, although in many variants, as Michael Weber's study of their evolution demonstrates.[55]

Cicúye-Cicuique, the largest pueblo of New Mexico during the sixteenth century, is described with great awe, in terms of its military prowess and architectural features.[56] The city within its wall is a square, perched on a steep rock in the center of a vast patio or plaza, with ovens, passageways, balconies, wooden ladders, and wells. "They pride themselves that no one has been able to subjugate them, while they dominate whatever pueblos they wish."[57]

Yet tucked away in this military sighting are fascinating observations about earlier interpueblo warfare at nearby villages in ruins. They see "big corn silos" that seem to have been recently destroyed and stones so large they look as if they have been hurled from catapults.[58] Castañeda comments that the Teyas had invaded the region decades earlier, laying siege to Cicúye, but when they were unable to take it, they destroyed neighboring pueblos.[59] This passage opens a fascinating window onto old and new regional frontiers that were not only places but also historical processes taking place on the eastern rim of the pueblos at the time of Spanish contact.[60] The representation of the Teyas, a plains tribe, perhaps Kiowas, who camped for the winter in the shelter of the walls of Cicúye, speaks to the symbiotic relationship of the eastern pueblos with plains Apaches or Kiowa traders and nomads who were moving onto their eastern flanks at the time of Spanish invasion.[61]

In the section of the itinerary entitled "Origins," the narrator draws a longer and wider conceptual frame for Cíbola and Quivira in which demography and topography converge in a list of sixty-six major indigenous settlements along the Río Grande. He ventures a theory of the origin of the Pueblo peoples through migration southward from Asia and the western mountain chain.[62] The information that Castañeda sets out at this point—that North America was a fourth great land mass located between "la Nuruega" (Europe) and "China" (Asia)—conveys the great epistemological challenges that defied European cartographers as they struggled to map the "grande anchura" of a fourth continent. Theirs was the task of visualizing and integrating the radical conceptual leap from medieval T-in-O maps and portolan charts of coastlines and islands to the confirmations of continental expanses that began to reach Europe.

Quivira: Saying, Seeing, and Knowing

The long itinerary of Part 2 ends at the remote point of Quivira, which is depicted as optimum for Spanish settlement.[63] Although Castañeda and his companions had planned to return to Quivira, "this did not happen because the Lord willed that these discoveries should wait (to be realized) by other people, and that those of us who went there had to be satisfied with being able to say that we were the first ones to discover it and obtain information about it."[64] Saying and knowing constitute the best recompense. Far Quivira lay beyond the reach and gaze of Spanish authorities or even the most intrepid prospectors. But they could learn about it by reading what Castañeda wrote. Writing created a bridge or mediating eye between the explorers and the viceroy. "Knowing was predicated on seeing,"[65] and seeing brought authenticity, legal force and, finally, possession. The men who had gone to Quivira knew what no others did because they had seen it and had long hoped to return there to settle.

The final analogy that Castañeda used to qualify the discovery of Quivira and the news about it was nothing less than the founding of Sevilla: "Just as Hercules made known the place where Julius Caesar was to found Sevilla, or Hispalis . . . it is plain that had it been [God's] will, Francisco Vázquez would not have returned to New Spain without just cause or reason nor would don Fernando de Soto's men have failed to settle such a fine land as they had found."[66] This powerful equation eliminates any lingering doubts about the success of the expedition by evoking an earlier epic act of imperial colonization, an act played out where the pillars of Hercules marked the last known frontier of the Greco-Roman Mediterranean world. By positioning the quest for Quivira in a direct line back to the earliest subjugation of Iberia, Castañeda raises this American endeavor to epic status, advancing its narrative as well as its political meaning from that of exploration to epic. Yet the old veteran cannot refrain from making a bitter comment about Coronado's abandonment of the territories "without just cause or reason." These were territories that neither Coronado nor do Soto had been able to hold or settle, lands that the narrator's textual map has filled with dense populations, large pueblos, rich soils, and wide rivers. Moreover, they have been consecrated by the blood of a martyr, fray Juan de Padilla, who had returned to the Wichita villages to attempt to establish a mission. Clearly the reason must be the divine will of God.

Conclusion

Part 2 of Castañeda's *Relación de la jornada de Cíbola* is an important example of the way written reports of Spanish exploration carried meaning that was crucial to cartography and, subsequently, expansion. Undoubtedly they implanted in cartographers' minds a landscape of North America seen through the eyes of the Spanish soldiers and central Mexican scouts who explored it, rather than through the eyes of the indigenous people who populated it. As the explorers renamed northern spaces with imperial toponyms in Nahuatl or Spanish, the people of the indigenous territories lost their power to represent themselves, a process that was already accelerating in New Spain. Through firsthand reports of observation and measurement, Cíbola and Quivira entered the American space that shattered Ptolemy's projections. First they were traced by connecting points that extended from the viceregal hub of Mexico City to vast northern prairies, and then they slid into focus in the chorographic views of their human and economic dimensions.

In epistemological terms, the second part of Castañeda's *Relación de la jornada de Cíbola* measures a continent, marking the passage from the island world of medieval and Columbian maps to a world of hemispheres in Ortelius's Renaissance atlas. It elevates the Coronado expedition to the status of an epic, in contrast to the fragmented reports of failure left by other contemporaries, in that no golden cities had been found. Castañeda also salvages the memory of the expedition from its forgotten and tainted status, even though his account was never published in his own time.

In discursive terms, Part 2 functions as a hinge that links the narrative space between two historic courses of exploration: the journey to Cíbola and the return from Quivira. As it traces itineraries, draws verbal maps, measures leagues, and translates toponyms, its cross references assemble an internal gloss or index that can be turned backward or forward to refer to places and peoples, resolve questions, mark routes, or inquire about other polities along the way across a vast land mass. In short, it makes sense of a continent.

Nonetheless, Castañeda is guilty of the same kind of fuzziness that other chroniclers of early northern frontiers have exhibited, judging from examples such as "the inhabitants of Quivira [the Wichitas] were of the same type and dress as the Teyas" (los de Quivira eran de la misma calidad y traje de las Teyas),[67] and the Hopis "were of the same as the people from Cíbola in dress, rituals and customs" (eran de la misma suerte, trajes, ritos y costumbres que los de Cíbola).[68] It is as though, as Hartog pointed out for Herodotus' representation of the Scythians, "elements that belong to the representation of peoples who lie on the margins of the world were altogether interchangeable."[69] Yet on other occasions, Castañeda does present positive or innovative representations of indigenous peoples that clearly go beyond the conventional binary divisions of Indian and Spaniard. For example, the pueblo of Cicuye is sharply distinguished from the plains and bison cultures of the Querechos and Teyas.

Moreover, this second segment of the *Relación* manifests the capacity rather than the incapacity to accommodate a model of representation comprising a plurality of terms: central Mexicans, Spaniards, Sonoran Desert and coastal peoples, western and eastern Pueblos, and the Plains groups, among whom nomadic bison hunters are differentiated from the more sedentary farmers. In ethnographic and representational terms, this opening toward a plurality of cultural appreciations constitutes an enormous step forward in comparison with the first account of Cíbola, written only two decades earlier by fray Marcos de Niza, in which the terms were purely binary—the Spaniards and their guides in contrast to the bellicose inhabitants of Cíbola.

The representation of nomadic peoples also evolves. In the initial chapters, dealing with the regions of northwestern Mexico, nomadism is presented as an aberrant and barbarous phenomenon associated with the eating of human flesh and the practice of sodomy, maximum signs of negativity for Spanish readers of the time.[70] In Castañeda's treatment of the Querechos and Teyas, however, nomadism becomes a conceivable notion. His detailed accounts of the mobile Plains peoples, their dominance of the bison, their teepees and dog-drawn travois are positive and admiring, no longer defining such groups by their deficiencies.[71]

Part 2 also has much to tell us about the interplay between the near and the far, represented by Cíbola and Quivira. Cíbola, which until Coronado's trek to Quivira had been the northernmost point of North America seen by Spanish eyes, now becomes near in terms of the remoteness of Quivira—forty-five days on horseback from the pueblos. Between these two poles there is constant interplay between the spaces of "despoblados," "poblados," and "llanos." Yet implicitly the near and the far are operating on still another level. Readers must perceive far Quivira to be "civilized" if the quest and Castañeda's articulation of it are to make political sense. Quivira must be recognized as a place of vast economic potential that is geographically positive and culturally intelligible in order to offer a political logic for the enormous investment of time and effort it cost Coronado's expedition to reach it and the still greater stake it will require to stay alive in the political imagination of the viceroyalty, if it is to merit a return there twenty years later. Therefore, Castañeda constructs his textual Quivira in terms that make it equal to Castile from an economic point of view and to Sevilla from a foundational and imperial perspective. The Wichita are sedentary, not nomadic, and they are "kind people" (gente amorosa) rather than cannibals or warriors. Now it will be worth the trouble to undertake the long and arduous journey from Culiacán by way of his itinerary, which can guide future settlers there.

A postcolonial appraisal of the *Relación* may also read it as an attempt by the principal narrator of the Coronado expedition to maintain possession of the landscape through textual mapping. Rendering the strange familiar enabled the Spaniards to make, in the words of David Weber, a "cognitive conquest of a world whose profound unfamiliarity might otherwise have overwhelmed them."[72] In this sense, the *Relacion* anticipates the extension of the *merced* and land grant process that Antonio de Mendoza had introduced to New Spain in 1535 as a way of rewarding services rendered to the crown,[73] an important factor for Coronado's officers, many of whom were still living at the time Castañeda was writing. A map was the prime requirement for filing their claims.

In sum, at the intersection of discourse and journey, the cartographic writing of the eight chapters of Part 2 of Pedro de Castañeda de Nácera's *Relación de la jornada de Cíbola* assumes a normative role in establishing a spatial and cultural order for resolving the articulation of alterity and territoriality from Culiacán to Quivira. It maps the "new" frontier of a "new" continent, transforming the faint islands of the medieval myth of the seven cities and the scribbled outlines of gulfs drawn by Cortés's pilots into the breadth of a densely populated land mass, a "seen" space that invited soldiers to become settlers and propelled cosmographers to integrate a northern American continent into their universal projects. The *Relación de la jornada de Cíbola* seized the epistemological challenges of a time when the chronicler functioned as cartographer and language stumbled before the plurality and vastness of the American terrain.

Notes

An earlier version of this essay appeared under the title "'Llevando el norte sobre el ojo izquierdo': Mapping, Measuring, and Naming in Castañeda's *Relación de la jornada de Cíbola* [1563]," in *Mapping Colonial Spanish America: Places and Commonplaces of Identity, Culture, and Experience,* eds. Santa Arias and Mariselle Meléndez (Lewisburg, Pennsylvania: Bucknell University Press, 2002), 24–50. I thank the editors for granting me permission to reproduce this modified and updated version. I wish to acknowledge research support from the Department of Spanish and Portuguese, Ohio State University, and express my gratitude to Ron McClean, Graphic Design, OSU, for reproductions and the expedition map.

1. Barbara E. Mundy, *The Mapping of New Spain: Indigenous Cartography and the Maps of the Relaciones geográficas* (Chicago: University of Chicago Press, 1996), 11.

2. Oswald A. W. Dilke and Margaret S. Dilke, "Ptolemy's *Geography* and the New World," in *Early Images of America: Transfer and Invention,* eds. Jerry Williams and Robert E. Lewis (Tucson: University of Arizona Press, 1993), 263–85.

3. J. Lennart Berggren and Alexander Jones, *Ptolemy's Geography: An Annotated Translation of the Theoretical Chapters* (Princeton: Princeton University Press, 2000), 20–21, 52.

4. Mundy, *Mapping of New Spain,* 13.

5. Jay A. Levensen, "Circa 1492: Art in the Age of Exploration," brochure of the exhibition

at the National Gallery of Art, Washington, D.C. October 12, 1991–January 12, 1992 (Washington, D.C.: National Gallery of Art, 1991), 7; Dilke and Dilke, "Ptolemy's *Geography*," 268–71.

6. Madeleine Turrell Rodack argues that what fray Marcos saw was the Zuni pueblo of Kiakima, not Hawikuh. See her "Cíbola: From Fray Marcos to Coronado," in Flint and Flint, *Coronado Expedition to Tierra Nueva,* 102–15.

7. The captain general's full family names were Vázquez de Coronado y Luxán, shortened in the documents of his time to Vázquez or Vázquez de Coronado. Nevertheless, English usage of simply Coronado is so entrenched that I have yielded to it in order to avoid confusion.

8. Maureen Ahern, "La *Relación de la jornada de Cíbola:* Los espacios orales y culturales," in *Conquista y contraconquista: La escritura del nuevo mundo,* eds. Julio Ortega y José Amor y Vázquez, Actas del XXVIII Congreso del Instituto Internacional de Literatura Iberoamericana (México, D.F: Colegio de México–Brown University, 1994), 187–98.

9. Nearly all the documents of the expedition, except the letters from Coronado to Viceroy Mendoza or the king, are summaries written well after the expedition took place and thus rely on distant memory. No diaries of day-to-day events survived. The original version of *Relación de la jornada de Cíbola* was lost. A copy dated Sevilla, 1596, which I have consulted, is in Case 63 of the Rich Collection at the New York Public Library in New York City. George Winship transcribed this Spanish text, although with deficiencies, and published it with his English translation in 1896 (see Winship, *Coronado Expedition,* 108–85). Hammond and Rey published their loose English translation in 1940 (see Hammond and Rey, *Narratives*). Carmen de Mora's edition in 1992 gives no folio numbers and seems to be based on the Winship transcription (see her *Siete ciudades*). Her notes contain errors regarding the indigenous groups and their territories and ignore the extensive research bibliography published by U.S. ethnohistorians. To date no reliable, Spanish-language, critical edition of the 1596 copy is available. The English translation of Castañeda's text in this chapter is my own, based in part on Winship's transcription of the 1596 copy. Quotations and page numbers for *Relación de la jornada de Cíbola* are for Winship's Spanish-language transcription. I have not modernized or changed spelling or punctuation.

10. There has been little critical discussion of the *Relación* as cultural discourse because to date it has been read nearly exclusively for the debate over the route of the expedition. William Brandon merely synthesized events; see his *Quivira: Europeans in the Region of the Santa Fe Trail, 1540–1820* (Athens, Ohio: Ohio University Press, 1990). Leónidas Emilfork pointed only to Part 3 as an example of verbal cartography; see his "Letras de fundación: Estudios sobre la obra americana de Oviedo y la Crónica de las Siete Ciudades de Cíbola" (Ph.D. diss., Johns Hopkins University, 1981). Clark Colahan focused on Renaissance ideals; see his "El cronista Pedro de Castañeda: Ideales renacentistas en la exploración de Nuevo México," in *Literatura Hispánica, Reyes Católicos y Descubrimiento,* Actas del Congreso, dir. Manuel Criado de Val (Barcelona: Promociones y Publicaciones Universitarias, 1989), 383–87. Carmen de Mora discussed the possible censorship of Castañeda's narrative; see her "Códigos culturales en la *Relación de la jornada de Cíbola* de Pedro Castañeda Nájera," *Nueva Revista de Filología Hispánica* 39, no. 2 (1991): 901–12. She also discussed its use of Iberian cultural codes; see Carmen de Mora, "La *Relación de la jornada de Cíbola* de Pedro Castañeda Nájera: Un texto censurado?" *Insula* 45, no. 522 (1990): 14–15. In the introduction to her edition she classifies Part 2 as a rupture that obstructs narrative coherence (see

Mora, *Siete ciudades,* 46–7), a point I seek to refute in this essay. Previously, I analyzed how Quivira displaced Cíbola as a quest myth (see Ahern, "Jornada de Cíbola").

11. Winship, *Coronado Expedition,* 154–69.

12. For the enormous changes in European and Spanish cartography and exploration frontiers during the fifteenth and sixteenth centuries, see Dilke and Dilke, "Ptolemy's *Geography*"; John B. Harley, Ellen Hanlon, and Mark Warhus, eds., *Maps and the Columbian Encounter* (Milwaukee: Golda Meir Library, University of Wisconsin, 1990); John B. Harley and David Woodward, eds., *The History of Cartography,* vol. 1, *Cartography in Prehistoric, Ancient, and Medieval Europe and the Mediterranean* (Chicago: University of Chicago Press, 1987); Robert Lawson-Peebles, *Landscape and Written Expression in Revolutionary America* (Cambridge: Cambridge University Press, 1988); Frank Lestringant, *Mapping the Renaissance World,* trans. David Fausett (Berkeley: University of California Press, 1994); Walter Mignolo, *The Darker Side of the Renaissance: Literacy, Territoriality, and Colonization* (Ann Arbor: University of Michigan Press, 1995); Mundy, *Mapping of New Spain;* J. Wreford Watson, *Mental Images and Geographical Reality in the Settlement of North America* (Nottingham: University of Nottingham, 1967); Weber, *Spanish Frontier;* Michael Frederick Weber, "*Tierra Incognita:* The Spanish Cartography of the American Southwest, 1540–1803" (Ph.D. diss., University of New Mexico, 1986); David Woodward, "Maps and the Rationalization of Geographic Space," in *Circa 1492: Art in the Age of Exploration,* ed. Jay A. Levenson (Washington, D.C.: National Gallery of Art; New Haven: Yale University Press, 1991), 83–87.

13. Harley and Woodward, *History of Cartography,* xvi.

14. Mundy, *Mapping of New Spain,* xiii. Many sixteenth-century maps blended the earlier cartographic traditions of the *mappaemundi,* structured in religious and symbolic space—as in the T-in-O maps that formed a cross with Jerusalem at the center—with the portolan charts that navigators drew of compass points along coastlines, incorporating Ptolemaic elements such as latitude scales. Woodward, "Maps," 84.

15. Winship, *Coronado Expedition,* 152.

16. "La discordançia de las notiçias porque aber fama tan grande de grandes thesoros y en el mismo lugar no hallar memoria ni aparençia de aberlo . . . hallar grandes despoblados y en lugar de ciudades populosas hallar pueblos." Winship, *Coronado Expedition,* 152.

17. "Dara materia para considerar y pensar en la bariedad de esta uida y para poderlos agradar les quiero dar relaçion particular de todo lo poblado que se bio y descubrio en esta jornada y algunas costunbres que tienen y ritos conforme a lo que de ellos alcançamos a saber y en que rumbo cae cada prouinçia para que despues se pueda entender a que parte esta la florida y a que parte cae la india mayor y como esta tierra de la nueba españa es tierra firme con el peru ansi lo es con la india mayor o de la china sin que por esta parte aya entrecho que la dibida ante es estan grande la anchura de la tierra que da lugar a que aya tan grandes despoblados como ay entre las dos mares." Winship, *Coronado Expedition,* 155.

18. "For the northern coast above Florida turns toward the Bacallaos [Land of the Cod] and then extends to Norway [Europe], the southern coast turns to the west, forming the other point to the south, almost like an arch which extends toward India. As a result the lands which extend among the mountains ranges on both coasts draw so far apart from one another that they form a center of great plains which are wilderness. For those reasons they abound in cattle and many other animals of various species." (Por que la costa del norte sobre la florida buelbe sobre los bacallaos y despues torna sobre la nuruega y la del sur a el

poniente haciendo la otra punta debaxo del sur casi como en arco la buelta de la india dando lugar a que las tierras que siguen las cordilleras de anbas costas se desbien en tanta manera unas de otras que dexen en medio de si grandes llanuras y tales que por ser inabitables son poblados de ganados y otros muchos animales de diberas maneras.) Winship, *Coronado Expedition,* 155.

19. Weber, *Spanish Frontier,* 41–42. Nevertheless, the Strait of Anian, the name of which derived from Marco Polo's travels, became a regular feature on late sixteenth-century maps of North America, beginning with Gastaldi (1546), Zaltieri (1556), and Ortelius's "Typva Orbis Terrarvm" (1564). See Miguel León-Portilla, ed., *Cartografía y crónicas de la antigua California* (Coyoacán, D.F.: Universidad Nacional Autónoma de México–Fundación de Investigaciones Sociales, 1989); Pierluigi Portinaro and Franco Knirsch, *The Cartography of North America: 1500–1800* (New York: Facts on File, 1987); Giovanni Battista Ramusio, *Terzo volume delle navigationi et viaggi* [1556] (Venice, 1556; facsimile edition with introduction by Raleigh A. Skelton, Amsterdam: Theatrvm Orbis Terrarvm, 1967); Dennis Reinhartz and Charles C. Colley, *The Mapping of the American Southwest* (College Station: Texas A&M University Press, 1987); Henry R. Wagner, "Quivira: A Mythical California City," *California Historical Society Quarterly* 3, no. 3 (1924), 267.

20. León-Portilla, *Cartografía y crónicas,* Lámina 12 of the Santa Cruz map preserved in the Real Swedish Academy, Stockholm.

21. Gonzalo Fernández de Oviedo (*Historia general,* vol. 4), Francisco López y Gómara (*La istoria de las Indias y conqvista de México* [Zaragoza: Casa de Agustín Millán, 1552]), and Ramusio (*Navigationi et viaggi*) provided the reports of Cíbola by fray Marcos de Niza and other toponyms of the region for Italian, English, and Dutch cartographers. Apparently López de Gómara's interpretation in *La istoria,* which first published news of the Coronado expedition in 1552, misplaced Quivira "to the northwest of Cíbola and this is what the cartographers did for many years" (Weber, "*Tierra Incognita,*" 56; see also Wagner, "Quivira," 262). For a striking example see Cordelis de Jode, one of the foremost Dutch cartographers of the sixteenth century. His map "Quivirae Regnum, cum aliius versus Bo"ream," 1593, from the edition of *Speculum Orbis Terrarum* of the same year, was one of the first regional maps of the American west coast, covering an area from the Tropic of Cancer to the Pole (see Portinaro and Knirsch, *Cartography of North America,* plate 56, 119). It placed Quivira along the western coast of the continent.

22. Charles W. Polzer, S.J., "The Coronado Documents: Their Limitations," in Flint and Flint, *Coronado Expedition to Tierra Nueva,* 39.

23. See Mundy's brilliant analysis of these concepts and their application to sixteenth-century Spanish maps.

24. See the discussions of Amerindian perspectives and coexisting territorialities in Mignolo (*Darker Side,* 289–313) and Mundy (*Mapping of New Spain,* 91–133). Ptolemy had defined geography as "pictures of the whole part of the known world," and cartographers and explorers of the sixteenth century eagerly adopted his concept of ordering space by representing it within a carefully measured and constructed geometrical framework. Folger Shakespeare Library, brochure of exhibition *Mapping Early Modern Worlds,* February 14–July 1, 1998 (Washington, D.C.: Folger Shakespeare Library, 1998).

25. Winship, *Coronado Expedition,* 156. "The Spanish league varied greatly, but in these early narratives the judicial league, equivalent to 2.634 English miles, is usually meant. Distances,

however, while sometimes paced, were generally loose guesses, as is often shown by the great disparity in the figures given by two or more chroniclers of the same journey." Frederick W. Hodge and Theodore H. Lewis, eds., *Spanish Explorers in the Southern United States, 1528–1543* (New York: Barnes and Noble, 1907), 22.

26. Henry R. Wagner, *The Cartography of the Northwest Coast of America to the Year 1800*, vol. 1 (Amsterdam: N. Israel, 1968), 24.

27. Maureen Ahern, "Articulation of Alterity on the Northern Frontier: The *Relatione della navigationi y scoperta* by Fernando de Alarcón, 1540," in *Coded Encounters: Writing, Gender, and Ethnicity in Colonial Latin America,* eds. Francisco Cevallos-Candau et al. (Amherst: University of Massachusetts Press, 1994), 46–61.

28. Winship, *Coronado Expedition,* 157. The meaning of *despoblado* in sixteenth-century texts about New Spain is roughly equivalent to that of the English term "wilderness"—not to "desert," as it appears in some translations. The despoblado on the Coronado route included dense pine forests, grasslands, and brush and scrub flora of the high deserts. Regarding the controversial route to Corazones or Suyo, see Daniel T. Reff, "The Location of Corazones and Senora: Archaeological Evidence from the Rio Sonora Valley, Mexico," in *The Protohistoric Period in the American Southwest, A.D. 1540–1700,* eds. David R. Wilcox and W. Bruce Masse, Arizona State Anthropological Research Papers no. 24 (Tempe: Arizona State University, 1981), 94–112.

29. David Spurr, *The Rhetoric of Empire* (Durham, North Carolina: Duke University Press, 1993).

30. Wagner, *Cartography of the Northwest Coast,* 21; Portinaro and Knirsch, *Cartography of North America,* 70–72.

31. León-Portilla, *Cartografía y crónicas,* Lámina 15. According to medieval legend, after the Moors defeated the last Visigoth king in 713, seven Portuguese bishops fled westward with other Christians and established seven cities on the island of Antillia. This tale and its images of walled cities circulated widely throughout the Iberian peninsula, appearing first on a Portuguese map in 1424, then on Behaim's globe in 1492 and on de la Cosa's map in 1501, and persisting on Martines's map in 1578 and in Herrera's official *Historia general* (1601–1615). Weber, "*Tierra Incognita,*" 48; Stephen Clissod, *The Seven Cities of Cíbola* (London: Clarkson N. Potter, 1962).

32. Fray Bartolomé de Las Casas, *Apologética histórica sumaria* (México, D.F.: Universidad Nacional Autónoma de México, 1967).

33. Lawson-Peebles argues that there is "no such thing as 'the unknown.' Those who are about to enter an undiscovered area project upon it a collection of images drawn from their personal experience, from the culture of which they are a part, from their reasons for traveling, and from their hopes and fears regarding their destination. On occasion these projections are so strong that they shape the terrain they encounter" (*Landscape,* 9).

34. Carroll L. Riley, "The Road to Hawikuh: Trade and Trade Routes to Cíbola-Zuni during Late Prehistoric and Early Historic Times," *Kiva* 41 (1975): 137–59.

35. Mundy, *Mapping of New Spain,* 138.

36. Alonso de Molina, *Vocabulario en lengua castellana y mexicana y mexicana y castellana,* ed. Miguel León-Portilla (México, D.F.: Editorial Porrúa, 1970), 19r.

37. Flint, "Armas de la Tierra," 60.

38. These records appear in the second part of the Códice Aubin (Charles E. Dibble, ed., *Historia de la Nación Mexicana: Códice de 1576 [Códice Aubin],* Colección Chimalistac 16 [Madrid: Eds.

José Porrua Turanzas, 1963], 90), composed around 1562, and in the *Anales Coloniales de Tlatelolco*, 1519–1633 (Jesús Monjarás-Ruiz, Elena Limón, and María de la Cruz Paillés-H., eds., *Tlatelolco: Fuentes e historia. Obras de Robert H. Barlow*, vol. 2 [México, D.F.: Instituto Nacional de Antropología e Historia; Puebla: Universidad de las Américas, 1989], 232, 242, 269).

39. Mundy, *Mapping of New Spain*, 167.

40. Jorge Klor de Alva, "Language, Politics, and Translation: Colonial Discourse and Classic Nahuatl in New Spain," in *The Art of Translation: Voices from the Field*, ed. Rosanna Warren, 143–62 (Boston: Northeastern University Press, 1989).

41. Weber, *Spanish Frontier*, 46. Cíbola has also been said to be an Aztec term meaning "bison," later applied by the Spaniards to the "cattle" they found on the plains, but it does not appear in the Nahuatl dictionaries compiled by Molina, Clavijero, and Simeon. According to Hallenbeck, the Zuni called their group of pueblos Shi-woh'-nuh. "Zuni of today, however, maintain that their pueblos were never known as Cíbola until they were so named by the Spaniards, and as they pronounce the word 'Shiwohnuh' I find very little suggestion of 'Cíbola'" (Hallenbeck, *Journey of Fray Marcos*, 87).

42. Weber, "*Tierra Incognita*," 67.

43. Winship, *Coronado Expedition*, 158.

44. "Tan sin señas como si estuvieramos engolfados en la mar." Francisco Vázquez de Coronado, "Carta de Francisco Vazquez de Coronado desde la provincia de Tiguex al Emperador, 20 de Octubre de 1541," in *Colección de documentos inéditos*, eds. Joaquín F. Pacheco and Francisco de Cárdenas (Madrid: Manuel B. de Quirós, 1864–1884), 3:364.

45. Maureen Ahern, "The Certification of Cíbola: Discursive Strategies in *La relación del descubrimiento de las siete ciudades* by Fray Marcos de Niza (1539)," *Dispositio* 14, nos. 36–38 (1989): 310–13.

46. On the Padrón Real, see Mundy, *Mapping of New Spain*, 15–17. On the possibility that Castañeda was addressing Zorita, see Flint and Flint, "*They Were Not Familiar.*"

47. François Hartog, *The Mirror of Herodotus: The Representation of the Other in the Writing of History*, trans. Janet Lloyd (Berkeley: University of California Press, 1988), 236.

48. Mignolo, *Darker Side*, 379.

49. To gain my own sense of this terrain, I have driven the route from the entry to the San Pedro Valley near the U.S.-Mexico border at Naco, Arizona, to Zuni. See Jerry Jacka's photographs in Stewart Udall's retracing of the complete route in *Arizona Highways* (Stewart Udall, "In Coronado's Footsteps," *Arizona Highways* 60, no. 4 [1984]: 1–47) and in Stewart L. Udall, *Majestic Journey: Coronado's Inland Empire* (Santa Fe: Museum of New Mexico Press, 1995).

50. Michel de Certeau, "Récits d'espace," in *L'invention du quotidien*, vol. 1, *Arts de faire* (Paris: Union Géneral de Editions, 1980), 205–7.

51. "The relationship between the human body and the world goes back at least as far as the Middle Ages, where the microcosm, the little body of man, was thought to replicate the macrocosm or large world around him." Folger, *Mapping*, n.p.

52. Lawson-Peebles, *Landscape*, 13.

53. Winship, *Coronado Expedition*, 160.

54. Winship, *Coronado Expedition*, 160.

55. See the maps by Gastaldi (1553), Ramusio (1556), Gutiérrez (1562), Zaltieri (1566), and Ortelius (1570) in Weber, "*Tierra Incognita*," 54–58.

56. Hodge and Lewis (*Spanish Explorers*, 355) classify its people as Tanoan. John Kessell (*Kiva, Cross, and Crown*, 48) notes that in 1591 some of Castaño de Sosa's soldiers began referring to the big eastern pueblo by an approximation of its Keresan name, Pecos, by which it has been known to outsiders ever since.

57. Winship, *Coronado Expedition*, 161–62.

58. Winship, *Coronado Expedition*, 161.

59. "They must have been powerful people who must have had war machines to batter down the pueblos. The natives of Cicuye could not tell from which way the invaders had come except to point to the north. . . . The Teyas whom the army met, although they were brave, were known by the people of the settlements as their friends. The Teyas often go to the latter's pueblos to spend the winter, finding shelter outside under the eaves of the walls, as the inhabitants do not dare to allow them inside" (pareçio debio de ser gente poderosa y que debian de tener ingenios para derriba los pueblos no saben decir de que parte binieron mas de señalar debajo del norte . . . porque los teyas que el campo topo puesto que eran ualientes eran cognoçidos de la gente de los poblados y sus amigos y que se ban a inbernar por alla los inbiernos debajo de los alaues de lo poblado porque dentro no se atreben a los reçebir). Winship, *Coronado Expedition*, 161–62.

60. Here I employ the concept of frontiers as a web of ethnic and territorial zones of interaction among a plurality of cultures over many centuries from central Mexico and across southwestern continental North America, as well as processes of contention and change, occurring at differing levels and times. It is an eclectic model that borrows largely from David Weber's rich formulation (*Spanish Frontier*, 11–13) and his concept that "it is the power of frontiers to transform cultures that gives them special interest" (*Spanish Frontier*, 13).

61. The Teyas encountered by Coronado may have been Jumanos who were enemies of the Querechos or Apaches (Hickerson, *Jumanos*, 25). Hodge and Lewis consider that the names Teyas or Tejas applied to Caddoan tribes (*Spanish Explorers*, 333).

62. Winship, *Coronado Expedition*, 162–63. "The lands from which these people come, according to location, are the beginning of greater India, although these are unknown and unexplored regions because as the coastline demonstrates, the region between Norway and China is very far inland. The distance from sea to sea is very great, as shown by the direction of both coasts, not only from what Captain Villalobos discovered by sailing this sea to the west in search of China but also from what has been discovered on the North Sea where the [land] turns toward the codfishing [grounds], which is up the coast from La Florida toward Norway" (las tierras de donde aquellas gentes proçeden que segun el rumbo es principio de la india mayor aun que parte innotas y no sabidas ni cognosidas porque segun la demostraçion de la costa es muy la tierra adentro entre la nuruega y la china en el comedio de la tierra de mar a mar es grande anchura segun de muestran los rumbos de ambas costas asi lo que descubrio el capitan uillalobos yendo por esta mar de poniente en demanda de la china como lo que sea descubierto por la mar del norte la buelta de los bacallaos que es por la costa de la florida arriba hacia la nuruega). López de Villalobos had sailed to the Philippine Islands from Mexico in 1542. Winship, *Coronado Expedition*, 167.

63. Winship, *Coronado Expedition*, 169.

64. "Porque fue dios seruido que estos descubrimientos quedasen para otras gentes y *que nos contentasemos los que alla fuimos con deçir que fuimos los primeros que lo descubrimos y tubimos notiçia de ello*" (emphasis added). Winship, *Coronado Expedition*, 169.

65. Hartog, *Mirror of Herodotus,* 352.

66. "Como hercules conoçer el sitio adonde jullio çesar auia de fundar a seuilla o hispales . . . sierto es que si su uoluntad fuera ni francisco uasques se bolbiera a la nueba españa tan sin causa ni raçon ni los de don fernando de soto dexaran de poblar tan buena tierra." Winship, *Coronado Expedition,* 169.

67. Winship, *Coronado Expedition,* 173.

68. Winship, *Coronado Expedition,* 159.

69. Hartog, *Mirror of Herodotus,* 44.

70. In the world of ancient Greek frontiers, "ultimately, as synonyms for nomads, the lexicographers simply give 'savages' 'barbarians.'" Hartog, *Mirror of Herodotus,* 206.

71. Winship, *Coronado Expedition,* 168.

72. Weber, *Spanish Frontier,* 57.

73. Mundy, *Mapping of New Spain,* 183.

SEVENTEEN

Two Colonies, Two Conquistadores:
Francisco and Juan Vázquez de Coronado

FÉLIX BARBOZA-RETANA

COLUMBUS'S LANDFALL IN THE AMERICAS in 1492 opened vast lands and opportunities for Spaniards and other Europeans. It set off a substantial flow of Iberians who journeyed to the new "paradise" to seek gold, glory, fame, and status. As the Costa Rican historian Carlos Meléndez Chaverri observed, "America exerted a strong seductive influence over young Spaniards, who found in the remote lands of the new continent the opportunity to prove their worthiness and to satisfy their aspirations and ambitions without colliding with the strong traditions and privileges of class and power that limited their lives on the peninsula."[1]

Two such young Spaniards, from a family of minor nobles in Salamanca, found in the Europeans' New World the opportunities of their lives. One sailed to New Spain in 1535, the other in 1540. The former, Francisco Vázquez de Coronado, led the first exploration and conquest of what is now the southwestern United States as captain general. The latter, Juan Vázquez de Coronado, his nephew, journeyed in 1561 to the Costa Rica de Cartago, where he became *alcalde mayor* and afterwards governor. Don Juan and don Francisco came to the land of opportunity, as Herbert Bolton put it, "to seek their fortunes, as did hundreds of other younger sons of noble families."[2]

Who were these two postmedieval men who navigated a wide ocean to seek hope, land, and political position? Who were these Spanish knights who, on behalf of king and God, came to the New World to reconnoiter and conquer lands and peoples for the Crown and add souls to heaven? Who were these proto-Quixotes who were willing to trade the comforts of their native city for rougher locales? What compelled them to search other horizons for the rumored El Dorado and the legendary seven cities?

Francisco Vázquez de Coronado y Luján (1510–1554)

Don Francisco was born into the hidalgo family of Vázquez de Coronado in Salamanca in about 1510. He was not unique in his aspirations; like many other young men of his station, he sailed to New Spain in search of opportunity and fortune. He was a representative of an epoch of Iberian political, economic, and religious expansion. Transplantation to the Americas was a common option in the middle 1500s. Beyond this, a more personal reason urged him west: the right of primogeniture made his older brother heir to the family patrimony and left him with little. That he had been granted "terminal settlements without further right to inheritance" was a powerful incentive to try to build a fortune an ocean away.[3] Thus, in 1535, at the age of twenty-five, he became a member of the entourage of New Spain's first viceroy, Antonio de Mendoza.

A few highlights of don Francisco's career in the New World are worth special note:

1536   Married doña Beatriz de Estrada,[4] daughter of wealthy Alonso de Estrada, treasurer of New Spain, and Marina Gutiérrez de la Caballería, descendant of advisors to the kings.

1537   On one of his administrative assignments, was sent by Mendoza to put down an Indian uprising.

1538   Became a *regidor,* or member of the city council, of Mexico City, a post he held until his death in 1554.

1538   Appointed "governor of the new province of Nueva Galicia on the Mexican west coast" by Mendoza.[5]

1538   In November, at age twenty-eight, charged by the viceroy with the enormous task of reconnoitering and conquering the lands and peoples reported by Álvar Núñez Cabeza de Vaca and his companions.

1540–42   With his lieutenants, explored the Southwest.

1542–54   After returning from Tierra Nueva, spent his last years in Mexico City.

1545, 1551   Served as *procurador mayor* of the Mexico City council.

1549   Received a royal grant of Indians in encomienda "for meritorious service in discovery and conquest."[6]

Juan Vázquez de Coronado y Anaya (1523–1565)

Don Juan (fig. 17.1), illegitimate son of don Francisco's brother, Gonzalo Vázquez de Coronado, and Catalina de Anaya, was born in Salamanca in 1523. In 1540, at seventeen and "having an uncle in New Spain" who was about to lead a major expedition in there,[7] he sailed for the Nueva España. As with his uncle before him, don Juan's exclusion from major inheritance—by reason of being a younger son, not because he was illegitimate—was a compelling reason behind his taking such a step.

Historians have located too few documentary sources to follow in detail don Juan's presence in New Spain. We know he arrived too late to accompany his uncle north. There is no indisputable evidence that nephew and uncle had personal contact in New Spain, though it seems unlikely that they did not. Don Juan definitely resided in the household of his young aunt, doña Beatriz, while the expedition to Tierra Nueva was away. And he must have been in New Spain for

Figure 17.1. Juan Vázquez de Coronado y Anaya. Drawing by
Carlos Moya B., inspired by a painting by Tomás Povedano.
Image in Carlos Meléndez Chaverri, *Juan Vázquez de Coronado,
Conquistador y fundador de Costa Rica.* Courtesy of Editorial Costa Rica.

some time. In his later letters he demonstrated familiarity with places there, such as Atrisco and Tlaxcala.[8] As further proof that his stay in New Spain must have been lengthy, some scholars point to his command of Nahuatl, the major native language of central Mexico.[9]

Furthermore, historians have not established why don Juan moved from Mexico City to Guatemala, though administrative assignment from Viceroy Mendoza, his uncle's patron, is likely. Nor is there agreement about exactly when he made the move.[10] But it must have been sometime in the middle 1540s. Once he has left New Spain, don Juan's career becomes much clearer:[11]

1548   Served as deputy of the cabildo of the city of Santiago de los Caballeros, Guatemala.

1549   Served as alcalde mayor of San Salvador.

1551   Served as interim *alcalde ordinario* of Guatemala.

1551   Married doña Isabel Árias Dávila, daughter of the wealthy captain Gaspar Árias de Ávila.

1552, 1554,

1558   Served as alcalde ordinario of Guatemala.

1552   Participated in an expedition to Sonsinate to subjugate and pacify the provinces of Izalcos, Caluco, and Nahulingo.

1556, 1560   Served as alcalde mayor of Honduras.

1561   At the age of thirty-eight, was appointed alcalde mayor of Nicaragua.

1562   Organized an expedition to pacify the Indians of Solentiname in the province of Nicaragua.

1562   Served as alcalde mayor of Nueva Cartago and Costa Rica.

1562–1564   Led the expedition that definitively extended Spanish sovereignty over Nueva Cartago and Costa Rica. For this don Juan is known as the founder of modern Costa Rica.

1565   On April 8, had conferred on him by the king the title governor of the province of Costa Rica.[12]

1565   While returning from Spain in October to his new post, died in a shipwreck at age forty-two.

The Relationship between the Two Vázquez de Coronado

Several genealogical studies have successfully reconstructed the family tree of Juan Vázquez de Coronado y Anaya. In Costa Rica, the Academia Costarricense de Ciencias Genealógicas and its members have been pioneers in this matter. Several publications of the Academia demonstrate its efforts in defining the

Vázquez de Coronado genealogy: Robert Luján 1955; Revello Acosta 1957; Castro y Tosi 1964; and Fuentes Baudrit 1981.[13] The Archivos Nacionales de Costa Rica have also promoted study of the Vázquez de Coronado family, which has resulted in several publications: Lines 1940; Castro y Tosi 1941 and 1948.[14] The Archivos Nacionales hold important primary documents, many originals and many copies, and are an excellent source for historians and genealogists studying the conquest and colonial periods and colonial society. This institution, founded in 1886, is currently working diligently to provide better facilities and access to its documentary collection to both scholars and the general public.

Recourse to such sources has been necessary to clarify the exact family relationship between don Francisco and don Juan. Norberto Castro y Tosi, one of Costa Rica's leading genealogists, has dedicated many years to delineating the family tree of the country's conquistador. Among the documents he consulted in particular was the *Minutas genealógicas* of don Josef Alfonso de Guerra y Villegas, a seventeenth-century chronicler.[15] Castro y Tosi revealed that don Juan was a nephew of don Francisco,[16] which has been confirmed more recently by the historian Carlos Meléndez.[17] These findings contravene statements to the contrary, namely, that the two conquistadores were brothers.[18]

The earliest member of the Vázquez de Coronado line who has been identified was Gonzalo Rodríguez de Cornado, who died in 1341 (fig. 17.2). Note that the

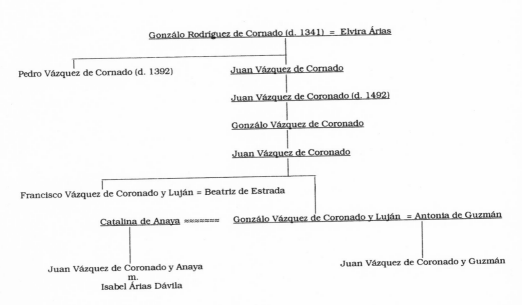

Figure 17.2. Genealogy of the Vázquez de Coronado family.

surname was Cornado, without the second "o." By the middle of the fourteenth century Vázquez de Cornado had become a single surname. One of Gonzalo's grandsons began using the spelling we are familiar with: Coronado.[19] Also disclosed by these researches was the fact that Juan Vázquez de Coronado was illegitimate. His father, don Francisco's brother, Gonzalo Vázquez de Coronado y Luján, married doña Antonia de Guzmán, with whom he had a son called Juan Vázquez de Coronado y *Guzmán,* half brother of the conquistador. Don Gonzalo had an extramarital relationship with doña Catalina de Anaya. It was their son, Juan Vázquez de Coronado y *Anaya,* who gained fame in Costa Rica.

The Expedition Led by Don Juan

Between 1560 and 1562, the enterprise of "pacifying" and colonizing the province of Costa Rica was carried out by Juan de Cavallón and Father Juan de Estrada Rávago, who bore the expense of the expedition. After nearly two years of conflict with the native peoples of Costa Rica and consequent failure to subjugate the province, Cavallón was replaced and transferred to Guatemala. Estrada Rávago, on the other hand, remained in Costa Rica for some time, awaiting the new alcalde mayor of the province.

On April 2, 1562, the Audiencia of Guatemala charged the alcalde mayor of Nicaragua, Juan Vázquez de Coronado y Anaya, with the daunting task of concluding the conquest of Costa Rica.[20] As the newly appointed alcalde mayor of the provinces of Cartago and Costa Rica, don Juan had charge of providing justice, keeping the peace, and indoctrinating and converting the natives. He had the authority to found towns and *villas* and to appoint members of local governments.[21] The eight alcaldes mayores under the Audiencia of Guatemala, including that of Costa Rica, "exercised the same power as a governor, but with greater emphasis on the military."[22]

Don Juan recruited people and gathered provisions and livestock for the expedition, utilizing funds from his own fortune and perhaps that of his wife as well (fig. 17.3). The expedition departed from León, Nicaragua, on August 18, 1562. En route to Costa Rica don Juan and his lieutenants traversed and reconnoitered much of the isthmian territory, encountering numerous indigenous groups. In accordance with royal dictates and instructions of the audiencia, don Juan and his subordinates recorded those encounters and described the native customs and Costa Rican landscapes. He dispatched parties to reconnoiter other areas and to seek gold, tracking down rumors of rivers full of the precious metal. Encounters with the Indians of Costa Rica were not always pacific. Even if don Juan eschewed using force, he saw it occasionally necessary in order to achieve

Acuña, Álvaro de
Abreo (Abreu), Melchor de
Adrada, Antonio de
Álvarez de Coy, Bartolomé
Amarilla, Pedro de
Andorra, Pedro de
Arias, Gaspar de
Armerico, Cipión
Arnialde (Yrnialde), Juanes de
Ávila, Juan de
Barrientos, Hernando de
Beltrán, Pedro
Betanzos, fray Pedro Alonso de
Bienvenida, fray Lorenzo de
Blázquez, Martín
Bonilla, Alonso
Bonilla, Francisco de
Bonilla, Juan de
Bonilla, fray Martín de
Bustillos, Juan de
Cabral, Gaspar
Cabrera, Miguel de
Calderón, Juan Francisco
Cano, Diego
Carvajal, Antonio de
Castellón, Marcos
Castillo, Juan del
Dávila, Juan
Díaz, Baltasar
Díaz de Loría, Pedro
Díaz Moreno, Francisco
Díez, Juan
Estrada, Pedro de
Fajardo, ?
Fajardo, Alonso
Fernández Navarrete, bachiller Gonzalo
Fonseca, Francisco de
Gallegos de Villavicencio, Francisco de
García, Miguel
García Carrasco, Pedro
Góngora, Miguel de
González, Baltasar
Gordillo, Gabriel
Guerrero, Juan
Guevara, Miguel de
Guido, Alonso de
Guillén, ?
Gutiérrez de Algava, Gaspar
Hernández, Diego
Hernández, bachiller Gonzalo
Hernández, Melchor
Hernández, Pedro
Hernández Camelo, Antonio
Hernández de Espinosa, Juan
Herrera, Antonio de
Hinojosa, Agustín de

Hinojosa, Juan de
Jiménez, Alonso
Juárez, Rodrigo
Lázaro, Rafael
León, Francisco de
León, Melchor de
Lidueña, Alonso de
Lobo de Gamaza, Francisco
López, Alonso
López, Miguel
López, Pedro
López de la Torre, Alonso
Lorenzo, Cristóbal
Madrigal, Cristóbal de
Manuel, Juan
Marín, Nicolás
Marmolejo, Francisco de
Martín, Diego
Martín, Juan
Mejía, Antonio
Mejía, Hernán
Mejía de Valladares, Juan
Mesa, Bernabé
Milanés, Vicencio
Miranda, Felipe de
Miranda, Martín de
Morales, Alonso de
Natarén, Tomás
Ortíz, Juan
Ovalle, Juan de
Paéz, Antonio
Parada, Luis de
Peralta, Antonio de
Pereira, Juan
Pérez Saavedra, Alonso
Porras, Diego de
Porras, Gregorio de
Puente Moreno, Juan de la
Ribero y de Escobar, Pedro de
Río, Nicolás de
Rivas, Alonso de
Rodríguez Chacón, Diego
Rojas, Gómez de
Salazar, fray Melchor de
Salcedo, Andrés de
Salinas, fray Diego de
Sánchez, Alonso
Sánchez, Hernán
Sánchez, Simón
Sánchez de Guido, fray Francisco
Torralba, Martín de
Valdivieso, Alonso de
Veneciano, Francisco
Vera Bustamante, Blas de
Villavicencio, Agustín de
Xaso, fray Alonso
Zárate, Juan de

Figure 17.3 List of 114 men who participated in the expedition of Juan Vázquez de Coronado y Anaya. Source: Meléndez Chaverri, *Conquistadores,* 259–78.

his goals. The enterprise of conquest took more than two years and involved journeys over "rough, unknown roads where the indispensable means of subsistence were not always to be found."[23]

In July 1563, don Juan and his expedition returned to Nicaragua so that he could attend to matters as alcalde mayor of the province. He did not return to the city of Cartago (formerly Garcimuñoz) in Costa Rica's central valley until April 1564. A lack of funds beset the expedition, especially don Juan, its major backer. This situation was one reason for his sailing for Spain in May 1564. There he sought to raise funds from friends and family, including his half brother, Juan Vázquez de Coronado y Guzmán. Another aim of the trip was to get full support from the Crown and to obtain a decision defining Costa Rica as a distinct political jurisdiction. Because of family ties with the king, don Juan also sought favors, political appointments, and financial support.

There are no known records of his journey from Panama to Spain, but he remained in his homeland for about eight months, from April until October 1565. While he was there, the title of governor of Costa Rica was conferred on him, and his term as governor of Nicaragua was extended for three more years. Further, the king named him *adelantado perpetuo* of Costa Rica. On July 6, 1565, a royal *cédula* extended the bishop of Nicaragua's ecclesiastical jurisdiction to Costa Rica. Finally, on August 17, the coat of arms of the city of Cartago was registered.

With all these appointments, cédulas, powers, privileges, and benefits in hand, don Juan set sail to return to his territories, his men, and his conquests. But destiny played its role and truncated the life and plans of the forty-two-year-old governor who had just spent almost three years taking control of a promising land. He died in a shipwreck in October 1565. His men in Costa Rica and Nicaragua waited and waited, but their captain general never returned.

Don Juan had many descendants. He and doña Isabel had five sons and a daughter. The oldest son became governor of the province of Costa Rica.[24] According to genealogical research conducted in Costa Rica in 1975 by Samuel Stone, 31 presidents and 285 legislators have traced their descent from don Juan. Many other descendants have been part of the Costa Rican social, economic, and political elite. As Stone put it, "from Vázquez de Coronado descend 16 generations whose members have occupied a great number of political positions in Costa Rica, during the colonial period as well as later."[25]

Violence and the Need for Corn

In Europe Spaniards ate wheat; in the New World they ate corn and other native products, but especially they relied on corn, or *maíz*. Such was the case for the expeditions led by the two Vázquez de Coronado. Neither the provisions don Juan carried with him from Nicaragua nor those don Francisco took from Mexico were sufficient for the entire duration of their expeditions and the large numbers of people who composed them. The search for provisions at Indian communities was constant and often desperate. Resort to force was not unusual.

Both Vázquez de Coronado made efforts to arrange for resupply from areas outside the territories they went to subjugate and, when that proved impossible, to "purchase" corn and other foodstuffs. Don Juan, writing to Felipe II in January 1563, said, "I have forbidden that anything be taken from them [the Indians]; they [the members of the expedition] only asked for food, which was given to them."[26] In the same month he reported to *licenciado* Juan Martínez de Landecho, "I am in need of food and corn and cattle; I am writing . . . so that, charged against my salary, they may send me eight hundred *fanegas* of corn."[27] In addition to this amount, don Juan sent requests for another six hundred fanegas between June 1562 and April 1563.[28]

Even after the establishment of Spanish towns in Costa Rica, the problem of a dependable supply of corn did not evaporate. As the Costa Rican historian Paulino González has written, "the problem of provisions was not definitively resolved, because upon the arrival of the new alcalde mayor, Juan Vázquez de Coronado, the settlers complained of the lack of sustenance."[29] Once he had founded Cartago, don Juan directed that the settlers "first of all, prepare cornfields for their sustenance, because until now I have brought all provisions from Nicaragua and other places at my own expense."[30]

Even if the primary aim of the conquistadores was to find wealth in the form of precious metals, when supplies ran low the first priority was to find corn and other food. The need for corn often soured relations between natives and invaders. "Across the whole continent, at the beginning of the conquest, Indians and Spaniards fought for possession of such a coveted grain, the ones to seize it, the others to defend it."[31]

Nevertheless, some historians call the conqueror of Costa Rica a peaceful leader who sought to discover and subjugate lands and peoples by pacific means.[32] We can say with some certainty that don Juan's style was different from that of his predecessor, Juan de Cavallón. The earlier conquistador's methods were often violent, and he readily resorted to force. Force raised the opposition of the natives and frustrated conquest and settlement of the province.

Juan Vázquez de Coronado, on the other hand, seems to have consistently preferred more pacific methods. He practiced *rescate,* trade of merchandise and other goods with the natives. At every settlement he approached the leaders with gifts. In reporting his journey to certain villages, don Juan remarked that he "gave them rescates and other things, which pacified them, so they deal peaceably with us as servants of Your Majesty living in this province. This event was good because it was bloodless. . . . I have not consented to do offense to the natives nor take anything without paying."[33] Likewise, he wrote, "Your Majesty possesses peacefully the province of Pacaca, and that of Accerri, and that of Botos, and that of Abra, and that of Guarco, and also that of Garabito without a drop of blood being spilled."[34] Meléndez observed, "The method follow by Vázquez [de Coronado] was to be happy in the presence of the chiefs, to flatter them and seat them at his table, and to give them abundant rescates such as shirts, bonnets, scissors, needles, necklaces, and other things the natives like."[35]

In comparison with his uncle during the expedition into the North American Southwest, don Juan resorted to military force less often, though both felt it necessary on occasion to confront Indian resistance. And certainly colonization has rarely been a peaceful process, even when it is bloodless. Violence is inherent from the moment an invading group arrives in a strange land and imposes its point of view, its cosmogony, religion, and government.

Neither don Juan nor don Francisco stinted in his efforts to achieve his aspirations of glory and fortune. Both searched and searched and interrogated the natives. And neither found appreciable wealth. That failure profoundly disappointed the Vázquez de Coronado and their followers. The two leaders were especially pained, both having spent considerable funds of their own to finance their expeditions. Don Juan, for instance, wrote, "I had spent fourteen or fifteen thousand pesos without having obtained any profits."[36]

The Value of the Reports of the Vázquez de Coronado

The letters and chronicles of the Vázquez de Coronados are unquestionably irreplaceable, though we must keep in mind that they were written in the sixteenth century. We cannot extract all the information we would like from those sources, but by linking them with other sources we can get a rich picture of the two conquistadores, their expeditions, and their deeds. It was not generally the chroniclers' intention to transmit the accounts of their expeditions to future generations. They were reporting to the king and other authorities their findings in new lands. Letters and reports, along with gifts, sent to the king and his viceroys were proof of the territories and peoples they had found and brought under Spanish control. The reports were also fundamental legal documents used by the conquistadores to claims land, rights, public appointments, and other rewards.

In the case of Costa Rica, nineteenth-century government officials used Juan Vázquez de Coronado's letters in litigations regarding the country's boundaries.

It was thanks to don Juan's descriptions that the frontiers were delineated. In addition, the cédula signed by Felipe II appointing don Juan as governor of Costa Rica defined the limits of the province and was used to defend the country's boundaries in international courts.[37]

Documents of the Vázquez de Coronado expedition have also been used extensively in studying the ethnography of Costa Rica. In the 1970s the historiography of Costa Rica underwent a thorough review; part of that process included a reevaluation of primary documents and how to use and interrogate them. Several of the resulting theses, articles, and books have utilized large numbers of primary documents.[38] Thanks to those documents, we now know more about our colonial history, material culture, religion, and society.

As but one example, there is *Las sociedades cacicales de Costa Rica (siglo XVI)* by Eugenia Ibarra, one of the most thorough works of ethnohistory focusing on Costa Rica during the Spanish conquest. Ibarra, relying heavily on sixteenth-century documents, including the letters of Juan Vázquez de Coronado y Anaya, has shown the spatial distribution of chiefdoms and indigenous routes of trade and travel as well as provided a "reconstruction of the lifestyles of the indigenous societies at the moment of contact with Europeans."[39]

This is similar to the use to which the documents of the expedition led by Francisco Vázquez de Coronado y Luján have been put in the United States. Much of the information recorded by members of the two Vázquez de Coronado expeditions has proved to be valuable anthropological and ethnological data, providing details on indigenous settlement, demographics, and lifeways.

None of the publications that relied on primary documents would have been possible without the contribution of early Costa Rican historians and scholars such as licenciado León Fernández, who transcribed hundreds of documents while in Spain and Guatemala.[40] He published a two-volume *Colección de documentos para la historia de Costa Rica* in 1881 and 1882. Among those transcribed documents were the letters of Juan Vázquez de Coronado y Anaya, which were afterwards published by León Fernández's son, Ricardo Fernández Guardia.[41] Because of the contributions of León Fernández, later scholars have been able to mine those documents to reconstruct the conquest and colonial histories of Costa Rica.

Archeology and the Expedition of Juan Vázquez de Coronado

With collaboration between scholars in anthropology and history, we are present at the birth of a new discipline: historical anthropology, or anthropological history. This new discipline is joining diverse techniques and concepts to deal with questions of the past. Today some archeologists consult historical documents, and some historians employ data recovered through excavation and archeological survey. Study of the expeditions of the two Vázquez de Coronado can benefit from this kind of integration. Historical and archeological collaboration has been particularly fruitful in recent years at the Jimmy Owens Site, a campsite of don Francisco's expedition near Floydada, Texas.

In Costa Rica, though, the situation is different: collaboration between the two disciplines is in its infancy. Historical research has focused on conventional documentary sources: letters, wills, reports, cédulas, sacramental records, diaries, chronicles, and so forth. And little archeology has been directed toward study of the Spanish conquest of the region.

To be fair, we must remember that the Costa Rican territory is small. It took Juan Vázquez de Coronado's company only a day or two to journey between native settlements. The expedition established itself in Garcimuñoz, the town founded by Juan de Cavallón, from which detachments were sent out in various directions. There was no need to set up numerous campsites. Furthermore, the high humidity, frequent rain, and heat of Costa Rica make preservation of items of material culture from the expedition poor. For these and other reasons, few attempts have been made to reconstruct the Vázquez de Coronado route archeologically. Indeed, the only significant archeological work undertaken in Costa Rica that has had a bearing on study of the expedition has dealt with the location of Garcimuñoz-Cartago, the colonial capital, which occupied several sites.

I believe that Costa Rican researchers need more feedback about strategies for archeological investigation in these harsh conditions, and those in the United States should take advantage of the genealogical studies of the Vázquez de Coronado family that have been carried out by Costa Ricans.

The Vázquez de Coronado are part of both of our pasts. More than four hundred years have elapsed since they made their marks on the history of Costa Rica and the North American Southwest. At that distance we have the opportunity to assess the activities of the two expeditions and their repercussions. We cannot alter the past, but we are entitled and have the responsibility to make those assessments. We cannot go back and change the facts, but we can and do adjust our perspectives. It would be unfortunate to keep silent about the conquest; by doing that, we are likely to misunderstand the past and bias our present and future.

Notes

Many people helped make this chapter possible. In Costa Rica, I thank my brothers Miguel and Gerardo Barboza-Retana, as well as Eugenia Zavaleta Ochoa and Joaquín Víquez, who sent me important materials. In Lubbock, thanks to Susan Shore, education director, Lubbock Lake State

Landmark, who scanned the illustrations. My special gratitude to Brooke A. Witcher, education intern at the Museum of Texas Tech University, who took the time to read the manuscript and correct the grammar.

1. Carlos Meléndez Chaverri, *Juan Vázquez de Coronado: Conquistador y fundador de Costa Rica* (San Jose: Editorial Costa Rica, 1966), 56.
2. Bolton, *Coronado*, 20.
3. Bolton, *Coronado*, 19–20.
4. Bolton, *Coronado*, 20.
5. Carroll L. Riley, "Introduction," in Flint and Flint, *Coronado Expedition to Tierra Nueva*, 5.
6. Bolton, *Coronado*, 406.
7. Meléndez Chaverri, *Juan Vázquez de Coronado*, 56; translation by author.
8. Fernández Guardia, *Cartas*, 55; Meléndez Chaverri, *Juan Vázquez de Coronado*, 58.
9. Meléndez Chaverri, *Juan Vázquez de Coronado*, 60.
10. Meléndez Chaverri, *Juan Vázquez de Coronado*, 61.
11. Meléndez Chaverri, *Juan Vázquez de Coronado*.
12. Raquel Guevara de Pérez, *Pedro Pérez Zeledón* (San José: Ministerio de Cultura, Juventud y Deportes [de Costa Rica], 1971), 177.
13. Enrique Robert Luján, "Descendencia del adelantado de Costa Rica don Juan de Vázquez de Coronado," *Revista de la Academia Costarricense de Ciencias Genealógicas* 9 (October 1955): 13–28; Julio E. Revello Acosta, "Algunos datos sobre la descendencia de doña Andrea de Vázquez de Coronado," *Revista de la Academia Costarricense de Ciencias Genealógicas* 2 (March 1957): 4–28; Norberto Castro y Tosi, "Los Vázquez de Coronado," *Revista de la Academia Costarricense de Ciencias Genealógicas* 11–12 (June 1964): 40–61; and Hernán Fuentes Baudrit, "Descendientes del adelantado de Costa Rica don Juan de Vázquez de Coronado," *Revista de la Academia Costarricense de Ciencias Genealógicas* 27–28 (November 1981): 371–78.
14. Jorge A. Lines, "Crónica de nuestro conquistador Juan de Vázquez de Coronado," *Revista de los Archivos Nacionales* (de Costa Rica) 9–10 (September–October 1940): 459–79; Norberto Castro y Tosi, "Ascendencia genealógica de Vázquez de Coronado," *Revista de los Archivos Nacionales* 12, nos. 1–2 (1948): 26–31; and Norberto Castro y Tosi, "Determinación y explicación de las armerías de la Casa de Vázquez de Coronado," *Revista de los Archivos Nacionales* 7–8 (July–August 1941): 348–54.
15. Meléndez Chaverri, *Juan Vázquez de Coronado*, 52.
16. Castro y Tosi, "Ascendencia genealógica," 26–31.
17. Meléndez Chaverri, *Juan Vázquez de Coronado*, 54.
18. Bolton, *Coronado*, 19–20; Carlos Monge Alfaro, *Historia de Costa Rica*, 23d ed. (San José: n.p., 1974), 83; and Rubén Yglesias Hogan, "Las siete ciudades doradas de Cíbola," *Revista de los Archivos Nacionales* (Costa Rica), 7, nos. 7–8) (1943): 372.
19. Meléndez Chaverri, *Juan Vázquez de Coronado*, 53.
20. Meléndez Chaverri, *Juan Vázquez de Coronado*, 88.
21. Meléndez Chaverri, *Juan Vázquez de Coronado*, 85.
22. Theodore S. Creedman, *Historical Dictionary of Costa Rica* (Metuchen, New Jersey: Scarecrow Press, 1997), 5.
23. Joaquín Bernardo Calvo, *Apuntamientos geográficos, estadísticos é históricos* (San José: Imprenta Nacional [de Costa Rica], 1887), 206.

24. Meléndez Chaverri, *Juan Vázquez de Coronado,* 63.
25. Samuel Stone, *La dinastía de los conquistadores: La crisis del poder en la Costa Rica contemporánea* (San José: EDUCA, 1975), 148.
26. Fernández Guardia, *Cartas,* 18; translation by author.
27. Fernández Guardia, *Cartas,* 23; translation by author.
28. Carlos Meléndez Chaverri, *Conquistadores y pobladores: Orígenes histórico-sociales de los costarricenses* (San José: EUNED, 1982), 61.
29. Paulino González Villalobos, *La empresa Cavallón-Estrada en la conquista de Costa Rica,* Avances de Investigación no. 27 (San José: Universidad de Costa Rica, 1987), 24; translation by author.
30. Fernández Guardia, *Cartas,* 55; translation by author.
31. Monge Alfaro, *Historia,* 82.
32. Meléndez Chaverri, *Juan Vázquez de Coronado* ; Meléndez Chaverri, *Conquistadores* ; Monge Alfaro, *Historia;* Calvo, *Apuntamientos.*
33. Fernández Guardia, *Cartas,* 43; translation by author.
34. Fernández Guardia, *Cartas,* 19; translation by author.
35. Carlos Meléndez Chaverri, *La Ciudad del Lodo,* Serie Historia y Geografía, no. 5 (San José: Universidad de Costa Rica, 1962), 96; translation by author.
36. Fernández Guardia, *Cartas,* 13; translation by author.
37. Guevara de Pérez, *Pedro Pérez Zeledón,* 178.
38. María Elena Rodríguez Molina and Félix A. Barboza-Retana, "Publicaciones sobre historia colonial realizadas en Costa Rica 1980–1987," *Revista de Historia* (de Costa Rica) 16 (July–December 1987): 219–92.
39. Eugenia Ibarra Rojas, *Las sociedades cacicales de Costa Rica (siglo XVI)* (San José: Editorial de la Universidad de Costa Rica, 1990), 13.
40. León Fernández, "Colección de documentos para la historia de Costa Rica," *Revista de los Archivos Nacionales* (de Costa Rica), 29, nos. 1–12 (1963), and "Colección de documentos para la historia de Costa Rica," *Revista de los Archivos Nacionales* (de Costa Rica), 31, nos. 1–12 (1965).
41. Fernández Guardia, *Cartas.*

Actas de Cabildo de la Ciudad de México. Edited by Ignacio Bejarano and others. 26 vols. México, D.F., 1889–1904.

Adorno, Rolena, and Patrick Charles Pautz. *Álvar Núñez Cabeza de Vaca: His Account, His Life, and the Expedition of Pánfilo de Narváez.* 3 vols. Lincoln: University of Nebraska Press, 1999.

Agricola, [Georg Bauer]. *De Re Metallica.* Translated from the First Latin Edition (1556) with Bibliographic Introduction, Annotations and Appendices upon the Development of Mining Methods, Metallurgical Processes, Geology, Mineralogy and Mining Law from the Earliest Times to the Late Sixteenth Century by Herbert C. Hoover and Lou H. Hoover. London: *Mining Magazine* [1912].

Ahern, Maureen. "Articulation of Alterity on the Northern Frontier: The *Relatione della navigationi y scoperta* by Fernando de Alarcón, 1540." In *Coded Encounters: Writing, Gender, and Ethnicity in Colonial Latin America,* edited by Francisco Cevallos-Candau et al., 46–61. Amherst: University of Massachusetts Press, 1994.

———. "The Certification of Cíbola: Discursive Strategies in *La relación del descubrimiento de las siete ciudades* by Fray Marcos de Niza (1539)." *Dispositio* 14, nos. 36–38 (1989): 310–13.

———. "*La relación de la jornada de Cíbola:* Los espacios orales y culturales." In *Conquista y contraconquista: La escritura del nuevo mundo,* edited by Julio Ortega y José Amor y Vázquez, 187–98. Actas del XXVIII Congreso del Instituto Internacional de Literatura Iberoamericana. México, D.F: Colegio de México–Brown University, 1994.

———. "'Llevando el norte sobre el ojo izquierdo': Mapping, Measuring, and Naming in Castañeda's *Relación de la jornada de Cíbola* [1563]." In *Mapping Colonial Spanish America: Places and Commonplaces of Identity, Culture, and Experience,* eds. Santa Arias and Mariselle Meléndez, 24–50. Lewisburg, Pennsylvania: Bucknell University Press, 2002.

Aiton, Arthur S. "Documents: Coronado's Muster Roll," *American Historical Review* 64 (1939): 556–70.

Aiton, Arthur S., and Agapito Rey. "Coronado's Testimony in the Viceroy Mendoza *Residencia.*" *New Mexico Historical Review* 12 (July 1937): 288–329.

Alvarado, Hernando de. "Narrative, 1540." AGI, Patronato, 26, R.23. In *"They Were Not Familiar with His Majesty": Documents of the Coronado Expedition, 1540–1542,* edited and translated by Richard Flint and Shirley Cushing Flint. In preparation.

[Alvarado, Pedro de]. "Contract between Antonio de Mendoza and the adelantado Pedro de

Alvarado, November 2, 1540." AGI, Patronato, 21, N3, R.2. In *"They Were Not Familiar with His Majesty": Documents of the Coronado Expedition, 1540–1542,* edited and translated by Richard Flint and Shirley Cushing Flint. In preparation.

Alvey, Richard L. "The Spring 1977 SPAS Field School." *Bulletin of the South Plains Archeological Society* 4 (1978): 39–51.

Anawalt, Patricia Rieff. *Indian Clothing before Cortés: Mesoamerican Costumes from the Codices.* Norman: University of Oklahoma Press, 1981.

Anderson, Charles Loftus Grant. *Old Panama and Castillo del Oro.* New York: North River Press, 1944.

Avellaneda, José Ignacio. *The Conquerors of the New Kingdom of Granada.* Albuquerque: University of New Mexico Press, 1995.

Bakewell, Peter. *A History of Latin America: Empires and Sequels, 1450–1930.* Oxford: Blackwell Publishers, 1997.

———. "Introduction." In *An Expanding World: The European Impact on World History 1450–1800,* vol. 19, *Mines of Silver and Gold in the Americas,* edited by Peter Bakewell, xiii–xxiv. Aldershot, U.K.: Variorum, 1997.

———. *Silver and Entrepreneurship in Seventeenth-Century Potosí.* Albuquerque: University of New Mexico Press, 1988.

Bandelier, Adolph F. *The Discovery of New Mexico by the Franciscan Monk, Friar Marcos de Niza, in 1539.* Translated by Madeleine Turrell Rodack. Tucson: University of Arizona Press, 1981.

———. "Documentary History of the Rio Grande Pueblos, Part 1, 1536–1542 (Concluded)." *New Mexico Historical Review* 2 (April 1930): 154–85.

———. *Final Report of Investigations among the Indians of the Southwestern United States, Carried on Mainly in the Years from 1880 to 1885,* Parts 1 and 2. Papers of the Archaeological Institute of America, American Series, 3 and 4. Cambridge, Massachusetts, 1890–92. Reprint, New York: AMS Press and Kraus Reprint Company, 1976.

Bandy, Philip, John Montgomery, William J. Mayer-Oakes, and Richard O. Keslin. *Archeological Mitigation at the Canyon Lakes Project, Texas.* Lubbock: Cultural Resources Institute, Department of Anthropology, Texas Tech University, 1980.

Bannon, John Francis, ed. *Bolton and the Spanish Borderlands.* Norman: University of Oklahoma Press, 1964.

Barnes, Thomas C., Thomas H. Naylor, and Charles W. Polzer. *Northern New Spain: A Research Guide.* Tucson: University of Arizona Press, 1981.

Barrett, Elinore M. *Conquest and Catastrophe: Changing Rio Grande Settlement Patterns in the Sixteenth and Seventeenth Centuries.* Albuquerque: University of New Mexico Press, 2001.

———. *The Geography of Rio Grande Pueblos as Revealed by Spanish Explorers, 1540–1598.* Research Paper Series 30. Albuquerque: Latin American Institute, 1997.

Beal, John D. "Foundations of the Rio Grande Classic: The Lower Chama River, A.D. 1300–1500." Manuscript on file, New Mexico Office of Cultural Affairs, Historic Preservation Division, Santa Fe. Southwest Archaeological Consultants, Inc., 1987.

Bell, William A. *New Tracks in North America.* London: Chapman and Hall, 1870. Reprint, Albuquerque: Horn and Wallace, 1965.

Benavente, fray Toribio de. "Relación postrera de Cíbola [1540s]." Benson Collection, University of Texas, Austin, JGI 31 XVI C. In *"They Were Not Familiar with His Majesty": Documents of the Coronado Expedition, 1540–1542,* edited and translated by Richard Flint and Shirley Cushing Flint. In preparation.

Benavides, fray Alonso de. *Fray Alonso de Benavides' Revised Memorial of 1634.* Edited by Frederick W. Hodge, George P. Hammond, and Agapito Rey. Albuquerque: University of New Mexico Press, 1945.

———. "The Memorial of Fray Alonso de Benavides, 1630." Translated by Mrs. Edward E. Ayer. *Land of Sunshine* 13 (1900) and 14 (1901).

Berdan, Frances, and Patricia Rieff Anawalt. *The Essential Codex Mendoza*. Berkeley: University of California Press, 1997.

Berggren, J. Lennart, and Alexander Jones. *Ptolemy's Geography: An Annotated Translation of the Theoretical Chapters*. Princeton: Princeton University Press, 2000.

Bermejo, Juan Sánchez. "Encomienda grant to Juan Sanchez Bermejo (1542)." AGN Mercedes. vol. 1.

Black, Craig C., ed. "History and Prehistory of the Lubbock Lake Site." *Museum Journal* 15. Lubbock: West Texas Museum Association, 1974.

Blakeslee, Donald J. *Along Ancient Trails: The Mallet Expedition of 1739*. Niwot, Colorado: University Press of Colorado, 1995.

———. "Which Barrancas? Narrowing the Possibilities." In *The Coronado Expedition to Tierra Nueva: The 1540–1542 Route Across the Southwest,* edited by Richard Flint and Shirley Cushing Flint, 302–19. Niwot, Colorado: University Press of Colorado, 1997.

Blakeslee, Donald J., Richard Flint, and Jack T. Hughes. "*Una Barranca Grande:* Recent Archeological Evidence and a Discussion of Its Place in the Coronado Route." In *The Coronado Expedition to Tierra Nueva: The 1540–1542 Route Across the Southwest,* edited by Richard Flint and Shirley Cushing Flint, 370–83. Niwot, Colorado: University Press of Colorado, 1997.

Bloom, Lansing B. "Was Marcos de Niza a Liar?" *New Mexico Historical Review* 16 (April 1941): 244–46.

Bolton, Herbert E. *Coronado: Knight of Pueblos and Plains*. Albuquerque: University of New Mexico Press, 1949. Reprint with foreword by John L. Kessell, Albuquerque: University of New Mexico Press, 1990.

———. "The Jumano Indians in Texas, 1650–1771." *Texas Historical Association Quarterly* 15 (1911): 66–84.

———. "The Mission as a Frontier Institution in the Spanish American Culture," in *Bolton and the Spanish Borderlands,* edited by John F. Bannon, 187–211. Norman: University of Oklahoma Press, 1974.

———. *Texas in the Middle Eighteenth Century*. Berkeley: University of California Press, 1915.

———, ed. *Spanish Explorations in the Southwest, 1542–1706*. New York: Scribner, 1908.

Booker, Rick, and Jeff Campbell. "An Excavation Report on Site 41LU6: Slaton Dump Site." *Bulletin of the South Plains Archeological Society* 4 (1978): 19–38.

Boorstin, Daniel J. *The Discoverers: A History of Man's Search to Know His World and Himself*. New York: Random House, 1983.

Boyd, Douglas K. *Caprock Canyonlands Archeology: A Synthesis of the Late Prehistory and History of Lake Alan Henry and the Texas Panhandle-Plains,* vol. 2. Reports of Investigations no. 110. Austin: Prewitt and Associates, 1997.

Boyd, Douglas K., Jay Peck, Steve A. Tomka, and Karl W. Kibler. *Data Recovery at Justiceburg Reservoir (Lake Alan Henry), Garza and Kent Counties, Texas: Phase III, Season 2*. Reports of Investigations no. 88. Austin, Texas: Prewitt and Associates, Inc., 1993.

Boyd, Douglas K., Jay Peck, Steve A. Tomka, Karl W. Kibler, and Martha Doty Freeman. *Data Recovery at Lake Alan Henry (Justiceburg Reservoir), Garza and Kent Counties, Texas: Phase III, Season 3*. Reports of Investigations no. 93. Austin, Texas: Prewitt and Associates, Inc., 1994.

Brandon, William. *Quivira: Europeans in the Region of the Santa Fe Trail, 1540–1820*. Athens, Ohio: Ohio University Press, 1990.

Breternitz, David A. *An Appraisal of Tree-Ring Dated Pottery in the Southwest*. Anthropological Papers of the University of Arizona 10. Tucson: University of Arizona Press, 1966.

Brinckerhoff, Sidney B., and Pierce A. Chamberlain. *Spanish Military Weapons in Colonial America, 1700–1821*. Harrisburg, Pennsylvania: Stackpole, 1972.

Brown, Claude. "Preliminary Report of the SPAS 41LU6." *Bulletin of the South Plains Archeological Society* 3 (1972): 2–3.

Brune, Gunnar. *Springs of Texas.* Fort Worth: Branch-Smith, 1981.

Bunzel, Ruth H. *Zuni Katchinas.* Annual Report of the Bureau of American Ethnology 47, 837–1108. Washington, D.C.: Government Printing Office, 1932.

Burrus, Ernest J. *Kino and the Cartography of Northwestern New Spain.* Tucson: Arizona Pioneers' Historical Society, 1965.

Calvo, Joaquín Bernardo. *Apuntamientos geográficos, estadísticos é históricos.* San José: Imprenta Nacional (de Costa Rica), 1887.

Carroll, H. Bailey. "The Texan Santa Fe Trail." *Panhandle-Plains Historical Review* (1951).

Castañeda de Náçera, Pedro de. "Castañeda's History of the Expedition." In *Narratives of the Coronado Expedition, 1540–1542,* edited and translated by George P. Hammond and Agapito Rey, 191–283. Coronado Cuarto Centennial Publications, 1540–1940, vol. 2. Albuquerque: University of New Mexico Press, 1940.

———. "The Narrative of Castañeda." In *The Coronado Expedition, 1540–1542,* edited and translated by George Parker Winship, 108–85. Fourteenth Annual Report of the Bureau of American Ethnology of the Smithsonian Institute, 1892–93, Part 1. Washington, D.C.: Smithsonian Institution, 1896. Reprint, Chicago: Rio Grande Press, 1964.

———. *Relación de la jornada de Cíbola compuesta por Pedro de Castañeda de Náçera donde se trata de todos aquellos poblados y ritos, y costumbres la qual fue el año de 1540* [1563]. Case 12, Rich Collection 63, Nuevo Mexico. Sevilla, 1596. 157 11, 4° bound. New York Public Library, Rare Books and Manuscripts Division. In *"They Were Not Familiar with His Majesty": Documents of the Coronado Expedition, 1540–1542,* edited and translated by Richard Flint and Shirley Cushing Flint. In preparation.

———. "Translation of the Narrative of Castañeda" [1896]. In *The Journey of Coronado, 1540–1542,* edited and translated by George Parker Winship. Reprint, New York: Dover, 1990.

Castro y Tosi, Norberto. "Ascendencia genealógica de Vázquez de Coronado." *Revista de los Archivos Nacionales* (de Costa Rica) 12, nos. 1–2 (1948): 26–31.

———. "Determinación y explicación de las armerías de la Casa de Vázquez de Coronado." *Revista de los Archivos Nacionales* 7–8 (July–August 1941): 348–54.

———. "Los Vázquez de Coronado." *Revista de la Academia Costarricense de Ciencias Genealógicas* 11–12 (June 1964): 40–61.

Certeau, Michel de. "Récits d'espace." In *L'invention du quotidien,* vol. 1, *Arts de faire,* 205–7. París: Union Géneral de Editions, 1980.

Cháves, José Antonio, and Captain Juan José Arrocha. *1829 Diaries of José Antonio Cháves and Captain Juan José Arrocha.* Mexican Archives of New Mexico, roll 9. New Mexico State Records Center and Archives, Santa Fe.

Chávez, Fr. Angélico. *Coronado's Friars.* Washington, D.C.: Academy of American Franciscan History, 1968.

Cieza de León, Pedro de. *The Discovery and Conquest of Peru.* Edited and translated by Alexandra Parma Cook and Noble David Cook. Durham, North Carolina: Duke University Press, 1998.

Clayton, Lawrence A., Vernon James Knight Jr., and Edward C. Moore, eds. *The De Soto Chronicles: The Expedition of Hernando de Soto to North America in 1539–1543.* 2 vols. Tuscaloosa: University of Alabama Press, 1993.

Clissod, Stephen. *The Seven Cities of Cíbola.* London: Clarkson N. Potter, 1962.

Códice Aubin. "Record of Mexican Indians Participating in the Expedition, 1576." In Códice Aubin, British Museum, Add MSS 31219, fol. 45v. In *"They Were Not Familiar with His Majesty": Documents of the Coronado Expedition, 1540–1542,* edited and translated by Richard Flint and Shirley Cushing Flint. In preparation.

Colahan, Clark. "El cronista Pedro de Castañeda: Ideales renacentistas en la exploración de Nuevo México." In *Literatura Hispánica, Reyes Católicos y Descubrimiento.* Actas del Congreso, dir. Manuel Criado de Val, 383–87. Barcelona: Promociones y Publicaciones Universitarias, 1989.

Collinson, Frank. *Life in the Saddle*. Norman: University of Oklahoma Press, 1963.

Columbus, Christopher. *The* Diario *of Christopher Columbus's First Voyage to America, 1492–1493*. Edited and translated by Oliver Dunn and James E. Kelley Jr. Norman: University of Oklahoma Press, 1989.

Cortés, Hernán. "Carta de Hernán Cortés a Cristóbal de Oñate." In *Documentos Cortesianos*, edited by José Luis Martínez, 4:148–49. México, D.F.: UNAM and Fondo de Cultura Económica, 1992.

————. *Cartas de Relación*. México, D.F.: Editorial Porrúa, 1993.

————. "Letter from Cortés to Mendoza, Cuernavaca, July 26, 1539." In Henry R. Wagner, "Fray Marcos de Niza." *New Mexico Historical Review* 9 (April 1934): 159–227.

Craine, Eugene R., and Reginald C. Reindorp, eds. and trans. *The Chronicles of Michoacán*. Norman: University of Oklahoma Press, 1970.

Creedman, Theodore S. *Historical Dictionary of Costa Rica*. Latin American Historical Dictionaries, no. 16. Metuchen, New Jersey: Scarecrow Press, 1997.

Crosby, Alfred W. *Ecological Imperialism: The Biological Expansion of Europe, 900–1900*. New York: Cambridge University Press, 1986.

Crown, Patricia L., Janet D. Orcutt, and Timothy A. Kohler. "Pueblo Cultures in Transition: The Northern Rio Grande." In *The Prehistoric Pueblo World, A.D. 1150–1350*, edited by Michael A. Adler, 188–204. Tucson: University of Arizona Press, 1996.

Cuevas, Juan de, scribe. "Muster Roll of the Expedition, February 22, 1540," AGI, Guadalajara, 5, R.1, N.7. In *"They Were Not Familiar with His Majesty": Documents of the Coronado Expedition, 1540–1542*, edited and translated by Richard Flint and Shirley Cushing Flint. In preparation.

Curry, W. Hubert. *Sun Rising on the West: The Saga of Henry Clay and Elizabeth Smith*. Crosbyton, Texas: Quality Printers and Typographers, 1979.

Day, A. Grove. *Coronado's Quest: The Discovery of the Southwestern States*. Berkeley: University of California Press, 1940.

Deagan, Kathleen. "Accommodation and Resistance: The Process and Impact of Spanish Colonization in the Southeast." In *Columbian Consequences*, vol. 2, edited by David H. Thomas, 297–314. Washington, D.C.: Smithsonian Institution Press, 1990.

Diamond, Jared. *Guns, Germs, and Steel: The Fates of Human Societies*. New York: W. W. Norton, 1997.

Díaz del Castillo, Bernal. *The Discovery and Conquest of Mexico, 1517–1521*, edited by Genaro García; translated by Alfred P. Maudslay. New York: Farrar, Straus and Cudahy, 1927.

————. *Historia verdadera de la conquista de la Nueva España*. Edited by Carmelo Sáenz de Santa María. México, D.F.: Alianza Editorial, 1991.

Dibble, Charles E., ed. *Historia de la nación mexicana: Códice de 1576 (Códice Aubin)*. Colección Chimalistac 16. Madrid: Eds. José Porrua Turanzas, 1963.

Dilke, Oswald A. W., and Margaret S. Dilke. "Ptolemy's *Geography* and the New World." In *Early Images of America: Transfer and Invention*, edited by Jerry Williams and Robert E. Lewis, 263–85. Tucson: University of Arizona Press, 1993.

Disbrow, Alan E., and Walter C. Stoll. *Geology of the Cerrillos Hills Area, Santa Fe County, New Mexico*. Bureau of Mines and Mineral Resources Bulletin 48. Socorro: New Mexico Institute of Mining and Technology, 1957.

Doolittle, William K. *Pre-Hispanic Occupance in the Valley of Sonora, Mexico: Archaeological Confirmation of Early Spanish Reports*. Anthropology Papers 48. Tucson: University of Arizona, 1988.

Duffen, William A., and William K. Hartmann. "The 76 Ranch Ruin and the Location of Chichilticale." In *The Coronado Expedition to Tierra Nueva: The 1540–1542 Route Across the Southwest*, edited by Richard Flint and Shirley Cushing Flint, 190–211. Niwot: University Press of Colorado, 1997.

Durán, Diego. *The History of the Indies of New Spain.* Edited and translated by Doris Heyden. Norman: University of Oklahoma Press, 1994.

Ellis, Bruce T. "Crossbow Boltheads from Historic Pueblo Sites." *El Palacio* 64, nos. 7–8 (1957): 209–14.

Ellis, Florence Hawley. "Hiways to the Past." *New Mexico Magazine* 53 (1975): 18–40.

———. "The Long Lost 'City' of San Gabriel del Yungue, Second Oldest European Settlement in the United States." In *When Cultures Meet,* papers from the October 20, 1984, conference held at San Juan Pueblo, New Mexico, 10–38. Santa Fe: Sunstone Press, 1987.

———. *San Gabriel del Yunque as Seen by an Archaeologist.* Santa Fe: Sunstone Press, 1989.

Ellis, Florence Hawley, and Andrea Ellis Dodge. "A Window on San Gabriel del Yunque." In *Current Research on the Late Prehistory and Early History of New Mexico,* edited by Bradley J. Vierra, 175–84. Albuquerque: New Mexico Archaeological Council, 1992.

Emilfork, Leónidas. "Letras de fundación: Estudios sobre la obra americana de Oviedo y la Crónica de las Siete Ciudades de Cíbola." Ph.D. diss., Johns Hopkins University, 1981.

[Escobar, Cristóbal]. "Proof of Service of Cristóbal de Escobar, 1543," AGI, Mexico 204, N14. In *"They Were Not Familiar with His Majesty": Documents of the Coronado Expedition, 1540–1542,* edited and translated by Richard Flint and Shirley Cushing Flint. In preparation.

Espejo, Antonio de. "Report of Antonio de Espejo." In *The Rediscovery of New Mexico, 1580–1594: The Explorations of Chamuscado, Espejo, Castaño de Sosa, Morlete, and Leyva de Bonilla and Humaña,* edited and translated by George P. Hammond and Agapito Rey. Coronado Cuarto Centennial Publications, 1540–1940, vol. 3. Albuquerque: University of New Mexico Press, 1966.

Ewen, Charles R., and John H. Hann. *Hernando de Soto among the Apalachee: The Archaeology of the First Winter Encampment.* Gainesville: University Presses of Florida, 1998.

Falconer, Thomas. *Letters and Notes on the Texan Santa Fe Expedition 1841–1842.* Chicago: Rio Grande Press, 1963.

Feathers, James K. "The Application of Luminescence Dating in American Archaeology." *Journal of Archaeological Method and Theory* 4 (1997): 1–66.

Ferguson, Leland. *Uncommon Ground.* Washington, D.C.: Smithsonian Institution Press, 1992.

Fernández, León. "Colección de documentos para la historia de Costa Rica." *Revista de los Archivos Nacionales* (de Costa Rica) 29, nos. 1–12 (1963).

———. "Colección de documentos para la historia de Costa Rica." *Revista de los Archivos Nacionales* (de Costa Rica) 31, nos. 1–12 (1965).

Fernández del Castillo, Francisco. "Alonso de Estrada: Su familia." *Memorias de la Academia Mexicana de la Historia* 1, no. 4 (1942): 398–431.

Fernández de Oviedo, Gonzalo. *Historia general y natural de las Indias.* 5 vols. Edited by Juan Pérez de Tudela Bueso. Madrid: Ediciones Atlas, 1992.

Fernández Guardia, Ricardo. *Cartas de Juan Vázquez de Coronado, Conquistador de Costa Rica.* Barcelona: la viuda de Luis Tusso, 1908).

Flannery, Tim. *The Eternal Frontier: An Ecological History of North America and Its Peoples.* Boston: Atlantic Monthly Press, 2001.

Flint, Richard. "Armas de la Tierra: The Mexican Indian Component of Coronado Expedition Material Culture." In *The Coronado Expedition to Tierra Nueva: The 1540–1542 Route Across the Southwest,* edited by Richard Flint and Shirley Cushing Flint, 57–70. Niwot: University Press of Colorado, 1997.

———. *Great Cruelties Have Been Reported: The 1544 Investigation of the Coronado Expedition.* Dallas: Southern Methodist University Press, 2002.

———. "The Pattern of Coronado Expedition Material Culture." M.A. thesis, New Mexico Highlands University, 1992.

Flint, Richard, and Shirley Cushing Flint. "The Coronado Expedition: Cicuye to the Rio de Cicuye Bridge." *New Mexico Historical Review* 67 (April 1992): 123–38.

———. "The Coronado Expedition: Cicuye to the Rio de Cicuye Bridge." In *The Coronado Expedition to Tierra Nueva: The 1540–1542 Route Across the Southwest,* edited by Richard Flint and Shirley Cushing Flint, 262–277. Niwot: University Press of Colorado, 1997.

———. "A Death in Tiguex, 1542." *New Mexico Historical Review* 74 (July 1999): 247–70.

———, eds. *The Coronado Expedition to Tierra Nueva: The 1540–1542 Route Across the Southwest.* Niwot, Colorado: University Press of Colorado, 1997.

———, eds. and trans. *"They Were Not Familiar with His Majesty": Documents of the Coronado Expedition, 1540–1542.* In preparation.

Florencio, Hernando, scribe. "Testimony of witnesses, Havana, November 1539." AGI, Patronato 21, N.2, R.4. In *"They Were Not Familiar with His Majesty": Documents of the Coronado Expedition, 1540–1542,* edited and translated by Richard Flint and Shirley Cushing Flint. In preparation.

Folger Shakespeare Library. Brochure of exhibition *Mapping Early Modern Worlds,* February 14–July 1, 1998. Washington, D.C.: Folger Shakespeare Library, 1998.

Foreman, Grant. *Marcy and the Gold Seekers.* Norman: University of Oklahoma Press, 1939.

———. *A Pathfinder in the Southwest.* Norman: University of Oklahoma Press, 1968.

Frazer, Robert. "Fort Butler." *New Mexico Historical Review* 43 (October 1968): 253–70.

Fuentes Baudrit, Hernán. "Descendientes del adelantado de Costa Rica don Juan de Vázquez de Coronado." *Revista de la Academia Costarricense de Ciencias Genealógicas* 27–28 (November 1981): 371–78.

García Icazbalceta, Joaquín, ed. "Fragmento de la visita hecha a don Antonio de Mendoza." In *Coleccion de documentos para la historia de México,* vol. 2. Mexico: Antigua Librería, 1866.

———. "Primera y segunda relaciones anónimas de la jornada que hizo Nuño de Guzman a la Nueva Galicia." México, D.F.: Chimalistac, 1952.

Gardiner, C. Harvey. *Martín López: Conquistador Citizen of Mexico.* Lexington: University of Kentucky Press, 1958.

Gates, Ted, and Alyce Hart. "The Garza Burial." *Transactions of the Twelfth Regional Archeological Symposium for Southeastern New Mexico and Western Texas,* 145–154. El Paso, Texas, 1977.

Gelo, Daniel J. "Comanche Land and Ever Has Been: A Native Geography of the Nineteenth-century Comancheria." *Southwest Historical Quarterly* 103, no. 3 (2000): 273–307.

Gerhard, Peter. *A Guide to the Historical Geography of New Spain.* Rev. ed. Norman: University of Oklahoma Press, 1993.

Gómez de la Peña, Fernando, scribe. "Testimony Taken at Culiacán, 1545." In "Criminal Process in the Audiencia of Mexico against Nuño de Chaves, Rebel in the Rebellion, Mexico City, 1566." AGI, Patronato, 216, R.2. In *Great Cruelties Have Been Reported: The 1544 Investigation of the Coronado Expedition,* edited and translated by Richard Flint, 344–431. Dallas: Southern Methodist University Press, 2002.

[Gómez de Paradinas, Juan]. "Proof of service of Juan Gómez de Paradinas, 1560." AGI, Patronato 63, R.5.

González Villalobos, Paulino. *La empresa Cavallón-Estrada en la conquista de Costa Rica.* Avances de Investigación, no. 27. San José: Universidad de Costa Rica, 1987.

Green, F. Earl. "The Lubbock Lake Reservoir Site: 12,000 Years of Human Prehistory." *The Museum Journal* 6 (1962): 83–123. Lubbock: West Texas Museum Association, Texas Tech University.

Greenberg, Joseph H. *Language in the Americas.* Stanford, California: Stanford University Press, 1981.

Gregg, Josiah. *Commerce of the Prairies.* Reprint, Norman: University of Oklahoma Press, 1954.

———. *Diary and Letters of Josiah Gregg: Southwestern Enterprises, 1840–1847,* vol. 1. Edited by Maurice Garland Fulton. Norman: University of Oklahoma Press, 1941.

Guevara de Pérez, Raquel. *Pedro Pérez Zeledón.* San José: Ministerio de Cultura, Juventud y Deportes (de Costa Rica), 1971.

Gunnerson, Dolores A. *The Jicarilla Apache.* De Kalb: Northern Illinois University Press, 1974.

Gunnerson, James H. "Documentary Clues and Northeastern New Mexico Archaeology." *New Mexico Archaeological Council Proceedings* 6, no. 1 (1984): 45–76.

Gunnerson, James H., and Dolores A. Gunnerson. "Apachean Culture: A Study in Unity and Diversity." In *Apachean Culture History and Ethnology,* edited by Keith H. Basso and Morris E. Opler, 7–27. Tucson: University of Arizona Press, 1971.

Haas, Jonathan, and Winifred Creamer. "Demography of the Protohistoric Pueblos of the Northern Rio Grande, A.D. 1450–1680." In *Current Research on the Late Prehistory and Early History of New Mexico,* edited by Bradley J. Vierra, 21–27. Albuquerque: New Mexico Archaeological Council, 1992.

Habicht-Mauche, Judith A. "Coronado's Querechos and Teyas in the Archeological Record of the Texas Panhandle." *Plains Anthropologist* 37 (1992): 247–59.

Habicht-Mauche, Judith A., Stephen T. Glenn, Homer Milford, and A. Russell Flegal. "Isotopic Tracing of Prehistoric Glaze-Paint Produce and Trade." *Journal of Archaeological Science* 27 (2000): 708–13.

Hackett, Charles W., ed. *Historical Documents Relating to New Mexico, Nueva Vizcaya, and Approaches Thereto, to 1773.* Collected by Adolph F. Bandelier and Fanny R. Bandelier. Carnegie Institution of Washington Publications 330; Monograph Series 2. Washington, D.C.: Carnegie Institution of Washington, 1926.

Hallenbeck, Cleve. *The Journey of Fray Marcos de Niza.* Dallas: Southern Methodist University Press, 1987.

Hammond, George P. *Coronado's Seven Cities.* Albuquerque: United States Coronado Exposition Commission, 1940.

———. "The Zúñiga Journal, Tucson to Santa Fe: The Opening of a Spanish Trade Route, 1788–1795." *New Mexico Historical Review* 4 (January 1931): 40–65.

Hammond, George P., and Agapito Rey, eds. and trans. *Don Juan Oñate, Colonizer of New Mexico, 1595–1628.* 2 vols. Coronado Cuarto Centennial Publications, 1540–1940, vols. 5 and 6. Albuquerque: University of New Mexico Press, 1953.

———. *Narratives of the Coronado Expedition, 1540–1542.* Coronado Cuarto Centennial Publications, 1540–1940, vol. 2. Albuquerque: University of New Mexico Press, 1940.

———. *The Rediscovery of New Mexico, 1580–1594: The Explorations of Chamuscado, Espejo, Castaño de Sosa, Morlete, and Leyva de Bonilla and Humaña.* Coronado Cuarto Centennial Publications, 1540–1940, vol. 3. Albuquerque: University of New Mexico Press, 1966.

Hanke, Lewis. *Los virreyes españoles en América durante el gobierno de la casa de Austria, México.* 2 vols. Madrid: Ediciones Atlas, 1976.

Harley, John Brian, Ellen Hanlon, and Mark Warhus, eds. *Maps and the Columbian Encounter.* Milwaukee: Golda Meir Library, University of Wisconsin, 1990.

Harley, John Brian, and David Woodward, eds. *The History of Cartography,* vol. 1, *Cartography in Prehistoric, Ancient, and Medieval Europe and the Mediterranean.* Chicago: University of Chicago Press, 1987.

Harper, Bob, and Emmett Shedd. "A Garza County Cave: SPAS-GR-269." *South Plains Archeological Society Newsletter* 22 (1969).

Hart, Alyce. "An Open Report on Probes and Digs of LY42 by Individuals and the Archaeological Society of Dawson County." *Transactions of the Eleventh Regional Archaeological Symposium for Southeastern New Mexico and Western Texas,* 111–120. Midland, Texas, 1976.

Hartmann, William K. "Pathfinder for Coronado: Reevaluating the Mysterious Journey of Marcos de Niza." In *The Coronado Expedition to Tierra Nueva: The 1540–1542 Route Across the Southwest,* edited by Richard Flint and Shirley Cushing Flint, 73–101. Niwot, Colorado: University Press of Colorado, 1997.

Hartmann, William K., and Richard Flint. "Migrations in Late Anasazi Prehistory: "Eyewitness" Testimony." *Kiva* 66, no. 3 (2001): 375–85.

Hartog, François. *The Mirror of Herodotus: The Representation of the Other in the Writing of History.* Translated by Janet Lloyd. Berkeley: University of California Press, 1988.

Haury, Emil W. "The Search for Chichilticale." *Arizona Highways* 60, no. 4 (1984): 14–19.

Hayden, Julian. *Excavations, 1940, at University Indian Ruin.* Southwestern Monuments Association Technical Services 5. Globe, Arizona: Gila Pueblo, 1957.

Hegmon, Michelle, Margaret C. Nelson, and Susan M. Ruth. "Abandonment and Reorganization in the Mimbres Region of the American Southwest." *American Anthropologist* 100, no. 1 (1998): 148–62.

Hickerson, Nancy Parrott. "Ethnogenesis in the South Plains: Jumano to Kiowa?" In *History, Power, and Identity: Ethnogenesis in the Americas,* edited by Jonathan Hill, 71–89. Iowa City: University of Iowa Press, 1996.

————. "Jumano: The Missing Link in South Plains History." *Journal of the West* 29, no. 4 (1990): 5–12.

————. *The Jumanos: Hunters and Traders of the South Plains.* Austin: University of Texas Press, 1994.

————. "The Linguistic Position of Jumano." *Journal of Anthropological Research* 44, no. 3 (1988): 311–26.

Hodge, Frederick W. *The History of Hawikuh: One of the So-called Cities of Cibola.* Los Angeles: Southwest Museum, 1937.

————. "The Jumano Indians." *Proceedings of the American Antiquarian Society for 1900–1910,* n.s. 20 (1911): 249–68.

Hodge, Frederick W., and Theodore H. Lewis, eds. *Spanish Explorers in the Southern United States, 1528–1543.* New York: Barnes and Noble, 1907.

Hoijer, Harry. "The Chronology of the Athapaskan Languages." *International Journal of American Linguistics* 22, no. 4 (1956): 219–32.

Holden, William Curry. "Blue Mountain Rock Shelter." *Bulletin of the Texas Archeological and Paleontological Society* 10 (1938): 208–221.

————. "Texas Tech Archaeological Expedition, Summer 1930." *Bulletin of the Texas Archeological and Paleontological Society* 3 (1931): 43–52.

Holliday, Vance T. *Paleoindian Geoarchaeology of the Southern High Plains.* Austin: University of Texas Press, 1997.

Hughes, Jack T. "The Canyon City Club Cave in the Panhandle of Texas." Manuscript on file. Austin, Texas: Office of the State Archeologist, 1969.

Hughes, Jack T., H. Charles Hood, and Billy Pat Newman. "Archeological Testing in the Red Deer Creek Watershed in Gray, Roberts, and Hemphill Counties, Texas." Canyon, Texas: Archeological Research Laboratory, Killgore Research Center, West Texas State University, 1978.

Hussey, Roland D. "Spanish Colonial Trails in Panama." *Revista de Historia de America* 6 (1939): 47–74.

Ibarra Rojas, Eugenia. *Las sociedades cacicales de Costa Rica (siglo XVI).* San José: Editorial de la Universidad de Costa Rica, 1990.

Icaza, Francisco A. de. *Conquistadores y pobladores de Nueva España: Diccionario autobiográfico sacado de los textos originales.* 2 vols. Madrid, 1923.

Ivey, James E. *In the Midst of a Loneliness: The Architectural History of the Salinas Missions.* Southwest Cultural Resources Center Professional Papers 15. Washington, D.C.: National Park Service, 1988.

Jaramillo, Juan. "Narrative [1560s]." AGI, Patronato, 20, N.5, R.8. In *"They Were Not Familiar with His Majesty": Documents of the Coronado Expedition, 1540–1542,* edited and translated by Richard Flint and Shirley Cushing Flint. In preparation.

Jeançon, John A. *Excavations in the Chama Valley, New Mexico.* Bureau of American Ethnology Bulletin 81. Washington, D.C.: U.S. Government Printing Office, 1923.

————. "Ruins at Peseduinque." *Records of the Past* 11 (1912): 28–37.

John, Elizabeth A. H. *Storms Brewed in Other Men's Worlds: The Confrontation of Indians, Spanish, and French in the Southwest, 1540–1795.* College Station, Texas: Texas A&M University Press, 1975.

Johnson, Douglas A. "Adobe Brick Architecture and Salado Ceramics at Fourmile Ruin." In *Proceedings of the Second Salado Conference, Globe, Arizona,* edited by Richard C. Lange and Stephen Germick, 131–38. Phoenix: Arizona Archaeological Society, 1992.

Johnson, Eileen, ed. *Lubbock Lake: Late Quaternary Studies on the Southern High Plains.* College Station: Texas A&M University Press, 1987.

Johnson, Eileen, Vance T. Holliday, Michael J. Kaczor, and Robert Stuckenrath. "The Garza Occupation at the Lubbock Lake Site." *Bulletin of the Texas Archaeological Society* 48 (1977): 83–109.

Jones, F. A. *Mines and Minerals of New Mexico, with Some Reference to the Geological Associations in the Various Camps of the Territory.* Santa Fe: New Mexico Bureau of Immigration, 1901.

Judd, Henry. "Report of a Scout along the Rio Pecos by Captain Henry Judd, March 30, 1850." Arrott's Fort Union Collection, 47:153–58. Donnelly Library, New Mexico Highlands University, Las Vegas, New Mexico.

Kalokowski, H. Paul, Jr. "Archeological Testing of the Fifth Green Site (A1363), Randall County, Texas." Manuscript on file. Canyon, Texas: Archaeological Research Laboratory, Killgore Research Center, West Texas State University, 1986.

Katz, Susana R., and Paul Katz. "Archeological Investigations in Lower Tule Canyon, Briscoe County, Texas." Office of the State Archeologist, Survey Report no. 16. Austin: Texas Historical Commission, 1976.

Kelley, J. Charles. "Juan Sabeata and Diffusion in Aboriginal Texas." *American Anthropologist* 57 (1955): 981–95.

————. "Jumano Indians." In *The Handbook of Texas,* edited by William P. Webb, H. Bailey Carroll, and Eldon S. Branda, 933–34. Austin: Texas State Historical Society, 1952.

Kelley, Vincent C. *Geology and Mineral Resources of the Española Basin, New Mexico.* Socorro: New Mexico Bureau of Mines and Mineral Resources, 1977.

Kendall, George W. *Across the Great Southwestern Prairies,* vol. 1. London: David Bogue, Fleet Street, 1845.

Kessell, John L. *Kiva, Cross, and Crown: The Pecos Indians and New Mexico, 1540–1840.* 2d ed. Albuquerque: University of New Mexico Press, 1987.

————. *Spain in the Southwest: A Narrative History of Colonial New Mexico, Arizona, Texas, and California.* Norman: University of Oklahoma Press, 2002.

————. "To See Such Marvels with My Own Eyes: Spanish Exploration in the Western Borderlands." *Montana: The Magazine of Western History* 41, no. 4 (1991), 68–75.

Kidder, Alfred V. *The Artifacts of Pecos.* Papers of the Southwestern Expedition, no. 6. New Haven: Yale University Press, 1932.

————. "The Glaze Paint, Culinary, and Other Wares." In *The Pottery of Pecos,* vol. 2, edited by Alfred V. Kidder and Anna O. Shepard, 1–388. New Haven: Yale University Press, 1936.

————. *Pecos New Mexico: Archaeological Notes.* Robert S. Peabody Foundation Archaeological Papers 5. Andover, Massachusetts: Phillips Academy, 1958.

Kidder, Alfred V., and Charles Avery Amsden. *The Pottery of Pecos,* vol. 1, *The Dull Paint Wares.* New Haven: Yale University Press, 1931.

Klor de Alva, Jorge. "Language, Politics, and Translation: Colonial Discourse and Classic Nahuatl in New Spain." In *The Art of Translation: Voices from the Field,* edited by Rosanna Warren, 143–62. Boston: Northeastern University Press, 1989.

Knaut, Andrew L. *The Pueblo Revolt of 1680: Conquest and Resistance in Seventeenth-Century New Mexico.* Norman: University of Oklahoma Press, 1995.

Lange, Richard C., and Stephen Germick, eds. *Proceedings of the Second Salado Conference, Globe, Arizona.* Occasional Papers. Phoenix: Arizona Archaeological Society, 1992.

Las Casas, Bartolomé de. *Apologética histórica sumaria*. México, D.F.: Universidad Nacional Autónoma de México, 1967.

———. *Historia de las Indias*. 3 vols. Edited by André Saint-Lu. Caracas, Venezuela: Biblioteca Ayacucho, 1986.

Lawson-Peebles, Robert. *Landscape and Written Expression in Revolutionary America*. Cambridge: Cambridge University Press, 1988.

LeBlanc, Steven. "The Mimbres Culture." In *Mimbres Pottery*, edited by J. J. Brody, Catherine J. Scott, and Steven LeBlanc, 23–37. New York: Hudson Hills Press, 1983.

Lee, Betty Graham. *The Eagle Pass Site: An Integral Part of the Province of Chichilticale*. Museum of Anthropology Publication no. 5. Thatcher: Eastern Arizona College, 1966.

Leonard, Irving A. *Books of the Brave: Being an Account of Books and of Men in the Spanish Conquest and Settlement of the Sixteenth-Century New World*. New York: Gordian Press, 1964.

Lekson, Stephen H. "Para-Salado, Perro Salado, or Salado Peril?" In *Proceedings of the Second Salado Conference, Globe, Arizona*, edited by Richard C. Lange and Stephen Germick, 334–36. Phoenix: Arizona Archaeological Society, 1992.

León, Juan de, scribe. "Hearing on Depopulation Charges, Compostela, February 26, 1540." AGI, Patronato, 21, N.2, R.3. In *"They Were Not Familiar with His Majesty": Documents of the Coronado Expedition, 1540–1542*, edited and translated by Richard Flint and Shirley Cushing Flint. In preparation.

León-Portilla, Miguel, ed. *Cartografía y crónicas de la antigua California*. Coyoacán, D.F.: Universidad Nacional Autónoma de México–Fundación de Investigaciones Sociales, 1989.

Lestringant, Frank. *Mapping the Renaissance World*. Translated by David Fausett. Berkeley: University of California Press, 1994.

Leubben, Ralph A. "The Leaf Water Site." In *Salvage Archaeology in the Chama Valley, New Mexico*, edited by Fred Wendorf, 1–33. School of American Research Monograph 17. Santa Fe: School of American Research, 1953.

Levensen, Jay A. "Circa 1492: Art in the Age of Exploration." Brochure of the exhibition at the National Gallery of Art, Washington, D.C., October 12, 1991–January 12, 1992. Washington, D.C.: National Gallery of Art, 1991.

Levine, Frances, and Kurt Anschuetz. "Adjusting our Scale of Analysis: Observations of Protohistoric Change in Pueblo Land Use." Paper presented at the annual meeting of the Society for American Archaeology, Seattle, 1998.

Lines, Jorge A. "Crónica de nuestro conquistador Juan de Vázquez de Coronado." *Revista de los Archivos Nacionales* (de Costa Rica) 9–10 (September–October 1940): 459–79.

Lingren, Waldemar, Louis C. Graton, and Charles H. Gordon. *The Ore Deposits of New Mexico*. USGS Professional Paper 68. Washington, D.C.: U.S. Government Printing Office, 1910.

Lockhart, James. *The Men of Cajamarca: A Social and Biographical Study of the First Conquerors of Peru*. Austin: University of Texas Press, 1972.

Loomis, Noel M., and Abraham P. Nasatir. *Pedro Vial and the Roads to Santa Fe*. Norman: University of Oklahoma Press, 1967.

López de Gómara, Francisco. *Cortés: The Life of the Conqueror by His Secretary*. Translated and edited by Lesley Byrd Simpson. Berkeley: University of California Press, 1964.

———. *Historia general de las Indias*. 2 parts. Barcelona: Editorial Iberia, c. 1954.

———. *La istoria de las Indias y conquista de México*. Biblioteca Nacional, Incunables y Raros, Madrid. Zaragoza: Casa de Agustín Millán, 1552.

López de Legazpi, Miguel, scribe. "Disposal of the Juan Jiménez estate, Puebla de los Angeles, 1550." AGI, Contratación, 5575, N. 24. In *"They Were Not Familiar with His Majesty": Documents of the Coronado Expedition, 1540–1542*, edited and translated by Richard Flint and Shirley Cushing Flint. In preparation.

Lorrain, Dessamae. "Excavation at Red Bluff Shelter (Sotol Site) X41CX8, Crockett County,

Texas." *Transactions of the Fourth Regional Archeological Symposium for Southeastern New Mexico and Western Texas,* 18–39. Iraan, Texas, 1968.

Luján, Enrique Robert. "Descendencia del adelantado de Costa Rica don Juan de Vázquez de Coronado." *Revista de la Academia Costarricense de Ciencias Genealógicas* 9 (October 1955): 13–28.

Lycett, Mark T. "Archaeological Implications of European Contact: Demography, Settlement, and Land Use in the Middle Rio Grande Valley, New Mexico." Ph.D. diss., University of New Mexico, 1995.

Lyon, Eugene. *The Enterprise of Florida: Pedro Menéndez de Avilés and the Spanish Conquest of 1565–1568.* Gainesville: University Presses of Florida, 1976.

Marcos de Niza, fray. "Narrative Account by Fray Marcos de Niza, Temistitán, August 26, 1539," AGI, Patronato 20, N.5, R.10. In *"They Were Not Familiar with His Majesty": Documents of the Coronado Expedition, 1540–1542,* edited and translated by Richard Flint and Shirley Cushing Flint. In preparation.

Marcy, Captain Randolph B. "Route from Fort Smith to Santa Fe: Report Prepared by Captain Randolph B. Marcy, February 21, 1850." Secretary of War, 31st Cong., 1st sess. Executive Document no. 45. Serial 577, 26–89.

Marshall, Michael P. "El Camino Real de Tierra Adentro: An Archaeological Investigation." Santa Fe: New Mexico Historic Preservation Division, 1990.

Marshall, Michael P., and Henry J. Walt. "Rio Abajo: Prehistory and History of a Rio Grande Province." Santa Fe: New Mexico Historic Preservation Office, 1984.

Mattingly, Garrett. *The Armada.* Boston: Houghton Mifflin, 1959.

McKenna, Peter J., and James A. Miles. "Bandelier Archaeological Survey Ceramic Manual." Manuscript on file at the Branch of Cultural Research, Southwest Regional Office. Santa Fe: National Park Service, 1991.

Meléndez Chaverri, Carlos. *La Ciudad del Lodo.* Serie Historia y Geografía, no. 5. San José: Universidad de Costa Rica, 1962.

———. *Conquistadores y pobladores: Orígenes histórico-sociales de los costarricenses.* San José: EUNED, 1982.

———. *Juan Vázquez de Coronado: Conquistador y fundador de Costa Rica.* San Jose: Editorial Costa Rica, 1966.

Mendoza, Antonio de. "Letter from Mendoza to Cortés, Mexico City, August 3, 1539." In Henry R. Wagner, "Fray Marcos de Niza." *New Mexico Historical Review* 9 (April 1934): 159–227.

———. "Letter to the King, Mexico City, December 10, 1537." AGI, Patronato, 184, R. 27.

———. "Viceroy's instructions to Hernando Alarcón, May 31, 1541." Biblioteca del Escorial, códice &-II-7, Docs. 66 and 67. In *"They Were Not Familiar with His Majesty": Documents of the Coronado Expedition, 1540–1542,* edited and translated by Richard Flint and Shirley Cushing Flint. In preparation.

———. "The Viceroy's Letter to the King, Jacona, April 17, 1540." AGI, Patronato, 184, R.31. In *"They Were Not Familiar with His Majesty": Documents of the Coronado Expedition, 1540–1542,* edited and translated by Richard Flint and Shirley Cushing Flint. In preparation.

[Mendoza, Antonio de.] "Contract between Antonio de Mendoza and the adelantado Pedro de Alvarado, November 2, 1540." AGI, Patronato, 21, N3, R.2. In *"They Were Not Familiar with His Majesty": Documents of the Coronado Expedition, 1540–1542,* edited and translated by Richard Flint and Shirley Cushing Flint. In preparation.

———. "Merits and services of Antonio de Mendoza—(1545)." AGI, Patronato 57, N2, R1.

———. "Probanza made in the name of don Antonio de Mendoza, Zacatula—(1546–47)," AGI, Justicia 263, pieza 1.

Mera, Harry P. *Population Changes in the Rio Grande Glaze Paint Area.* Laboratory of Anthropology Technical Series, Bulletin 8. Santa Fe: Museum of New Mexico, 1940.

————. *A Proposed Revision of the Rio Grande Glaze Paint Sequence.* Laboratory of Anthropology Technical Series, Bulletin 5. Santa Fe: Museum of New Mexico, 1933.

————. *A Survey of the Biscuit Ware Area in Northern New Mexico.* Laboratory of Anthropology Technical Series, Bulletin 6. Santa Fe: Museum of New Mexico, 1934.

Mignolo, Walter. *The Darker Side of the Renaissance: Literacy, Territoriality, and Colonization.* Ann Arbor: University of Michigan Press, 1995.

Milford, Homer E. *Cultural Resource Survey for the Real de los Cerrillos Abandoned Mine Lands Project, Santa Fe County, New Mexico.* New Mexico Abandoned Mine Land Bureau Report 1996-1. Santa Fe: Mining and Minerals Division; Energy, Minerals, and Natural Resources Department, 1996.

Milford, Homer E., Richard Flint, Shirley Cushing Flint, and Geraldine Vigil. *Nuevas leyes de las minas de España de Juan de Oñate.* Congreso Internacional de Historia de la Minería. Facultad de Minas. Guanajuato, Mexico: Universidad de Guanajuato, 1998.

Mills, Jack P., and Vera M. Mills. *The Curtis Site: A Pre-Historic Village in the Safford Valley.* Self published, 1978.

————. *The Kuykendall Site: A Prehistoric Salado Village in Southeastern Arizona.* Special Report for 1967, no. 6. El Paso, Texas: El Paso Archeological Society, 1969.

Molina, Alonso de. *Vocabulario en lengua castellana y mexicana y mexicana y castellana.* Edited by Miguel León-Portilla. México, D.F.: Editorial Porrúa, 1970.

Monge Alfaro, Carlos. *Historia de Costa Rica.* 23d ed. San José: n.p., 1974.

Monjarás-Ruiz, Jesús, Elena Limón, and María de la Cruz Paillés-H., eds. *Tlatelolco: Fuentes e historia. Obras de Robert H. Barlow,* vol. 2. Mexico: Instituto Nacional de Antropología e Historia y Universidad de las Américas, Pueblo, 1989.

Mora, Carmen de. "Códigos culturales en *La Relación de la jornada de Cíbola* de Pedro Castañeda Nájera." *Nueva Revista de Filología Hispánica* 39, no. 2 (1991): 901–12.

————. "*La Relación de la jornada de Cíbola* de Pedro Castañeda Nájera: Un texto censurado?" *Insula* 45, no. 522 (1990): 14–15.

————, ed. *Las siete ciudades de Cíbola: Textos y testimonios sobre la expedición de Vázquez Coronado.* Sevilla: Ediciones Alfar, 1992.

Morison, Samuel Eliot. *The European Discovery of America: The Southern Voyages, 1492–1616.* New York: Oxford University Press, 1974.

Morris, John Miller. *El Llano Estacado: Exploration and Imagination on the High Plains of Texas and New Mexico, 1536–1860.* Austin: Texas State Historical Association, 1997.

Mundy, Barbara E. *The Mapping of New Spain: Indigenous Cartography and the Maps of the Relaciones Geográficas.* Chicago: University of Chicago Press, 1996.

Myers, Harry C. "Meredith Miles Marmaduke's Journal of a Tour to New Mexico, 1824–1825." *Wagon Tracks* 12 (November 1997): 8–16.

Myers, Harry C., and Michael Olsen. "'We Found the Rocks Very Troblesom': The Taos Trail in New Mexico." In *The Prairie Scout,* vol. 6, 80–97. Abilene: Kansas Corral of the Westerners, 1996.

Nallino, Michel, and William K. Hartmann. "A Supposed Franciscan Exploration of Arizona in 1538: The Origins of a Myth." Paper presented at the conference "Contemporary Vantage on the Coronado Expedition through Documents and Artifacts." Las Vegas, New Mexico, 2000.

Northern, Martin James. "Archaeological Investigations of the Montgomery Site, Floyd County, Texas." M.A. thesis, Texas Tech University, 1979.

Núñez Cabeza de Vaca, Álvar. *Castaways: The Narrative of Álvar Núñez Cabeza de Vaca* [1555]. Edited by Enrique Pupo-Walker. Reprint, Berkeley: University of California Press, 1993.

————. *Naufragios y comentarios con dos cartas.* 9th ed. México, D.F.: Espasa-Calpe Mexicana, 1985.

Obregón, Baltasar de. *Historia de los descubrimientos antiguos y modernos de la Nueva España* [1584]. Reprint, México, D.F.: Editorial Porrúa, 1988.

Orcutt, Janet D. "Chronology." In *The Bandelier Archaeological Survey*, vol. 1, edited by Robert P. Powers and Janet D. Orcutt, 85–116. Washington, D.C.: National Park Service, 1999.

Oroz, fray Pedro. *The Oroz Codex*. Edited and translated by Angélico Chávez. Washington, D.C.: Academy of American Franciscan History, 1972.

Parker, Wayne. *Archaeology at the Bridwell Site*. Crosbyton, Texas: Crosby County Pioneer Memorial Museum, 1982.

———. "The Bridwell Site (41CB27)." *Transactions of the Twenty-fifth Regional Archeological Symposium for Southeastern New Mexico and Western Texas*, 99–114. Midland, Texas, 1990.

Parry, William J., and John D. Speth. "The Garnsey Spring Campsite: Late Prehistoric Occupation in Southwestern New Mexico." Technical Reports no. 15. Ann Arbor: Museum of Anthropology, University of Michigan, 1984.

Parsons, Mark L. "Archeological Investigations in Crosby and Dickens Counties, Texas, during the Winter, 1966–1967." Archeological Program Report 7. Austin, Texas: State Building Commission, 1967.

Pattie, James O. *The Personal Narrative of James O. Pattie* [1831]. Reprint, Lincoln: University of Nebraska Press, 1984.

[Paz Maldonado, Rodrigo de]. "Proof of service of Rodrigo de Paz Maldonado, 1571." AGI, Patronato 117, R.5.

———. "Proof of service of Rodrigo de Paz Maldonado, Quito, 1564." AGI, Patronato 112, R.2.

Penman, Shawn L. "Colonowares at Pecos: A Study in Acculturation." Ph.D. diss., University of New Mexico, 2002.

[Pérez, Melchior]. "Melchior Pérez's Petition for Preferment, 1551." Bancroft Library, University of California, Berkeley, manuscript M-M 1714. In *"They Were Not Familiar with His Majesty": Documents of the Coronado Expedition, 1540–1542*, edited and translated by Richard Flint and Shirley Cushing Flint. In preparation.

Pérez de Luxán, Diego. "Diego Pérez de Luxán's Account of the Antonio de Espejo Expedition into New Mexico, 1582." In *The Rediscovery of New Mexico, 1580–1594: The Explorations of Chamuscado, Espejo, Castaño de Sosa, Morlete, and Leyva de Bonilla and Humaña*, edited and translated by George P. Hammond and Agapito Rey. Albuquerque: University of New Mexico Press, 1966.

Perry, Richard J. "The Apachean Transition from the Subarctic to the Southwest." *Plains Anthropologist* 25 (1980): 279–96.

———. *Western Apache Heritage*. Austin: University of Texas Press, 1991.

Pierce, Christopher. "Toward Explaining Complex Patterns of Cooperation and Conflict during the Protohistoric Period in the American Southwest." Paper presented at the Summer Workshop on Modeling Complexity in Social Systems at the Colorado Center for Chaos and Complexity. Boulder: University of Colorado, 1998.

Pierce, Christopher, and Ann F. Ramenofsky. "Investigating Patterns of Cooperation and Conflict during the Contact Period in New Mexico." Paper presented at the Sixth Biennial Southwest Symposium, Hermosillo, Mexico, 1998.

[Pino, Juan Estevan]. Merced del Sitio del Ojito del Rio de las Gallinas dada a favor de Don Juan Esteban Pino con el tiendo de Hacienda de San Juan Bautista del ojito del rio de las Gallinas. Año de 1823. Preston Beck (Juan Estevan Pino) Grant. Spanish Archives of New Mexico 1. Land Records of New Mexico, 1824, SG 1, Roll 12. Santa Fe.

Polzer, Charles W., S.J. "The Coronado Documents: Their Limitations." In *The Coronado Expedition to Tierra Nueva: The 1540–1542 Route Across the Southwest*, edited by Richard Flint and Shirley Cushing Flint, 36–43. Niwot, Colorado: University Press of Colorado, 1997.

Pope, Leon. "The Hogue Site (41TY2)." *Transactions of the Twenty-seventh Regional Archeological Symposium for Southeastern New Mexico and Western Texas*, 4–8. Lubbock, Texas, 1991.

Portinaro, Pierluigi, and Franco Knirsch. *The Cartography of North America: 1500–1800*. New York: Facts on File, 1987.

Portis, John, Fern Portis, Pat Bills, and Nelda Bills. "A Surface Site in Scurry County (41S.C.)." *Transactions of the Fourth Regional Archeological Symposium for Southeastern New Mexico and Western Texas,* 60–64. Iraan, Texas, 1968.

Posada, Alonso de. *Alonso de Posada Report, 1686.* Edited by Alfred Barnaby Thomas. Pensacola, Florida: Perdido Bay Press, 1982.

Priestley, Herbert Ingram. *The Luna Papers: Documents Relating to the Expedition of don Tristán de Luna y Arellano for the Conquest of La Florida in 1559–1591.* 2 vols. Freeport, New York: Books for Libraries Press, 1971.

Probert, Alan. "Bartolomé de Medina: The Patio Process and the Sixteenth-Century Silver Crisis." In *An Expanding World: The European Impact on World History 1450–1800,* vol. 19, *Mines of Silver and Gold in the Americas,* edited by Peter Bakewell, 96–130. Aldershot, U.K.: Variorum, 1997.

Quigg, J. Michael, Christopher Lintz, Fred M. Oglesby, Amy C. Earls, Charles D. Frederick, W. Nicholas Trierweiler, Douglas Owsley, and Karl W. Kibler. "Historic and Prehistoric Data Recovery at Palo Duro Reservoir, Hansford County, Texas." Technical Report no. 485. Austin, Texas: Mariah Associates, Inc., 1993.

Ramenofsky, Ann F. "Decoupling Archaeology and History: Northern New Mexico." In *The Entangled Past: Integrating History and Archaeology. Proceedings of the Thirtieth Chacmool Archaeological Conference,* edited by Matthew Boyd, J. C. Erwin, and M. Hendrickson, 5–64. Calgary: University of Calgary, 2000.

Ramenofsky, Ann F., and James K. Feathers. "Documents, Ceramics, Tree-Rings, and Luminescence: Estimating Final Native Abandonment of the Lower Chama Region." *Journal of Anthropological Research* 58, no. 1 (2002): 121–59.

[Ramírez de Cárdenas, García]. "Report extracted from the affidavit prepared for don García Ramírez de Cárdenas." AGI, Justicia, 1021, N.2, Pieza 2. In *Great Cruelties Have Been Reported: The 1544 Investigation of the Coronado Expedition,* edited and translated by Richard Flint, 437–456. Dallas: Southern Methodist University Press, 2002.

Ramusio, Giovanni Battista. *Terzo volume delle navigationi et viaggi.* Venice, 1556. Facsimile edition with introduction by Raleigh A. Skelton. Amsterdam: Theatrvm Orbis Terrarvm, 1967.

Reff, Daniel T. "The Location of Corazones and Senora: Archaeological Evidence from the Rio Sonora Valley, Mexico." In *The Protohistoric Period in the American Southwest, A.D. 1540–1700,* edited by David R. Wilcox and W. Bruce Masse, 94–112. Arizona State Anthropological Research Papers no. 24. Tempe: Arizona State University, 1981.

Reid, Jefferson, and Stephanie Whittlesey. *The Archaeology of Ancient Arizona.* Tucson: University of Arizona Press, 1997.

Reinhartz, Dennis, and Charles C. Colley. *The Mapping of the American Southwest.* College Station: Texas A&M University Press, 1987.

"Relación del suceso [1540s]." AGI, Patronato, 20, N.5, R.8. In *"They Were Not Familiar with His Majesty": Documents of the Coronado Expedition, 1540–1542,* edited and translated by Richard Flint and Shirley Cushing Flint. In preparation.

Requena, Pedro de, scribe. "Proceso de Francisco Vázquez, 1544." AGI, Justicia, 267, N.3. In *Great Cruelties Have Been Reported: The 1544 Investigation of the Coronado Expedition,* edited and translated by Richard Flint, passim. Dallas: Southern Methodist University Press, 2002.

Revello Acosta, Julio E. "Algunos datos sobre la descendencia de doña Andrea de Vázquez de Coronado." *Revista de la Academia Costarricense de Ciencias Genealógicas* 2 (March 1957): 4–28.

Rhodes, Diane Lee. "Coronado Fought Here: Crossbow Boltheads as Possible Indicators of the 1540–1542 Expedition." In *The Coronado Expedition to Tierra Nueva: The 1540–1542 Route Across the Southwest,* edited by Richard Flint and Shirley Cushing Flint, 44–56. Niwot, Colorado: University Press of Colorado, 1997.

———. "Coronado's American Legacy: An Overview of Possible Entrada Artifacts and Site Types and a Discussion of Texas Sites." *Bulletin of the Texas Archeological Society* 63 (1992): 27–51.

Ridgway, William Ryder. "Billy the Kid Killed First at Bonita." *Journal of Graham County History* 5, no. 1 (1969): not paginated.

———."Eureka Springs Ranch." *Eastern Arizona Courier,* March 24, 1976. Reprint in *Mt. Graham Profiles,* vol. 2, edited by Glenn Burgess, 82–83. Stafford, Arizona: Graham County Historical Society, 1976.

Riemenschneider, Larry. "The David Hackberry Spring Site (41ST87), Sterling County, Texas." *The Cache: Collected Papers of Texas Archeology* 3 (1996): 13–16.

Riggs, Aaron D., Jr. "Comments on a Hearth." *South Plains Archeological Society Newsbulletin* 16 (1968): 2–3.

———. "The Reed Shelter." *Transactions of the Second Archeological Symposium for Southeastern New Mexico and Western Texas,* 45–58. Midland, Texas, 1966.

Riley, Carroll L. *The Frontier People: The Greater Southwest in the Protohistoric Period.* Rev. and exp. ed. Albuquerque: University of New Mexico Press, 1987.

———. "Introduction," in *The Coronado Expedition to Tierra Nueva: The 1540–1542 Route Across the Southwest,* edited by Richard Flint and Shirley Cushing Flint, 1–28. Niwot: University Press of Colorado, 1997.

———. *Rio del Norte: People of the Upper Rio Grande from Earliest Times to the Pueblo Revolt.* Salt Lake City: University of Utah Press, 1995.

———. "The Road to Hawikuh: Trade and Trade Routes to Cíbola-Zuni during Late Prehistoric and Early Historic Times." *Kiva* 41 (1975): 137–59.

Roberts, Lt. Col. Benjamin S. "Report from Hatch's Ranch, New Mexico, December 8, 1860, to Captain Dabney H. Maury, Asst. Adjutant General, Department of New Mexico, Santa Fé." *Letters Received by the Department of New Mexico.* Microfilm. Washington, D.C.: National Archives and Record Service.

Robinson, William J., and Richard L Warren. *Tree-Ring Dates from New Mexico C–D: Northern Rio Grande Area.* Laboratory of Tree-Ring Research. Tucson: University of Arizona, 1971.

Rodack, Madeleine Turrell. "Cíbola: From Fray Marcos to Coronado." In *The Coronado Expedition to Tierra Nueva: The 1540–1542 Route Across the Southwest,* edited by Richard Flint and Shirley Cushing Flint, 102–15. Niwot, Colorado: University Press of Colorado, 1997.

[Rodríguez, García]. "Proof of service of García Rodríguez and his grandson, 1617." AGI, Patronato 87, N.1, R.5.

Rodríguez de Montalvo, Garci. *Las Sergas de Esplandián.* Zaragosa: Casa de Simon de Portonariis, 1587. Facsimile, Madrid: Ediciones Doce Calles, 1998.

Rodríguez Molina, María Elena, and Félix A. Barboza-Retana. "Publicaciones sobre historia colonial realizadas en Costa Rica 1980–1987." *Revista de Historia* (de Costa Rica) 16 (July–December 1987): 219–92.

Rolland, Vicki L., and Keith H. Ashley. "Beneath the Bell: A Study of Mission Period Colonowares from Three Spanish Missions in Northeastern Florida." *Florida Anthropologist* 53, no. 1 (2000): 36–61.

Runkles, Frank A. "The Garza Site: A Neo-American Campsite near Post, Texas." *Bulletin of the Texas Archeological Society* 35 (1964): 101–125.

Runkles, Frank A., and E. D. Dorchester. "The Lott Site (41GR56): A Late Prehistoric Site in Garza County, Texas." *Bulletin of the Texas Archeological Society* 57 (1987): 83–115.

Sánchez, Joseph P. "A Historiography of the Expedition of Francisco Vázquez de Coronado: General Comments." In *The Coronado Expedition to Tierra Nueva: The 1540–1542 Route Across the Southwest,* edited by Richard Flint and Shirley Cushing Flint, 31–35. Niwot, Colorado: University Press of Colorado, 1997.

———. "A Historiography of the Expedition of Francisco Vázquez de Coronado: Compostela to Cibola." In *The Coronado Expedition to Tierra Nueva: The 1540–1542 Route Across the Southwest,* edited by Richard Flint and Shirley Cushing Flint, 138–48. Niwot, Colorado: University Press of Colorado, 1997.

————. "A Historiography of the Expedition of Francisco Vázquez de Coronado: Cibola to Río de Çicuye." In *The Coronado Expedition to Tierra Nueva: The 1540–1542 Route Across the Southwest,* edited by Richard Flint and Shirley Cushing Flint, 215–24. Niwot, Colorado: University Press of Colorado, 1997.

————. "A Historiography of the Expedition of Francisco Vázquez de Coronado: Río de Çicuye to Quivira." In *The Coronado Expedition to Tierra Nueva: The 1540–1542 Route Across the Southwest,* edited by Richard Flint and Shirley Cushing Flint, 281–301. Niwot, Colorado: University Press of Colorado, 1997.

Sauer, Carl O. "The Credibility of the Fray Marcos Account." *New Mexico Historical Review* 16 (April 1941): 233–43.

————. "The Discovery of New Mexico Reconsidered." *New Mexico Historical Review* 12 (July 1937): 270–87.

————. *The Road to Cíbola.* Ibero-Americana 3. Berkeley: University of California Press, 1932.

Sauer, Carl O., and Donald Brand. "Pueblo Sites in Southeastern Arizona." *University of California Publications in Geography* 3, no. 7 (1930): 415–58. Berkeley: University of California Press.

Scholes, France V. *Church and State in New Mexico.* Publications in History 7. Albuquerque: Historical Society of New Mexico, 1937.

————. *Troublous Times in New Mexico 1659–1670.* Publications in History 11. Albuquerque: Historical Society of New Mexico, 1942.

Scholes, France V., and Harry P. Mera. "Some Aspects of the Jumano Problem." *Contributions to American Anthropology and History* 6, no. 34. Carnegie Institution of Washington Publication 523. Washington, D.C., 1940.

Schroeder, Albert H. "Pueblos Abandoned in Historic Times." In *Handbook of North American Indians,* vol. 9, *Southwest,* edited by Alfonso Ortiz, 236–54. Washington, D.C.: Smithsonian Institution Press, 1979.

Schroeder, Albert H., and Dan S. Matson. *A Colony on the Move: Gaspar Castaño de Sosa's Journal, 1590–1591.* Santa Fe: School of American Research, 1965.

Schurz, William Lytle. *The Manila Galleon.* New York: E. P. Dutton, 1959.

Schwaller, John Frederick. *Origins of Church Wealth in Mexico: Ecclesiastical Revenues and Church Finances, 1523–1600.* Albuquerque: University of New Mexico Press, 1985.

Schwartz, Marion. *A History of Dogs in the Early Americas.* New Haven: Yale University Press, 1997.

Scott, Glenn R., compiler. "Sectional Map of Colfax and Mora Counties, New Mexico, Compiled from the Original Plats in the Surveyor General's Office at Santa Fe, New Mexico, and from Private Surveys by the Maxwell Land Grant Company, 1889." In *Historic Trail Maps of the Raton and Springer 30' by 60' Quadrangles, New Mexico and Colorado.* Miscellaneous Investigations Series, Map I-1641. U.S. Geological Survey, 1986.

Sedwick, Frank. *The Practical Book of Cobs.* 2d ed. Maitland, Florida: Frank Sedwick, 1990.

Shepard, Anna O. *Rio Grande Glaze Paint Ware.* Publication no. 528. Washington, D.C.: Carnegie Institution of Washington, 1942.

Simmons Marc, and Frank Turley. *Southwest Colonial Ironworks: The Spanish Blacksmithing Tradition from Texas to California.* Santa Fe: Museum of New Mexico Press, 1980.

Simpson, Lt. James H. "Coronado's March in Search of the 'Seven Cities of Cibola' and Discussion of their Possible Location." *Annual Report of the Board of Regents of the Smithsonian Institution for 1869,* 309–40. Washington, D.C.: Smithsonian Institution, 1869.

————. *Maps of the Route from Fort Smith to Santa Fe, Made by Lieut. James H. Simpson of the Corps of Topographical Engineers, January 14, 1850.* Secretary of War, 31st Cong., 1st sess., Senate Executive Document no. 12, Serial 554.

————. "Route from Fort Smith to Santa Fe." In "Route from Fort Smith to Santa Fe: Report Prepared by Captain Randolph B. Marcy, February 21, 1850,", 1–25. Secretary of War. 31st Cong., 1st sess., Executive Document no. 45. Serial 577.

Skinner, S. Alan. "Goals for the 1975 TAS Field School." *Texas Archeology* 19, no. 2 (1975): 3–5.

Smith, Marvin T., and Mary Elizabeth Good. *Early Sixteenth-Century Glass Trade Beads in the Spanish Colonial Trade.* Greenwood, Mississippi: Cottonlandia Museum Publications, 1982.

Snow, David. "A Note on Encomienda Economics in Seventeenth-Century New Mexico." In *Hispanic Arts and Ethnohistory in the Southwest,* edited by Marta Weigle, 347–58. Santa Fe: Ancient City Press, 1983.

———. "'Por alli no ay losa ni se hace': Gilded Men and Glazed Pottery on the Southern Plains." In *The Coronado Expedition to Tierra Nueva: The 1540–1542 Route Across the Southwest,* edited by Richard Flint and Shirley Cushing Flint, 344–64. Niwot, Colorado: University Press of Colorado, 1997.

South, Stanley, Russell K. Skowronek, and Richard E. Johnson. *Spanish Artifacts from Santa Elena.* Occasional Papers of the South Carolina Institute of Archeology and Anthropology, Anthropological Studies no. 7. Columbia: University of South Carolina, 1988.

Speth, John D. *Bison Kills and Bone Counts: Decision Making by Ancient Hunters.* Chicago: University of Chicago Press, 1983.

Speth, John D., and William J. Parry. *Late Prehistoric Bison Procurement in Southeastern New Mexico: The 1977 Season at the Garnsey Site.* Technical Reports 8 and Research Reports in Archaeology Contribution 4. Ann Arbor: Museum of Anthropology, University of Michigan, 1978.

———. *Late Prehistoric Bison Procurement in Southeastern New Mexico: The 1978 Season at the Garnsey Site (LA18399).* Technical Reports 12. Ann Arbor: Museum of Anthropology, University of Michigan, 1980.

Spielmann, Katherine A. "Coercion or Cooperation? Plains-Pueblo Interaction during the Protohistoric Period." In *Farmers, Hunters, and Colonists: Interaction between the Southwest and the Southern Plains,* edited by Katherine A. Spielmann, 36–50. Tucson: University of Arizona Press, 1991.

———. "Colonists, Hunters, and Farmers: Plains-Pueblo Interaction in the Seventeenth Century." In *Columbian Consequences,* vol. 1, edited by David H. Thomas Jr., 101–14. Washington, D.C.: Smithsonian Institution Press, 1989.

———, ed. *Farmers, Hunters, and Colonists: Interaction between the Southwest and the Southern Plains.* Tucson: University of Arizona Press, 1991.

———. "Inter-societal Food Acquisition among Egalitarian Societies: An Ecological Analysis of Plains/Pueblo Interaction in the American Southwest." Ph.D. diss., University of Michigan, 1982.

———. "Late Prehistoric Exchange between the Southwest and Southern Plains." *Plains Anthropologist* 28, no. 102 (1983): 257–72.

Spurr, David. *The Rhetoric of Empire.* Durham, North Carolina: Duke University Press, 1993.

Stone, Samuel. *La dinastía de los conquistadores: La crisis del poder en la Costa Rica contemporánea.* San José: EDUCA, 1975.

Sudbury, Byron. "A Sixteenth-Century Spanish Colonial Trade Bead from Western Oklahoma." *Bulletin of the Oklahoma Anthropological Society* 33 (1984): 31–36.

Ternaux-Compans, Henri. *Voyages, relations et memoires originaux pour servir a l'histoire de la decouverte de l'Amerique.* vol. 9. Paris: A. Bertrand, 1838.

Tichy, Marjorie Ferguson. "The Archaeology of Puaray." *El Palacio* 46, no. 7 (1939): 145–63.

Toulouse, Joseph H., Jr. *The Mission of San Gregorio de Abo: A Report on the Excavation and Repair of a Seventeenth-Century New Mexico Mission.* School of American Research Monograph 13. Albuquerque: University of New Mexico Press, 1949.

Treece, Abby C., J. Michael Quigg, Kevin Miller, and Christopher Lintz. "Elm Creek Site, 41CN95." In *Cultural Resource Investigations in the O. H. Ivie Reservoir, Concho, Coleman, and Runnels Counties, Texas.* Technical Report no. 346-IV in *Data Recovery Results from Ceramic Sites,* vol. 4, by Abby C. Treece, Christopher Lintz, W. Nicholas Trierweiler, J. Michael Quigg, and Kevin A. Miller, 307–86. Austin, Texas: Mariah Associates, Inc., 1993.

Troyano, Juan. "Letter by Juan Troyano, Dec. 20, 1568." AGI, Mexico, 168.

Turcios, Antonio de, scribe. "Proof of service of Juan Troyano—(1560)." AGI, Mexico 206, N12. In *"They Were Not Familiar with His Majesty": Documents of the Coronado Expedition, 1540–1542*, edited and translated by Richard Flint and Shirley Cushing Flint. In preparation.

Tuthill, Carr. *The Tres Alamos Site on the San Pedro River, Southeastern Arizona*. Amerind Foundation Paper no. 4. Dragoon, Arizona: Amerind Foundation, 1947.

Tylecote, R. F. *The Prehistory of Metallurgy in the British Isles*. London: Institute of Metals, 1986.

Udall, Stewart L. "In Coronado's Footsteps." Photographs by Jerry Jacka; illustrations by Bill Ahrendt. *Arizona Highways*, Special Commemorative Issue, 60, no. 4 (1984): 1–47.

———. *Majestic Journey: Coronado's Inland Empire*. Photographs by Jerry Jacka. Santa Fe: Museum of New Mexico Press, 1995. Re-edition of *To the Inland Empire*, Garden City, New York: Doubleday, 1987.

Upham, Steadman. "Population and Spanish Contact in the Southwest." In *Disease and Demography in the Americas*, edited by John W. Verano and Douglas H. Ubelaker, 223–36. Washington, D.C.: Smithsonian Institution Press, 1992.

U.S. Department of the Interior, National Park Service. *Coronado Expedition: Arizona/New Mexico/Texas/Oklahoma/Kansas (March 1992)*. National Trail Study and Environmental Assessment. Denver, 1992.

Vargas, Victoria D. *Copper Bell Trade Patterns in the Prehistoric U.S. Southwest and Northwest Mexico*. Arizona State Museum Archaeological Series 187. Tucson: Arizona State Museum, University of Arizona, 1995.

Vargas Machuca, Bernardo de. *Milicia y descripción de las Indias*. 2 vols. Madrid: Librería de Victoriano Suárez, 1892.

Vaughan, C. David. "Investigation of Spanish Colonial Mining and Metallurgy." In *Summary Report of the 2000 Season of Archaeological Research at San Marcos Pueblo (LA98) by the University of New Mexico*, edited by Ann Ramenofsky, 66–80. Santa Fe: New Mexico Historic Preservation Division, 2001.

Vaughan, David, and Ann F. Ramenofsky. "Mining Slag for Knowledge." Poster presented at "Founders, Smiths and Platers: An International Conference on Metal Forming and Finishing from the Earliest Times," sponsored by the Materials Science–Based Archaeology Group, Department of Materials, St. Catherine's College, University of Oxford, Oxford, U.K., 1999.

Vázquez de Coronado, Francisco. "Carta de Francisco Vazquez de Coronado desde la provincia de Tiguex al Emperador, 20 de Octubre de 1541." In *Colección de documentos inéditos relativos al descubrimiento, conquista, y organización de las antiguas posesiones españoles in América y Oceanía*, 42 vols., edited by Joaquín Pacheco y Francisco de Cárdenas, 3:363–69. Madrid: Imprenta de Manuel B. de Quirós, 1864–1888.

———. "Letter of Coronado to Mendoza, from the city of Granada, province of Cíbola, August 3, 1540." In *Narratives of the Coronado Expedition, 1540–1542*, edited by George P. Hammond and Agapito Rey, 163–84. Coronado Cuarto Centennial Publications, 1540–1940, vol. 2. Albuquerque: University of New Mexico Press, 1940.

———. "Letter of Coronado to the King from the Province of Tiguex, October 20, 1541." In *Narratives of the Coronado Expedition, 1540–1542*, edited and translated by George P. Hammond and Agapito Rey, 186–87. Coronado Cuarto Centennial Publications, 1540–1940, vol. 2. Albuquerque: University of New Mexico Press, 1940.

———. "Letter to the King, Compostela, July 15, 1539," AGI, Guadalajara, 5, R.1, N.6. In *"They Were Not Familiar with His Majesty": Documents of the Coronado Expedition, 1540–1542*, edited and translated by Richard Flint and Shirley Cushing Flint. In preparation.

———. "Letter to the King, Tiguex, October 20, 1541." AGI, Patronato, 184, R.34. In *"They Were Not Familiar with His Majesty": Documents of the Coronado Expedition, 1540–1542*, edited and translated by Richard Flint and Shirley Cushing Flint. In preparation.

————. "Letter to the Viceroy, Cíbola, August 3, 1540." In Giovanni Battista Ramusio, *Terzo volume delle navigationi et viaggi,* fol. 359v–63r. Venice: Stamperia de Giunti, 1556. In *"They Were Not Familiar with His Majesty": Documents of the Coronado Expedition, 1540–1542,* edited and translated by Richard Flint and Shirley Cushing Flint. In preparation.

[Vázquez de Coronado, Francisco]. "Residencia of Francisco Vázquez de Coronado, Guadalajara, 1544–45." AGI, Justicia 339, N.1, R.1.

Vernon, Richard H., and Ann S. Cordell. "A Distribution and Technological Study of Apalachee Colono-Ware from San Luis de Talimali." In *The Spanish Missions of La Florida,* edited by Bonnie McEwan, 418–43. Gainesville: University Press of Florida, 1993.

Vierra, Bradley J. "A Sixteeth-Century Spanish Campsite in the Tigues Province: An Archaeologist's Perspective." In *Current Research on the Late Prehistory and Early History of New Mexico,* edited by Bradley J. Vierra, 165–74. Albuquerque: New Mexico Archaeological Council, 1992.

————. *A Sixteenth-Century Spanish Campsite in the Tiguex Province.* Laboratory of Anthropology Note 475. Santa Fe: Museum of New Mexico, 1989.

————, ed. *Current Research on the Late Prehistory and Early History of New Mexico.* Albuquerque: New Mexico Archaeological Council, 1992.

Vierra, Bradley J., and Stanley M. Hordes. "Let the Dust Settle: A Review of the Coronado Campsite in the Tiguex Province." In *The Coronado Expedition to Tierra Nueva: The 1540–1542 Route Across the Southwest,* edited by Richard Flint and Shirley Cushing Flint, 249–61. Niwot, Colorado: University Press of Colorado, 1997.

Vint, James M. "Ceramic Artifacts." In *The Bandelier Archeological Survey,* vol. 2, edited by Robert P. Powers and Janet D. Orcutt, 389–467. Washington, D.C.: National Park Service, 2000.

Vivian, R. Gordon. *Gran Quivira: Excavations in a Seventeenth-Century Jumano Pueblo.* Archaeological Research Series no. 8. U.S. National Park Service, 1979.

Wagner, Henry R. *The Cartography of the Northwest Coast of America to the Year 1800,* vol. 1. Amsterdam: N. Israel, 1968.

————. "Fray Marcos de Niza." *New Mexico Historical Review* 9 (April 1934): 184–227.

————. "Quivira: A Mythical California City." *California Historical Society Quarterly* 3, no. 3 (1924): 262–67.

Walker, Dale L. "'Dear Soapy' Letters from Will Henry." *Roundup Magazine* 7, no. 4 (2000): 8–14.

Walsh, Jane MacLaren. "Myth and Imagination in the American Story: The Coronado Expedition, 1540–1542." Ph.D. diss., Catholic University of America, 1993.

Ward, Christopher. *Imperial Panama: Commerce and Conflict in Isthmian America, 1550–1800.* Albuquerque: University of New Mexico Press, 1993.

Watson, J. Wreford. *Mental Images and Geographical Reality in the Settlement of North America.* Nottingham: University of Nottingham, 1967.

Watts, Pauline Moffitt. "Prophecy and Discovery: On the Spiritual Origins of Christopher Columbus's 'Enterprise of the Indies.'" *American Historical Review* 90 (February 1985): 73–102.

Webb, Walter Prescott. *The Great Plains.* New York: Grosset and Dunlap, 1931.

Weber, David J. "Reflections on Coronado and the Myth of Quivira." In *Myth and the History of the Hispanic Southwest,* 1–17. Albuquerque: University of New Mexico Press, 1988.

————. *The Spanish Frontier in North America.* New Haven: Yale University Press, 1992.

————. "Turner, the Boltonians and the Spanish Borderlands." In *Myth and the History of the Hispanic Southwest,* 33–54. Albuquerque: University of New Mexico Press, 1988.

Weber, Michael Frederick. "*Tierra Incognita:* The Spanish Cartography of the American Southwest, 1540–1803." Ph.D. diss., University of New Mexico, 1986.

Wedel, Waldo R. "Coronado's Route to Quivira, 1541." *Plains Anthropologist* 15 (August 1970): 161–68.

Wendorf, Fred. "Excavations at Te'ewi." In *Salvage Archaeology in the Chama Valley, New Mexico,* edited by Fred Wendorf, 34–124. School of American Research Monograph 17. Santa Fe: School of American Research, 1953.

———. "A Reconstruction of Northern Rio Grande Prehistory." *American Anthropologist* 56, no. 2 (1954): 200–27.

Wendorf, Fred, and Eric Reed. "An Alternative Reconstruction of Northern Rio Grande Prehistory." *El Palacio* 62, nos. 5–6 (1955): 37–52.

West, Robert C. "Early Silver Mining in New Spain, 1531–1555." In *An Expanding World: The European Impact on World History 1450–1800,* vol. 19, *Mines of Silver and Gold in the Americas,* edited by Peter Bakewell, 41–56. Aldershot, U.K.: Variorum, 1997.

Wheat, Carl I. *Mapping the American West, 1540–1857.* Worcester, Massachusetts: American Antiquarian Society, 1954.

———. *Mapping the Trans-Mississippi West, 1540–1861,* vol. 1, *The Spanish Entrada to the Louisiana Purchase, 1540–1804.* San Francisco: Institute of Historic Cartography, 1957.

Wheat, Joe Ben. "Two Archaeological Sites near Lubbock, Texas." *Panhandle-Plains Review* 28 (1955): 71–77.

Windes, Thomas. "Report on Excavations at Tsama LA 908 near Abiquiu, New Mexico: West Mound, West Rooms, and West Mound Kiva." Manuscript, 1970.

Winship, George Parker, ed. and trans. *The Coronado Expedition, 1540–1542.* Fourteenth Annual Report of the Bureau of American Ethnology of the Smithsonian Institution, 1892–93, Part 1. Washington, D.C.: Smithsonian Institution, 1896. Reprint, Chicago: Rio Grande Press, 1964.

Wood, J. Scott. "Toward a New Definition of Salado: Comments and Discussion on the Second Salado Conference." In *Proceedings of the Second Salado Conference, Globe, Arizona,* edited by Richard C. Lange and Stephen Germick, 337–44. Phoenix: Arizona Archaeological Society, 1992.

Woodson, M. Kyle. "Migrations in Late Anasazi Prehistory: The Evidence from the Goat Hill Site." *Kiva* 65 (1999): 63–84.

Woodward, David. "Maps and the Rationalization of Geographic Space." In *Circa 1492: Art in the Age of Exploration,* edited by Jay A. Levenson, 83–87. Washington, D.C.: National Gallery of Art; New Haven: Yale University Press, 1991.

Word, James H. "The 1975 Field School of the Texas Archeological Society." *Bulletin of the Texas Archeological Society* 60 (1991): 57–106.

———. "Floydada Country Club Site (41FL1)." *Bulletin of the South Plains Archeological Society* 1 (1963): 37–63.

———. "The Montgomery Site in Floyd County, Texas." *Bulletin of the South Plains Archeological Society* 2 (1965): 55–102.

Ximénez, fray Jerónimo. "Carta de fray Jerónimo Ximénez de San Esteban a Santo Tomás de Villanueva." In *Cartas de religiosos de Nueva España, 1539–1594,* edited by Joaquín García Icazbalceta, 187–88. México, D.F.: Editorial Salvador Chávez Hayhoe, 1941.

Yglesias Hogan, Rubén. "Las siete ciudades doradas de Cíbola." *Revista de los Archivos Nacionales* (Costa Rica), 7, nos. 7–8 (1943): 373–84.

[Zaldívar, Juan de]. "Proof of service of Juan de Zaldívar, Guadalajara, 1566." AGI, Patronato 60, N5, R4.

Zaldívar Mendoza, Vicente de. *Zaldívar and the Cattle of Cíbola: Vicente de Zaldívar's Report of His Expedition to the Buffalo Plains in 1598.* Edited by Jerry R. Craddock; translated by John R. Polt. Dallas: William P. Clements Center for Southwest Studies, Southern Methodist University, 1999.

Zaragosa, Juan de, scribe. "Testimony of Coronado's Purchasing Agent, Juan Fernández Verdejo, Guadalajara, 1553." AGI, Justicia, 336, N.1, fol. 3v. In *"They Were Not Familiar with His Majesty": Documents of the Coronado Expedition, 1540–1542,* edited and translated by Richard Flint and Shirley Cushing Flint. In preparation.

———. "Testimony of Juan Bermejo, Guadalajara, 1553." AGI, Justicia, 336, N.1. In *"They Were Not Familiar with His Majesty": Documents of the Coronado Expedition, 1540–1542,* edited and translated by Richard Flint and Shirley Cushing Flint. In preparation.

Zumárraga, fray Juan de. "Letter to unknown recipient, Mexico City, August 23, 1539." In Henry R. Wagner, "Fray Marcos de Niza." *New Mexico Historical Review* 9 (April 1934): 184–227.

Maureen Ahern is a professor of Spanish and Latin American literatures and cultures at Ohio State University, Columbus, Ohio. Her studies of the sixteenth-century narratives of early expeditions into the Greater Southwest have appeared in major journals and collections of essays. She is co-translator (with Daniel Reff and Richard Danford) of the critical edition of Andrés Pérez de Ribas's *History of the Triumphs of Our Holy Faith* (1999). She is currently working on a project on frontier martyrdom.

Félix Barboza-Retana is a historian and museologist from Costa Rica. He holds a B.A. in history from the Universidad de Costa Rica and an M.A. in Museum Science from Texas Tech University. He has taught history at the Universidad Nacional Autónoma in Costa Rica and is an international advisor for the Museo de Cultura e Identidad Nacional. Currently he is an education specialist at the Museum of Texas Tech University.

Jay C. Blaine is an avocational archeologist with interests in both the Paleoindian period and the Spanish colonial era. He is a widely recognized authority on the metal artifacts of the early historic period. He is a past president of the Dallas and Texas Archeological Societies and was elected a Fellow of the Texas Archeological Society in 1989.

Donald J. Blakeslee is a professor of anthropology at Wichita State University, where he has taught for twenty-five years. His interest in the archeology of Indian trails led him to investigate the route of the Coronado expedition.

Dee Brecheisen, a Kansas native, received a B.S. from Kansas University in 1964 in aeronautical engineering. He served as a fighter pilot in the U.S. Air Force and the New Mexico Air National Guard for twenty-six years and as a pilot for TWA for twenty-nine years. During deployments in Panama with the New Mexico Air National Guard, Brecheisen became interested in the similarity between Spanish colonial artifacts there and in New Mexico. He is retired and lives in Peralta, New Mexico.

Douglas K. Boyd received a B.A. from West Texas State University in 1983 and an M.A. from Texas A&M University in 1986. He is currently a vice president at Prewitt and Associates, Inc., a cultural resources contracting firm in Austin, Texas. A native of the Texas Panhandle, he conducted extensive archeological research at Lake Alan Henry, Garza and Kent Counties, Texas, from 1987 to 1997.

Richard Flint is co-director of the Documents of the Coronado Expedition Project at New Mexico Highlands University in Las Vegas, New Mexico. The project will produce the first comprehensive, dual-language edition of thirty-five documents deriving from the expedition, fourteen of which have previously been unavailable in English. Flint's most recent book is *Great Cruelties Have Been Reported: The 1544 Investigation of the Coronado Expedition,* a documentary edition and study of the record of judicial inquiry into the expedition's treatment of native peoples of the Greater Southwest.

Shirley Cushing Flint is a research faculty member at New Mexico Highlands University, Las Vegas, New Mexico, co-director of the Documents of the Coronado Expedition Project, and co-director of the 2000 conference "Contemporary Vantage on the Coronado Expedition through Documents and Artifacts." She is also currently at work on a book-length manuscript exploring the network of social, political, and economic alliances engineered by Marina Gutiérrez Flores de la Caballería, mother-in-law of Francisco Vázquez de Coronado.

Frank R. Gagné Jr., after a nearly twenty-year business career, returned to Wichita State University, receiving both his B.A. and M.A. degrees in anthropology. Gagné has been an active participant in the Blanco Canyon excavations since they began in 1995. Married with one son and two grandsons, he is currently project director of archeology for Wichita State University.

Judith Habicht-Mauche is an associate professor of anthropology at the University of California, Santa Cruz. Her research interests include study of the organization of production and exchange of ancient pottery in the American Southwest and southern Great Plains. She earned her Ph.D. in anthropology from Harvard University in 1988. Her doctoral research on interaction between Pueblo farmers of the Southwest and bison-hunting nomads of the southern plains was awarded the Society for American Archaeology Dissertation Prize.

William K. Hartmann is a Tucson astronomer, writer, and painter with an interest in Southwestern history. His research at the Planetary Science Institute has involved planetary origin and evolution. He served on two NASA missions exploring the geological history of Mars and was named first recipient of the Carl Sagan Medal of the American Astronomical Society. His books include *Desert Heart: Chronicles of the Sonoran Desert* (1989) and a forthcoming novel, *Cities of Gold,* dealing with both the Coronado expedition and the modern Southwest.

Nancy P. Hickerson has taught cultural and linguistic anthropology at Texas Tech University since 1971 and is the author of *Linguistic Anthropology* (2000). In the past decade her interests have also included ethnohistory, resulting in the book *The Jumanos: Hunters and Traders of the South Plains* (1994) and several related articles. Her current plans include a book tentatively titled *Cabeza de Vaca and the Indians of Texas.*

Jack T. Hughes was professor emeritus of anthropology at West Texas A&M University. His numerous publications include *Prehistory of the Caddoan-Speaking Tribes.* He participated in many organizations, including the American Society of Conservation Archaeology, the Society for Historical Archaeology, and the Society of Professional Archaeologists. Hughes's specialties were the archeology of Texas, the Great Plains, North America, and early man. He was instrumental in defining the Garza and Tierra Blanca complexes of the Texas Panhandle.

John L. Kessell, professor emeritus, founding editor of the Vargas Project at the University of New Mexico, and historian, resides near Durango, Colorado. His most recent book is *Spain in the Southwest: A Narrative History of Colonial New Mexico, Arizona, Texas, and California* (University of Oklahoma Press).

Betty Graham Lee received a B.A. in anthropology from the University of Arizona. She is an instructor emeritus at Eastern Arizona College in Thatcher, Arizona, and has served as director of its Museum of Anthropology. She has prepared reports on the Eagle Pass Site and other sites in southeastern Arizona for Eastern Arizona College, the Bureau of Land Management, and other agencies. In 1994 she received a National Meritorious Achievement Award from the Oregon/California Trails Association for her work as chair of its archeology committee.

John H. Madsen has been involved for twenty-six years in all aspects of archeological research, including site inventory, data recovery, analysis, and publication. He is currently a senior research specialist and administrator of the Arizona Antiquities Act permits program at the Arizona State Museum, University of Arizona. His professional interests include the archeological assessment of prehistoric and historic American Indian trade trails and their use by Spanish expeditions.

John Miller Morris, a native son of the Texas Panhandle, is the author of *A Private in the Texas Rangers* and the award-winning *El Llano Estacado: Exploration and Imagination on the High Plains of Texas and New Mexico*. A historical-cultural geographer, he is an associate professor at the University of Texas at San Antonio.

Harry C. Myers is the National Park Service planning coordinator for El Camino Real de Tierra Adentro National Historic Trail. The early routing of Southwestern trails is a particular interest of Myers's that has sparked new geographical insights. Cartography and investigating actual trail sites are his present interests.

Ann F. Ramenofsky is an associate professor of archeology in the Department of Anthropology at the University of New Mexico. Her research interests attend the period of European contact in the Americas. She is currently working on a long-term research project on Spanish-Native interaction at San Marcos Pueblo, New Mexico.

Carroll L. Riley received a Ph.D. in anthropology from the University of New Mexico in 1952. He is currently distinguished professor emeritus at Southern Illinois University and a research associate at the Laboratory of Anthropology, Museum of New Mexico. Riley has done field and archival research in both North and South America and in Europe. His major interest at present is in the archeology and ethnohistory of the Greater Southwest, and his recent books, reflecting that interest, include *The Frontier People, Rio del Norte,* and *The Kachina and the Cross.*

C. David Vaughan is a doctoral candidate in anthropology at the University of New Mexico. His dissertation topic is Spanish mining and metallurgy in colonial New Mexico. Vaughan also holds a law degree from Emory University.

Page numbers in bold type indicate photos, illustrations, graphs, or tables.

Agnese, Battiste, 273
Aiton, Arthur, 59, 62, 69
Alarcón, Hernando de, 49
alarde. See muster roll
Alvarado, Diego de, 68
Alvarado, Hernando de, 69
Alvarado, Pedro de, 42; investment in expedition, 20, 45; provisioning of ships, 51
Álvarez, Lorenzo, 51, 61
Amangual, Francisco, 230–31
amazons, 24–25
Amerind, as ethnic designation, 189
anthropological history, birth of, 300–301
Antillia, Seven Cities of, 13, 22; conflated with Aztlán, 24; conflated with Tejo's account, 27
antimony, 128
Anza, Juan Bautista de, 17, 18
Apachean language, 189
Apaches, 15, 109; conflict with Jumanos, 192; independent bands, 165; in-migration of, 179; invasion by, 188, 190; and numerical superiority, 197; and pottery, 174–75; Querechos linked to, 177; and raids, 193–94; and South Plains environment, 195; southward and westward spread of, 176; technological advantages, 196. *See also* Querechos

Aravaipa River, 88; headwaters of, 84–85
archaeological sites in Chichilticale region (Arizona), **86**; 76 Ranch Ruins, 92; Citadel Ruin, 98; Eagle Pass Ruin, 100, **101**; Eastern Arizona College Field School Site, 99; Eureka Springs Ranch, "Crescent Ruin", 94–97; Eureka Springs Ranch House Site, 92–94; Fort Grant Eastern Ruins, 92; Fort Grant Ruins, 90–92; Haby Ranch Site (Garden Springs Site), 85–86, 88–89; Haby Ranch Site, Older Eastern Outlier, 90; Klondyke Cemetery Site, 99–100; "Pentagon" Ruin Site, 97; Pottery Hill Site, 100; Rattlesnake Mesa Ruin, 98; Skinner Site, 101–2; Wooten-Claridge Terrace Site, 97–98
archaeology, historical, 117–18; limited contribution of in the Southwest, 117–18
Arellano, Tristán de (Luna y), 118
armor: lack of on expedition, 74–75; native, 76; recovered in southeastern Arizona, 111, 113; crossbow penetration of, 241
arquebuses, 211
arrow points: triangular and side-notched, 168; Garza, Lott, Fresno, and Washita, 170, 180, 183; Clovis, 222
artifacts: of Clovis bands, 222; distribution of, **110**; from Blanco Canyon, 205; temporal mixture of, 207; from Panama, 253–64; Spanish colonial in southeastern Arizona, 109–15, **112**, characteristic of the Coronado expedition, 210–13; Tierra

Blanca sites, 168; use of metal detectors to locate, 206–8

Athapaskanization of areas in the Southwest, 176–77

Athapaskans: on Llano Estacado, 167; migration from Asia, 189, 225

Aztlán, 24, 39, 273; conflated with Antillia, 24. *See also* seven caves

Baja California (Mexico): as a peninsula, 16, 272; Cortés to, 26

Bandelier, Adolph, F., 3; opinions of, 128, 188, 190

Barrionuevo, Francisco, 118–19

Bastidas, Rodrigo de, 254

bells, copper: as evidence of regional trade, 27; in Sulfur Springs Valley, 91, 96; received and heard of by Cabeza de Vaca, 26–27, 39

Benavente, Toribio de, 60

Benevides, Alonso de, 195

Bermejo, Juan de, 51

Bernalillo (New Mexico): Coronado campsite near, 2

bison, 26, 164, 188; coevolution with humans, 224; dressing in skins of, 51; and fear of stampedes, 159–60; as food source, 144; herding behavior of, 224; and hides, 166; hunted to near extinction, 232; sighting of, 156–57

Blanco Canyon (Texas): visited by Coronado expedition, 216–17, 227; Anglo settlement in, 233, 235–38; livestock and, 231–32; loss of megafauna in, 223–24

Bodega y Quadra, Juan Francisco de la, 18

body painting, 166, 181, 199–200

bragging documents: as sources of information on the conquest, 68

Brand, Donald, 82

Bridwell, John, 88

Cabello, Domingo, 18

Cabeza de Vaca, Álvar Núñez, 12, 26, 27, 39, 42, 104

calendars: change from Julian to Gregorian, 153–54

Camino Real: in Panama, 253–57, **255**

Caprock Canyonlands, **169**, 180, 182–83

Cárdenas, Luis, 24

cartography of North America, sixteenth century, 269; relation to territorial expansion, 279

Casa de Contratación, 11, 265, 270

Casas, Bartolomé de las, 22, 273

Castañeda de Nájera, Pedro de: relación of, 2, 21, 34, 62, 265, 268; geographical insights of, 22, 34, 83, 84, 269–82; quotations from, 35; speculation about origin of Pueblo people, 228; provided evidence about servants, 67; on native ceramics, 124, 127–28; and sense of discovery, 220–21; and shiny metal, 118–33

Castillo Maldonado, Alonso del, 26

Cavallón, Juan de, 295, 298, 301

ceramics: distribution in northern New Mexico, **126**; glaze-paint ware, 124–27; Plains Village, 172; at Tierra Blanca sites, 173

Chichilticale, 38, 81–108, 274; environment, 84–85; Late Pueblo ruins, 102–5; location of, 83–84. *See also* archeological sites in Chichilticale region

Chichilticale Pass (Arizona), 104

Cíbola (New Mexico), 29–30, 275–78; false assumptions about gold at, 33–35; Guzman's search for, 25; mapping of, 273; relation to the Orient, 22; size of advance guard on arrival at, 63; tales of wealth in, 20–21; two waves of information about, 36–37

Cicuique (New Mexico), 156, 273. *See also* Pecos Pueblo

Cieza de León, Pedro de: regarding importance of Indians to entradas, 65; regarding women on entradas, 68

Clovis bands, 222–23

Clovis Gravel Site, 222

Clovis points, 222, 224

clyster pumps, 260

Codex Aubin, 64

coevolution of bison and humans, 224

Collinson, Frank, 231–32

Columbus, Christopher, 12, 22

comancheros, 232

Comanches, 18, 187

Compostela (Mexico): muster conducted at, 58

Cona: geographical extent of, 159–60; 164, 179, 180, 181; origin of name, 165; springs of, 227

The Conquest of Mexico (Prescott), 3

conquistadors, **75**; and Navajos, 225

Contreras, Alonso de, 67

Coppo, Pietro: world map by, **266**

corn: reliance of entradas on, 297–98; scarcity of during expedition, 51

Coronado. *See* Vázquez de Coronado, Francisco

Coronado: Knight of Pueblos and Plains (Bolton), 69

Coronado expedition's route, **268**; in southeastern Arizona, 83, 113; across Texas, 204, 213–17, **214**; Bosque Redondo trails, 147; in northern New Mexico, 118–19; Pecos Pueblo to Llano Estacado, 120, 141–50, **142**, 152; uncertainties about, 226

Coronado expedition: appearance of, 74–77; "balance sheet" for, **46**; calendars and dating problem, 151–63; contribution to geography, 226; encounter with Na-Denes, 225; as epic, 279–80; estimated cost for, 44–48; expansion of geographic knowledge, 265; failure of, 37, 52–53, 220; geographic scale of, 226; investors in, 44–48; Llano Estacado ascension point, 173; major investors in, 20; multicultural makeup of, 77, 226; organization of, 58–59, 69–73; preparations for, 43; rate of travel of, 160; recruitment for, 62; religious component of, 226; slaves and servants on, 66–67; stops for rest and recovery, 163n. 32; as story of preconceived expectations, 38; supplying, 49–52, 51, 252n. 14, 298; time line, **155**; travel in separated units, 154, 156; travel time, 154–61; two campsites near Llano Estacado, 215–17; violent conflict with Pueblo Indians, 263; women on, 67–68. *See also* Coronado's route; muster roll

Cortés, Hernán, 23; and Gulf of California, 25–26; curbing power of, 42–43

rivalry with Mendoza, 32; expenditures of, 52

Costa Rica, 301; ethnography of, 300; role of Vázquez de Coronado's letters in, 299–300

Costa Rica expedition, 295; lack of funds for, 297; list of men on, 296

Cotter, John L., 222

Crosby, Alfred W., 230

cross: as indication of good news, 29

crossbows: absent from Oñate's expedition, 241; penetration of armor, 241; reliability of, 240; replaced by firearms, 211, 240. *See also* crossbow boltheads,

Cuevas, Juan de, 58, 66, 69

crossbow boltheads, 205, 208–11, 216, 227, 240–52, **262**; analysis data, **247**; comparison of, 242–44, **249**; four basic types of, 246; measurement of, 245–48; missing in Panama, 263; scattergram of, **246**; use of copper for, 241, 250–51

Bolton, Herbert E.: opinion of regarding barrancas, 227, 116–17, 227; distortion introduced by, 68–69, 116–17

Culiacán (Mexico), 21

cultural spaces, 265–82

culture groups in South Plains (Texas), **191**

Dees, Thomas, 111

Díaz del Castillo, Bernal, 23

Díaz, Melchor (or Melchior), 35, 59–60, 63, 66, 105

diseases: effect of on indigenous peoples, 167, 229, 230

dogs: as beasts of burden, 196

Domínguez, Francisco Atanasio, 17

Dorantes, Andrés, 26

Dorantes, Esteban de, 26, 29–31

Durán, Diego, 24

ecological imperialism, 230, 234

ecological release, 223, 228–31

El Turco, 157, 238

Escalante, Silvestre Vélez, 17

Escandón, José de, 16

Escobar, Cristóbal de, 47

Escobar, Francisco, 11, 14

Espejo, Antonio de, 65

Espejo expedition, 193

Esteban. *See* Dorantes, Esteban de.

Estrada, Beatriz de, 73, 291

Estrada Rávago, Juan de, 295

ethnographic evidence: instances of misuse of, 174; paucity of regarding Teyas and Querechos, 171

exploration, Spanish: conducting and financing, 42–53; licensed but not funded by Crown, 43–44; number of Spanish-led expeditions, 1, 25, 42, 57; three periods of, 12–18

extinction of Pleistocene fauna, 223–24

Farfán de los Godos, Marcos, 14

Fernández, León, 300

Fernández, Santiago, 145

first arrivals, 219–39; American, 231–38; Eurasian, 221–25; Spanish, 225–31

Folsom Man, 224

Folsom points, 224

Forbes, Jack D., 176

Fragoso, Francisco, 145

alena (lead ore), 127–28, 132, 133. *See also* lead.
Gallego, Juan, 64
Gálvez, José de, 17
Garay, Francisco de, 52
Garcés, Francisco, 17
Garza sites (Texas, New Mexico), 164, **169**, 170, 171; and cultural and historical origins, 173; and linkage with Teyas, 175; location of, 177; sampling problems and inadequate data sets limit understanding of, 171
gold: evidence in New World, 22–24; evidence and lack thereof from Marcos de Niza, 29, 30, 33–34; in Central American and Peru, 254–55, 295; suggestion of at Quiviria, 269
Goodnight, Charles, 232
Gregg, Josiah, 145
Guadalupe Mountains (Texas, New Mexico), 190
Gutiérrez de la Caballería, Diego, 73–74
Guzman, Nuño Beltrán de, 21, 25, 67

Haby, Margaret, 88
hailstorms: during the expedition, 215, 250; during 1890s, 234
Hammond, George P.: documents published by, 57, 59, 69; misinterpretation of name and term by, 74, 75; remarkable scholar, 77
Harahey knives, 170, 172
hearths: in Blanco Canyon, 208–9, 210
Henry, Will, 221
historical anthropology: birth of, 300–301
historical archaeology: limited contribution of in Southwest, 117–18
Honorato, fray, 28, 30
Hodge, Frederick W., 227
Hopi trail (Arizona), 84, 88
horizon markers: of Coronado expedition, 210–13; caret-head nails as, 211; crossbow boltheads as, 210–11, 242
horses, 229; and access to water, 232
horseshoes and muleshoes, 212–13, 257–58
Howard, Edgar B., 222
Hozes, Francisca de, 67, 70
Hughes, Jack T., 162, 168, 204

Ibarra, Eugenia, 300
Ibarra, Francisco, 53
Indian allies: of Coronado expedition, 59–66; functions of, 65; numbers of, 62–63, 274; on other expeditions, 65
Indian trails, 204, 205, 216

Inquisition, 15
Inuit (people), 189
irrigation: in and around caprock Canyons, 236, 237, 238
Isopete, 158

Jaramillo, Juan de: narrative of, 62; evidence of slaves from, 67; on location of Chichilticale, 83; on the Llano Estacado, 156; on travel along streams, 223
Jemez province (New Mexico), 119
Jesús de la Coruña, Martín de, 23
Jiménez de San Esteban, fray, 34
Jiménez, Francisco, 65
Jiménez, Juan, 51, 75–76
Jimmy Owens Site (Texas), 73; as campsite in one of the barrancas, 175, 181, 210–13; crossbow boltheads from, 242, 243, 247, 249–51; discovery and investigation of, 203–10; hearth remnant and animal bone at, 210; historical marker to commemorate, 227; lack of lead shot at, 263; location and structure of, **206**; methodology used in investigation of, 204; size of, 210
Jumanos, 182, 183, 188, 193–200; abandonment of Llano Estacado, 193; assimilated by conquerors, 198; conflict with Apaches, 192; factors leading to decline of, 195–98; maintenance of bases, 191–92; and South Plains environment, 195; ubiquity of, 190; use of body decoration, 199

Kelley, J. Charles, 176
Keres (people of New Mexico), 119–20, 181
Kino, Father Eusebio Francisco, 15–16

Lackner, Don and Kim, 95
Las Cruces Trail (Panama), 256
lead, 131, 133. *See also* galena.
lead shot: at Santiago Pueblo, **261**; absence of at Jimmy Owens Site, 263
Lee, Betty Graham, 82, 88–89
León, Alonso de, 15
León, Luis de, 65
Lewis and Clark, 18
Life in the Saddle (Collinson), 231
Llano Estacado, 158–60, **214**; as inhospitable for settlement, 159–60; demographic and economic transition in, 167
longitude, 265–66
López de Cárdenas, García, 70, 158

López de Villalobos, Ruy, 13
López, Diego, 35, 61, 158–59
López, Martín, 67
López, Nicolás, 194
Lubbock Lake Landmark (Texas), 222, 223, 235
luminescence dating of ceramics (Chama Valley, New Mexico), 123–24

Madden Lake Campsite (Panama), 257–59
Maldonado, María, 67
Maldonado, Rodrigo, 159
Mallet expedition, 204
Mallet, Paul and Pierre, 143
mammoths on Llano Estacado, 223
maps: misplacement of toponyms learned by Coronado expedition, 226; Padrón Real, 265; sixteenth-century examples, 266, 267, 271
Marcos de Niza, fray, 25, 152; Chichilticale discovered by, 84; cursed by expedition members, 35; final report of, 33–34; and myth of Cíbola, 20, 275; no evidence of fraudulent intent, 37; talked with people who had been to Cíbola, 105
Marcy, Randolph B., 145, 146
Mares, José, 144
Massanet, Damián, 15
measurement of distances (from Mexico City), 272
Medina, Bartolomé de, 129
Melgares, Facundo, 18
Mendoza, Antonio de (viceroy), 13, 31–33, 42, 57–58, 276, 291; dispatched a reconnaissance party, 27–29; investment in expedition, 20, 45–48; no evidence fraudulent intent, 37; instructed Marcos to send interim reports, 38; sent a second reconnaissance party, 35
Menéndez de Avilés, Pedro, 13, 44, 45, 52
mesquite trees: clearing of in Blanco Canyon, 206
metal detectors: use of at Blanco Canyon, 206–8
mica (at Yunque Yunque), 128, 133
Michoacán: gold at, 23–24, 25
Miera y Pacheco, Bernardo de, 17
mineral deposits: in the Upper Rio Grande area, 131–32
mining and metallurgy: lack of knowledge of on entradas, 129–30
Mixtón War: effects of, 49, 51, 53
Moho (New Mexico), 263–64

Montesclaros, Marqués de, 14
Mora, Carmen de, 59
mules: on Camino Real in Panama, 256–57
mule shoes. See horseshoes and muleshoes, 257–58
muster roll: format of and ordering of names on, 70; incompleteness of, 59, 66, 76; page from, **71**; prepared at Compostela, 58, publication of, 59; purposes of, 58

Na-Dene migrants, 225
Nahuatl language: used by expedition, 274–75
nails: from Jimmy Owens Site, 208–9, 211–13; carat-head, 211, **212**; 257–58; from Panama, 253
names: use of saints' names as toponyms, 14; change in spelling of Coronado, 295; invention of topography, 274, 275; lists of in sixteenth century, 70
Narratives of the Coronado Expedition (Hammond and Rey), 59; mistranslation in, 73–74; page from, **72**
Niza, fray Marcos de. See Marcos de Niza, fray
nomadism: as represented as Castañeda, 281

Ogallala Aquifer (Texas), 225, 236, 237
Olid, Cristóbal de, 24
Oñate, Cristóbal de, 26
Oñate, Juan de, 12, 120; absence of crossbows in expedition of, 241; expedition to the Great Plains, 141–43, 199; as mining engineer, 130; statue of, 116; sought silver ore, 53
Oviedo y Valdés, Gonzalo Fernández de, 26
Owens, Jimmy, 205. See also Jimmy Owens Site

Padilla, Juan de, 13, 65, 230, 279
Padrón Real, 11 (official map), 265, 276
Palo Duro Canyon (Texas), 177, 204, 227
Panama, 253–64; as transit point for gold and silver, 255; use of mules in, 256–57
Paradinas, Juan de, 47, 61
Pawnee Indians, 145
Paz Maldonado, Rodrigo de, 47, 51
Pecos Pueblo (New Mexico), 147, 156, 177. *See also* Cicuique.
Pecos River (New Mexico): bridge built across, 147, 156, 161
Peñalosa, Diego de, 15
Pérez, Juan, 18
Pérez, Melchor (or Melchior), 47, 48, 51
Pérez de Luxán, Diego, 65
Pike, Zebulon Montgomery, 18

Plains Indians, 18; and community organization, 165; death of Juan de Padilla among, 13, 65, 230, 279

Plains Villagers, 184; Antelope Creek people, 167; relation to Garza complex, 173; ceramics of, 172

Portolá, Gaspar de, 17

Posada, Alonso de, 196

pothunting: and damage to Crescent Ruin (Arizona), 95

Prescott, William H., 3

Pueblo Indians, 14–15, 16

pueblo retreats: for people of Yunque Yunque, 121–22

pueblos: abandonment of along southeastern flank of Rocky Mountains, 178

Querechos: relation to Apaches and Tierra Blanca complex, 164–87; indistinctness of in archaeological record, 177; location of in 1540s, 148, 157–58, 159–60; seasonal activities, 178

Quesada, Cristóbal de, 47

Quitaque Canyon (Texas), 168

Quivira (Kansas), 64, 65, 141, 199, 279; mapping of, 273; as place of economic potential, 281

raid-and-trade theory: of relations between Plains Indians and Pueblos, 178

Relación de la jornada de Cíbola (Castañeda), 62, 118, 156, 265–82; description of Pueblo ceramics in, 124; dating discrepancy with Vázquez de Coronado's letter, 152–53; measured itinerary in, 276; Ternaux-Compans's French translation, 2; Winship's English translation, 3

rescate (trade with indigenous peoples), 298–99. See also trade.

Rey, Agapito: documents published by, 57, 59, 69; misinterpretation of name and term by, 74, 75; remarkable scholar, 77

Riley, Carroll L., 229

Rio Chama pueblos, lower, 121–22, **123**

Rio del Norte (Riley), 229

Rodríguez Cabrillo, Juan, 13

Rodríguez, García, 48, 51, 61

Romero, Diego, 15

Sabeata, Juan, 193, 196, 198

Sacramento Mountains (New Mexico), 190

Saint Denis, Louis Juchereau de, 16

Salado Pueblos (Arizona), 81–82

Salas, Juan de, 192

Saldaña, Gaspar de, 61

Sandoval, Francisco Tello de, 62

Sangre de Cristo mountain range (New Mexico), 189, 192

San Juan Pueblo (New Mexico), 121. See also Yuque Yunque.

Santa Cruz, Alonso de, 270

Santiago Pueblo (New Mexico): as Moho, 263–64

Sauer, Carl, 82

seeing and authenticity, 279

Sergas de Esplandián (Rodríguez de Montalvo), 24

Serra, fray Junípero, 17

seven caves: Atzlán, 24

seven cities: of Antillia, 21–22, 24–25, 28–29; of Cíbola, 275–76

shiny metal: at Yuque Yunque, reported by Castañeda, 118; galena as, 127; mica as, 128, 133

silver: presence of suggested by shiny metal, 127–28; sources of in middle Rio Grande Valley, 131–32

Simpson, James H., 3, 145, 146, 226

Singer, George Washington, 235

Smith, Hank, 233–34

Sonoran uprising (1541–42), 53

Soto, Hernando de, 13, 42

South Plains (Texas): culture groups in, 191

springs: in caprock canyons, 231, 232, 236–37

style: as archaeological concept, 166, 173

Sulfur Springs Valley (Arizona), 81–84; ceramic assemblages at site in, 87; and Late Pueblo sites, 85, **86**, 105

sustainability paradigms: for the Llanco Estacado, 238

Tapia, Andrés de, 24

tattooing: used to mark ethnic difference, 166, 180. See also body painting.

Tejada, Lorenzo de, 61, 67

Tenochtitlán (Mexico), 23–25

Ternaux-Compans, Henri, 2

Teyas: as Caddoes, 183–84; location of, 179; equation with Jumanos, 182, 184, 187, 190; linguistic stock of, 183–84; linkage with Garza sites, 175; location of, 159–60; use of tattooing, 181; relations with neighbors, 184

Thaxcaltecas, 64

Tierra Blanca sites (Texas), 164; as distinct from Garza sites, 172; ceramics from, 173; cultural and historical origins of, 173; linkage with Querechos, 171, 175; list of, 170; location of, **169**, 177; sampling problems and inadequate data sets limit understanding of, 171; two types of, 168

Tiguex people: division of labor and gender roles among, 277

Tiguex province (New Mexico), 75, 119, 147, **268**

Tiguex war, 6fi

Tlatelolco (Mexico), 64–65

Tlaxcaltecas, 64

Tompiros people (New Mexico), 199

tool kits: of Tierra Blanca and Garza, 172

trade: between indigenous groups, 27, 102–5, 141, 184–85, 192–93; between Spaniards and Indians, 15, 298; Apaches as mediators, 178; fairs in Panama, 256; indigenous routes of, 300; Jumanos and, 198; linking of areas as basis for alliance, 188

trail segments: search for in southeastern Arizona, 114. *See also* rescate.

tree-ring dating, 122, 124

Troyano, Juan, 45, 51, 67

Ulloa, Francisco de, 31

Urdaneta, Andrés de, 13

Vargas, Diego de, 16

Vázquez de Coronado, Francisco, 13, 31–32, 57; biographical highlights, 291; compared to nephew Juan, 290; dating discrepancy between his letter and Castañeda's *Relación*, 152–53; indebtedness of, 48; investment in expedition, 20, 45–47; letter to Mendoza, 276; marriage to Beatriz de Estrada, 73; testimony before *visitador*, 62; testimony concerning Indian allies, 61; use of wife's dowry, 48

Vázquez de Coronado family: genealogy of, 294; letters and chronicles of, 299–300; spelling of name changed, 295

Vázquez de Coronado, Juan, 291–93; biographical highlights, 293; compared to uncle Francisco, 290; descendants of, 297; expedition led by, 295–97; letters of, 300; as peaceful leader, 298–99; portrait of, **292**

Velasco, Luis de, 14

Verdejo, Juan Fernández, 45

Vial, Pedro, 18, 143, 145

Villasur, Pedro de, 16

Vizcaíno, Sebastián, 12, 14

war: between native groups on South Plains (Texas), 187, 190

water: as determinant for expedition campsite and course of travel, 140, 206, 223; for livestock, 227–28, 232

Whipple, Amiel W, 146

White River (Texas), 221

Winship, George P., 57, 77, 227

women: on Coronado expedition, 67–68; on other expeditions, 68 and dirty work, 170; warlike, 25

Yellow House Canyon and Draw (Texas), 175, 204, 217, 222, 235–38; loss of megafauna in, 223

Yuque Yunque (New Mexico), 116–39; Castañeda's description of, 120; identification of, 120–32. *See also* San Juan Pueblo.

Zacatecas silver strike, 53

Zaldívar, Juan de, 47, 61, 66, 67, 69

Zaldívar Mendoza, Vicente de, 144

Zaltieri, Bolognino: map by, **271**

Zorita, Alonso de, 276

Zumárraga, fray Juan de, 32

Zúñiga, José de, 113–14; journal of, 114

Zuni Pueblo (New Mexico), 114

Zuni Salt Lake (New Mexico), 114